*On Bata*

1995

SUNY series,
Intersections: Philosophy and Critical Theory
Rodolphe Gasché, editor

# On Bataille
# Critical Essays

Edited and translated, with an introduction by
## Leslie Anne Boldt-Irons

Published by
State University of New York Press, Albany

© 1995 State University of New York

Printed in the United States of America

For information, address State University of New York Press,
State University Plaza, Albany, NY 12246

Production by Cynthia Tenace Lassonde
Marketing by Fran Keneston

We gratefully acknowledge the following for permission to reprint copyrighted material:
Lionel Abel, for "Georges Bataille and the Repetition of Nietzsche";
l'Association des publications de la Faculté des Lettres de Nice, for "Georges Bataille and the Challenge
to Think" by Robert Sasso;
Les Editions de Minuit, publishers of *Critique*, for "Bataille and the World: From 'The Notion of
Expenditure' to *The Accursed Share*" by Jean Piel;
*French Literature Series* and the University of South Carolina Press for "Bataille's Erotic Writings and the
Return of the Subject" by Paul Smith, and "...And a Truth for a Truth: Barthes on Bataille" by Michael
Halley;
Groupe de la Cité, for "From Beyond Hegel to Nietzsche's Abscence" by Denis Hollier, "Bataille and
Science: Introduction to Inner Experience" by Jean-Louis Baudry, and "Bataille, Experience, and
Practice" by Julia Kristeva;
Harvard University Press, for "Transgression and the Avant-Garde: Bataille's Histoire de l'oeil" by Susan
Robin Suleiman. Reprinted by permission of the publishers from SUBVERSIVE INTENT: GENDER, POLI-
TICS, AND THE AVANT-GARDE by Susan Suleiman, Cambridge, Mass.: Harvard University Press,
Copyright © 1990 by the President and Fellows of Harvard College;
The Hebrew University Studies in Literature and the Arts (*HSLA*) for "On the Eve of Legibility: Illegibility
in Georges Bataille's Story of the Eye" by Mikhal Popowski;
Pierre Klossowski, for "Of the Simulacrum in Georges Bataille's Communication";
*Raison Presente*, for "On Georges Bataille: An Escape from Lameness?" by Jean Borreil;
*The Romantic Review*, for "Unemployed Negativity (Derrida, Bataille, Hegel)" by Tony Corn;
*Studies in Twentieth Century Literature*, for "The Maze of Taste: On Bataille, Derrida, and Kant" by
Arkady Plotnitsky;
Tilgher-Genova, publishers of *Nuova Corrente*, for "The Heterological Almanach" by Rodolphe Gasché;
The University of Wisconsin Press, publishers of *SubStance*, for "Bataille and Communication: savoir,
non-savoir, glissement, rire" by Joseph Libertson.

Library of Congress Cataloging-in-Publication Data

On Bataille : Critical Essays / edited and translated, with an
    introduction, by Leslie Anne Boldt-Irons.
        p.  cm — (SUNY series, Intersections)
    Includes bibliographical references and index.
    ISBN 0-7914-2455-3 (HC : alk. paper). — ISBN 0-7914-2456-1 (PB :
alk. paper)
    1. Bataille, Georges, 1897–1962. I. Boldt-Irons, Leslie Anne,
1954– II. Series: Intersections (Albany, N.Y.)
B2430.B33905  1995
128—dc20
                                                        94-22405
                                                        CIP

10 9 8 7 6 5 4 3 2 1

# Contents

## III. Alterity, Heterology, and Communication

## IV. Inner Experience and the Subject

## V. *Histoire de l'oeil* and Bataille's Fiction

# Acknowledgments

The idea for this book arose when I prepared the introduction for my translation of George Bataille's *L'experience intérieure* (published as *Inner Experience* by SUNY Press in 1988). It became clear that there would not be enough scope, within the space of that introduction, for any detailed discussion of critical reaction to Bataille's work. Accordingly, I made the decision to limit that introduction to a general discussion of *Inner Experience*. Rodolphe Gasché and Mark Taylor suggested that I put together a collection of previously published articles on Bataille's *oeuvre*, translating many of them for the first time into English and reserving general discussion of critical reaction to his work for the present introduction. I thank Rodolphe and Mark for that suggestion.

This book has taken several years to complete. I wish to thank the editors and publishers of the journals and books in which the articles originally appeared for their cooperation and positive response to my request for permission to reprint them. Given the complexity surrounding the terminology used in the French articles, much time was needed to attend to their translation.

Finally, the publication of this book has been delayed by the birth of my second daughter, Juliette. I thank her, my eldest daughter, Nastasia, and my husband Glen Irons for the many ways in which they have sustained me during the years of work on this volume, and for gifts that remain unspeakable, always *in excess*.

## Editor's Note

My choice of English articles for this volume was dictated by the novelty and importance of their respective positions on various aspects of Bataille's work, and by the fact that they had sometimes appeared in less well-known journals or in books on subjects other than that of the work of Georges Bataille. In all cases, I felt that their juxtaposition with the French articles added freshness and interest to the aspect of his work under study in each section of this book.

# Introduction

When Bataille first published *Histoire de l'oeil* in 1928, he did so under the pseudonym of Lord Auch. Clearly, Bataille knew that he risked scandal and outrage in publishing this erotic tale and therefore chose, as a librarian at the Bibliothèque Nationale, to adopt a fictitious name as author. After years of collaboration in various journals, Bataille published his first philosophical work, *Inner Experience*, in 1945. Reaction to this work was also mixed, and prominent intellectuals of the time responded to this text in both detailed and dismissive fashion. While much has been made of Bataille's influence upon the work of celebrated poststructuralist and postmodern theorists, less attention has been paid to these early responses to Bataille's work.[1]

The first part of this introduction will therefore examine these early responses to Bataille's fiction and philosophical work, for he risked dismissal and incomprehension on the part of his critics, writing as they were from the Surrealist and Existentialist perspectives that informed their work. I will begin, then, with the notorious and rather predictable reactions of Breton, Sartre, and Marcel to certain of Bataille's texts, texts that troubled and provoked them enough to include passages and chapters on Bataille in their own manifestos and critical and philosophical texts. My examination of these three early responses will then lead to a discussion of Bataille's influence upon the poststructuralist and postmodern theorists who regarded Bataille as a precursor and as a "contemporary" *avant la lettre*.

As mentioned, one of the earliest and most noteworthy responses to Bataille's work can be found in André Breton's *Second manifeste du surréalisme*.[2] There Breton responds to Bataille's accusations that the Surrealists had "a sordid thirst for all integrities." In a passage at the end of *Sur Nietzsche*, Bataille intensifies his criticism by accusing Breton and his Surrealists of idealism, in that the destruction of objects and words at which they aim does not go so far as to subvert the value of nothingness (*le néant*), which retains its superiority and transcendence, conferring this value ultimately upon the Surrealist search itself and the experience of those that engage in it.

Breton's relationship to idealism is indeed a complex one.  In the *Premier manifeste du surréalisme*,[3] he seems to decry the fact that we "are still living under the reign of logic" (22), suggesting instead that the processes of abstraction be modified and subverted by the illogic of dream as well as by material from the unconscious.  Yet he later proposes that these very illogical forces be controlled by reason: "If the depths of our mind are receptive to strange forces capable of augmenting those of the surface, or of fighting victoriously against them, it is in everyone's interest to capture them, to capture them first, in order to submit them later, if necessary, to the control of our reason" (23).

While Breton in the *Second manifeste du surréalisme* maintains that it was necessary to "do away with idealism per se" (172), and that, along with "historical materialism," Surrealism takes as its point of departure "the colossal abortion of the Hegelian system" (171), it is precisely the move-ment's idealist tendencies that inform Bataille's criticism of Breton. Breton's famous definition of the "ideal point" is indicative of the move-ment's tendency towards idealism:

> Everything would lead one to believe that there exists a
> certain point in the mind where life and death, the real and the
> imaginary, the past and the future, the communicable and the
> incommunicable, the high and the low cease to be perceived
> as contradictory. Now it would be vain to seek in Surrealist
> activity a motivation other than the hope of determining this
> point. (134)

It is highly significant that Bataille—who was acquainted with the Surrealists but who refused adherence to their movement—would write in Inner Experience of a similar point, but with one important modifica-tion: while Breton seeks to determine this point, Bataille writes of its ability to cut, with the trenchancy of catastrophe, like the blade of a razor.  Thus one can compare Breton's desire to determine, and no doubt contemplate, the point—and this, despite its supposed goal of "annihilating being in a blind and inner brilliancy"—with Bataille's desire to be the fabric torn by the experience of the point. "To summon all of man's tendencies into a point, all of the "possibles" which he is, to draw from them at the same time the harmonies and violent oppositions, no longer to leave outside the laughter tearing apart the fabric of which man is made, on the contrary to know oneself to be assured of insignificance as long as thought is not itself this profound tearing of the fabric and its object—being itself—the fabric torn."4 Where Breton envisages being's "annihilation" (or culmination) in a brilliancy, Bataille dramatizes its "tearing."

The polemic between the two authors is also oriented by the prefix "sur" of Surrealism. In the *Premier manifeste du surréalisme*, Breton writes: "I believe in the future resolution of those two states, those of dream and reality, into a sort of absolute reality, a *surreality*, as it were" (27). But other quotations from the *Manifeste* suggest that Breton was more interested in a sort of absolute reality of *thought*, not one which would incorporate lived, and at times obscene or vulgar experience into this equation. This tendency is manifest in his defense of Surrealism's power to "wrench thought away from an increasingly difficult bondage" in order to "put it back on the path of total comprehension, to return it to its original purity" (155).

It is this intoxicated quest for the purity of thought—unsullied by baser attributes, which it refuses—that leads Breton to write utopically of the poet who will "rise above the momentary feeling of living dangerously and dying." Breton continues: "May he use, in contempt of all prohibitions, the venging weapon of *the idea* against the bestiality of all beings and of all things and may he one day—vanquished—but vanquished only if the *world is world*—welcome the discharge of sorrowful guns, like the return of volley fire" (221).

This intoxication with the purity and the transcendence of the *idea* also leads Breton to criticize Bataille's fascination with the "sullied, senile, rancid, sordid, ribald, imbecilic" (218) aspects of the very reality that Breton's *absolute* reality seems intent on eclipsing.

Hence Bataille's accusation that the Surrealist enterprise is essentially Icarian, disdaining all that is base and vulgar: "From one who speaks across the heavens, full of aggressive respect for heaven and its lightning bolts, full of disgust for this too base world that he believes he scorns— scorns more than anyone has ever scorned it before him—after touching Icarian naïveté has betrayed his desire for the miraculous, we can only expect... the betrayal of the vulgar interests of the collectivity, which have become simply filth, a pretext to rise with cries of disgust."5

This disagreement between the two authors—the one accused of a penchant for idealism, the other of a morbid preoccupation with filth and the obscene—is resumed in their discussion of the rose, metaphor for ideal beauty and love. In "The language of flowers," Bataille reminds one that "even the most beautiful flowers are spoiled in their centers by hairy sexual organs. Thus the interior of a rose does not at all correspond to its exterior beauty; if one tears off all of the corolla's petals, all that remains is a rather sordid tuft... But even more than the filth of its organs, the flower is betrayed by the fragility of its corolla: thus, far from answering the demands of human ideas, it is the sign of their failure. In fact, after a very short period of glory the marvelous corolla rots indecently in the sun, thus becoming, for the plant, a garish withering" (*Visions*, 12). Breton, for his part, comments in the *Second manifeste du surréalisme* that Bataille "must surely not be well"; for "the rose, deprived of its petals, remains the *rose*" (219). Bataille decries the tendency to idealize an object by eliminating its *base* elements, while Breton clings to the transcendence and identity of the *idea*, despite its abstraction from the base and the particular.

A second early and noteworthy response to Bataille's work may be found in Sartre's article "Un Nouveau mystique."[6] In the first section of this text, Sartre accuses Bataille of putting forward a "totalitarian thought," one that is "syncretic" in approach. Sartre writes: "In contrast to the analytic processes of philosophers, one might say that Bataille's book presents itself as the result of a totalitarian thought" (149). According to Sartre, Bataille's thought "does not construct itself, does not progressively enrich itself, but, indivisible and almost ineffable, it is level with the surface of each aphorism, such that each one of them presents us with the same complex and formidable meaning seen from a particular light" (149).

Sartre seems to be accusing Bataille of not being systematic, of not elaborating a *system* beginning from *founding principles*. He appears to be dissatisfied with the exposition of Bataille's thought because it refuses to be *linear*. One can suppose that Bataille's response to this accusation would, in itself, issue from various points of departure, thus once again refusing linearity and system.

To put forward this hypothetical response to Sartre, one might first refer to the sections of *Inner Experience* which deal with Descartes and Hegel. In Bataille's eyes, Descartes' philosophy is driven by the project to establish a ground or foundation for knowledge. This *project* begins in the spirit of contestation—"the tormenting genius of Descartes"—but a contestation that is assuaged by the assurance of knowledge methodically accumulated in the interests of *project*: "Without activity linked to *project*, Descartes would not have been able to maintain a deep assurance, which is lost as soon as one is no longer under the spell of *project*" (106). Were Descartes to allow the spirit of contestation to torment him unabated, he would direct it to the need for *project*, to the need to provide a foundation for a system of thought: "It is henceforth less a question of the well or poorly founded nature of accepted propositions than of deciding, once the best understood propositions are established, if the infinite need for knowledge implied in the initial intuition of Descartes could be satisfied" (106). To allow the spirit of contestation, as opposed to the need for *project* to drive one's philosophical quest causes the ground or foundation of the resultant system to give way. The systematic thought which Sartre seems to be advocating in his criticism of Bataille is thereby rendered impossible.

Both Descartes and Hegel are viewed by Bataille as being unable to sustain the unknowability of the unknown and the unknowable. The systems of both philosophers envisage the project of appropriating the unknown to the known. "Which supposes either a solid ground upon which everything rests (Descartes) or the circularity of knowledge (Hegel). In the first case if the ground gives way... in the second, even if assured of having a well-closed circle, one perceives the unsatisfying nature of knowledge. The unending chain of things known is for knowledge but the completion of oneself" (108). In Bataille's view, the movement of Hegel's system towards closure of the circle denies the moment of negativity to which the entire circle could be subjected. "But this circular thought is dialectical. It brings with it the final contradiction (affecting the entire circle): *circular absolute knowledge is definitive non-knowledge*" (108). As was the case with Descartes, it is once again the satisfaction of knowledge obtained through the accomplishment of project that drives Hegel's philosophical system. The systematic thought which Bataille's thought *denies* is only possible under these conditions: either a ground or a closure are needed to satisfy the demands of the project to sustain a philosophic "system."

Keeping Bataille's view of the systems of Descartes and Hegel in mind, we might now respond to Sartre's accusation that Bataille's thought is not systematic, that it does not "construct itself" or "enrich itself," with Bataille's identification with Nietzsche: "In relation to him I am burning, as through a tunic of Nessus, with a feeling of anxious fidelity. That in the path of inner experience he advanced, inspired, undecided, does not stop me—if it is true that, as a philosopher he had as a goal not knowledge but, without separating its operations, life, its *extreme limit*, in a word experience itself..." (26).

What Sartre cannot seem to accept in Bataille's thought is its very point of departure in *experience*—"sole value, sole authority"; his deliberate decision to let "experience... lead where it would, not to lead it to some end point given in advance. And [Bataille] say[s] at once that it leads to no harbor, (but to a place of bewilderment, of nonsense)" (3). Thus to Sartre's critique that Bataille's thought, in its nonlinearity, does not "construct itself" or "enrich itself," Bataille would reply that : "Inner experience, not being able to have principles either in a dogma (a moral attitude) or in science (knowledge can be neither its goal or its origin), or in a search for enriching states (an experimental, aesthetic attitude), it cannot have any other concern nor goal than itself" (7).

Another point of departure for Bataille's hypothetical response to Sartre's accusations may be found in Bataille's admitted deliberate use of reason to deconstruct its own constructions. Without the use of reason as the privileged tool of deconstruction, the latter would lose much of its significance. Madness is ineffectual as a means of deconstruction; mystic and ecstatic release would not be directed or stable enough in their undoing: "Reason alone has the power to undo its work, to hurl down what it has built up... Without the support of reason, we don't reach dark incandescance" (47). What Sartre cannot seem to tolerate is Bataille's use of reason to undo any "system" that depends on self-construction and self-enrichment from principles it carefully elaborates. Indeed Bataille's thought is transgressive vis-à-vis traditional philosophical enterprise by virtue of its very ludic nature. "I set out from notions which were in the habit of closing off certain beings around me, and I played about with them [*je m'en suis joué*]" (349), announced Bataille in a *Discussion sur le péché*[7] held with Sartre, among other intellectuals. In this discussion, Bataille declares his desire to escape the limits of all notions so as to "surpass them infinitely," and this with gaiety, irony, and a certain lack of deference [*désinvolture*]. Given his desire for a playful thought, one bent on its own expenditure, it is difficult to accept Sartre's accusation that Bataille's thought is "totalitarian."

As a final rejoinder to Sartre's criticism, one might turn to Bataille's recognition in himself and in all others of the inevitable desire to "carry his person to the pinnacle," to identify with the desire to be everything. This desire is countered and undermined by the impossibility, by defini-tion, of embracing this everything: "Being is *nowhere*" (82) he writes in

*Inner Experience*, there is but a labyrinthine composition of beings, each composition a composite of other compositions, themselves composites... The recognition of a composition of beings, transcended by no totality, but which is rather composed by mobile groups in provisional positions of transcendence and immanence—this recognition that "Being is *nowhere*" would preclude the establishment of a system reflecting a totality. In short, it is Sartre's seeming need to identify a linear, systematically developed thought, there where he sees one that is only "totalitarian" and "syncretic," that Bataille would qualify as totalitarian.

Sartre's criticism of Bataille is also informed by principles laid out in *L'existentialisme est un humanisme*,[8] where he makes the following declaration: "...man exists first, then he encounters himself, surges forth into the world and defines himself after" (21). This subsequent definition which man gives himself is *willed* according to conceptions made of his future life and actions. But no matter what form these conceptions take, man is ultimately nothing other than what he makes of himself. In this sense, man is project and arises from project. Sartre writes: "...man is first of all that which throws itself toward a future and which is conscious of projecting itself into the future. Man is first of all a project that is lived subjectively...nothing exists prior to this project...man will be first of all what he will have projected to be" (*EH*, 23).

It is the primordial role that Sartre gives to project that causes him to criticize Bataille for his assertion that inner experience is the opposite of project. Bataille writes in *Inner Experience*: "I come to this position: inner experience is the opposite of action. Nothing more. Action is utterly dependent upon project... Project is not only the mode of existence implied by action, necessary to action—it is a way of being in paradoxical time: *it is the putting off of existence to a later point*" (46).

Not surprisingly, Sartre takes issue with Bataille's view that one must escape from project to gain access to inner experience, where one might finally become what one truly *is*. While Bataille sees loss of man's essence in project, Sartre sees the impossibility of loss within the experience of the *cogito*. For Sartre, man *is* project. He cannot escape from project, for it constitutes his subjectivity. Thus Bataille's invitation to loss in an experience of "*l'instant*,"—outside of project (which simply postpones this experience indefinitely)—is seen by Sartre as residing still within the experience of a *cogito* for which the experience of loss, of Night, and the abyss is impossible. In "Un nouveau mystique," Sartre explains: "Once one has found oneself through the *cogito* it can no longer be a question of losing oneself: no longer is there an abyss, a night, man carries himself everywhere with himself, wherever he may be he illuminates, he sees only what he illuminates, it is he who decides what meaning things will take" (185).

Bataille and Sartre could not fail to disagree on the importance of project to experience and the possibility of experience outside of project. Where Bataille sets as a "principle of inner experience: to emerge through project from the realm of project" (46) and this, through laughter, through intoxication, *désoeuvrement,* and loss in eroticism, Sartre views project as constitutive of subjectivity, a condition from which one cannot escape, even by means of project. To Bataille's will to experience *"l'instantanéité,"* Sartre opposes the existentialist invocation to action, the call to a responsible use of one's time, the realization of acts conceived within and through project, acts whose ultimate meaning would be the search for freedom *en tant que telle.*

Given the existentialist call to commitment, to *la bonne foi,* and responsibility, Bataille's invocation of childishness, of glory, and irresponsibility, of the exuberant love of the present instant can only be seen by Sartre to be an "unuseable experience" (187). "...[T]he joys to which we are invited by M. Bataille, if they are not to be integrated into a fabric of new enterprises, or to contribute to the formation of a new humanity that would surpass itself by striving towards new goals, are worth nothing more than the pleasure of having a drink, or of sunning one's body at the beach" (187).

The third early response to Bataille's work that I wish to discuss may be found in a chapter of *Homo Viator*[9] written by the Christian existentialist Gabriel Marcel in 1943 and entitled "The Refusal of Salvation and the Exaltation of the Man of Absurdity." In this chapter, Marcel accuses Bataille of, among other things, abrogating for himself a "patent of superiority" when he (Bataille) declares that "spiritual life can only be founded upon an absence of salvation." In the face of this alleged "patent of superiority," Marcel responds that Bataille cannot "install [himself] in an authentic world beyond"; on the contrary, what he does is "merely limit [himself] to playing a game of which the inspiration is boundless pride merging into a will to intimidate" (200).

Marcel is referring here to the passages of *Inner Experience* in which Bataille discusses the role that salvation plays in the religious life of the Christian. In Bataille's view, salvation fulfills a function not dissimilar to that of project in the philosophical investigations of Descartes and Hegel: it affords the value of a positive object which orients questioning and ultimately assuages the spirit of contestation. Just as Descartes refuses this spirit, which had incited his questioning, so the Christian, in dramatizing the sacrifice of Christ, stops short of an experience of anguished loss of self by recuperating this anguish in the project of salvation:

> It is doubtful...if salvation is the object of a true faith or if it is only a convenience permitting one to give the shape of a project to spiritual life (ecstasy is not sought for its own sake, it is the path of a deliverance, a means)...salvation for the faithful is "becoming everything"... (22)

Marcel counters this view of salvation with his own: where Bataille views salvation as a value permitting Christians to satisfy their desire, and one shared by all beings, of "carrying their person to the pinnacle," of "wanting to be everything," Marcel argues that salvation delivers one from the egotism of the self:

> But how is it possible not to recognize that spiritual life is found in the renunciation of ambition?...The aspiration to salvation is seen to be...different in character because in its principle it is not and cannot be a will, and it thus escapes from the world of the project which the author never tires of excommunicating. Salvation can only be deliverance, but deliverance from what, if not from the principle of the egotistical self ruled over by avarice? (195)

It is noteworthy that Marcel, while denying the possibility of a "will" to salvation, speaks in this passage of an "aspiration to salvation." He thus seems to be suggesting that salvation is something that is accorded by God, not made to materialize by the practising Christian. Yet he cannot deny that the "aspiration" for salvation is there. Bataille's point is not that the Christian "wills" his reward, but that he desires to be "saved" and not "lost" to the abyss of nothingness, of forgottenness after death. It is in this sense that salvation responds to the "*will to be everything*"—to which Bataille opposes the opposite will: "where the will to become everything would be regarded as an obstacle to that of losing oneself...To lose oneself in this case would be to lose oneself and *in no way to save oneself*" (22). Christians, if they lose themselves in the dramatization of Christ's sacrifice, do so, Bataille argues, safe in the knowledge that they will ultimately be saved from radical loss. It is to this difference between his and the Christian experience that Bataille refers when he writes: "I feel that I am situated with respect to [the Christian] as the opposite of one who calmly looks from the shore at a dismasted ship. I am sure that the ship is dismasted. And I must insist upon this. I am amused and I look at the people on the shore much more joyfully than those on the shore can look at the dismasted vessel, because, in effect, despite everything, I cannot imagine anyone so cruel that, from the shore, he could observe someone dismasted with a joyous laughter. The act of sinking, however, is something else: one can give oneself fully to this experience with a joyful heart" (*Discussion*, 359). Unlike the Christian, who fears for his salvation, Bataille gives himself freely to loss without salvation.

As for Marcel's criticism that Bataille "installs himself in an authentic world beyond" from which he uses his "boundless pride" to "intimidate," one must respond to these remarks from various perspectives. First of all, Bataille can hardly be said to "install himself," since he writes repeatedly of the impossibility of knowing the extreme limit attained: "I can only, I suppose, reach the extreme limit in repetition, for this reason, that I am never sure of having attained it, that I will never be sure" (42–43). That Marcel should believe Bataille to consider his experience as an "authentic" "beyond" is a remark that also demands clarification. Bataille prefers to use the term "authority," rather than "authentic," since he can never guarantee the "authenticity" of his having attained the extreme limit of experience. He writes, rather, of inner experience as "sole value, sole authority," refusing to submit it to any value or authority affixed in advance and from without. This authority, however, eludes canonization as authority; in Blanchot's words, it is an authority that "expiates itself." Nor can one say that experience is really "beyond," for this would once again imply the objectification of it, in order to situate it vis-à-vis what is this side of it. Rather than access to a "beyond," Bataille writes of experience as spiraling, agitated, culminating in supplication: "The extreme limit of the possible assumes laughter, ecstasy, terrified approach towards death; assumes error, nausea, unceasing agitation of the "possible" and the impossible and, to conclude—broken, nevertheless by degrees, slowly desired—the state of supplication, its absorption into despair" (39).

Finally, to Marcel's accusation that Bataille suffers from a "boundless pride" that is intent on "intimidation," one must respond with passages from *Inner Experience* in which Bataille speaks of the "vanity of vanity" and of "community." That "vanity" (pride) should be "vain" (idle, useless) is what Bataille suggests as he intertwines the two meanings in the following passage. He begins by showing that vanity and pride are the catalysts that engage one in project: "...vanity is...only the condition for a project, for a putting off of existence until later...One has egotistical satisfaction only in project; the satisfaction escapes as soon as one accomplishes..." (49). Given that vanity and pride engage one in projects that merely put off existence, and given that they are dissipated upon the completion of projects, inciting one to a further postponement of existence in renewed projects, they can only be recognized as "vanity"—emptiness, what is inessential. It is only "vanity" *recognized* as "vanity" (a celebration of idleness), that, paradoxically, permits one to escape "vanity" (as both pride and inanity). "In the anguish enclosing me, my gaiety justifies, as much as it can, human vanity, the immense desert of vanities, its dark horizon where pain and night are hiding—a dead and divine gaiety" (49). This is playfulness, joyful expenditure, idleness, the *désoeuvrement* unknown to pride in project, be it surrealist, existentialist, Christian, or other. It is this disdain for pride that leads Bataille to write: "Infinite surpassing in oblivion, ecstasy, indifference, towards myself, towards this book..." (59).

This indifference toward the self which arises when the "vanity of vanity" is recognized is doubled by the desire for a community composed of beings lost as waves among waves. Thus, to Marcel's accusation that Bataille engages in "intimidation," one can only respond with the passages where he writes of "the passage of warmth or of light from one being to another" (94). In a direct address to his reader which is hardly characteristic of one who "intimidates," Bataille writes of this passage "from you to your fellow being or from your fellow being to you (even at the moment when you read in me the contagion of my fever which reaches you)...Thus we are nothing, neither you nor I, beside burning words which could pass from me to you, imprinted on a page: for I would have lived in order to write them..." (94). This desire for communication, this disdain for pride and vanity leads him to add at a later point: "I find in myself nothing, which is not even more than myself, at the disposal of my fellow being. And this movement of my thought which flees from me—not only can I not avoid it, but there is no movement so secret that it doesn't animate me. Thus I speak—everything in me gives itself to others" (128–129). These are hardly the words of one whose "boundless pride" is used to "intimidate."

⋘⋙

Since the publication of these early reactions to Bataille's writings, the interest which his work has sollicited has resulted in conferences given in his honor (from the 1971 Colloque de Cerisy to one held 20 years later at the University of London[10]), journal editions devoted entirely to his work (notably those of *Critique, Arc,* and more recently, *Yale French Studies* and *Stanford French Review*[11]) as well as articles and books, in increasing numbers, on various aspects of his work.

Although viewed at times as "no more than a shadowy (if crucial) precursor of such poststructuralists as Derrida, Foucault, Baudrillard, and Kristeva,"[12] Bataille has also been judged instrumental in effecting a "mutation" in modern epistemology and theories of classification. "A veritable culture hero of the French literary and philosophical avant-garde," writes Susan Suleiman, "Bataille's writings functioned as a major intertext in the theories of cultural subversion and of (literary) textuality that were being elaborated around the *Tel Quel* group during the years immediately following the explosion of May 1968."[13]

My intention in this section of the introduction is to stimulate an examination of the way in which Bataille's work may be situated with respect to the aforementioned mutation in modern epistemology and theory, although to define with some accuracy and precision the nature of this "mutation" is, of course, an impossible task which, given the variety and complexity of perspectives on this question, can only be dealt with peremptorily in the space of this introduction. In the interest, however, of opening discussion on the nature of this mutation which has come to be associated with the onset of "postmodernism"— in order to better situate Bataille's work vis-à-vis this phenomenon and question the extent to which his singular and idiosyncratic work risks distortion once again, this time in order to accommodate the concerns of contemporary theorists—I will, in the next few pages, refer to the arguments of Foucault, Derrida, and Lyotard (although many others could have been chosen): Foucault, because he refers directly to Bataille's contribution; Derrida, because of his articulation of what he identifies as the closure of Western metaphysics; and Lyotard, because his controversial views on the nature of postmod-ernism have in turn stimulated a variety of responses which together attempt to define the nature of the postmodern and its relationship to the modern.

Foucault's *The Order of Things*[14] ends with passages that refer to the phenomenon, in our day, of a literature fascinated by the being of language, a literature in which *finitude* posits itself in *language*. "And it is indeed in this space thus revealed that literature, first with surrealism (though still in a very much disguised form), then, more and more purely, with Kafka, Bataille, and Blanchot, posited itself as experience: as experience of death (and in the element of death), of unthinkable thought (and in its inaccessible presence), ... as experience of finitude (trapped in the opening and the tyranny of that finitude)" (383–384). Foucault's book ends with his famous suggestion that the return of a preoccupation with language in literature and in the human sciences heralds the disappearance of "man" as the epistemological figure that appeared at the beginning of the nineteenth century when man first "constituted himself as a positive figure in the field of knowledge" (326). This figure of man first emerged in the form of an "empirico-transcendental doublet"—the being in whom knowledge would be attained of what makes knowledge possible (318). For Foucault, this new figure appeared only after a major epistemological shift, for in the classical period, from the beginning of the seventeenth century to the end of the eighteenth century, knowledge was ordered by representation, a system in which "the subject is kept at bay."[15] In this classical period, the relationships between things and their representations were articulated and understood in tabular form, but the knowing subject did not have a place in this network of representation. It was only at the beginning of the nineteenth century that historical depth was given to what were formerly viewed as the "surface regularities of classical knowledge" (*F*, 51). It is only in this new, dynamic, historical space that the figure of man as knowing subject could be postulated. As the new "empirico-transcendental doublet," man is now recognized as the knowing subject in whom the conditions of knowledge arise and are met. The phenomenological enterprise epitomizes this search, in its effort to grasp both the empirical and transcendental elements of experience. As J. G. Merquior observes, this was an epistemological requirement almost impossible to meet in a satisfactory way. "No wonder, then, such an ambiguous figure of knowledge [man, the empirico-transcendental doublet] is threatened by the prospect of dissolution" (*F*, 53).

This threat is also fired by inquiries launched by the new human sciences—particlarly the "counter-sciences" of psychoanalysis, ethnology, and linguistics which turn their critical attention to man's Other, his unthought [*impensé*] and in so doing, "ceaselessly 'unmake' that very man who is creating and re-creating his positivity in the human sciences by revealing the concrete figures of finitude...Desire, Law and Death."[16] In his discussion of the emergence of linguistics as a counter-science, Foucault points to the "reunification of language" which had taken on a variety of forms and modes of being when man first emerged as a positive epistemological figure. It is this reunification of language and its

increasing importance in our day, together with the way in which
linguistic categories are extended and applied to a growing number of
disciplines and areas of study that heralds the "end of man" in its present
epistemological configuration (382), for "linguistics no more speak[s] of
man himself than do psychoanalysis and ethnology" (381). Foucault notes
that the return of language and the disappearance of man are perceptible
in philosophy and literature as well, for the question of language is posed
more and more not only within philosophic reflection, but outside and
"against" it in literature (385).

Bataille's fiction, from *Histoire de l'oeil* (1928) to *L'Abbé C.* (1950),
contains numerous passages that indeed exemplify what Foucault has
identified as the positing, within literature, of the 'experience of death, of
finitude, and of unthinkable thought (in its inaccessible presence)'. One
can also discern the questioning of language throughout the corpus of his
work, and this is a questioning which often arises within his literature,
where one could even say, with Foucault, that it is played out and
directed *against* the reflections contained in his own philosophic texts.
But to situate Bataille's thought vis-à-vis Foucault's postulation of the
"disappearance of man" is more difficult. Bataille referred to his works as
"un anthropomorphisme déchiré",[17] but never ceased to meditate upon
what it was that made experience *human*, writing in the Preface to
*Eroticism* that he had "sacrificed everything to the search for a point of
view from which the unity of the human spirit emerges…"[18] From his
early articles in *Documents* to his later texts *Eroticism* and *The Accursed
Share*, Bataille examined the rituals and practices that showed the
inevitable *human* need for expenditure and participation in the sacred.
At the same time, Bataille's work, as precisely this "anthropomorphisme
déchiré," privileged the phantasmagorical figure of *Acéphale*, the headless
being whose sovereign experience culminated in a blinding and all-
consuming non-knowledge. In this sense, this figure already stands in
complete opposition to the epistemological figure of man as Foucault has
defined it, the empirico-transcendental doublet whose objective, as
subject, is to secure and master knowledge of himself as object in and of
the world. The figure *Acéphale* delivers an experience of the *impossible*
auto-mutilation or blinding to which one could say that the figure of the
"empirico-transcendental doublet" fantasmagorically subjects itself. It is
not surprising, therefore, that the singularity of Bataille's work, a work
that claimed to both rupture anthropomorphism and to bear witness to an
inner experience, should be difficult to place in the context of Foucault's
discussion of the "disappearance of man" in *The Order of Things*.

Derrida's article entitled "The Ends of Man"[19] also addresses the way in which contemporary French thought has witnessed a mutation of sorts: where existentialism (both Christian and atheist) *and* Marxism could be said to share a common ground of humanism, it is the critique of humanism and anthropologism that united and dominated much of French thought since the 1960s. In this article, however, Derrida emphasizes that contemporary philosophical language and, by extension, the language of this critique, is still marked by Hegelian discourse, a discourse that subsumes humanism, for Hegelian *Aufhebung* already designates the end of man—both its achievement and its end, "the appropriation of its essence" (121). Derrida writes that, despite the critique of anthropologism, "the infinity of *telos*" (123) continues to regulate our discourse. He then indicates the following signs of a "trembling" that informs this French thought, a trembling that threatens the "co-belonging and co-propriety of the name of man and the name of Being" (133). These signs are *the reduction of meaning*, which, in opposition to the phenomenological reduction to meaning, seeks to determinine the "possibility of a meaning on the basis of a 'formal' organization which in itself has no meaning" (134) and what he calls *the strategic bet*—two strategies to mark the effects of this trembling "from the inside where 'we are'." These strategies can only be to "attempt an exit and a deconstruction without changing terrain" (the Heideggerean strategy) and "to decide to change terrain, in a discontinuous and irruptive fashion" (the strategy of much of this French thought) (135).

To place Bataille's work in the context of this description of recent French thought requires that one ask to what extent he engaged in a critique of anthropologism and if there is evidence in his work of this "trembling" that appears to dislocate the name of man from the name of Being.

Once again, his remark in *L'Amitié* that his work constituted "un anthropomorphisme déchiré" comes to mind. While it is true that his language, like Hegelian discourse and our own, is necessarily regulated by "the infinity of *telos*," and by a discourse that subsumes humanism, his was a singular meditation upon the Hegelian moment of "unemployed negativity." In his letter to Kojève,[20] Bataille writes of the man who, at the end of history, would no longer have anything to do, who would recognize the negativity within him as being empty of content; such a man would be unable to escape either his negativity, or the uneasiness he would feel in facing it, for at that moment, there would be no way out, no action would be possible any longer (371). As a manifestation of

Bataille's *anthropomorphisme déchiré*, this meditation is meant as an extension and completion of the process implied by Hegelian *Aufhebung*, inserting unemployed negativity there where Hegel had envisioned satisfaction through work as the *end of man* (meant in both senses of the word).   Thus, while Bataille's discourse, like our own, is marked by Hegelian discourse, it extends the latter by imagining, in *désoeuvrement*, the culmination of productivity at the end of History, a productivity that Hegel had identified as the "end-point" of man.   Tony Corn addresses the singularity of Bataille's meditation on this moment of unemployed negativity in an article of this volume.

As Derrida argues in his own well-known article on Bataille,[21] the major writing which the latter's works enclose engage in a reduction *of*, and not *to* meaning, and it is in this sense that his *Inner Experience*—which, among other things, could be construed as a sort of critique of phenomenological bracketing—aligns itself with the critique of anthropologism of which Derrida writes. In addition, Bataille's thought—which recognized *ipse's* impossible attempt to enclose a Being that was precisely *nowhere*—may be said to take account of that "trembling," or the dislocation of the name of man from the name of Being, and no doubt this is accomplished in Bataille's text more from within, "without changing terrain," than by doing so in a "discontinuous, irruptive fashion."

A third text which addresses the question of an epistemological "mutation"—in whose context the works of Bataille can only be placed with some difficulty—is Lyotard's *The Postmodern Condition*.[22]   There Lyotard argues that the postmodern "is undoubtedly a part of the modern" (79).   Whereas many theorists situate the postmodern as *following* the modern, Lyotard believes that it is inscribed within the *beginnings* of a constantly evolving "modern": "A work can become modern only if it is first postmodern.  Postmodernism thus understood is not modernism at its end but in its nascent state, and this state is constant" (79).

Lyotard essentially distinguishes between the modern artist, who attempts to "present the unpresentable," given that the real has become less accessible to representation, and the postmodern artist whose work still inheres in the modern tradition in its attempt to present the unpresentable, but who tries to situate the unpresentable within presentation itself.  Whereas the modern artist expresses his powerlessness to present the unpresentable—often exhibiting a certain nostalgia for lost presence—the postmodern artist situates the unpresentable within his work, and does so without the assistance of preestablished rules or aesthetic categories to guide the formation of his work of art.

To put the matter differently, Lyotard views the modern artist as making explicit or visible the fact that there is something which cannot be made visible. There are two ways of realizing this task: on the one hand, there are artists like Chirico and Proust who allow the unpresentable to be invoked as "missing contents" without, however, inventing "new rules" of expression to convey the existence of these missing contents. On the other hand, there are artists like Joyce and Duchamp who invoke the unpresentable not as "missing contents," but within presentation itself. These postmodern artists experiment with new forms, inventing new rules of the game which, in fact, serve only to heighten, within their work, the invocation of the unpresentable. The works of these postmodern artists remain, strictly speaking, within the framework of modern art, by virtue of their quest to invoke, negatively, the unrepresentable, a quest that they share with modern artists. What distinguishes their work from the latter is, then, the fact that their experimentation with forms and with new rules of the game in their invocation of the unpresentable takes place without their reliance upon conventions and consensus of taste that would make their chosen form of expression recognizable to its addressees. This recognition and the consensus that accompanies it would, ostensibly, be forthcoming in time, hence Lyotard's statement that the postmodern is part of the modern, that it is modern art in its nascent state.

Criticism of Lyotard's theory has most often been directed to his placement of the postmodern *within* an always evolving modern,[23] and it is this criticism that has helped to focus the debate on what distinguishes the postmodern from the modern.

Frederic Jameson, for example, suggests that postmodernism arises from a break with modernity.[24] Whereas the modern looks "for new worlds," the "postmodern looks for breaks,...for shifts and irrevocable changes in the *representation* of things and of the way they change" (ix). Thus moderns, who are still preoccupied with the essence of the *things* that have changed and the results of these changes, are, according to Jameson, more apt to be caught in a substantialist, Utopian, or essentialist perspective (ix). Postmoderns, on the other hand, explore the *changes* in representation themselves, since they view the contents of these variations as capable of an endless variation according to context. This postmodern lack of concern for the "essence" of things leads Jameson to attribute to postmodern works "a new depthlessness, which finds its prolongation...in a whole new culture of the image or the simulacrum" (6), a depthlessness accompanied by a general diminution or waning of "affect," for the new de-centered "subject" is free of the anxiety experienced by its modern counterpart. In fact, Jameson argues that the postmodern subject becomes liberated from other feelings as well, "since there is no longer a self present to do the feeling..."(15).

The distinction (or break) between modernism and postmodernism is also argued by Boyne and Rattansi,[25] who nonetheless attribute lines of continuity between the two, since, for them, postmodernism "extends and deepens the critique already begun by modernism" (8). To define what they understand by the term "modernism," Boyne and Rattansi quote Lunn,[26] who sees in modern texts the belief that it is possible to locate and recover the world's essential truth, hidden as it is beneath appearances. But for this revelation to be accomplished, more "complex, inventive and self-reflexive" strategies than those used in realist or naturalist art are needed. These strategies include an aesthetic of self-reflexiveness; a juxtaposition or montage permitting the simultaneous existence of various points of view; paradox, ambiguity, and uncertainty; and the waning and displacement of the centered, individual subject.[27] Thus, the modern belief in the world's essential and recoverable truth obtains, despite the apparently contradictory tendency to fragment the narrative voice and to highlight paradox, ambiguity, and uncertainty. Boyne and Rattansi view *postmodernism* as deepening and extending this process through its "commitment to heterogeneity, fragmentation and difference" (9). Although the moderns believe that it is possible to uncover the essential truth of the world, the postmoderns, sceptical of such a possibility, believe that literary theory, philosophy, and the social sciences are essentially unable "to deliver totalizing theories and doctrines or enduring answers to fundamental dilemmas and puzzles posed by objects of inquiry..." (12).

The views of Lyotard, Jameson, Boyne, and Rattansi indicate the multiplicity of perspectives from which a certain "epistemological mutation" known as the onset of postmodernism has been represented; within the perspective of these views, it is once again not easy to situate Bataille's work. One could argue, for example, that, while he did not experiment with new forms *per se* in the manner of a Duchamp or a Joyce, he does tend to situate the unpresentable rather immediately within presentation itself (a phenomenon which Lyotard associates with postmodern art). Witness to this are the numerous passages of his literary texts, punctuated as they are by silence, and where, in the words of

Foucault, the subject engaged in unthinkable thought is "thrown by it, exhausted, upon the sands of that which he can no longer say" (39). There is also, however, in Bataille's work something suggestive of a desire which locates the unpresentable *outside* of the text, an unpresentable which orients from afar the text's movement. This is the dead star, NIGHT, the impossible death that would wash him—what his readers would one day know and to which he would not, but for one fleeting instant, gain access. That Bataille's work both attempts to situate the unpresentable immediately within presentation itself and evinces a desire for the unpresentable, located outside of the text, makes it somewhat difficult to place within the perspective of Lyotard's categories.

Jameson's formulations also render the situation of Bataille's writings problematic. While it is true, as Klossowski has shown, that Bataille could have recourse only to "simulacra" of notions in his communication of the incommunicable, this use of the simulacrum is not evidence of a certain "depthlessness" seen in a "new culture of the simulacrum." While his work does not point to a depthlessness, neither does it manifest an unequivocal essentialism. For Bataille, it will be remembered, "Being is *nowhere...It is only "grasped" in error...*" (82).

The theories of Boyne, Rattansi, and Lunn help to focus the debate on postmodernism and its distinction from modernism, but once again Bataille's work seems to elude classification. One can find evidence of self-reflexiveness, ambiguity, and paradox (strategies of the centered, modern text) as well as a movement towards decentering which, in the postmodern text, is accompanied by a "commitment to heterogeneity, fragmentation and difference." While it is true that Bataille's work announces the inability of sociology, philosophy, and literary theory to "deliver totalizing theories and doctrines or enduring answers to fundamental dilemmas and puzzles posed by objects of inquiry," it is also accurate to note Bataille's comment that "*[t]he world is given to man as if it were a puzzle to solve*" (xxxiii). He writes: "*My entire life—with its bizarre dissolute moments as well as deep meditations—has been spent solving this puzzle*" (xxxiii). Once the elements of a "*disciplined emotional knowledge*" had come in contact with a "*discursive knowledge,*" and once thought had dissolved before being rediscovered again "*at a point where laughs the unanimous throng,*" Bataille awakened before a new enigma: "*one [he] knew at once to be unsolvable...*" (xxxiii). With these statements, Bataille seems to exhibit neither a belief in the hidden, recoverable truth of the world, nor in a scepticism that would disengage him from his interest in the "world's enigma."

That Bataille should occupy a singular position vis-à-vis those of the theorists mentioned above is no doubt further complicated by the indeterminacy characterizing the "break" or "mutation" separating modernism from postmodernism. This indeterminacy is problematized by Barry Smart who is perhaps more concerned with the phenomenon of *postmodernity* than he is with the *postmodern per se*. He sees postmodernity as a "contemporary social, cultural and political condition…as a form of reflection upon and a response to the accumulating signs of the limits and limitations of modernity… as a more modest modernity, a sign of modernity having come to terms with its own limits and limitations.[28] Smart's observations about postmodernity and its relation to modernity point, as well, to the difficulty which inheres in any discussion of the postmodern and its relation to the modern. Does the postmodern constitute a break with the modern, or is it really and more properly a feature of high modernism, modernism radicalized by an extension/recognition of its own features and limitations? Do the heterogeneity and difference associated with the postmodern not arise naturally from modernism, whose relentless "pursuit of order and control, promotion of calculability, affirmation of the 'new' [and] preoccupation with 'progress'…are necessarily articulated" with a simultaneous range of negatively viewed experiences and conditions such as "the risk of chaos, the persistent presence of chance or threat of indeterminacy…" (92–93)? In response to these questions, Smart is inclined to agree with Lyotard that the postmodern is undoubtedly part of the modern. "In consequence," he writes, "the postmodern does not so much signal the end of the modern, but rather the pursuit of 'new rules of the game'" (116). Whether or not one accepts this view, or any of the others enunciated previously, Bataille's writings cannot, I believe, be situated firmly on either one or the other side of the "division" distinguishing the modern from the postmodern. Rather, his texts are perhaps uniquely equipped to problematize the question of the division, for they bear elements attributed to both sides, while escaping reduction to either.

Thus despite the impossibility of determining, without equivocation, the nature of the epistemological mutation under discussion—a phenomenon still very much the subject of controversy in countless books and articles devoted to the question of postmodernism—it is my expectation that the articles in this volume will help to situate Bataille's work vis-à-vis this troubling epistemological "mutation." In particular, I believe that the articles in this volume will help to address the issue of Bataille's "subversive intent"[29] vis-à-vis traditional ideology and philosophical discourse.

While Libertson writes, in his article in this volume, that the "contemporary student of Bataille confronts a critical tradition …[which] has declared with urgent sympathy the immediate relevance of Bataille's thought to contemporary philosophical issues"—a relevance, moreover, which the authors in this book do not question—this critical tradition has "attributed to his categories a radical, violently subversive opposition to the categories of a 'traditional' discourse" (55). While it is true that many readers of Bataille are quick to adopt the latter position, at least two of the authors included in this volume challenge the extremity of this view.

In order, then, to highlight the various aspects of Bataille's contribution to the aforementioned "epistemological mutation," I have grouped the present articles into five categories, although it is true that Bataille's writing defied classification into easily recognized and separate domains of investigation. For this reason, my discussion of the points of conjuncture between articles in each category could be extended to a discussion of links between articles drawn from various categories.

## BATAILLE AND PHILOSOPHICAL INQUIRY

As the four articles in this section suggest, Bataille's philosophical writings appear to occupy a frontier position in that through them the investigation of the relationship of thought and experience to traditional philosophical inquiry is radicalized: Bataille's questionings lead critics to reformulate the relationship of Bataille's texts to those of Nietzsche and Hegel, which leads in turn to a reformulation of the Nietzsche/Hegel relationship. This incitement to reformulation extends through Bataille's texts to those of his critics as well: readings of readings of Bataille have led to reformulations of, for example, the relationship of Derrida's texts to those of Hegel and Bataille, causing one critic to suggest that Derrida is "less Bataillean than he thinks."[30]

For Robert Sasso, Bataille's thought is one which aims to defy all finitude—that of things, practice, and knowledge: it is a thought intolerant of the tendency of philosophical inquiry to lock out any operation that it deems to exist "this side of" or "beyond" the horizon or arena of its own activity. Sasso points to Bataille's conviction that thought originates "in a collapse" (for man to think, he must experience a rupture from his continuity with nature and animality). Despite the acrobatics of traditional philosophical reasoning, thought cannot escape from its own violence, a violence into which it ultimately collapses in the end.

In an early and important article, Lionel Abel examines Bataille's relationship to Nietzsche in light of their respective positions on action and consciousness—Bataille views action, while Nietzsche, consciousness, as limiting life's possibilities. He also looks at the respective views of Sartre and Bataille on commitment (to life and to death), noting that there is always a "remainder"—neither innocent nor guilty—an irritant in the form of a hesitation or an afterthought, that stands in the way of total commitment. It is this "remainder" that Bataille tries to eliminate in himself by undertaking to repeat Nietzsche and his experience, knowing all the while that an authentic repetition of Nietzsche is impossible, for it means accepting death, his own and Nietzsche's, there where Nietzsche had affirmed life. For Abel, the impossibility of this repetition is no doubt what incites Bataille to undertake it.

Once again we see a thought originating in a collapse, this time Bataille's thought as a collapse of his experience into that of Nietzsche, the potential collapse of their difference (its possibility and impossibility), and the desire for a collapse of the "remainder" separating him from Nietzsche and inciting him to repeat the latter's experience.

Denis Hollier reflects on the relationship of Bataille's texts to those of both Nietzsche and Hegel, noting that if the texts of the two philosophers do not explicitly confront each other, this is because the double but separate play of Nietzschean and Hegelian thought within Bataille's text can be distinguished as obeying separate rules. Where Bataille speaks *of* Hegel, occupying a position of transcendence vis-à-vis the latter's texts, he does so in order to correct the misunderstandings to which Hegel's texts have been subject. He does not speak *of* Nietzsche but rather, from his position of immanence vis-à-vis Nietzsche's texts, tries to make Nietzsche speak in his own discourse. For Hollier, the return of Nietzsche/of Nietzsche's return entails the return of sacrifice (the one who returns has already lost his identity). The return can therefore not be *recognized.* Non-recognition is, paradoxically, the condition for an authentic reading of Nietzsche's return, for the return of sacrifice cannot be thematized; if Nietzsche is in Bataille, Bataille must be in Nietzsche's absence; immanence in absence will lead inexorably to (and indeed already implies) Bataille's absence. Bataille, suggests Hollier, is only the means for a repetition of Nietzsche, but since this repetition cannot be thematized, Bataille is its means only to the extent that the means fail him. This collapse of means enables a collapse of difference in repetition—the return of a thought in which identity has been sacrificed.

Tony Corn extends the question of authenticity and recognition in reading *within* Bataille's texts to that of Bataille's *critics.* Derrida's reading of Bataille's reading of Hegel is examined for its metonymic moves—if, as

Corn suggests, Derrida "plays Bataille against Bataille in order to play Bataille against Hegel," then Corn plays Derrida's Bataille against Hegel in order to play Derrida against Derrida. If one can assume that the crux of Derrida's argument in "A Hegelianism Without Reserve" is that Bataille feigns to repeat Hegel in order to play Hegel's concept of unemployed negativity against that of closure, Corn asks "why not extend the presumption of feint to Hegel himself?" In other words, why assume that Hegel did not himself feign within his own logos to play the concept of unemployed negativity against closure? Such an assumption, argues Corn, is closer to the position of the later Derrida in *Glas*.

Corn also comments upon Bataille's metonymic reading of Hegel (the master/slave dialectic being only one part of the *Phenemonology*, itself only one part of Hegel's *Oeuvre*) and upon Derrida's metonymic reading of this reading: he attempts to arrive at a decisive reading of Bataille's relationship to Hegel only through a formal study—one that brackets the *becoming* of this relationship. In this neglect of the Hegelian moment of *becoming*, Corn finds Derrida's reading of a "Hegelianism Without Reserve" to be not Hegelian enough.

## EXPENDITURE, GENERAL ECONOMY, AND POLITICAL COMMITMENT

Jean Piel's article (which originally appeared in the aforementioned special edition of *Critique* entitled "*Hommages à Georges Bataille*") begins this section, for it provides a succint description of Bataille's theory of expenditure and the relationship of this theory to those outlining a general economy in *The Accursed Share*. Piel summarizes Bataille's notion of expenditure, whose point of departure is the fact that the sun, source of all earthly energy, gives without receiving, for it emits an energy that can never be entirely recovered by consumption for productive ends. The surplus of global energy cannot but be spent in part unproductively; indeed at the basis of all energy exchange, and therefore of all economy, is the movement of expenditure—production and acquisition are *secondary*, an attempt to capture and channel this expenditure of energy in the interest of utility.

Piel draws some very interesting and significant conclusions from the Bataillean notion of expenditure. He shows how Bataille, "in a bold reversal alone capable of substituting dynamic overviews in harmony with the world for the stagnation of isolated ideas," puts forward a view of a general economy which, contrary to economic theories tied to political considerations, is conceived not as a separate system, but as an economy of the "living masses" in their "entirety." The limited notion of (politically determined) economy, like other notions in Bataille's work, is opened beyond itself until, in a movement engaging it in the freedom of thought, it operates in a way that is finally consonant, in its freedom, with the "movement of the world." This world—both open to and a product of chance—is bound in its "destiny" to expenditure, and despite (or perhaps thanks to) a myriad of productive accomplishments which outstrip and at times annul one another, it can only culminate in a "useless and infinite realization." Use-less because no moment of production can withstand the pressure towards expenditure and thus maintain the integrity of its "use." Bataille, writes Piel, views man as a summit—attained through his capacity and inevitable indulgence in the squandering of energy—energy that can never *entirely* be channeled for productive ends.

Arkady Plotnitsky takes as his point of departure Bataille's notion of expenditure when he asks whether or not Bataille avoids idealizing waste, which he opposes to consumption for productive purposes. While Plotnitsky points to Bataille's tendency at times to "subordinate the effects of exchange and consumption" (to a somewhat idealized insistence on the primordiality of waste), he also underlines Bataille's awareness that to privilege expenditure unconditionally is just as untenable as to not account for its loss. Plotnitsky argues that Bataille's "insistence on waste is saved by his labyrinthine complexity of inscription of these theories." In writing of an exchange *of* expenditures, Bataille avoids reducing his view of economy to either an exchange economy or to one that is entirely free of exchange; the exuberance of the sovereign operations which he describes always involves more than mere waste or expenditure.

The "lameness" to which the title of Jean Borreil's article refers is, in a sense, not unrelated to the questions surrounding the general economy, for what is at issue is the tendency to compartmentalize existence by adherence to the various "fetishizing" functions of science, art, politics… These disciplines or domains, like all others, cause one to become lost in their individual, *restricted* economies. They tend to supplant man, to reduce him to a "link on the chain," rather than to return him to the unpredictability of life and its chances, a movement whose openness links it to a *general* economy of energy.

Borreil is particularly interested in the dilemma with which the intellectual outside of the Communist Party is faced after the 1917 revolution, when Marxist theory became the science of revolution. The theory, having been recognized as successful, eliminated the need for theoreticians. How was Bataille, who wanted to save the autonomy of the masses and therefore, by the same token, the autonomy of the intellectual, to account for the Marxist position of centrality, its "horizon of unsurpassability"? Borreil writes that Bataille's answer was to fight against intellectuals in the name of the "whole man."

By means of a detour which examines the significance of Bataille's analysis of fascism, Borreil suggests that the centrality of Marxism (which ensures the "lameness" of the propogandist) was surpassed in Bataille by a Nietzschean centrality. Nietzsche addressed free spirits who were "incapable of letting themselves be used." Fascism, on the other hand, which is far more capable of fascinating the masses than Marxism, uses and betrays the energy (sollicited by Nietzsche) as a means to control and discipline, thereby homogenizing the heterogeneous. For Bataille, Nietzsche's thought allows one to "reestablish the play of excess that fascism confiscates." Borreil shows that Nietzsche's invocation of the free spirit permits Bataille to return to the "whole man"—having escaped the "lameness" awaiting the artist or the propogandist—and to emerge from Marxism, having surpassed (not negated) it, in his substitution of Nietzschean centrality for Marxist centrality.

## ALTERITY, HETEROLOGY, AND COMMUNICATION

The invocation of the "free spirit," the desire to return to the "whole man," is directly related to the "voyage to the end of the possible" upon which Bataille embarks in *Inner Experience*. In that text, Bataille describes the paradoxical desire of "wanting to be everything," therefore of escaping the experience of discontinuous *ipseity*, while maintaining the limits and integrity of the latter in order that the escape from discontinuity be savored. Alterity, or "a being otherwise" is desired by *ipse*, which at the same time fears loss in this otherness. The articles that follow address themselves to the way in which this otherness is experienced and communicated in Bataille's texts.

Pierre Klossowski's article, "Of the Simulacrum in the Communication of George Bataille," begins with a definition of sorts: atheology (which appears in the title of Bataille's *Summa Atheologiae*) designates, for Klossowski, a vacancy of the site held by God, "guarantor of the personal self." Atheology therefore designates as well the vacancy of the self "whose vacancy is experienced in a consciousness that, since it is not this self, is its vacancy." The "communication" of this vacancy can only be realized through simulacra of notions, the simulacrum being the "sign of an instantaneous state" that does not permit the exchange of ideas between one mind and another. Indeed, the simulacrum does not communicate; it "mimics" the incommunicable. Klossowski asks, "How can the contents of experience keep their 'sovereign' character of an expenditure tending towards pure loss?" particularly since "inner" experience implies "profit" taken for the self? A further question arises: "How can [the contents of experience] escape sufficiently from notional language to be recognized as simulacra?" This is an apt transcription of the dilemma with which Bataille was faced, using words, "their labyrinths, the exhausting immensity of their 'possibles'" (*IE*, 14) to give to the 'secret of movements leading to interiority' that "sort of resting place where they will finally disappear, the silence which is no longer anything" (*IE*, 16) and which Klossowski likens to "complicity."

Rodolphe Gasché's article, "The Heterological Almanac" examines Bataille's attempt to arrive at a theory of the science of heterology. Just as alterity is seen as a state that disengages ipseity from its rootedness in integral and discontinuous selfhood, so the heterogeneous is viewed by Bataille as invading and intruding upon the homogeneous, upsetting the equilibrium upon which the homogeneous depends and to which it directs itself. Bataille was interested in the description of a science that would have as its object the heterogeneous; Gasché explores the dilemma he faced in attempting to use a homogenizing scientific discourse to present that which can only be foreign to science—the heterogeneous, at first glance, would appear to refer to that which science must eliminate as an unassimilable "waste product."

But Gasché examines with painstaking attention the relationship of science and philosophy (and the homogeneous) to the heterogenous. The heterogeneous is shown to be fissured, comprising a low or left (base) aspect and a high or right (pure) aspect. Homogeneity, which embraces only the continuous and the stabilized, is already limited by what it rejects. It may therefore be seen to lack internal authority or justification for its state, since, in order to exist as such, it depends on an evacuation of what it cannot tolerate. Gasché shows that it is the heterogeneous that exudes this authority, that appears to be sufficient unto itself. But it is in effect only the high heterogeneous that attracts the homogenous, the high heterogeneous having excluded or evacuated from its realm the base, miserable, apparently formless and weaker base elements. Gasché shows that the "sacred core" of the heterogeneous, initially comprised of unequal and mobile, attractive, and repulsive forces, is subjected to a mediation or transformation of the left (base) sacred into the right (high) sacred which allows the homogeneous to become attracted to the high sacred and to abrogate for itself the power of the latter, thus, paradoxically, subordinating it. While the high sacred draws its energy and subsistence from the low sacred which it rejects, it moves towards exhaustion in its affiliation with the homogeneous, thereby becoming vulnerable to a subversive movement arising from the low, base sacred.

Of great significance in this article are the detailed elaborations of this complex relationship between the heterogeneous and the homogeneous and the implications of this relationship for the homogenizing discourses of science and philosophy. Gasché shows that there can be no heterological *object* before the "appropriating" operation of philosophy or of science; thus, heterology must be viewed as a science that must evacuate heterology as its own waste product.

In "Bataille and Communication: *Savoir, Non-savoir, Glissement, Rire,*" Joseph Libertson asks whether Bataille was indeed one whose "heterological practice" subverted and interrupted traditional philosophical discourse, or whether in fact Bataille saw this possibility as already conditioning this discourse, rather than supervening from without, as it were. Libertson opts for the second possibility. He begins his article by describing the frequent oppositional configuration in the Bataillean text. A first term of the opposition designates an ineluctable and negatively viewed closure (prohibition, discontinuity). This first term exists in a relation of "compressed intimacy" and non-tolerance vis-à-vis the second term, one that designates violence (transgression, continuity). The violence of the relationship between the two terms always exceeds the violence of the second term and never effects a synthesis between the two terms that remain in strict opposition. Libertson sees the two terms as "contaminating" and "conditioning one another" and it is in this mutual conditioning that Libertson's views differ from those of Derrida. There where Derrida writes of an "irruption of discourse" effected by Bataille's laughter, Libertson sees laughter as conditioning philosophy's very discourse. There where Derrida champions a defiant, efficacious subversion of traditional discourse, Libertson detects an overestimation of the violent efficacy of Bataille's thought, arising from a misinterpretation of the prohibition/transgression opposition and their mutual conditioning in Bataille's formulations.

## INNER EXPERIENCE AND THE SUBJECT

The question of the "whole man" who avoids the lameness or the restricted domain of the artist, intellectual or party-member, and the question of alterity or complicity "experienced" or "communicated" by a discontinuous self that "contains more than it can contain"—these questions are not unrelated to the issues explored in this section; what is the status of the "subject" in inner experience and can this subject be represented? In his short article entitled "Inner Experience and the Return of the Subject," Paul Smith notes that Bataille, whose text *Histoire de l'érotisme* appeared after the publication of Levi-Strauss' *Structures élémentaires de la parenté*, was not satisfied with the latter's exclusion of the life of the individual from his representation of the dialectic between nature and culture—a dialectic that was to become a founding principle of structuralism. Whereas structuralism tended to relegate the "individual to the status of an abstract bridge between the natural and the cultural," Bataille's focus on erotic experience, as constitutive of a tension between the animal body and the civilized body, highlights an instability within the nature/culture opposition, thus undermining the structuralist attempt to keep these categories mutually exclusive. Smith in fact argues that Bataille's work, in highlighting this instability and in problematizing the question of the life of the individual, runs counter to the structuralist enterprise, for his elaboration of inner experience as characteristic of a "life outside of all intellectual systematization" "acts as the locus for a battle against the agents of systematic thought."

Yet Smith is also quick to argue that the erotic experience that Bataille's texts re-present allows him to disrupt and empty the "assumed plenitude of the individual"; having outlined Bataille's exemplary resistance to structuralist systematization, Smith's article, far from arguing for a return to the subject's plenitude, argues for its problematization.

In his text, *Discerning the Subject*,[31] Smith maintains that the subject is presently conceived in such a way that it has tended to remain purely theoretical, disconnected in general from the "political and ethical realities" in which it is always implicated (xxix). Smith suggests that it is time to find new ways to look at and conceive of the subject by disrupting "both the conceptual and representational modes in which [it is] cast" in the interest of "opening up possibilities for new relations of knowledge and thus for new representations of the subject" (xxxi).

Julia Kristeva, author of "Bataille, Experience and Practice," is in fact given detailed consideration in a chapter of Smith's book. Noting her insistence that a theory of the subject be included in any elaboration of systems of language or representation, Smith then refers to her privileging of literature as the intersection of subject and history—for its ability to highlight "the ideological tearings in the social fabric."[32]

In addition to viewing the literary text as a sort of "borderline or an interface" that separates an individual's social from his subjective existence, Kristeva views the literary text as providing evidence for the way in which the subject confronts and is constituted by the semiotic and the symbolic.

As Paul Smith has observed, Kristeva models her use of the symbolic order upon the symbolic order as outlined by Jacques Lacan, but differs from the latter by showing the symbolic to be comprised of the "semiotic" and the "thetic." Whereas the "thetic" is defined as fulfilling the legalistic and "paternal" functions of the symbolic, the "semiotic" is conceived as upsetting these very repressive functions of the thetic, a thetic that had demanded that the subject submit to its laws (121).

The symbolic and the semiotic are both involved in the constitution of the subject, though neither are able to thoroughly control it. Literature is unique in its ability to "introduce, across the symbolic, [the semiotic] which works, crosses it, and threatens it" (121). Kristeva maintains that the thetic cannot be entirely dissolved or done away with by the semiotic—constrained by both the symbolic and the semiotic, the "subject" for Kristeva is always engaged in the conflict between these two irreconcilable functions. This is why Kristeva uses the formulation of the "sujet en procès: the 'subject' not only in process, but also as it were on trial, put to the test as to its ability to negotiate this contradictory tension" (121).

In "Bataille, Experience and Practice," Kristeva writes that it is necessary to "postulate in order to expend, the affirmative moment in the process creating meaning…" In her view, modern literature, despite the stress it places upon rupture, dissolution, and death, has too often remained wedded to and simply the reverse side of the "monotheistic" (Christian), "substantialist," and "transcendental" authority that it tries to displace.

For Kristeva, Bataille's texts, *unlike* those of his contemporaries, postulate the thetic moment in order to traverse it, in a reverse direction , leading back to the "movement preceding discourse and the subject." This process of first postulating and then traversing the thetic is necessary for any displacement of the monotheistic and transcendental authority mentioned earlier. It is a process—avoided by many "transgressive" works of modern literature—that "exceeds the thetic" and brings about an "adequation of the subject with its movement." This Bataillean process is unlike the process characteristic of Hegelian dialectics that "postulates division, movement and process," only to dismiss them "in the name of a superior metaphysical process."

Like Smith, Kristeva writes of the "recasting" of the subject: in Bataille's work, the subject is affirmed only in order to disappear as such through eroticism and desire; what emerges as the subject is recast is a fusion with the other. But it is only a literature of themes that allows this recasting of the subject to be represented. Philosophy and science cannot arrive at this representation for they rely upon a unary subject from which the possibilities of jouissance and sacrifice have been excluded. Unlike philosophy and science, whose truth-gathering activities depend on specularization arising from the subject, a literature of themes requires the positing of the *thetic* moment in subjective experience, while permitting the backwards traversal of specularization to the "initial moment in the constitution of the subject."

Baudry's article, "Bataille and Science: Introduction to Inner Experience," is also of interest in its questioning of the subject's role in science and in inner experience. Like Kristeva, Baudry refers to Bataille's view of science and philosophy as requiring the establishment of identities ("bringing the other back to the same"): philosophy merely homogenizes and assimilates what science rejects as unassimilable.

It is Bataille's reflections upon the science of heterology and upon the discipline of sociology that bring his theories on the subject into focus. Unlike other sciences, the science of heterology is comprised of heterogeneous elements that directly and concretely affect the subject; these elements therefore elude the pure objectivity necessary for the formulation of scientific laws. Similarly, sociology as a "human science" cannot "reflect on its own position," since its study of the sacred and the profane contains elements that put the subject into play: the subject that studies these givens is altered in the course of its study and in the act of studying. Thus, sociology forces science out of its position as "neutral observer." These reflections on sociology and on the science of heterology both reinforce Bataille's view that science is distortive of experience when it makes an abstraction of the subject. As opposed to the usual "scientific" method, Bataille seeks another method which will lead him to the *heterogeneous* subject. He seeks a "beyond science" which is not its renunciation but its transformation; this is achieved by situating science within the general economy.

Baudry concludes that inner experience for Bataille is this "beyond science"—science's "other" where theory and practice *are no longer opposed.* As opposed to science, inner experience postulates the subject; as opposed to philosophy, which uses the subject to "guarantee being," inner experience postulates the moment of the subject's negation. For Baudry, inner experience is inconceivable outside of a *practice.*

## Histoire de l'oeil and Bataille's fiction

Since the articles in this final section discuss Bataille's fiction and the way in which his literary images operate, it is perhaps not surprising that *Histoire de l'oeil* should be chosen, as the work which represents most clearly and shockingly what is at stake in the Bataillean literary text. *Histoire de l'oeil* was written under a pseudonym in 1928 and its pornographic nature has been discussed by critics like Sontag and Suleiman who examine the significance of this work in light of the transgressive literary production of the avant-garde. Whether critics like Barthes choose to address themselves to the "metonymic" eroticism of this text, or whether feminist critics like Dworkin stress its exemplariness in revealing "the particular truth of *male* desire, or the male imagination of sex, in our culture,"[33] Bataille's representation of erotic experience, in its most extreme and shocking form, cannot be ignored.

In "...And a Truth for a Truth: Barthes on Bataille," Halley puts forward his criticism of Roland Barthes' famous reading of the text.[34] Halley's criticism is that Barthes reads Bataille's eroticism as an "exclusively rhetorical phenomenon." A purely intratextual interpretation centering on "two distinct and autonomous, in fact parallel metaphorical chains," Barthes' reading does not refer to or acknowledge any atextual concept of the erotic. Halley links Barthes' exclusion of such a concept of the erotic from the scene of Bataille's writing to his "indiscriminate rejection of thematic criticism," to his refusal to see in literature a "mirroring of human activity." Just as Smith had seen in Bataille's work a challenging of structuralism's inability to problematize the life of the individual as existing outside of its abstraction in a systematizing thought, so Halley views Bataille's representation of eroticism as constituting a challenge to the tendency of formalist criticism to subsume such a theme in a "formal proliferation of semantic structures which replaces it without ever recording it."

Mikhal Popowski's article, "On the Eye of Legibility: Illegibility in *Story of the Eye* by Georges Bataille," might at first glance appear to return Bataille's text to the "story of an eye," thus eliminating, as had Barthes, any atextual concept of eroticism from the scene of his writing. It is true that Popowski is not concerned with the question of the "themes" of eroticism and death in Bataille's fiction. The object of his study is, rather, the way in which what he calls the "thematics" of the eye and seeing are rendered opaque on the productive level of *Histoire de l'oeil*, and result in illegibility on its receptive level.

Popowski begins his study by noting that, given its "thematic" frequency, the eye seems to occupy the entire space of the text. Since the language of spatial relations (up/down, before/behind) often symbolizes non-spatial relations (good/bad, desirable/undesirable), Popowski is interested in the way that the eye generates spatialization in this text. He examines the preponderance of "face-to-face" configurations, in which the "eye of retention, the eye of interruption, the eye of hypnosis, the eye centered on itself returning to itself in a moment of closure and rupture" ceases to see, and triggers a fixity that limits the surrounding visual field, thereby limiting knowledge. One will note already that this eye is not the eye which Barthes circulated in an endless series of substitutions. If anything, the "thematics" of the eye in this text are viewed by Popowski as a metaphor for the problematic of illegibility encompassed by and originating in the text.

A second set of configurations at work in the text are marked in French by the prepositions "*à*" and "*sous.*" While these prepositions might suggest a "gradation" of levels and distances in the text opening the fixity of the eye's stare into the legibility of seeing/knowing, Popowski shows that this apparent spatial gradation "does not lead to meaning any more than does the face-to-face of the eye."

Popowski concludes that it is not a question in *Histoire de l'oeil* of a "textual polysemia, but of an atrophy of meaning," which suggests once again that his reading departs from that of Barthes. His belief that the text maintains both its legibility and illegibility, the former grasped only negatively and indirectly, leads him to state that *Histoire de l'oeil* is a text that must be "read and un-read in a simultaneous movement"; the reader is obliged, paradoxically, "to look in opposite directions at the same time."

Susan Suleiman's article "Transgression and the Avant-Garde: Bataille's *Histoire de l'oeil*" ends this section on Bataille's fiction. In her article, Suleiman addresses the question of the ways in which Bataille's fiction has been read by practitioners of both "textual" and "ultra-thematic" criticism; she suggests her own model for a "thematic" reading that both "accords the work all due respect" without "letting respect inhibit it" (84).

Suleiman's article begins with important statements on the significance of Bataille's transgressive fiction for the theorists of "cultural subversion and (literary) textuality" (the *Tel Quel* group) whose work came to prominence in the 1960s. These writers (whom Libertson accuses of often overestimating Bataille's subversive "intent" and the efficacy of this intent) practice a "textual" reading of Bataille's work, which integrates his erotic fiction with his philosophical writing. Suleiman correctly notes, however, that with the exception of Barthes (who views eroticism in Bataille's text as a"textual" phenomenon), these writers devote very little if any space to an analysis of the erotic in Bataille's text.

Since every interpretation is "an appropriation of a text for its own purposes" and since every interpretation has its own "blind spot," Suleiman uses the blind spot of the feminist reading of *Histoire de l'oeil* to reveal the blind spot in the "textual" reading of Bataille's text as practiced by the members of the *Tel Quel* group. The blind spot of the "textual" reading is also used to reveal the blind spot in the "ultra-thematic" feminist reading.

Whereas the blind spot of the "textual" reading arises from the fact that it "averts its gaze from the representational or fantasmatic content of Bataille's erotic fiction," Dworkin's feminist and "ultra-thematic" reading is blind to the *framing* of the text: "those aspects of a fictional narrative that designate it, directly or indirectly, as constructed, invented, filtered through a specific medium: in short as a text rather than as life itself." Seizing upon the representation of the female body in Bataille's text, to the exclusion of the philosophic, personal, and intertextual framework within which it arises, Dworkin engages in a "flattening" of Bataille's fiction which, however, leads Suleiman to ask a very important question in her "thematic" reading of this text: Given that the dominant culture has been "not only bourgeois but also patriarchal," "to what extent are the high-cultural productions of the avant-gardes of our century in a relation of complicity rather than in a relation of rupture vis-à-vis dominant ideologies?" Suleiman's conclusion in this article is that the complicity cannot be denied, particularly since the works of this avant-garde fiction, including the works of Georges Bataille, continue to stage their dramas through a model of sexuality that passes through "the son's anguished and fascinated perception of the duplicity of the mother's body" (86).

This observation is necessary to complete an overview of the critical perspectives encompassed by this volume. While many of the articles in this volume refer, either explicitly or implicitly, to Bataille's role in the "mutation in modern epistemology" and its concomitant "theories of classification" mentioned earlier in this introduction, at least two authors suggest either that Bataille's work continues to operate in a relation of complicity vis-à-vis the dominant ideologies within which it is situated or that it is not accurate to attribute to it a defiant, violently efficacious subversion of traditional discourse. I will conclude this introduction with an examination of what the articles in this volume may reveal about Bataille's position with respect to the mutations and restructurings of theories of classification in question.

His philosophical writings are considered to occupy a frontier position, in that they put into question philosophy's tendency to exclude or "lock out" that which it considers to be "short of" or "outside of" its horizon of operation. The relationships between the writings of other philosophers are reformulated through the readings he offers and through the readings that his readers offer. His writing can be seen to inhabit the writing of others and to effect a mutation, from within, upon the way they are viewed from without.

Questions of an economic order are also subject to the same mutation and spirit of contestation. Where these questions were formerly seen to reside within their own restricted economy, Bataille, in a "reversal [of thought] alone capable of substituting dynamic overviews...for the stagnation of isolated ideas," inserts this restricted economy of economic questions within a general economy of global energy exchange, accumulation, and expenditure. Within this reformulation, which reflects the "useless and infinite realization of the world," expenditure is accorded its rightful place at the basis of all exchange and economies; it is no longer seen as secondary to production and acquisition.

In addition, just as his work gives evidence of his desire to free the "whole man" from reduction to a restricted "use" as propagandist or intellectual, so does it resist the structuralist epistemological mutation which, in its abstraction and near subsumption of the subject, accords little place to the "life of the individual." Bataille's insistent inclusion of eroticism in his representation of subjectivity both highlights an "instability within structuralism's nature/culture opposition" and disrupts and empties what was traditionally the "assumed plenitude of the individual." Bataille's work permits and attempts a "recasting" of the subject because his is a literature of "themes" which does not proceed quickly and cavalierly to a naive rejection of monotheistic and transcendental authority. Unlike philosophy and science, whose restricted economies exclude the sacrifice and jouissance of the subject, and unlike much modern a-thematic literature and poetry, Bataille's literature of themes traverses the subject (*as well as* the monotheistic and transcendental authority which inhabits it) in a backward movement to that which precedes it.

In this traversal, Bataille's work perhaps stops short, however, of the radical subversion with which his work is often associated. It is no doubt more precise to say that this traversal and its resultant mutations are more radically accomplished in some directions than in others. But this is often because an absolute or more radical subversion is naive and illusory, given, for Bataille, the inevitable movement of "decline" that is attendant upon the reaching of any "summit." Thus, Plotnitsky finds within Bataille's writings on the notion of expenditure, the tendency to idealize "waste," but this idealized expenditure is always ultimately inscribed within an "*exchange* of expenditures." Similarly, the moment of radical interruption of discourse attributed to Bataille's representation of sovereign laughter is shown by Libertson to be the *impossibility* of this radical interruption. For Libertson, Bataille's *impossible* is the relation, of and *within* discourse, to the latter's unraveling, not a radical unraveling itself. Finally, for Suleiman, there is in Bataille's work a relation of complicity vis-à-vis dominant ideologies that continue to represent the drama of a "confrontation between an all-powerful father and a tramautized son, a confrontation staged across and over the body of the mother" (87).

This moment, at first glance, appears to be more complicitous with *ideology* than the others; "Is there a model of *textuality*," Suleiman asks, "that would not necessarily play out, in discourse, the eternal Oedipal drama of transgression and the Law—a drama which, always, ultimately, ends by maintaining the latter?" Or does the sovereign operation consist, as Kristeva suggests, of "traversing Oedipus [the constitution of the unary subject as knowing subject] by *representing* Oedipus and what exceeds it" namely, "pre-Oedipal free energies"? For Kristeva, "the traversal of Oedipus is not its lifting, but its knowledge," for "all fictional themes and all fiction share the economy of a traversal of Oedipus." The vantage points of Suleiman and Kristeva on this issue are interesting, for they lead to the question of the efficacy of Bataille's "subversive intent" vis-à-vis *ideologies*—a question asked earlier with respect to the *philosophical* and *economic* notions contested in his writing. Is it accurate to attribute to Bataille's work the defiant *radical* subversion of the discourse within which it was produced—a radical subversion with which, in the articles of many current theorists, his work risks being identified—or is one perhaps more loyal to the spirit and singularity of Bataille's thought by liberating it from the appropriating tendencies of a new discourse, one that would like to read it in ways befitting its own purposes? It is in this context that the significance of Suleiman's comment arises: "Bataille's writings functioned as a major *intertext* in the theories of cultural subversion and of (literary) textuality...elaborated in the years immediately following the explosion of May 1968" (my emphasis).

"On the one hand the theological encyclopaedia and, modeled upon it, the book of man. The question could be opened only if the book was closed...The opening into the text was adventure, expenditure without reserve.

And yet did we not know that the closure of the book was not a simple limit among others? And that only in the book, coming back to it unceasingly, drawing all our resources from it, could we indefinitely designate the writing beyond the book?

...A book which is the interfacing of a risk...(294–295)[35]

## NOTES

1.   Two texts that address themselves to the relationship between Bataille and his critics Breton and Sartre are Michèle Richman's *Reading Georges Bataille: Beyond the Gift* (Baltimore: The Johns Hopkins University Press, 1982) (see chap. 5) and Francis Marmande's article "Sartre et Bataille: Le Pas de deux" in Burgelin, Claude (ed.), *Lectures de Sartre* (Lyon: Presses Universitaires de Lyon, 1986).

2.   A. Breton, *Second manifeste du surréalisme. Manifestes du surréalisme* (Paris: J-J. Pauvert, 1962).

3.   A. Breton, *Premier manifeste du surréalisme. Manifestes du surréalisme* (Paris: J-J. Pauvert, 1962).

4.   G. Bataille, *Inner Experience*, trans. L.A. Boldt (Albany: SUNY Press, 1988). Unless otherwise specified, all further quotations from Bataille will be taken from this book.

5.   G. Bataille, "The "Old Mole and the Prefix *Sur*," *Visions of Excess* (Minneapolis: University of Minnesota Press, 1985), 42. This work will be referred to hereafter as *Visions*.

6.   J-P. Sartre, "Un nouveau mystique," *Situations I* (Paris: Gallimard, 1947).

7.   G. Bataille, "Discussion sur le péché," *Oeuvres complètes*, vol. VI (Paris: Gallimard, 1973), 358. This text will be referred to hereafter as *Discussion*.

8.   J-P. Sartre, *L'existentialisme est un humanisme* (Paris: Les Editions Nagel, 1946). This work will be referred to hereafter as *EH*.

9.   G. Marcel, *Homo Viator*, trans. E. Craufurd (New York: Harper and Row, 1962).

10.   The Colloque de Cerisy was held from June 29 to July 9, 1972; its proceedings were published as *Bataille/Artaud: vers une culture révolutionnaire*. Direction: P. Sollers. Coll. 10/18, no. 805 (Paris: Union générale d'éditions, 1973).   The presentations of Julia Kristeva, Denis Hollier, and Jean-Louis Baudry have been translated for this volume.   Twenty years later in May, 1992, an International Conference on Georges Bataille was held at Birkbeck College, University of London, England.   Present were Denis Hollier and Susan Suleiman, among others.

11.   *Hommages à Georges Bataille. Critique*, no. 195–196 (Aug.–Sept. 1963), 672–832; *Georges Bataille. l'Arc*, no. 32 (1967).   Henri Ronse, ed.; *Yale French Studies*, no. 78, 1990. *On Bataille*. Allan Stoekl, ed.; *Stanford French Review*, vol. 12 (1), Spring, 1988.

12.   This quotation appears on the back cover of *Visions of Excess*.

13. S. Suleiman, *Subversive Intent* (Cambridge: Harvard University Press, 1990), 73. The reference reappears on page 000 of our text.

14. M. Foucault, *The Order of Things* (London: Tavistock Publications, 1970).

15. J.G. Merquior, *Foucault* (London: Fontana Press, 1985), 47. This book will be referred to hereafter as *F.*

16. B. Smart, *Postmodernity* (London: Routledge, 1993), 49.

17. G. Bataille, *L'Amitié, Oeuvres complètes*, vol. VI (Paris: Gallimard, 1973), 295.

18. G. Bataille, *L'Erotisme* (Paris: Edition de minuit, 1957), 10.

19. J. Derrida, "The Ends of Man," *Margins of Philosophy*, trans. A. Bass (Chicago: The University of Chicago Press, 1982).

20. G. Bataille, "Lettre à X, chargé d'un cours sur Hegel...," *Oeuvres complètes*, vol. V (Paris: Gallimard, 1973), 369–371.

21. J. Derrida, "From Restricted to General Economy: A Hegelianism Without reserve," *Writing and Difference*, trans. A. Bass (Chicago: The University of Chicago Press, 1978), 251–278.

22. J-F. Lyotard, *The Postmodern Condition: A Report on Knowledge*, trans. G. Bennington and B. Massumi (Minneapolis: University of Minnesota Press, 1984).

23. Another source of criticism is Lyotard's appropriation of the Kantian notion of the sublime, "which is shifted away from the aesthetic concern with transcendence, characteristic of modern art, and toward a sociological and psychological impulse to find new moves within the language games of social life." R. Boyne and A. Rattansi, "The Theory and Politics of Postmodernism," *Postmodernism and Society*, R. Boyne and A. Rattansi, eds. (London: Macmillan, 1990), 18. In *The Postmodern Scene: Excremental Culture and Hyper-aesthetics*, A. Kroker and D. Cook, eds. (Montreal: New World Perspectives, 1986), Arthur Kroker makes the following critique of Lyotard's use of the sublime: "Lyotard sinks into the spectator sport of witnessing the sublime and the beautiful: the art world propped up by Kant's salvage job of uniting terror and taste to the market of abuse beyond use" (14).

24. F. Jameson, *Postmodernism, or, The Cultural Logic of Late Capitalism* (Durham: Duke University Press, 1991). Charles Jencks, in his well-known text on postmodernism, *What is Post-modernism?* (New York: St. Martin's Press, 1986) tends to view the latter as a "continuation of modernism and its transcendence." He defines as 'late' modernism what Lyotard describes as 'post' modernism: in his view, Lyotard's postmodernism is not really distinguishable from avant-gardism. Jencks sees late modernism as an exaggeration of modernism [the latter characterized by the value of abstraction and by the primary role of aesthetics (28)], while postmodernism is characterized by the reincorporation of previously existing forms, a "double coding, the combination of modern techniques with something else..." (14). While Jencks separates late modernism from postmodernism, he admits that both react to modernism in decline.

While it may be true that the distinction between modernism and postmodernism may be more significant when discussed on the level of what it "does" rather than what it "is" [cf. Suleiman, *Subversive Intent*, (186)], I am interested, for the purposes of this introduction, in the distinction between the two on a thematic or aesthetic level as well, in order to better situate Bataille's work in the context of these two ways of articulating lived experience in fiction and their respective effects upon the reading experience.

25. R. Boyne, A. Rattansi, eds. *Postmodernism and Society* (London: Macmillan, 1990).

26. E. Lunn, *Marxism and Modernity* (London: Verso, 1985).

27. R. Boyne and A. Rattansi, *Postmodernism and Society*, 7. These ideas, originally expressed in Lunn's book, are echoed to a certain extent by those of Linda Hutcheon in *Narcissistic Narrative: the Metafictional Paradox* (New York: Methuen, 1980). There she writes: "the heritage of the modernist text's formal complexity was not just an awareness of the activity needed on the part of the reader to make texts mean: there was also an intense self-awareness regarding the process of artistic production itself. While modernist texts may have worked to combat the imposition of single, authoritative meaning, postmodernist meta-fiction tends more to play with the possibilities of meaning (from degree zero to plurisignification) and of form ...Some have argued that postmodernist art does not aim, as did modernist, at exploring the difficulty, so much as the impossibility, of imposing that single determinate meaning on a text (xiii).

28. B. Smart, *Postmodernity*, 12.

29. I have borrowed this expression from the title of Susan Suleiman's book (from which her contribution to this volume has been drawn). *Subversive Intent: Gender, Politics, and the Avant-garde* (Cambridge: Harvard University Press, 1990).

30. See Tony Corn's article in this volume: "Unemployed Negativity (Derrida, Bataille, Hegel)."

31. P. Smith, *Discerning the Subject* (Minneapolis: University of Minnesota Press, 1988).

32. Smith here quotes Kristeva on p. 119 of his book. The next three page references appearing in the body of my introduction are taken from Smith's book.

33. Quoted from Susan Suleiman's article in this volume.

34. R. Barthes, "La Métaphore de l'oeil" *Essais critiques* (Paris: Editions du Seuil, 1964), 238–246.

35. J. Derrida, "Ellipsis," *Writing and Difference*, trans. A. Bass (Chicago: The University of Chicago Press, 1978), 294, 295.

# I. Bataille and Philosophical Inquiry

# 1

# Georges Bataille and the Challenge to Think

**Robert Sasso**

> I propose a challenge, not a book.
> For insomnia, I offer nothing.[1]

The principal interest of Bataille's work resides, in our[2] opinion, in the very stakes of its possibility. How can the rational be challenged *theoretically* by means of its very contradiction? How is it possible to discern, to *make explicit*, "the effects, in our human life, of the fading of the discursive real"?[3] How can one be understood, without misunderstandings, when one prides oneself, when all is said and done, in having "shuffled the deck"?[4]

The following extract from a posthumous *Autobiographical Note*, written by Bataille in the third person likely near the end of his life, suggests that the challenges of the work are necessarily linked to that other challenge that consists in wanting to think at the extreme limit of the thinkable:

> If thought and the expression of thought have become his
> privileged domain, this is only after he had, to the limit of his
> resources, multiplied the apparently incoherent experiences,
> whose intolerance indicates his effort to embrace the totality

of possibilities—more precisely, to reject untiringly any one possibility exclusive of others. Bataille's ambition is for a *sovereign* existence, freed from all limited searching. For him, it is actually a question of *being*, and of being *sovereignly*. It is a question of going beyond merely implementing the means: it is a question, beyond the means, of reaching the end, even at the price of a disrespectful disorder. Philosophy, for example, is reduced, for Bataille, to an acrobatics—in the worst sense of the word. It is not a question of attaining a goal—but of escaping from the traps that the goals represent."[5]

On the basis of these declarations, let us try to make clear what is at stake in this game.[6]

Because it is a question of "embracing the totality of possibilities," the stakes of a "sovereign existence" become the concern of thought: the exercise and expression, in language, of thought—the only human power capable of infinitely *transgressing* and *summoning* the finite.

Yet one must not confuse the question of thought with the psychological, in a descriptive approach, or with logic, aimed at the normative. What is in question is the total thought of everything, meta-psychic and onto-logical, which ventures to defy all finitude—that of things, that of practices, that of knowledge.

To raise oneself up in this way to the lofty and vertiginous perspectives of the site of thought seems to require heroes and madmen. And if the history of philosophy is that "succession of noble minds," that "gallery of reason's heroes who think," whose object is the "everything" or the "absolute"—according to Hegelian definitions[7]—how could Bataille break free from philosophy and its "acrobatics," all the while pretending to embrace the "totality of possibilities," short of being "mad"?

However, what is more reasonable, what is wiser, from the viewpoint of philosophical tradition, than the questioning from which Bataille sets out? "My answer to anyone," he confides, "is first of all a question. I hope to ask, from one man to another, whether he has ever suspected some hoax. On the surface, everything is in order, foreseen and defined, but none of this is certain."[8] Now already this suspicion, without causing a stir, can cause one to be suspicious about the person who evokes it. If it only takes one "philosopher" to wonder about what ultimately founds this apparently ordered world in which Hippias is more useful than Socrates, then it only takes one philosopher to believe, or to pretend to believe, that this astonishment shouldn't astonish: "Personally, what I speak of is simple and we all experience it at every moment: I am speaking of life that consumes itself, independently of any *use* to which this self-consuming life can be put. Therefore what I say should never surprise. It is always in front of us *all.* But always a little secretly."[9]

Up to this point, nothing particularly outrageous, although the incitement to ask oneself what is really happening, despite the "evidence" of the "well known," might have appeared as a sufficient motive for accusing and condemning Socrates. Without running the same deadly risk, Bataille jeopardizes his case to no less of an extent when he refuses to be satisfied with the very solutions of philosophy. To the philosophic questioning of "common sense" is added, then, a questioning of what one could call the "sense constructed" by the philosophers. A double challenge, consequently, which will be translated by the extreme attempts to escape from "doxa" as well as from the abusive jurisdiction of "reason," that is, from any "police/regulation/policy [*police*] of thought."[10]

As a result of such a position, an intellectual practice *without restraint* is developed. If one understands by intellectual practice the indissociable exercise of the couple thought/writing, it is not surprising, from Bataille's perspective, that to the phrase "I think like a girl takes off her dress,"[11] there hangs this resolution: "How to write? if not as a woman accustomed to honesty but undressing at an orgy."[12] The acceptance of the *impudence,* of the *obscenity* of thought, at the extremity of its movement,[13] orders a work dedicated to the thematics of excess and of violence, according to a triple register (novelistic text, theoretical essays, and "meditations"), in which each type of "discourse" can coexist with its "other" or be transposed there: this erotic tale will provide the opportunity to quote Hegel while that work on "economy" will end with a note on the "madness" of its author, and on the importance he attributes to mysticism.[14] From then on, this "work" can appear quite unseemly, a source of unending equivocations (without purpose) hardly qualified to measure up to its inordinate pretentions. It is however an undertaking that—even were it to be declared "impossible"—makes rigorously explicit its own conditions for possibility.

In order to stay in the race in the challenge to think, Bataille was successful in withstanding a disqualified trial whose grounds lie in three motives for accusation: madness, perversion (or barbarity of feeling), and mysticism (or delerious brilliancy and thinking enthusiasm). Refusing to elevate the "anomalies" witnessed in certain of his texts to sufficient reasons or to absolute neo-values,[15] protesting his humanity, after having catalogued and analyzed the excesses of which man is capable,[16] Bataille—many barely take this into account—has vigorously excluded from his *inner experience* "a mediocre mysticism lending its approbation to poetic imagination."[17]

But the question of the "discursive status" of project is asked all the more. For to pretend to get out of the "intellectual prison"[18] subservient to the authority of "reason," all the while rejecting the "literary route"[19] and the easiness of the *schwärmerei*, is inevitably to accept neither one (the philosophers) nor the other (the poets and literati). What remains would be an intellectual pseudopractice, which is aimed at the formless and at impasses, at least if one believes Hegel who, with respect to "intuitive and poetic thought" "too good for the concept," speaks of *"fantastiqueries"* which are neither flesh, nor fish, nor poetry, nor philosophy.[20]

In Bataille's work, the question of thought thus amounts to the possibility of putting thought doubly to the test, in both its rational and irrational registers. This assumes that each one of them is as "true" as the other and *through* the other, without ever having to yield to the other or dominate it. Thus, the rational, in opposing itself to the irrational, would only "absolutely" constitute itself to the extent that it would paradoxically liberate the latter with some commotion. Given that this "theoretical" position implies a recognition of "negativity," but refuses the hypothesis of its "dialectical" annulment, it no doubt permits one to declare that one is Hegelian, and even "Hegelian more than anything else" provided that one add: "without being so through and through."[21] These are nonetheless affirmations that require some explanation.

The question of thought, in philosophic tradition, often amounts to determining thought instrumentally, based on what it does and what it is capable of; later, the problematic of its competence and of its performances, in its realization, takes precedence over all others, and thought is only taken into account if it insures a project of mastery. At times philosophy envisages the mastery of what begins with an absolute foundation (such as the *Cogito*); at others, it envisages the mastery of what derives from the dialectical subsuming of the "real" in the process of the "rational" (such as the *Phenomenology of Spirit*), right up to the closure of an absolute circularity. In one case, it is the *foundation* that gives all its power to the exercise of thought; in the other case, it is its teleonomic *development*. From both perspectives, in a certain way, philosophy is assured of the real and of its meaning, by a lockout this side of which, or beyond which, the "practice" of thought is no longer to be envisaged;

horizons of thought determining simultaneously both the definition and the disappearance of the question of thought.

However, one can and one must take up the "question" again because, in the preceding hypotheses, the primordial question, providing the "dimensions" of all interrogations about what is called thinking, hasn't been asked. Heidegger formulates it in these terms: What calls us, what commands us, as it were, to think? What calls us to thought?[22] From this angle, the challenge to think in Bataille's writing takes on its true dimension as an opening to the pro-vocation of thought, that is to what solicits it, to which it corresponds and of which it is the intimate understanding.

Bataille's theoretical attempts to broach this question are generally placed within the framework of genealogies of humanity: history of art, of religion, of societies, of eroticism. At the "origin" is always "thought," a real phenomenon whose transformations will constitute History. But the very structure of this manifestation, its reflexivity, is the indication of an event literally without foundation: thought only originates in a collapse. More precisely, it only really takes place to the extent that man is no longer in continuity with nature and animality. Man's truly prehistoric immanence to natural life, still witnessed by the Lascaux paintings, is made progressively impossible by the splitting of the given and by the "ontological" scission resulting from objectifying activity. The entire drama of History that necessarily ensues, stems from this paradox: by his transforming action, man can experience and prove his essence only by negating all present states of things, without being able to recognize and assert himself entirely within the result of this negation, for this would risk equating his being with the "object." Arising from a violence, exerting its violence with regard to every *dasein*, whether "given" or "produced," thought is able neither to rest upon an "unshakeable foundation," ground or base, nor find rest in an "absolute knowledge," which would mean the completion of its "realization," without deceptively betraying its nature and its destiny.

On the contrary, according to Bataille, thought can never really escape from the violence from which it proceeds, and which always finishes by *unleashing* it by wrenching it from the ordered concatenations to which it temporarily submits in order to respond to the (necessarily) pragmatic requirements of praxis. The *lost intimacy* of supposed immanence engages man in transcendence, that is in the process of a contradictory quest: to attain *oneself* in the end by suppressing one's transcendence, although the latter is the condition for ipseity. To attain *oneself* thus would amount to destroying *oneself* as *self*, in other words as non-object.

Will one say, however, that the experience of the *Cogito* is beyond question and that the certitude of the *"ego sum res cogitans"* assures me of the objective solidity and consistency of the thinking self? According to Bataille, the experience of the "self-that-dies"—for example, in "Christian meditation before the cross"—would more likely establish the contrary. In this circumstance, the self, turning away "from any application to the world," is revealed as a *catastrophic object,* a "thing" brutally removed from the order of things: "In this position of the object as *catastrophe,* thought experiences the annihilation that constitutes it as a vertiginous and infinite fall: thus it doesn't simply have *catastrophe* as object: its very structure is *catastrophe*: it is itself absorption into the Nothingness that supports it and that at the same time is elusive."[23]

Will one say, in another context, that thought is not alienated in the objective results of rational action and that, on the contrary, it realizes itself fully in it? Or that it finds itself there with a complete *satisfaction*? Bataille sees the absurdity of these conjectures. To say that thought *must submit itself* to the conditions and constraints correlative to rational sense and to the production of the object is to recognize that it is not from the outset synonymous with useful or usable rationality. But how can one admit to the total adequation of thought and its result, as soon as meaning and the *object* are produced, without seeing that this involves the disappearance of the disjunctive conditions of reflexivity? Pushed to its extreme, thought would only be able either to extinguish itself in the dazed beatitude of its having-become-world, or to find itself again in a total liberation with regard to all "meaning" and to all project for realization. A "liberation" which is that of an unemployed negativity, irrecuperable in the sphere of useful production and consumption: a "liberation" delivering thought to the violence that, genealogically, constitutes it. If it is true, for example, that sacrifice (thus all religion) is an attempt to reintegrate the sacred sphere (that of naked violence)—separated from the profane sphere, in which violence is *used* and *neutralized* in the position of the object—then in the same way: "At an extreme point of its development, thought aspires to its own 'putting to death': it is precipitated as though by a leap into the sphere of sacrifice (...) its plenitude carries it right to where a wind blows that knocks it down, right to where the definitive contradiction of minds prevails."

What conclusions can be drawn from all of this? Must one content oneself with saying, sardonically, that Bataille's reflexion and work *serve no purpose*? In that case, it wouldn't matter if the judgment came laughingly, from some young Thracian servant girl, but if it were pronounced by a modern Thales, then it would not be lacking in irony.

Rather, let us see once again, by simplifying, in what sense it is possible to speak of a "challenge to think" in Bataille's work.

In this work, the so-called challenge is essentially presented: 1) as the "provocation" (shocking, for most readers) of the content and form of his "work"; 2) as an ambiguous attempt to exercise and express the thought-limit, at the limit of "philosophy" as of "poetry"—at their breaking point. As for the first point, the justification of the provocation would be dependent less on biographical anecdotes than on the "objective" demands of all thought responding to the violence that founds and that summons it. With regard to the second point, one must insist on the fact that Bataille envisages the arrival of thought at the gates of non-knowledge only to the extent that thought would have exhausted its "resources";[24] in other words, on the condition that it have first yielded to the ascesis of philosophy proceeding to "absolute knowledge." Certainly "[t]he greatest effort of thought is necessarily that which condemns effort *in general*";[25] and "only in excess does thought (reflexion) complete itself in us."[26] This is no idle argument, for thought "demands a meticulous relentlessness and it only yields to violence—its opposite—in the end."[27] Such a "completion"[28] of thought puts an end to knowledge. What is manifested, then, has strictly speaking no status, is "ecstatic," in the flash of an instant, with no possibility of being grasped intuitively or enunciated discursively, unless it is subject to a comic illusion. Extreme tension can only be followed by an emotional or linguistic release (more generally in symbols); hence the inevitable disappointment of the experience that follows thought, in as much as it is doomed to absolute contradiction: "As I sink into night, poetry, sobbing, tears together rob me of the *impossible*. Philosophy disguises it, and love or laughter finish deluding me."[29] Such is non-knowledge, which is never "super-knowledge" in Bataille's work. It is true that shortly after the sentences just quoted, Bataille follows in the same text with this: "However we might grasp, finally, the trap into which, in various ways, man in his entirety has fallen. We have searched for it on all sides." However, this is in order to immediately add: "But there where the *impossible* prevails (where convulsive emotion—but at the limit of reason—follows upon clarity) all explanation eludes us."

No doubt one will be willing to grant that Bataille was not "mad." Must one, in return, award him the quality of a hero, for having alone taken up the challenge to think? One declaration, among others, suffices to bring things back to more fitting proportions: "I personally don't presume to think that in a small number of years I have managed to solve, by myself, a problem that has up to this point disarmed humanity in its entirety."[30]

The fact remains that it appears difficult to lessen the provocation of an undertaking so zealous in the most general questioning of "what is," and so stubborn regarding the compromises of all forms of rest in thought, that is to say of all forms of its death, in the illusory reign of coherence. The sovereign exercise of a thought without reserve, because it is accomplished teleologically in "incoherence,"[31] can be exhausting and frustrating, unless it provides one with the opportunity to joyously give one's assent to a shattered and unguided world, to measure up to its excessiveness: "sovereign ek-sistence."

The trap, for Man, is to "reflect," to lead a "tedious"[32] interrogation. But to think, in this sense, is a challenge that cannot be challenged, like the invitation to a certain stone guest: "The hope never abandoned me," admitted Bataille in *The Impossible*, "of clasping in my hand the stone hand of the *Commandeur*."[33]

## NOTES

1. Unedited notes referring to *Inner Experience*, in *Oeuvres Complètes*, vol. V (Paris: Gallimard, 1973), p. 443. The references to this edition, in publication since 1971, will be made using the abbreviation *O.C.*, followed by the volume in Roman numerals, and the pagination in Arabic numerals.

2. The present article schematizes the arguments of a presentation made in Nice, under the same title, on the 4th of March, 1982. In this article, one will find an echo, but not simply a repetition or a resume, of my essay, *Georges Bataille: le système du non-savoir. Une ontologie du jeu*. Editions du Minuit, 1978.

3. *O.C.*, V, 231 (Post-scriptum, 1953).

4. An interview held in the spring of 1961 (Bataille died on the 8th of July, 1962), and published in *Les écrivains en personne*, by Madeleine Chapsal, U.G.E., coll. 10/18, 1973, p. 29. [Trans. note: the expression "brouiller les cartes" is often used to mean "to mystify or confuse."]

5. *O.C.*, VII, 462 (The editors situate this notice around 1958).

6. [Trans. note]: The original French reads "de la partie qui se joue." "Partie" in French means both "a part" and "a game, in the sense of match." "Se jouer" means both "to be played" and "to be at stake." I have tried to incorporate as many of these various meanings as possible in my translation.

7. Hegel, *Introductions aux leçons sur l'histoire de la philosophie*, trad. fr. Gibelin, (Paris: Gallimard, 1954), 20.

8. *O.C.*, VIII, 598 (Notes pertaining to *La Souveraineté*).

9. Ibid., 599.

10. *O.C.*, VI, 484 (Posthumous notes).

11. *O.C.*, V, 200 (*Méthode de méditation*).

12. *O.C.*, VII, 456 (*Les problèmes du surréalisme*). The metaphors correspond, by a sort of coupling, to that other figure: "to think in a virile way/ to turn away from nothing,"

*O.C.*, IX, 410 (*Dossier William Blake*). In other words, not to fear a laying bare and to bear "seeing."

13. *O.C.*, V, 200.

14. Respectively: *Madame Edwarda*, with its 1956 *Preface* (cf. *O.C.*, III); *La part maudite* (cf. *O.C.*, VII, 179).

15. He gives, as an example, these precisions, in 1957, in the Avant-propos to *Le bleu du ciel*, a novel written in 1935: "A torment that ravaged me is alone at the source of the monstrous anomalies of *Le bleu du ciel*. But it is so foreign to me to think that this basis justifies worth, that I gave up the idea of publishing this book" (*O.C.*, III, 382). Such specifications are not rare in Bataille's work, underlining an unequivocal distancing from the ambiguities of the work—or from its readers. See, among other sources, *O.C.*, III, 13, 101, 251, 359, 510–511; V, 495.

16. "I have proposed the friendship of man with himself (...) and in the most rigorous exercise of life possible," *O.C.*, V, 426 (Unpublished notes referring to *Inner Experience*).

17. *O.C.*, V, 427 (id.). One will notice what links this challenging of thought to that attempted by a Valéry or an Antonin Artaud (practicing it in "entire thought"). With this exception, that Bataille did not want to merely present the *states* of *his* thought, but to understand the *vocation* of all thinking thought.

18. *O.C.*, II, 128 (Posthumous text).

19. *O.C.*, VIII, 583 (Posthumous notes).

20. *Phénoménologie de l'esprit*, Préface, trad. fr. Hyppolite, Aubier, 1939, t. I, p. 58.

21. *O.C.*, VI, 348 (*Discussion sur le péché*).

22. *Qu'appelle-t-on penser?* trad. fr. Becker and Granel, P.U.F., 2nd ed. 1967, 128.

23. *O.C.*, I, 94 (Sacrifices).

24. *O.C.*, VIII, 584 (Posthumous notes).

25. Ibid.

26. *O.C.*, III, 12 (Preface à *Madame Edwarda*).

27. *O.C.*, V, 232 (Post-scriptum, 1953).

28. *O.C.*, VIII, 563 (Posthumous notes).

29. *O.C.*, III, 513 (Posthumous notes for *L'Impossible*).

30. *O.C.*, VIII, 596 (Posthumous notes).

31. Ibid., 584.

32. *O.C.*, V, 209 (*Méthode de méditation*).

33. *O.C.*, III, 166.

# 2

# Georges Bataille and the Repetition of Nietzsche

*Lionel Abel*

Georges Bataille's *Sur Nietzsche, volonté de chance* is a curious work. Partly a journal, possibly a system of philosophy, it is certainly not a commentary *on* Nietzsche. For the German philosopher is present on every page, even when not expressly quoted, present as the accomplice, the conscience, the intimate of the author. Georges Bataille's relation to Nietzsche is not that of a commentator or a disciple; it is something much more striking and exceptional. The key to this relationship is to be found in the theory of "communication" which Bataille discussed in his previous books *Le Coupable* and *L'Expérience intérieure*. "Existence," he wrote in *Le Coupable*, "is not present where men regard themselves in isolation: it begins with conversations, shared laughter, friendship, eroticism, and arises only in passing from the one to the other." According to this view any true experience of human existence requires and implies the relationship of togetherness, of being-with-another. *Sur Nietzsche, volonté de chance* is at once an assertion of this view and a realization of it; not a commentary on Nietzsche, it is rather a work undertaken in his company, an expression of Georges Bataille's attempt at being-with-Nietzsche, of his attempt even at being-Nietzsche-with-Nietzsche.

What is interesting about Bataille is his attitude. He presents himself as a thinker who expresses himself "as chance wills." "The very

movement of my intelligence is unbridled ... it is to fugitive moments of
relaxation that I owe a minimum of order, a relative erudition." As an
appendix to *Sur Nietzsche, volonté de chance* he publishes a criticism of
*L'Expérience intérieure* by the philosopher, Sartre, and in reply to Sartre's
objections to his views, objections which seem perfectly reasonable,
Bataille pleads that precisely because Sartre's argument is reasonable it is
unjust to his thought, which, proceeding by "uncoordinated flashes,"
cannot be judged conceptually. Bataille insists that he is not expressing
general ideas, but making notations of a certain kind of experience, in fact,
that he is able to make these notations only insofar as he is inadequate to
his experience. To the degree that he can express himself clearly the way
is dark before him, and what might illumine the way for him could make
nothing clear to anybody else....

Is this view not in contradiction with the view that true "existence"
involves shared experience, intimate and communicative relations with
others? I think not. For Bataille's whole enterprise in expression is directed
towards involving the reader in his own fever and tension. He wants to
establish a bond with the reader, but that bond is not to be one of clarity,
but to follow from a companionable readiness to be with him in the dark.
He asks for friendship, but one has to be friendly to his friends, which are
the night, the not-known Nietzsche.

Now precisely because I feel friendly to Bataille's friend,
Nietzsche—if not to the night and the not-known—I think it necessary to
insist on a certain clarity, and to distinguish carefully between Nietzsche's
criticism of action, and the criticism of action Bataille presents in his
book as his own elaboration of Nietzsche's ideas. Nietzsche's analysis of
the problem of action might be summarized as follows: consciousness
makes us aware of a multiplicity of problems, actualities and events, of
countless fields of enterprise, but when we have to do something, it is
impossible for us to take into account all that our consciousness has told
us. Action means limitation. The world is too large for us to live in it.
We can know it in its breadth, but this breadth is contradictory to the
depth implicit in resolute activity, which cannot have for its stage all of
the world that we know, but must occupy a limited sector of the world, a
fragment of the world. To act means to be part of a plot, and since the
universe cannot be the background of any one plot, the depth of action
is cut off from the breadth of consciousness, and consciousness is cut off
from the intensity of action. The pathos of existence, its alternate flatness
and artificiality may be expressed as follows: a story is true to the degree
that it is not a story.

The contradiction between action and consciousness, Nietzsche believed, could be solved only by the strong, resolute individual, various in his interests, like the men of the Renaissance capable of limiting his consciousness when necessary, and of acting without taking into account all of his knowledge. But in the modern world of specialization and group dominance, of weaklings and hysterics, the problem was unsolvable.

So Nietzsche. Now for Bataille. He asserts that the acceptance of any aim, of any morality, is an expression of a resignation to being less than the totality. To play a part means to be a part, and he wants to be all. This is madness, perhaps, he grants, but is not madness superior to compromising with a situation that is in fact senseless? For he argues that whenever men in the past acted resolutely, and took sides in the world, they were able to invest that part of the world they identified themselves with and for the sake of which they were willing to be less than everything, with what he calls transcendence: that is to say, they made sacred the ends at which they aimed, assumed that these ends were absolute and in this way avoided the humiliating admission that they were resigned to being less than the totality. But, says Bataille, in the modern world, now that we can no longer believe that the good of the city is anything more than the good of the city; now that the defense of the Fatherland, the achievement of the revolution, are merely the defense of the Fatherland and the achievement of the revolution; now that, on the one hand the increasing trend towards specialization limits the range of what we can do, and on the other hand the equally pronounced tendency to see the tasks we have to perform in their exact limits deprives these tasks of any unseizable and hence satisfying signification; how can we act at all without a feeling of mutilation and fragmentation? Bataille writes:

> But what does this fragmentation signify, if not that which causes it? If not that need to act which specializes and limits one to the horizon of a given activity? Even when of general interest, which is not customarily the case, activity, subordinating each of our moments to some precise result, effaces the total character of being. He who acts substitutes for that *raison d'être*, which he is himself as a totality, such and such an end, which might be in less objectionable circumstances, the grandeur of a state, the triumph of a party. Every action specializes, in so far as any act must be limited. Ordinarily a plant does not act and is not specialized: it is specialized when it swallows flies!

I can exist *totally* only by transcending the field of action in
some way. (*Sur Nietzsche, volonté de chance*)

Now let us see what Bataille has made of Nietzsche's criticism of the
possibilities of action that life presents. The first thing to be noted is that
Nietzsche did not, by his very way of formulating the problem, preclude
the possibility of a solution by any kind of individual under any social
conditions. Having in mind the men of the Renaissance and the Greeks,
who combined in their lives a great many different kinds of activities,
Nietzsche, protesting against the fragmentation of the individual in the
modern world, wanted a wider horizon, a larger theater, and while recognizing a contradiction between action and consciousness regarded
consciousness rather than action as the evil for which remedies were to
be found. But Bataille's animus is directed not against some specialized
form of life, but against life because it specializes; not against some
incomplete form of action, but against action because it renders incomplete. And the question arises, what norm can he be invoking in making
this criticism, since from his point of view even the Renaissance men and
the Greeks, whom Nietzsche admired, would also be instances of "torn"
incompleteness?

Now the only norm antagonistic to life and commensurable with it
is death. And, in fact, it is from the point of view of death that Bataille
has restated Nietzsche's criticism of the incomplete man and his demand
for a fuller and more satisfying life. Bataille unhesitatingly asserts that his
conception of totality is linked with the idea of death. "Only in the halo
of death," he says, "can the self found its kingdom" (*L'Expérience
intérieure*). In *Le Coupable* he writes: "The only element which links
existence to *everything else* is death: he who envisages death stops
belonging to a room, to those near him, and is ready to give himself to
the freeplay of the skies." But now if Bataille is speaking from the point
of view of death how can he make a distinction between the incomplete
and the complete man considering that from such a point of view all
human affairs are blotted out in a radical indistinction: death makes "the
odds all even." From Bataille's perspective any kind of difference
between men should not even be visible. To speak of the "whole man"
is to make some kind of social criticism. But one cannot make social
criticism from the point of view of death. The truth is that death has
nothing to say. That is what it says and so saying is most eloquent.
When it tries to say more all it can do is quote from life and that means to
give up its one supreme advantage.

Is Georges Bataille, in fact, throughout all of his books, restating the meditation on life, which was Nietzsche's philosophy, as a meditation on death? And what could be the motive for such an enterprise? For on the question as to whether philosophy should be a meditation on life or on death, there would seem to be no possible compromise... But death again seems to be the norm when Bataille transforms Nietzsche's criticism of complete commitment to any one goal, into a criticism of any kind of partial commitment. Bataille is for absolute non-commitment. Much more on guard against the meaningful than against the meaningless and, characteristically modern in this, Bataille asserts that the only goal he can accept is the goal of having no goal, which he calls the project of having no project. To have a project of any sort is to be *staged*, but on the other hand, not to have a project, a cause, thrusts one into solitude: " ...it means the sickness of the desert, a cry losing itself in a great silence." In taking this position he is certainly not naive. He knows perfectly well, as Jaspers has put it, that one is always in a situation, and that one can only get out of a situation by way of a situation. But what he knows Bataille will not accept, but protests against, staking everything on the possibility that the impossible can occur, that what he knows-not can be experienced, and that there is a practice of not-knowing whereby this experience, which he names at different times "torn anthropomorphism," "the sacrifice," "the desert," and "inner experience," can be approached. The logic of his position might be stated thus: I can not-know, therefore I can be.

Now the project of having no project, and the insistence on the possibility of impossibility, are equivalent, at a certain point, to complete commitment to one project, and the acceptance of the impossibility of further possibility. Both attitudes imply the acceptance of death. Bataille asserts that the I-that-lives is always compromised, while only the I-that-is-about-to-die can have knowledge of totality. So total non-commitment means commitment to death, as total commitment means commitment to death, though the philosophers of *engagement*, Sartre and Simone de Beauvoir, have not told us that frankly. For the truth is that it is impossible for anyone to be completely committed to any action, just as it is impossible for anyone to act without any degree of commitment, if he holds fast to the values of life. If I am not ready to die, I am ready to live in different ways, and will not be completely faithful to any one of them. If I am always in a situation, I am also always not completely in that situation. If I am always on the stage, I am also always partly off the stage, overlooking the action, trying to find out the direction of the plot, and criticizing the very lines I am reciting. I carry with me always a "remainder" which is not committed, not involved, which is neither innocent nor guilty, however I think or act. This "remainder" is an irritant and a trouble in all my moments of decision and determination, which it continually threatens to render comical. It is my resolve not to be resolved, and since I want my acts to be authentic, I would like to get rid of it; it gives me the lie, saps my gall, betrays my motives, but I can only liquidate it by being ready to die; with such readiness, the "remainder"—what Hamlet called "the rest"—is silenced. But should not philosophy help us to live authentically by some resource other than death? And were not Nietzsche as well as Kierkegaard precisely artists and experts in dealing authentically with this "remainder," using it as a touchstone for false acts of heroism and determination in others, retreating into it, recuperating by means of it, extracting from it humor and poetry? Are not rather absolute commitment and absolute non-commitment the easier and more conventional courses, requiring the least inventiveness, the least degree of tension? At this point in the discussion of commitment one must commit oneself. I am for the "remainder."

*My Remainder:* Are you for me one hundred percent?

*I:* Don't bother me. I am writing an essay on Georges Bataille. I must be serious. Your presence is disturbing.

*My Remainder:* I just wanted to remind you that whatever you have said so far in this essay is not said irrevocably, that you may well change your mind in the future, that is, I may change it, and a certain tone of decisiveness in some of the statements you have been making goes against my grain. Let me warn you. Look at Earl Browder. Who would have thought that there was even a tiny bit of him that didn't belong to Stalin? And now he is in business.

*I:* But I am writing about a very unusual thinker who has expressed views on some of the most profound problems of human existence. I have to be serious, I have to commit myself.

*My Remainder:* You want to say something profound, I suppose?

*I:* Yes. And that's what you object to, that's why you have intruded. You know very well that profundity means limitation, and that limitation means your liquidation.

*My Remainder:* True enough. Just the same, I know more about the problem you are discussing than you do. The fact is that you can say little on the problem that will be interesting without consulting me, although once you have consulted me, or adopted a suggestion of mine, you will not be able to be completely convinced of it.

*I:* You think there is no way of circumventing you!

*My Remainder:* There are many ways, and I know them all. As a matter of fact, one of the methods of getting rid of me is in question here. I mean that Georges Bataille is concerned almost entirely with circumventing his version of me. You see, one of the interesting ways by which I might be suppressed would be if you were to repeat the life of someone past, if you were to substitute for me, who am alive with possibilities, someone dead. I believe that what Georges Bataille is doing is something of this sort. He is attempting to substitute for that being within him, which corresponds to my being within you, and which I will call not-being-Bataille, Nietzsche. He is attempting nothing less than a repetition of the German philosopher, not merely a repetition of his philosophy, but of his experience.

*I:* I recollect that in *L'Expérience intérieure* Bataille wrote: "One cannot, I suppose, achieve the ultimate, except in repetition, for the reason that one can never be sure of having attained it, that one can never be certain...."

*My Remainder:* And Bataille wants the ultimate.

*I:* And that is why Nietzsche is so present in all his books in the form of quotations, as a stylistic model....

*My Remainder:* As an accomplice, a conscience, and an intimate, if you don't mind my quoting you....

*I:* And that is why he is restating as a meditation on death, the meditation on life that is Nietzsche's philosophy...

*My Remainder:* Your unpersuader seems to have persuaded you.

If Georges Bataille is indeed attempting nothing less than a repetition of the experience of Nietzsche, then certainly no purely logical criticism of his ideas, alert for contradictions in the detail, but indifferent to the real premises of Bataille's effort can be valid. For what he presents us with is not an analyis, but a drama, not another conception of existence, but another, and a very unfamiliar, kind of existence, one most mysterious.

How can the experience of another human being be *repeated?* And what is meant by saying that someone has undertaken such a repetition? All I can say here is that there is very little exact knowledge about this matter, which in the nature of the case, can probably not even be examined in a wholly objective way, and that if Bataille is, as I am assuming, trying to repeat Nietzsche, he is at least presenting us with some further data for the answering of these questions.

The problem of repetition is surely one of the most intriguing in the world. It should first of all be noted what repetition is not. The word *imitation,* for example, is not adequate to convey the sense of repetition, although in a repetition there may well be an element of an imitation. Moreover, while repetition is a disvalue from the point of view of thought, since it involves a certain refusal to think—the mind tends to put everything aside that it has formulated into a law—in experience repetition is a value and a sign not of a weak nature but, on the contrary, of a strong and highly original nature: without great character no one will ever attempt a repetition. In French poetry we have one wonderful example of such a mysterious reduplication of one man's life and work by an entirely different life and work: I mean the repetition of Mallarmé by Paul Valéry. And it might be remarked here that repetition is not *influence:* would it not be absurd to say that Valéry was influenced by Mallarmé? And when we think of the relationship between these two men, does it not seem most probable that a third was necessary to unite them, that Valéry was only able to repeat Mallarmé after he had discovered Leonardo? And would Bataille have attempted a repetition of Nietzsche without having read Kierkegaard? All this is sheer speculation, and any hypothesis about these matters is fairly dubious, but I am struck by this fact which I will set down for whatever it is worth: while Valéry never expressed the slightest criticism of either Mallarmé or Leonardo, never wrote of them without eloquence, nor without conceding to them the utmost that could be conceded, Bataille has not refrained, in his book on Nietzsche, from occasionally finding something to object to in the German philosopher he is trying to repeat. He also makes it clear that he does not wholly admire Kierkegaard, who, I believe, enabled him to attempt the repetition. This suggests a certain unsatisfactoriness, an element of the unlucky in Bataille's *will to chance*. I said before that Valéry had never criticized Mallarmé. Now was Mallarmé perfect? To say that would be to imply that he did not exist, that he had distilled his being into some essence, and that there was no remainder left over which could live or err. To say that Mallarmé was uncriticizable is to say that he was, or gave the appearance of being, not human but a kind of form, which could be exactly what it was and never appear to be something else again.... So that Valéry, in repeating Mallarmé, was repeating not a life, really, which by its very nature is unduplicable, but a form capable of being repeated, though implicated in the life of a particular man in we cannot say what way... But Nietzsche, who is wholly existent, who contradicts himself, makes fun of himself, forgets who he is, who is ready to think of himself as a clown at one moment and as a God at another, who is a very flux of thoughts and feelings; Nietzsche, who was all life, who was a continual repudiation of form—how could he be reduplicated? How could this man who makes us so interested in his failings be regarded by anyone as uncriticizable? And it would seem, too, that only a man, the sight of whom would make one think that he had been *seen before*, could be repeated, repetition being repetition of a repetition. And finally, does not this immolation of the self to another require the sacrifice of existence, the acceptance of death? But then, the one repeating Nietzsche would become the very opposite of Nietzsche, so that in the nature of the case, an authentic repetition of Nietzsche would be impossible.

> *My Remainder:* At this point you need a hint from someone who understands this subject. The reason Bataille is attempting a repetition of Nietzsche is precisely the fact that a repetition of Nietzsche is impossible. A miracle will have to take place if he is to succeed, a miracle not within the limits of human power, as in the magical substitution of himself for Mallarmé which Valéry makes us believe in by a kind of conjuror's trick, but a miracle in the literal sense of the word, the intervention of some transcendent influence unknown to man. Bataille's whole aim is to provoke the appearance of such a power.
>
> *I:* But in that case he is bound to fail.
>
> *My Remainder:* That's the very reason for his excitement.

# 3

# From Beyond Hegel to Nietzsche's Absence

**Denis Hollier**

*In the end, I accepted my extraordinary obsession with the names Hegel, Nietzsche; I laughed in vain—I could no longer become excited unless I accepted or pretended to imagine a fantastic composition which would confusedly link my most disconcerting steps with theirs.*

*I should at first, without Hegel, have been Hegel: and the means fail me.*

*No-one can read Nietzsche authentically without "being" Nietzsche.*

*I would like first of all to excuse myself: firstly for the number of quotations that my presentation will entail; next, for having preferred not to identify them on each occasion, given their number.*

*Nothing is more foreign to me than a personal mode of thought. At the very most, when I put forward a word, I play upon the thought of others. Up to the present time, the thought of Bataille in particular. And it is in order to speak of this thought that I have been asked to attend this colloquium.*

*I have come, then, to speak of Bataille. Of Bataille and not of myself. Of Bataille and not of Artaud at this colloquium devoted to Artaud and Bataille. A colloquium moreover in which it has seemed to me that we have not spoken of Artaud, that we have rather made it evident that there is a certain impossibility of speaking of Artaud, an impossibility in the face of which it became necessary either to speak of something else, or to do Artaud, to redo Artaud.   Such that what took place could be regarded as that second birth of Artaud...*[1] *But I came to speak of Bataille and not of Artaud.   Nor of myself.   I will not do Bataille. I will not redo Bataille.   Perhaps in the presence of any of Bataille's texts, I have never had that desire—of which Barthes speaks—of having written them.   That is why I will speak of them.*

*As much as is possible without taking too many risks.   I am not a writer.   Rather, I would, at least remotely, be something like an academic. And it is in order to diminish those risks that I yesterday wrote the lines I am reading to you.   I wrote them, driven, I imagined, by the fear of panicking before you, of going mad...*

*I had thought of reading you an old text, written two or three years ago.   It was the second part of a sort of diptych entitled:* "The Hegel/ Nietzsche Mechanism in Bataille's Library." *The first appeared in* Arc's *special edition devoted to Bataille.   This title referred to a text by Ponge on Lautréamont:* "The Maldoror/Poésies Mechanism," *a reference which was at the same time the recognition of a debt with respect to the borrowed model.*

*Supply your personal library with the only mechanism that will allow it to be scuttled and to resurface at will.*

...

*Open Lautréamont! And then suddenly you have all of literature turned inside out like an umbrella!*

*Close Lautréamont! And everything immediately returns to its place...*

...

*In order to enjoy complete intellectual comfort at your home, adapt the Maldoror/Poésies mechanism to your library.*

*This oscillation between scuttling and resurfacing, between opening and closing, annulment and profit, that Ponge had put into play based on the Lautréamont/Ducasse (Maldoror/Poésies) couple—this oscillation also described the double Hegelian and Nietzschean play of Bataille's writing. Hegel closes; he closes the library back upon itself with the identity of the subject and the object, an identity produced when the long journey accomplished by discourse reaches its end point at the moment of absolute knowledge.   Nietzsche, on the contrary, undermines the library, causes it to explode, puts fire to it.   A double register, then, for this library which, on the one hand, evokes Bataille's work place—Bataille, the conserver of knowledge, a Hegelian civil servant at the library, which, as one knows, was the National Library; but on the other hand, the latter evokes the place worked through [travaillé] by Bataille, that space of the book that he transgressed, even though this meant damning several of his own works.*

*Now Pleynet has distributed an unpublished page of Artaud that begins with some notes on Lautréamont. One of these notes: "To close everything and no longer open anything" is, apparently, according to Pleynet, a response to Ponge's* Maldoror/Poésies Mechanism *which had appeared right after the war in a special edition of* Les cahiers du Sud *devoted to Lautréamont, an edition whose abstract contained a* Letter on Lautréamont *by Artaud. To close everything and no longer to open anything.*

*Close it. Close the library. This is also the cry of the miswritten, uttered by the box in which Denis Roche had at first put it before putting us in it, remade by Artaud. The performance/representation is over; we're closing. We are laying into a box,[2] a jack-in-the-box and the family's burial vault, and we are covering it (up) again: as Miro, according to Bataille, would have done with the painting that he wanted to kill—no longer leaving anything but "some vaguely formed spots on the cover (or on the family tombstone, as it were) of the jack-in-the-box." He was speaking of the canvasses painted by Miro in the 1920s, in other words, right after* La ferme.[3] *Close, then, the performance/representation, the box of perspectives with the more or less tricky illusions; close Narcissus' tomb.*

*Not to speak of Artaud: one must do him (it) [le faire] redo him (it) [le refaire] for no one can read Artaud authentically without "being" Artaud. This of course complicates the Artaud/Bataille relationship, a relationship at once necessary and disunited, uneven and asymmetrical, but an inevitable relationship. (Will an Artaud/Bataille mechanism emerge, then, from this colloquium, a mechanism that we can suggest, for the intellectual comfort of our contemporaries, as an addition to their libraries?)*

*Lautréamont/Ducasse, Maldoror/Poésies, Hegel/Nietzsche—or rather Nietzsche/Hegel, since the order is Artaud/Bataille. Bataille is worked through by "Artaud"—by what is not easily "spoken of"—in the Hegel/Nietzsche relationship. And just as one doesn't speak of Artaud, in order to give rise to that second birth which permits him to take (have taken) place so Bataille doesn't speak of Nietzsche and through this gesture permits him, even though his thought has up to this point remained null and void, to at last take (have taken) place. The disjointed [déboîtée][4] series of these couples (disjointed because there is no point of escape: the jack-in-the-box has closed) indicates the work of contradiction such that the number one divides itself into two, such that the subject emerges in the rupture of proper names. For these couples of proper names are never twice times one: if Nietzsche has never masked his masks, behind Hegel one must discern the pseudo-Hegel. A scissiparous operation that constitutes dualist materialism in as much as, resolutely antiatomistic, it characterizes matter through productive scission. Matter is always matter-for-contradiction.*

*"In a certain way, the Hegel–Kierkegaard dilemma completes and pushes to the extreme the dilemma implied in Hegelian thought itself." The Hegel/Nietzsche mechanism is already programmed all the more by the contradiction that opposes Hegel to the immutable Hegel. Like a negative mark, the name Nietzsche denies the Hegelian pretention of being at once the incarnation of absolute knowledge and the subject of its discourse. It is the bar that separates him from himself, the bar–between–him: Nietzsche = Hegel/Hegel. When he was still young, Hegel believed himself to be going mad; he then worked out the system, one can imagine, in order to escape, so that what forced him to write, I imagine, was the fear of going mad. But once the system was completed, he again thought that he was going mad. Nietzsche is Hegel's madness, the return of what Hegel repressed, the insufficiency of the whole that provokes the scissiparous opening after which narcissistic identity remains nothing more than a broken corpus. Hegel is not Hegel and this "is not" is Nietzsche. A disordering of the relationship between signified and signifier that passes through the impropriety of the proper name and produces an effect of silence in the text. A suspension of discourse: breath cut short, tightened throat. The anguish into which the subject sinks ruptures the discourse that fled from it. This is night, one that is also a sun, at whose setting Minerva's bird does not take flight but falls asleep. The* Commandeur *has reopened the tomb. Nietzsche speaks in Hegel...*

*"Nietzsche is to Hegel what the hatching bird is to the one that quite happily absorbed the inner substance." The scission of Hegel as the appearance of Nietzsche makes itself heard through a silence, that of the "moment of genius": when a nascent universe rises above the sound of the old universe, this universe demands that silence be felt... Through a silence or through a sound. That of a broken egg/ shell. Cracked like the voice of the system. Very low, very light. A small cracking that opens a still accessible world... Or sharp and dull. As when, forcing that other circular enclosure—the arena in Madrid on the 7th of May 1922—the horns striking the boards with great force, in order to produce flat, macabre sounds: the three strokes of death. The* Commandeur *emerges*

*from the box. Here, excuse me, we need music. Vivan le femine. Viva il buon vino. And may the wind open the windows, so that on a stormy night a damp sheet flaps, lit by the moon. But I will read this reworked text:*

## FROM BEYOND HEGEL TO THE ABSENCE OF NIETZSCHE

I. Dramatis Personnae

Bataille's discourses on Hegel and on Nietzsche do not obey the same rules, do not belong to the same zones of his writing and this is why—something which cannot fail to be strange, given the qualitative and quantitative importance of the references he makes to both—he has almost never explicitly confronted them: from one to the other, the absence of a relationship, the strangeness of the zones prevents a meeting, an articulation in form. With the exception of some attempts that confirm this impermeability, like the note from *Inner Experience* in which Bataille draws attention to Nietzsche's relative ignorance of Hegel's thought; like that unpublished text where one reads, *Nietzsche's thought, that of Hegel and mine*, where what strikes one at first is the impossibility of grasping them both in the same discourse.

The discourse on Hegel is marked by transcendence: Bataille speaks *of* Hegel. He speaks of him, one might say, in order to make up for an error, an injustice. Hegel is misunderstood. "It seems to me," he writes, "that the pursuits of present-day thought are generally falsified by the misunderstanding, which we perpetrate, regarding Hegel's general representation of Man and the human spirit from 1806 onwards" (*Hegel, Man and History*). It is a question here, then, of making up for a delay, for a cultural gap in a movement of intellectual honesty, in all objectivity. Following Kojève, Bataille provides the elements of this rectification even if it means benefiting from them in order to rectify and bring to light certain detailed points of the Hegelian edifice. Nietzsche, on the contrary, is known, quoted abundantly, translated, commented upon. And even too much. But this Nietzschean inflation is itself the cause of a misreading that his beneficiary suffers from, a misreading for which remedies must be sought, remedies that are the inverse of those used for Hegel: one must actualize Hegel but hide Nietzsche.

Not to speak of Nietzsche: transcendence is replaced by a certain form of immanence. To speak with or in Nietzsche, to make Nietzsche speak in his own discourse, a discourse whose stakes are to become Nietzsche's discourse. Ultimately, one might say that Bataille's discourse takes up that of Hegel once again on the level of the signified, of ideological content; it identifies itself with that of Nietzsche through the position of the subject that it implies (and Nietzsche functions well from this point of view as the system of ruptures, of gaps, and of everything that *escapes* from Hegelian discourse). Bataille speaks of Hegel; he becomes Nietzsche's madman.

If he speaks *of* Nietzsche, it is purely in a negative manner, in order to denounce misunderstandings. On the occasion, for example, of reviews of works that are devoted to him, and which he will not criticize so much for having at times misinterpreted, as for being in themselves irreparable misinterpretations, the misinterpretation that arises from any intention to speak of Nietzsche. Among many examples, this judgment: "An honest, conscientious work, repeating everything that might arise from an immediate analysis, like many other authors (for example Ch. Andler whose study he calls admirable), this one situates himself *outside of* Nietzsche." To speak of—in a certain way, this would be the structure of Hegelian discourse to the precise extent that it implies an exteriority, one that condemns any attempt to apply it to Nietzsche "from the outside" as being "completely penetrated by Hegelianism."

"To speak of Nietzsche makes sense only from the inside." But from the inside of whom? Who is in whom? That the operation is directed towards two terms nevertheless excludes a simple structure of interiority. It can only be a question of an inside whose interiority will be compromised. And it is on the basis of this compromise that it will be possible to think inner experience as it is carried out electively as *Nietzsche's experience.*

One can qualify Hegel's position, given many of its attributes, as being paternal. Nietzsche, on the contrary, gives the impression of a son. Or rather, of a child: of a fatherless child, of a homeless child. Hegelian patriotism or paternalism dies, suffocating under the weight of a past which he wants so much to conserve that he no longer has the strength to surpass it. On the contrary, "the marvelous Nietzschean *Kinderland* is nothing less than the place where the challenge directed towards each man's *Vaterland* takes on a meaning that ceases to be an impotent negation"; a *Kinderland* that is not an ideal fatherland but an absence of fatherland in the sense implied by Nietzsche when he declared himself (and the rest of us) stateless, in other words, without a past, without a father, without an inheritance. Of an unknown father: the stateless are in fact the sons of the future, in other words, the sons, precisely, of the unknown. A true child and a true childhood are only those of an unknown father.

But the fatherless child will be childless; he will not be a father. Born of a rupture with the reproductive system, he will not reproduce himself. "Nietzsche's work is an abortion." All parents are sons of the past that they reproduce; only childhood is the son of the future.

## II. The imitation of Mr. Nietzsche

Hegel is surpassed by his reversal, annulled by his repetition. Now, if surpassing was the essential character of Hegel, the return is that of Nietzsche: 1) Nietzsche is only on the condition that he return and is himself already only the return of former existences, their repetition. 2) Reading Nietzsche demands that the reader identify himself with Nietzsche's experience, that he undergo Nietzsche's experience.

A. Many realities arise from the law of all or nothing. This is the case with Nietzsche (1937). "I continue to think that one cannot gain access to the meaning of Nietzsche's thought and experience any more than one can to Christian thought and experience: in both cases, it is a question of *all or nothing* (1951)." Thus if the distance from which Bataille speaks of Hegel tolerates, even implies several restrictions or contestations (major or minor), communication with Nietzsche implies a total adherence; it is submitted to that law of all or nothing that Bataille will nevertheless immediately call into question by expressing the most explicit reservations regarding certain decisive points of Nietzsche's thought: in the first place, the notions of the will to power and the overman which, in a certain way, would remain this side of the mastery that Hegel put in place with the dialectic of the master and the slave ("Nietzsche knew barely more of Hegel than a standard popularization. *The Geneology of Morals* is the singular proof of the ignorance in which the dialectic of the master and the slave is held and remains to be held..."). It is not the Nietzschean will to power but rather Hegelian mastery that will be submitted to the tremor from which sovereignty will draw what one could call its existence.

The same thing more or less holds for the notion of the eternal return. As if Nietzsche's return was carried out only on the condition that the theme of the eternal return be excluded. As if the axis of this return was at the same time to remain its blind spot; as if the return could not be thematized. "For just about anybody, the idea of the *return* is ineffectual. It does not on its own provide a feeling of horror. It could amplify this if it existed, but it doesn't... Nor is it any more able to produce ecstasy." What is actually named, what is thematized, is not the Nietzschean return but, through a significant displacement,

Kierkegaardian repetition. However, Bataille's reservations regarding the eternal return cease to be assimilable to his refusal of the other Nietzschean philosophemes: it is a question precisely of producing the return as a destruction of philosophemes.

The concept of the eternal return leaves one cold, the experience of the return burns, dissolves, melts. This is what appears in an aphorism of the *Post-scriptum to the Torment* (fourth part of *Inner Experience*) where:

1) The experience during which Nietzsche underwent that of the eternal return is renewed for Bataille by means of dramatization:

> Given that Nietzsche had of the eternal return the vision with which one is familiar, the intensity of Nietzsche's feelings made him laugh and tremble at the same time. He wept too much: these were tears of jubilation. Traversing the forest, the length of Lake Silvaplana, he had stopped near an enormous rock which stood in the form of a pyramid, not far from Surlej. I imagine myself arriving at the shore of the lake and, at imagining it, I weep…. (*IE*, 154)

2) But where the repetition of the Nietzschean experience, the return of the return, is no less accompanied by the most complete indifference vis-à-vis the idea which, in his view, would determine it:

> I imagine myself arriving at the shore of the lake and, at imagining it, I weep. Not that I have found in the idea of the eternal return anything which might move me in my turn. The most obvious aspect of a discovery which was to make the ground give way beneath our feet—in Nietzsche's eyes a sort of transfigured man alone would know how to overcome the horror of it—is that before it the best will is immaterial. (*IE*, 154)

For 3) this experience is that of sacrifice which cannot be represented by the notion. It stages the asymmetrical opposition between the experience and the discourse within whose structure experience both implies and excludes discourse: there is no experience without discourse even if experience is still the experience of what discourse cannot represent, of what cannot be converted into conceptual space. Experience "opens notions beyond themselves." Thus, before the idea of the eternal return:

...the best will is immaterial. Only the object of his vision—
what made him laugh and tremble—was not the return (and
not even time), but what the return laid bare, the impossible
depth of things. And this depth, should one reach it by one
path or another, is always the same since it is night and since,
perceiving it, there is nothing left to do but collapse (become
agitated right to the point of fever, lose oneself in ecstasy,
weep). (*IE*, 154)

What was to make the ground give way beneath our feet...lays bare
the impossible depth of things, the bottomless nature of being, the
absence of a ground. By refusing the return as notion, Bataille produces
the same effect as Nietzsche when he postulated it.

Bataille declares elsewhere that he experiences "nothing but a
breathless interest for the philosophies of time" among which he
numbers the theory of the eternal return which proposed "a circular
hypothesis" of it. Philosophical models—this is what Hegel proposes
and Bataille uses them; the relationship to Nietzsche is situated in
another space. Hypotheses, models, theories define scientific thought
(discursive and objective), thought submitted to the calculation of
meaning, to the domination of reason, and it is in their refusal that
Bataille situates the common ground of his writing and that of Nietzsche:
"He rejected the reign of things, and science could not be for him the
limit and the objective of man since, assumed in this way, it guarantees
the mind's subordination to the object."

Thus Bataille, like Nietzsche, sacrifices the notion. He sacrifices the
notion of the eternal return such that it makes way, not for a philosophy of
time, but *for the experience of sacrifice.* In this operation, it will become
evident that the return is in itself always the return of sacrifice because it
implies the loss of identity on the part of one experiencing it; that the
return, like sacrifice, leads first of all to the deterioration of personal identity. There is, then, a return only on the condition that the one who returns
and the one in whom he returns communicate within this deterioration;
there is a return only on the condition that the one who returns return as
one sacrificed, to the extent that he has already lost his identity. The return
is always the return of the return and Bataille only repeats Nietzsche
because the latter repeated Christ, who repeated Dionysius or so many
other avatars of the Dianus figure.

It will also become evident that the sacrifice does not take place in
any other form than that of the simulacrum as such, the simulacrum of

sacrifice and the simulacrum of the notion. First of all, because, as *Inner Experience* makes clear, "death is in a sense an imposture" (this is the title of the version of *Sacrifices* that he repeats in this volume). Next because sacrifice is not the experience of something, but the experience of *nothing* (and in this sense *Inner Experience* is no more an experience than it is inner).

B. Thus that which Nietzsche named eternal return has nothing fundamental about it: based on it, nothing is fundamental any longer, it is the loss of a foundation, the irruption of the bottomless. The foundation of Nietzsche's thought gives way, can no longer be grasped, mastered by conceptual representation and resumed under its own name. In Bataille's resumption of Nietzsche's thought, the eternal return will not be *recognized*. But this non-recognition, paradoxically, is the condition for an authentic reading; it is implied in the functioning of the Nietzschean text itself. The eternal return is only a simulacrum and to recognize it would be to recognize *nothing*. A nocturnal point in which the unknown gains access as such to the consciousness that has sacrificed the notion, the whole of the known; one can only fail to recognize it although this failure may occur in two ways: unrecognized because one speaks of it or because one doesn't speak of it.

Recognition (*Anerkennung*)—the Hegelian concept and operation *par excellence*—does not function vis-à-vis Nietzsche with whom the community will never present itself as a means of overcoming separation, but as the renewed experience of the impossible depth of things which achieves reality from this separation. If one remembers that Hegel's slavery/mastery opposition rests on the struggle for recognition, the non-recognition that marks the relationship to Nietzsche is no doubt the condition for getting around this alternative.

Hegel himself knew separation ["no-one more than Hegel placed importance on the separation of men among themselves" (*IE*, 150)]. He knew it since it is one of the composite elements of the experience of supplication that he repressed in working out his system, and he was to overcome it through the implementation of a community politics whose decisive moment was to be military service. It is "compulsory military service" which seems to him to guarantee the return to that communal life, without which there was, according to him, no possible knowledge.

Knowledge alone can be made communal, shared, recognized. Not ignorance or non-knowledge which, by this fact are associated with the separation of beings, with the failure to recognize: they can only go unrecognized. In the non-recognition of what Nietzsche called the focal point of his thought, in the sacrifice of the notion of the eternal return, experience is thus realized for Bataille, as loss of the fundamental, which is a repetition of Nietzsche's experience. "If one proceeds right to the end, one must efface oneself, undergo solitude, suffer from it severely, renounce the wish to be *recognized*."

C. Absolute knowledge is the identity of the subject and the object. This is an accepted fact, recognized by Bataille. Recognized, at least from a distance, in other words, like an object. From the outside. Without recognizing oneself in it. To speak of Hegel, is decidedly, up to a certain point, to speak like Hegel. But Bataille does not do so himself; this is done in a certain way without him. Repeating Hegelian discourse is the inverse of repeating Nietzsche—it only takes place by means of its subject's foreclosure. "I can resume Hegel's thought in myself by developing it around a point, but despite this, it is not mine (in other words, I don't have the right to oppose this thought, like *another* thought, to that of Hegel)." To take up Hegel again means both to repeat what he has said and to resume/make repairs [*faire des reprises*⁵] where the texture of his discourse demands it; but the first meaning always takes the upper hand [*reprend toujours le dessus*] and any *reprise*, in the sense of touch up, of Hegel's discourse will always be taken up again [*reprise*] by the fabric of this discourse. Another thought does not arise from these *reprises* per se; these *reprises* don't need another thought; they are only the repetition of the same. Thus Bataille doesn't do it "himself." Moreover someone else undertook this, someone within the economy of its reflections, played the same game vis-à-vis Hegel, as he did with Nietzsche. We are referring to Kojève whose "thought," he said, "wishes as much as possible to be Hegel's thought, as much as a contemporary mind, knowing what Hegel didn't know…could contain and develop it. It must be said that the originality and the courage of Alexandre Kojève is to have perceived the impossibility of going any further; the necessity, as a result, of renouncing the plan of working out an original philosophy, and, through this, the unending renewal which admits the vanity of thought."

Absolute knowledge, as identity of subject and object, is thus recognized as an object (an objectivity) by Bataille who does not recognize himself in it, leaving this task to Kojève—a lame recognition which was to unseal absolute knowledge. The identity of Bataille's discourse on Hegel and Hegel's discourse assumes the objective existence of Hegel (it is necessary that Hegel be, that he be something and that one know what he is); it is necessary that the discourse directed toward him confer the status of a concept upon the name of Hegel. Now Bataille only takes on this task to a certain point, a point only beyond which the name Hegel will be worked upon by an operation that he will no longer be able to resume, an operation that then escapes from him irreversibly and by which he escapes from himself: he is sacrificed in his turn, like all notions. Hegel opposes the immutable Hegel. Hegel opened beyond himself, the absence of Nietzsche appears. The objectivity of absolute knowledge "dissolves in the *nothing* of non-knowledge" under the action of a discourse that refuses to recognize itself in it and to allow itself to be taken up again by it. The failure to recognize the unknown reacts upon the recognition of the known. The fabric is not repaired; on the contrary, it is ripped apart and in the place of the identity of the subject and of the object, the absence of object is shown as fading thought: "Nietzsche alone described it in the 'death of God' (*Joyful Wisdom* #125)."

This fading thought—expenditure and sacrifice—which only maintains itself upon its own ruin, is therefore "Nietzsche's thought." In other words, on the one hand, what Nietzsche thought: that God is dead and that we have killed him—something that cannot be thought by any objective and rational scientific thought, for the latter believes only what it sees and the death of God is not seen, is not a spectacle; it is lived—or it dies. But also, on the other hand, what one thinks when one thinks (of) Nietzsche, since to think (of) Nietzsche is to repeat him and to repeat Nietzsche is to sacrifice, with God, the guarantee of all identities. To repeat Nietzsche is to renew the sacrifice in which "everything is victim" right to the sacrificial destruction of Nietzsche himself.

The experience of Nietzsche (an expression in the genitive whose subjective and objective values must be maintained), as experience of the loss of the subject in the absence of object is just as much that of Nietzsche's absence. Nietzsche is not. Let us leave Mr. Nietzsche there.

1. "Those who read him or admire him scoff at him (he knew it, he said it). *Except me?* (I am simplifying). But to attempt, as he asked, to follow him is to abandon oneself to the same trial, to the same bewilderment as his."

2. "Since no-one has been prepared to die for Nietzsche's doctrine, it is null and void."

3. "I am the only one to present myself, not as an interpreter of Nietzsche, but as being the same as he. Not that my thought is

always loyal to his: it is often removed from it, especially when I envisage the meticulous developments of a theory. But this thought places itself within the conditions where Nietzsche's thought placed itself."

The absence of Nietzsche: in Bataille's works this is the form taken by what Derrida called the absence of a transcendental signified. At first because if it imports the stamp of an exteriority, of a foreign source to Bataille's text, this stamp is above all one of the constitutive elements lending its play to this text: not a reference to a referential exteriority, but self-presence of the forbidden text. Nietzsche is often cited; he is quoted at length (*Joyful Wisdom* #125) and many of these quotations are not followed by any commentary. Nietzsche is inside Bataille's text; he (his absence) is the heart of the experience Bataille called inner ("I spoke of *inner experience* [...] by putting this vague title forward, I didn't intend to confine myself to the inner aspects of this experience") and which—its further development bears moreover the title *Sur Nietzsche*—might just as well have been called the experience of Nietzsche. Nietzsche is "in" Bataille; Bataille is "in" Nietzsche or in Nietzsche's absence which will then at the same time lead necessarily to Bataille's absence.

Bataille calls this operation "dramatization," an operation that has a religious origin, for it is also a dramatization that leads in particular to mystical ecstasy. In this last case it gains support from myths evoking divine presence: it is a "meditation upon objects having a history (pathetic and dramatic) like God." But the dramatic meditation of Nietzsche in Bataille ("I imagine myself ... and in imagining it, I weep") is distinguished from it in that it finds no foundation in divine presence since, on the contrary, it brings about sacrifice to the point where it can in the end do nothing more than lose itself in its absence. Dramatization makes presence burst forth. It makes it burst out laughing. Laughter: "If we hadn't known how to dramatize, we would not know how to laugh." Ecstasy: "If we didn't know how to dramatize, we wouldn't be able to leave ourselves." Dramatization: "One only attains states of ecstasy or of rapture by *dramatizing* existence in general."

As an example, there is the meditation on the word "silence." But perhaps it recurs too often to be only an example. And perhaps the function of the example itself is implicated in this type of operation. "I limit myself to the word *silence*. It is already, as I have said, the abolition of the sound which the word is" (*IE*, 16). The meditation leads to a silencing of the word, to its reduction to silence, in a putting to death that is brought about by the dissolution of the unit, of its body and its soul, of its tangible materiality (the sound) and the ideal nature of its signification, a dissolution that leads to the confrontation of a sound and of a nonsense. (*Comment*: such indeed is the concluding movement of several of Bataille's texts, a conclusion marked not by the delivery of a meaning, but by a sort of acceleration of the signifier liberated by an earlier meditation. cf. the end of *The Solar Anus* "The solar ring is the intact anus of her body..." All of these conclusions, these finales have an ejaculatory character, closer to glossolalia than to thesis.) Silence is, then, stifled beneath the sound of the word that means it. This dramatization puts into play the self-transgressing quality of certain words (silence, God, Nietzsche, etc.) on the basis of which the opposition between major and minor will alone be able to function: therefore between the silence that remains minor when it is simply the word's meaning and which becomes major when it has become its nonsense. "A dictionary would begin starting from the moment when it would no longer provide the meaning but the tasks of words." Sacrifice places words in the space of the senseless.

This is the title of aphorism #125 of the *Joyful Wisdom,* a passage in which the empty place of atheology is inscribed in Bataille's text but under the name of Nietzsche. *The Summa Atheologiae* or *The Imitation of Mr. Nietzsche.*

D. The repetition of the Nietzschean experience is implied in every "authentic" reading of Nietzsche because this experience—and it is in this sense that it is "authentic," in other words authentic right to the negation of authenticity, right to the dissolution of the identity and the affirmation of the mask—is unreservedly exposed to sacrifice, exposed as sacrifice: right to madness.

1. It is true that this "madness" is, in its turn, a slipping notion, a notion whose meaning, whose relationship to meaning (to "its" own meaning as to meaning in general) is particularly perverse.

Nietzsche's madness, writes Bataille, "would appear to be somatic in origin." This is a phrase which, at first reading, can lead from the outside to a certification of nonsense, of a nonsense that as a result is objective, minor. Yet it causes a distinction between the somatic and the psychic to intervene, a questioning that, according to Bataille, is one of the decisive results of the Nietzschean experience, a result that causes the question of madness to reemerge, but this time in its major form. Bataille gives Nietzsche the name incarnate, in other words, to a man who:

...could not be satisfied, in fact, with thinking or with speaking, for an inner necessity forced him to live what he thinks and what he says. Such an incarnate would thus know such a great liberty that no language would suffice to reproduce its movement (and dialectics would suffice no more than others). Only human thought incarnated in this way would become a festival whose drunkenness and licentiousness would be unleashed no less than the feeling of anguish and of the tragic. This leads one to recognize—without leaving any way out—that the incarnate man should also go mad.

The insane: the incarnate. Major non-sense was the disordering of the relationships constitutive of the sign surrounding the absence of the transcendental signified. Nietzsche's madness is the refusal of terms whose distinction served as a metaphor for the traditional thought of the sign. Nietzsche's madness "(it would appear to be somatic in origin): one must say, however, that a first movement towards the whole man is the equivalent of madness."

2. "What forces me to write, I imagine, is the fear of going mad." These are the last words of *Sur Nietzsche*. And elsewhere: "Given that we are the reasonable men we are forced to be, we would insist that anyone who doesn't speak according to the rules of language is *mad*. We ourselves are afraid of going *mad* and we observe the rules with a great uneasiness."

Bataille, then, writes and in writing he trusts the guardrails that are rules. At least that is what he says. So as not to go mad. As Nietzsche had done. But how can one reconcile these rhetorical defenses against madness with the requirement to repeat Nietzsche's experience?

One of Blake's proverbs says that *if others hadn't been mad, we would have to be.* Madness cannot be rejected outside of human *integrality*, which would not be complete without the madman. Nietzsche going mad—in place of us—has made this integrality possible—madmen who had lost their reason before him had not been able to do it with so much flair. But the gift of madness which man makes to his fellow man, can it be accepted by them without its being payed back with interest? And if this interest is not the insanity of one who receives the madness of another like a royal gift, what can its counter-offer be?

Therefore, what counter-offer can one make in this potlach inaugurated by Nietzsche's own madness sent out as a challenge to his fellow men? What counter-offer can one make that, without being madness (for Nietzsche's madness exempts us from this) nevertheless marks the gradation of the contributions essential to the development of potlach?—The "Community"?

E. The Nietzsche-Bataille relationship is played out around five elements:

1. Repetition, as return of the return—that redoubling which removes it from all thematization: faithfully, jealously, Bataille repeats Nietzsche who repeated faithfully, jealously, etc.

2. Separation, in as much as it is at the heart of the repetition that divides it and produces it as originarily redoubled—it forbids all self-presence previous to the return, all positivity in the repetition that finds itself, as a result of this fact, dispersive and innumerable. What returns, through it, is the impossible as the depth or the bottomlessness of things, is the unknown as the reverse side of an unavoidable misinterpretation, an irreversible, unrepresentable reverse side.

3. Writing or communication, in other words non-communication—in it repetition is brought about, but in it separation is brought about as well. It is the means for communication, but communication only takes place when the means fail.

4. Inauthenticity (or madness, duplicity, mask, etc.)—which means that experience, communication, repetition *does not take place*: does not take place because one must include the means and with the means repetition is impossible; the means separate it from "itself."

5. The "Community" (?)

Let us resume: "It is from a feeling of community linking me with Nietzsche and not from an isolated originality that the desire to communicate arises in me." Bataille is only the means in (and for) the repetition of Nietzsche and a means to the extent that the means fail: fail their goal, on the one hand (because they are means) which means that on the other hand, as the means for nothing, they are not means, but rather a lack of means. There is nothing original.

> I should have, without Hegel, been at first Hegel: and the means fail me. Nothing is more foreign to me than a personal way of thinking. My hatred for individual thought (the mosquito that asserts itself: "I think differently") attains calmness, simplicity: when I put forward a word, I play upon

the thought of others, something that I have gleaned by chance from human substance around me.

Failing the means: not to be Hegel, to be Nietzsche. Nietzsche who is the end of Hegel, his death and his madness. Hegel, who had the means and who became enslaved to them, who identified himself with them. No end is attained by means, but against them and despite them: there where they are wanting. If they provide the possible, they can do nothing either for or against the impossible.

It is natural for children to be impossible. This is all the more so for fatherless children, for children without parents like Nietzsche, who only wanted to be recognized by and in terms of the unknown to come, to the extent that this future would not follow him but would repeat his inconsequentiality. "Nietzsche's doctrines have this strange quality about them," writes Batille, "that they cannot be followed." Strange like the difference between the conclusion (the consequence) and the repetition, like the opposition between the means and the end when it is insurmountable, in other words when it is inscribed in an ateleological work where the meaning of meaning is marked by an unsettling strangeness.

On the one hand, Bataille writes that "the absence of goal is inherent in Nietzsche's desire" (or yet still: "he never lost that Ariadne's thread *of having no goal whatsoever*"). But, on the other hand, he wrote as well: "the desire for a community never stopped troubling him" (and: "I know how to respond to Nietzsche's desire when he spoke of a community").

How is it possible to say at the same time that this work pursues no goal, that it has avoided work as production or search for meaning, that in it language thwarts and undoes all that which would subjugate it and yet that if it hadn't been repeated it wouldn't even have taken place, that it is obsessed by this desire for a community which its repetition would introduce, etc.? A question which is that of the advent of non-meaning in a space of meaning. Which is that of the status of play in writing/reading to the extent that if meaning is no longer in play, play does not for all that affirm itself; it can only risk itself, remain in play. A question which is that of ateleology in general: it is not a system of clauses, for all systems of clauses are situated within the perspective of a meaning; it can only be a certain mode of work, of pressure exerted upon the system of clauses in order to disarticulate it.

"Contrary to what is normally observed, language is not communication but its suppression." "When the extreme limit is there, the means which serve to attain it are there no longer." One passes from one to the other, even if one cannot do without one in order to obtain the other.

Communication is a result of interrupted speech. It interrupts discourse. Communication is realized not in plenitude, but in emptiness, not on the basis of a being, but on the basis of its lack, of that lack which it is, of its unoccupied wound. If meaning is the continuity of discourse (an infinitely reversible clause: if continuity is the meaning of discourse, if discourse…), communication thwarts it, undoes it. Let us say that it dislocates it in order to indicate that such a desertion of meaning is not the constitution of a new space which would be that of non-meaning; it cannot be a question of providing a ground for non-meaning, for what pulls the ground out from under our feet.

Repetition is a break in discourse. In that of Bataille in particular which it interrupts like a quotation: of Nietzsche for example (for example?). In effect, it is always return of the lack to the self, of the lack of means as extreme limit. And the extreme limit "is never entirely attained unless communicated." It is only attained when communicated—this implies that it doesn't exist outside of the process of its communication, that it is therefore not that which is communicated (a status that would endow it with the possibility of being what it is, without taking account of the process). The extreme limit is, in effect, the invalidation of communication, and this is why "if one proceeds right to the end, one must efface oneself, undergo solitude, suffer from it severely, renounce being *recognized*." The extreme limit, repetition: unending, the unending absence of means. The game is not over, potlach continues. Always in excess of our means. What would be the counter-offer to Nietzsche's madness? To accept it/him [*l'accepter*] without the recognition that would put us out of play?

—The "community"?

## TRANSLATOR'S NOTES

1. I have abridged those sections of the original text of Denis Hollier's introduction which pertain specifically to Artaud.

2. *mettre en boîte* not only means to "put into a box," but to "trick," to "pull someone's leg."

3. *La Ferme* (The Farm) extends the linguistic play in this passage surrounding the verb "fermer"—"to close." It is also the colloquial expression for demanding silence: ("shut up").

4. In a similar fashion, the verb *déboîter* plays with the earlier expressions "*mettre en boîte*"—to "lay in a box," to "pull someone's leg," and "*boîte à malice*"—"jack-in-the-box."

5. In the following passage, I will use the original French word *reprise* when it is required to develop both senses of the word—to "resume" and to "make repairs."

# 4

# Unemployed Negativity
# (Derrida, Bataille, Hegel)

### Tony Corn

The end of Metaphysics is our unavowed metaphysics…(Levinas)

What can I know? What must I do? What may I hope?

One will remember that these are the three questions by which, at the threshhold of our modernity, Kant defines the concerns of Reason in their entirety. With time, and the Hegel episode, Reason has become Spirit: "that I which is an us, that Us which is an I." With time as well, modernity has created out of the Hegel episode a reason for itself, and the question, then, which haunts this massive Kantian repetition more or less from the underground could be the following: what must we do (indeed, in these distressing times: what may we hope) once Hegel has answered the first question?

For absolute knowledge has taken place: with or without denial, avoidance, surpassing, overturning or displacement, we live in (if not *from*) this *belief*, that it will be necessary to really *think* one day. Though it has been just barely recognized as such by our very recent modernity,[1] this belief demands to be thought in a logic that is itself Hegelian (supposing that there were others), as *certitude* of absolute knowledge's *reality*. Do what one will, it thus determines, as such, the powerful recitatives of our modernity, not the least of which is that of a "becoming-literature of philosophy."

One is only too aware that this certitude of *reality* is not translatable, far from it, into a certitude of the *truth* of absolute knowledge. It is even always on the basis of that reality that the non-truth of the Hegelian system is ultimately inferred.[2] Yet, even though Hegel finds himself reinscribed in a problematic that is foreign to him (whether it be a question of a History of Being, or of human Praxis), this certitude of *reality* (of its having-taken place as "thought") is doubled by a certitude of its *realization* (of its becoming-world) through/in modernity. Must we see indicated there, in that paradox, a certitude of Hegel's truth, but only "in itself"? And for which "for us"?

With respect as much to the doxa (which undertakes to sort out "what is dead and what is living in Hegel") as to those major readings by modernity (which are indicated here by the names Heidegger, or Adorno,[3] Foucault or Derrida), the singularity of the position taken by a certain Bataille risks not becoming immediately apparent. Even and above all if one wanted to restrict oneself only to the French intellectual scene of the last fifty years, and to the definition that it was thought possible to propose of that scene:

> In 1945, everything that is modern comes from Hegel...In 1968, everything that is modern is hostile to Hegel. The difference between the two generations is in this inversion of the sign under which the relationship to Hegel is declared: a *minus* sign replaces the *plus* sign. What doesn't change, on the other hand, is the point of reference...[4]

That the relationships are in fact more complex can be demonstrated simply by taking such a text from "1968" which, on the grounds of a *Hegelianism without reserve*, examines such a text from "1945." Indeed, what is henceforth Derrida's classic study on Bataille opens with this remark:

> Often Hegel seems to me to be self-evident, but the self-evident is a heavy burden. (*Le Coupable*) Why today—even today—are the best readers of Bataille among those for whom Hegel's self-evidence is so lightly borne?[5]

But if, *mutatis mutandis*, this remark by Derrida can be applied even today to the best(?) readers of Derrida, this is because his own relationship to Hegel, although constantly reaffirmed and "practiced" throughout his work, takes on an ambiguity that is, moreover, irreducible to the declared motive of a "double science," and of which the study on Bataille, as we will try to show, constitutes the most *critical* moment of inscription.

The disconcerting manner of Derrida's text stems first from the fact that it challenges not only the "best" readers of Bataille for whom Hegelian evidence is lightly borne (to be brief, let us say the *Tel Quel* group), but also the "worst" readers (Sartre), for whom Hegelian evidence would, moreover, seem a bit more heavily borne if it did not rest on the anthropological misunderstanding with which one is familiar (that is to say, of which one is unaware). Since one is, at one and the same time, reminded of the impossibility of circumventing Hegel and of the infinitesimal excess characterizing the position of Bataille, Derrida is forced to *play Bataille against Bataille* (Bataille: "Hegel didn't realize to what extent he was right"; Derrida: "Bataille is even less Hegelian than he thinks") in order to *play Bataille against Hegel.*

Now, what is least surprising is not that the text curiously resembles *two possible readings* of Hegel (what the future itinerary of Derrida will only confirm): thus, measuring what separates the "sovereignty" of one of them from the "mastery" of the other ["it cannot even be said that this difference has a sense: it is the *difference of sense,* the *unique* interval which separates meaning from a certain non-meaning"(254)], Derrida affirms:

> Describing this simulacrum [of the Aufhebung, of Mastery], philosophy's blind spot, Bataille must, of course, say it, feign to say it, in the Hegelian logos. (257)

Assuming—rightly or wrongly, let one be the judge—that the essence of the demonstration of a "Hegelianism without reserve" derives ultimately only from this *"presumption of feint,"*[6] one can only put forward a double question: what is the philosophical status of the "feint"? But also, already, without prejudice for what could maintain it in a certain psychologism: what prevents one from extending this *"presumption of feint"* to Hegel himself? In other words, what if Hegel had "feigned" saying it in the Hegelian logos? (i.e., the logos itself?)

It is moreover this direction that Derrida's future itinerary will take, at the very time when the "feint" is found thought *as such,* i.e., as that space, always already there, separating *prescription* from *description.* Thus, in *Glas* ("of absolute knowledge/as absolute knowledge"), one finds Hegel's feint described in the following way:

But can the at least apparent prescriptive mode of his discourse
be regularly transformed into the descriptive mode? And if this
possibility regularly presents itself, does it not belong to the very
structure of the text?...Rigorously considering writing can henceforth make the oppositions vacillate, even up to those received
here, for example, between prescription and description. A
discourse that is (or develops the) metaphysical can always be
treated as if it contented itself with describing metaphysics, its
norms and its effects.[7]

With this rigorous attention given to Hegel's writing, one is here
quite removed from the cherished project of the young Derrida;[8] and as a
result of a necessity that will have to be thought through, the history of his
relationship to Hegel is not dissimilar to that of Heidegger to Hegel—
according to Derrida himself ["to let Hegel's word be magnified and
spoken, the word of metaphysics in its entirety (Hegel included or rather
including itself entirely within Hegel)"].

That this destiny was to be *also*, perhaps, that of a certain Bataille, is
something that Derrida's study does not permit one to even ask. Far from
putting the "best" readers back to back with the "worst," this text seems to
us to accompany their respective unthought [*impensé*] through a radicalization, which is first of all a precipitation and a blinding vis-à-vis the
Hegelian text; hence its exemplarity *a contrario*. Thus, should the difference between "sovereignty" and "mastery" *have* a meaning (which those
who are skilled in the anthropological folding back of "writing" upon literature continue to say today) or, more cautiously and according to Derrida,
should it *be* the difference of meaning, this difference of difference is decisive only upon the outcome of a double, communal presupposition that
will be the center of our questioning here:

> 1) the possibility of *attaining* (in all senses of the word) the whole
> of absolute knowledge through one of its parts. Or yet still, as is
> here the case, one part of its parts (the Master/Slave dialectic in
> the *Phenomenology* alone). The question is of course that of the
> possibility of a "metonymic" reading, and of its modalities. As
> such, it holds for any reader of Hegel, and as one knows, it has
> received various answers in modernity: a centering on "the
> unhappy consciousness" for Wahl, on the "Master and the Slave"
> for Kojève, on the "moral conscience" for others, etc.; and more
> generally, a centering on the *Phenomenology* at the expense of
> the *Logic* or the *Encyclopaedia*.[9]

2) the possibility of attaining decisively the relationship of Bataille to Hegel through a *formal* study of the motif of "sovereignty" (i.e., that of "abstract negativity" according to Hegel). Is one true to Bataille's intention, to what he says or to what he does? But above all: can one restrict oneself to a *formal* reading, bracket the *becoming* of this relationship (or refer to Queneau's article, which amounts to the same thing)—and hope thus to understand, indeed to demonstrate a "Hegelianism without reserve," while for "ordinary" Hegelianism the result is nothing without its becoming? And is it not for not having thought in a Hegelian fashion this "Hegelianism without reserve" that one is henceforth blinded vis-à-vis the singular position of a Bataille?

These questions obviously exceed the mere reading relationship (or not) of Derrida to Bataille, and the scope of this article. By restricting ourselves, however, to a "minor" text (minor by its format, but major by what it puts at stake), we will now attempt to sketch out what makes Bataille's answer exemplary.

> I should have, without being Hegel, been at first Hegel, and the means fail me. (*Le Coupable*)

More or less, something else in any case, than a drama that is above all "textual,"[10] the relationship of Bataille to Hegel is in fact explicitly situated at the level of an *experience* ("sole authority, sole value," Bataille will say) which, if it is reinscribed[11] in the Bataillean *text*, remains above all a *reading* experience: at once immediate—that of an individuality confronted with Hegelian discourse—and mediated, as Queneau reminds us, by the reading of Hegel at the time:

> During almost twenty years, he confronted Hegel, or rather the different Hegels that the French public discovered one after the other. By eventually discovering the *true one*, he came to know himself—know himself as radically non Hegelian, but by knowing that this self-knowledge could only take place after he had knowledge of a doctrine which he claimed was comparable to no other, and by thus finding himself once again, mediated, but not reduced.[12]

At the logical (if not chronological) outcome of his experience as reader, it would appear that Bataille discovered the truth of Hegel and, at the same time, his own truth.  Or to put it another way: subscribing in this way to an entirely Hegelian logic, he will only have been able to "go through the economy" of absolute knowledge after having *gone through* its *economy* (i.e., only after having played out again and traversed, in his very experience of reading, the different figures of the experience of consciousness described by Hegel).  Such is Queneau's conclusion regarding the *becoming* of this relationship to Hegel, a conclusion that Derrida takes up again and intends to verify *structurally,* so to speak, at the level of the Bataillean text.  In fact, as one will see, it is the inverse that is produced: and Queneau's affirmation only represents the "ideal" point attained by any reading of Hegel.  Somewhat more cautious, Bataille himself does not claim to have attained it, but contents himself with problematizing it.[13] Which, for all intents and purposes, is to say that this end point remains "merely aimed at," to speak in Hegelian terms.

If it appears very early in Bataille's work, the motif of "sovereignty" is not originally thought, in near or distant proximity to Hegel (to "mastery" or to "absolute knowledge"): its determination is first of all formal, without a precise philosophical status, and is elaborated outside of this reading experience (it is, at the very least, not referred to it explicitly).  It is only several years later that such an articulation takes place—with respect to absolute knowledge—and, at the same time, that "sovereignty" finds its *truth* (for the time being, in the Hegelian sense) as "unemployed negativity."  As is indicated by the letter to Kojève,[14] where "unemployed negativity" is elaborated, the *logical* outcome of Bataille's reading experience, far from marking a liberation vis-à-vis Hegel, is presented, rather, as the exact determination of what the beginning of this experience should be. To put things differently: at the *outcome* of this *empirical* reading experience, the *logical beginning* of this experience is correctly determined. But, rather, let us read:

> Your taking me to task helps me express myself with a greater precision.
>
> I can assume (as a likely hypothesis) that from this point on history has been completed (with the exception of its outcome).  I however represent things to myself differently than you do...
>
> If action ("doing") is—as Hegel says—negativity, the question then arises as to knowing if the negativity of one who "no longer has anything to do" disappears or remains in the state of

"unemployed negativity." I can only accept one of these possibilities, since I am myself this very "unemployed negativity" (I couldn't define myself any more precisely).

With respect to the fragmentary readings of the philosophical institution, the singularity of Bataille's position stems at first from the radicality of this "beginning": no doubt only a non-philosopher could have *taken Spirit to the letter* to that point, and have determined his own negativity as a function of absolute knowledge's having-taken place (immediately transcribable then as "the end of history"). That such a "beginning" is not the result of an arbitrary choice, but that it should proceed from a logical necessity renders it all the more consequential. No doubt there is no text that manifests so radically the certitude of absolute knowledge's reality, and assumes it in its most immediate consequences: what can I do, now that "it" has taken place?

But there is as well no text that accentuates so seriously the gap between the certitude of the *reality* of absolute knowledge, and its *truth*. In effect, what one could have taken for the surest indication of a Hegelianism without reserve is immediately converted into a disqualification of Hegelian discourse:

> I accept that Hegel may have foreseen this possibility [of my unemployed negativity]: he didn't, however, situate it *at the outcome* of the processes he describes. I imagine that my life—or its abortion, even better, the open wound that is my life—by itself constitutes the refutation of Hegel's closed system.

Bataille who, "without being Hegel, should have been Hegel," disqualifies Hegel for not having been able, or having wanted, without Bataille, to be Bataille. The objection is obviously untenable, and this on three levels.

First, and most immediately, in that Bataille's unemployed negativity is *no longer* unemployed negativity as soon as it thinks itself *as such*—which it does, here, now (in as much as it is used to reflect upon itself in reference to a discourse which does not fail to remind that, when consciousness determines itself in a position, it at the same time goes beyond that position. A classical example: when the animal determines itself as such, it ceases by this very act to be what it is; it becomes man). This (false) refutation is, moreover, only the first moment of that reflexion

*of* unemployed negativity which, as prospective and individual as it was
(what can I do?), becomes retrospective and universal (what has happened
since Hegel, and what is its meaning?):

> It is no longer really a question of misfortune or of life, but
> only of what becomes of "unemployed negativity," if it is true
> that it becomes something. I am this negativity in the forms
> that it engenders not at first in myself, but in others. Impotent
> negativity most often makes itself into a work of art: this
> metamorphosis, whose consequences are usually real,
> responds poorly to the situation left by the completion of
> history (or by the thought of its completion). A work of art
> responds through elusion or, to the extent that the response is
> prolonged, it responds to no situation in particular; it
> responds the most poorly to that of the end, when elusion is
> no longer possible.

Art (i.e., literature as well) draws, then, its logical finitude from this
impossibility of responding to/from the End. Bataille, certainly, is led to
distinguish art that is *prior to* the end of history (where the metamor-
phoses are real, but where negativity is introduced into a system that
annuls it, and where only the affirmation is recognized) from art that
*follows* the end of history, as it were, (where negativity is indeed recognized as such, but as a negativity "empty of content"); but this "fundamental difference" is rapidly reabsorbed:

> Thus there is a fundamental difference between the objec-
> tivization of negativity, such as the past has recognized it, and
> that which remains possible *at the end.* In effect, since the
> man of "unemployed negativity" does not find in art an answer
> to the question that he himself is, he can only become the man
> of "recognized negativity." He has understood that his need to
> act no longer had a use. But since this need could no longer
> be duped by the enticements of art, one day or another it is
> recognized for what it is: as negativity empty of content….He
> stands before his own negativity as before a wall. Whatever
> uneasiness he experiences, he knows that nothing can hence-
> forth be dismissed, since from negativity there is no longer a
> way out.

Thus ends the letter to Kojève: one is far removed, then, from the triumphant attitude of certain modern commentators, and from the powerful recitatives of the "becoming-literature of philosophy." Coming after Bataille's reflexions, it would appear inversely that *since* Hegel "all the rest is only literature"... And if Bataille's text seems to possess certain Hegelian resonances, this is because it comes closest to the *Lectures on Aesthetics*, and this not only with respect to the determination of the art-to-come as "negation of art" (i.e., negation of that "negation of negativity" that Bataille situates in "pre-Hegelian" art). The most visible proximity is realized around the famous Hegelian thesis of the end of art: if it is true that in relation to *finality*, "the highest destination of art is that which it has in common with religion and philosophy,"[15] art however remains tainted for Hegel by a *finitude*, and "in the hierarchy of means used to express the absolute, religion and the culture arising from reason occupy the highest degree, well superior to that of art. The work of art is thus incapable of satisfying our ultimate need for the Absolute."[16] Once the art-religion-philosophy trio is not simply *affirmed* as a logical necessity, but also *performed* by Hegel, once absolute knowledge has therefore taken place, what may one hope for art? Before and without Bataille, Hegel answers: "it is permissible to hope that art will continue to rise and perfect itself, but its form has ceased to satisfy the most elevated need of the spirit."[17] For one as for the other, modernity is indeed the moment of *historical* inscription of the *logical* finitude of art. With the following consequence: not only does Bataille's conclusion not disturb in any way the Hegelian reading of art, but it renders irrelevant the original objection addressed to Hegel of not having situated Bataille's unemployed nega-tivity "at the outcome of the processes he describes": since the end of art signifies above all *logical finitude*, there is no point in searching *at the outcome of absolute knowledge* what is already situated (because of this finitude) as simply the first *moment* of absolute Spirit. To put things differently, the error in Bataille's reading ultimately stems from the very determination of the concept of "negativity." His misreading of the Work *of* Hegel [*l'Oeuvre* de *Hegel*] is reflected most visibly in a "metonymic" fashion in his misreading of Hegel's Work [*l'Oeuvre* chez *Hegel*][18] where one finds articulated a *double* negativity: far from being situated at the *historical* level, as Bataille would have it ("before/after" Hegel), this double negativity is at first of a *logical* order: negativity *in being* and negativity *of the performing*, through whose dialectic the Work is engen-dered. Even when Bataille seems to place this double negativity at that logical level which is his, he inscribes it only *within* the negativity of the performing, through a distinction that is somewhat reminiscent of the opposition *praxis/poesis* (and which is already obliquely indicated in the definition of his negativity as "that of a man who no longer has anything to do and not that of a man who prefers to speak").

What would continue to exist, after the impossibility—once absolute knowledge/the end of history have taken place—of a negativity as action (*praxis*), is the possibility of a negativity as work (*poesis*), in which it would be recognized as such. Though it is naive, this false alternative is however decisive for Bataille's later itinerary, leading as it does to that master work which is *The Accursed Share*, which marks less the passage from a restricted economy to a general economy than its opposite: the final aporia of a theorization/*thesaurization of expenditure.*[19] In the letter to Kojève, Bataille's inaugural question (what becomes of the negativity of one who no longer has anything to do?) is quite simply not pertinent, given that the initial axiom ("if action...is negativity") only takes into account the negativity of the performing. Now the latter is indissociable from negativity in being, always already there, whatever the historical context or the project of an individuality. One will certainly say that Bataille finds it again inspite of himself in his answer, since he affirms that the negativity of one who no longer has anything to do "subsists in the *state* of unemployed negativity" (my italics). In other words, that the negativity of the performing becomes negativity in being: the error is at once that of blocking in a relationship of a *causal* nature this *dialectical* movement (by which the work is engendered—including that of Bataille) *and* of relating it to a determined historical moment (in this case, absolute knowledge's having-taken-place).

Even in this very misreading of Hegel's Work [*l'Oeuvre* chez *Hegel*] (which, at least at first, is only equalled by its certitude in the Work of Hegel [*l'Oeuvre de Hegel*]), Bataille's position remains exemplary, though negatively: it indicates *a contrario* that the only legitimate and pertinent "metonymic" reading, and one which would permit one to attain the truth of the Work of Hegel [*l'Oeuvre de Hegel*], would be that of Hegel's Work [*l'Oeuvre chez Hegel*].

From the viewpoint of that letter to Kojève, however, it is less on a synchronic level that the error in reading is ultimately situated. Bataille's error is in effect that of adhering to a certitude of absolute knowledge's having-taken-place/the end of history in the form of a *Here, Now* in the past—and against which Bataille will immediately play, as one has seen, another *Here, Now* (his own, his "life")—instead of surpassing this very position of *sense certainty* (whose critique in fact opens the presentation of the figures of the experience of consiousness which, in the *Phenomenology*, "lead" to absolute knowledge). All of the later objections addressed to Hegel, all of the contradictions supposedly revealed in "absolute knowledge," remain saddled with this initial position.

Let us resume: by "beginning" in such a radical manner, Bataille didn't know to what extent he was right; but because he remained with this *sense certainty* (first of absolute knowledge, and then of its own "self-presence"), he will remain with "the richest and the poorest" reading of Hegel. Derrida is therefore less Bataillean than he thinks when, forty years later, he opens *Glas* with this reversion:

> What to make of what remains, today, for us, here, now, of a Hegel?

> For us, here, now: from now on that is what one will not have been able to think without him.

> For us, here, now: these words are citations; already, always, we will have learned that from him.[20]

Between "1945" and "1968," "Bataille" and "Derrida" mark decisive moments (as much chronological as logical) in the historicity of Modernity's reading of Hegel. And paradoxically, it is really since the *Glas* "of absolute knowledge/as absolute knowledge" that it will be possible to undertake, at new costs, a Hegelian reading of Hegel, which, in its reading *practice*, goes through the different figures of "the experience of consciousness" exposed by Hegel. One has the feeling that something other than a contribution to the advancement of Hegelian studies is at stake: far from being "regional," this historicity in effect puts into play the whole of Modernity (and its "postmodern" variations) since through Derrida (which is here less a proper name than the exemplary indication of an attitude and a moment), what tolls is nothing less than the bell [*le Glas*] of "Modernity" itself (the concept and the thing), that strange "Here, now, for us" placed under the sign of the spacing of time, the temporalization of space, and anthropological fading.

That the Kantian problematic (in its original version or subtitled as "modern") should bear the cost of such an operation is what is already indicated when a certain psychoanalytical discourse—which one has been able to define as a "*negativised* Hegelian system"[21]—suggests that the three Kantian questions constitute the entire concerns...of Unreason.[22]

We will end on a joyful note, by way of a conclusion: if Bataille questioned himself about his own "unemployed negativity," and about that of his predecessors, at no moment did he ask himself what became of Hegel's negativity, once absolute knowledge had been accomplished. Strictly speaking. Hegel is indeed the first man of "unemployed negativity." On the most empirical, even anecdotal level, it is known that once the Work was finished, Hegel passed the rest of his life playing cards...more precisely, at achieving "successes." Moreover one has not refrained (Bataille among the first) from invoking the image of the old Hegel playing cards in order to cast doubt upon the validity of his enterprise. Closer to us, in Bataille's time, it is Art's turn to find its completion; and Duchamp ceased all artistic activity, though symbolically, in order to devote himself...to "chess" [*aux échecs*].[23] The highly problematical question is then the following: why are Hegel's "successes" considered to be the indication of his failure [*son échec*] while Duchamp's chess [*les échecs*] are considered to be the proof of his success?

## NOTES

1. "In this sense, *within* the metaphysics of presence, within philosophy as knowledge of the presence of the object, as the being-before-oneself of knowledge in consciousness, we believe, quite simply and literally, in absolute knowledge as the *closure* if not the end of history. And we believe *that such a closure has taken place.*" [J. Derrida, *Speech and Phenomena*, trans. D. Allison and N. Garver, (Evanston: Northwestern University Press, 1973), 102]. And the recognition *a contrario* by Foucault: "our entire era, whether it be through logic or through epistemology, whether it be through Marx or through Nietzsche, is trying to escape from Hegel" (*L'ordre du discours*, 74).

2. It is already on the grounds of this "internal contradiction" that the first critique of Hegel, i.e., that of Feuerbach, is presented: "if Hegelian philosophy were the absolute reality of the idea of philosophy, then the arresting of reason in Hegelian philosophy should of necessity entail the arresting of time: for if time continued as if following its sad course, then Hegelian philosophy would lose its predicate of absoluteness." (*Manifestes philosophiques*, 26). Reexamined by our modernity, this naive critique is put in its proper place by J.-R. Seba in "Histoire et fin de l'histoire dans la *Phénoménologie de l'Esprit* de Hegel," in *Revue de Métaphysique et de Morale*, Jan–Mar 1980.

3. Of Heidegger, cf. in particular Introduction *à la métaphysique* and "Hegel and his concept of experience," in *Chemins*; of Adorno, *Trois études sur Hegel*.

4. Vincent Descombes, *Le Même et l'autre*, 24. Assuming that such an affirmation were exact, it would still remain to be *thought*: either, as the author seems to do, by privileging the structural point of view, like an "antinomy" of Modernity vis-à-vis Hegel; or, from a diachronic point of view, like a growing scepticism vis-à-vis Hegel—but since, for Hegel, History is the history of scepticism completing itself, this growing scepticism of Modernity would only confirm Hegel. Things become more complicated in that this "declaration" by Descombes on French modernity is already almost word for word, and

thirty years earlier, that of Ernst Bloch vis-à-vis the preceding (German) generation (cf. *Sujet-objet*, 361).

5. J. Derrida, "From Restricted to General Economy: A Hegelianism without Reserve," in *Writing and Difference*, trans. A. Bass (Chicago: University of Chicago Press, 1978), 251.

6. In effect, it is from this presumption that the future demonstration can be developed: "neither can nor may be inscribed in the nucleus of the concept itself...the space which separates the logic of lordship and, if you will, the nonlogic of sovereignty will have to be inscribed within the continuous chain (or functioning) of a form of writing..." (267). A demonstration that concludes with this enormity, surprising from the pen of Derrida: "...even differing from the Hegelian *Book* which was Kojève's theme, Bataille's writing, in its major instance, does not tolerate the distinction of form and content" (267). In *Dissemination*, then in *Glas*, Derrida will be led to reconsider Hegel's writing more rigorously (on this question, cf. as well *La patience du concept* by Gerard Lebrun, and *La remarque spéculative* by Jean-Luc Nancy).

7. J. Derrida, *Glas*, trans. J. Leavey, Jr., R. Rand (Lincoln: University of Nebraska Press, 1986), 197-198.

8. "The extreme audacity would consist here in returning against Hegel the accusation of formalism and of denouncing speculative reflexion as logic of understanding, as tautological. One can imagine the difficulty of the task" ("Violence et Metaphysique," in *Ecriture et la différence*, p. 135).

9. A temptation from which Derrida himself will not have escaped for a time: in effect, the demonstration (cf. "The Ends of Man in *Margins of Philosophy*) of the anthropologism of the Hegelian system is only valid for the *Phenomenology* alone, as Lyotard very strongly indicates (cf. "Phraser après Auschwitz," in *Les fins de l'homme*, Colloque Cerisy). For memory, let us remember the different metonymic readings attempted by Derrida: "semiology" of Hegel (in *Margins*), "Prefaces" (*Dissemination*), "Family" (*Glas*)...

10. J. Derrida, op. cit., "One could describe as a scene, but we will not do so here, the history of Bataille's relations to Hegel's different faces...But let us leave the stage and the players. The drama is first of all textual" (253).

11. [trans. note]: Here Corn uses the verb "se re-marquer" which I have translated as "reinscribed" but which also bears the meaning "to be noticed."

12. R. Queneau, "Premières Confrontations avec Hegel," *Critique*, 195–196. As the title indicates, this article concerns only the period between the first articles in *Documents* (1929) and *Inner Experience* (1943).

13. Even *supposing* that I were to attain it [absolute knowledge], I know that I would know nothing more than I know now (...) If I "mimic" absolute knowledge, I am at once, of necessity, God himself (...) *Supposing* then that I were to be God (...) at precisely that moment, the question is formulated which allows human, divine existence to enter...the deepest foray into darkness without return: why must there be *what I know*? (*Inner Experience*, trans. L. Boldt (Albany: State University of New York Press, 1988), 109 (my italics). And it is precisely because it is only aimed at that the final objection is not pertinent (cf. further).

14. Written in 1937, this letter to Kojève was published as an appendix to *Le Coupable* (*Complete Works*, vol. V, 369–371), and reproduced in a slightly different version by Denis Hollier in *Collège de sociologie* (Gallimard, 1979). It would be necessary (but we cannot do it within the framework of this article) to take into account the draft version of this letter, and in particular Bataille's declarations about Hegel's belonging to the "Geistige Tierreich"...

15.  G.W.F. Hegel, *Aesthetics*, vol. I, 32.

16.  Ibid., 33.

17.  Ibid., 155.

18.  Such as it is determined in the *Phenomenology of Spirit*, in the chapter of the "animal reign of the Spirit," at the decisive moment of articulation between Reason and Spirit (i.e., between the formal determinations of the figures of the experience of consciousness, and their inscription *in* history).  It is about at the same time that Blanchot publishes under the very title of the "Règne animal de l'esprit" (taken up again in *La Part du feu*, as the first part of "La littérature et le droit à la mort"), an article which, inversely, questions Hegel's Work (l'Oeuvre *chez* Hegel) without relating it to the Work of Hegel (L'Oeuvre *de* Hegel). Cf. our study "Hypocrite de la Raison—Pure," in *L'Esprit Créateur*, Fall 1984 (*Blanchot et l'éthique de la littérature*).

19.  One may assume that Bataille was perfectly aware of this, since he defined *The Accursed Share* as a book "which the author wouldn't have written if he had followed its lesson to the letter" (C.W., vol. VII, 21).

20.  J. Derrida, *Glas*, (op. cit.), 1.

21.  Cf. the only reading of Lacan "recognized" by Lacan (in Seminar XX): *Le Titre de la lettre*, by Lacoue-Labarthe and Nancy.

22.  Cf. *Télévision*, by Lacan.

23.  On this question, cf. the article by Damisch, "The Duchamp Defense," in *October 10*, Fall 1979.

# II. Expenditure, General Economy and Political Commitment

# 5

# Bataille and the World From "The Notion of Expenditure" to The Accursed Share

*Jean Piel*

In the presence of Georges Bataille I have always felt, since our first meeting around 1927—at the home of Raymond Queneau, who lived at that time at Desnouettes Square—an impression of extraordinary brotherhood, an impression that was never proven wrong right up to our last conversation a few days before his death. I can see once again the outburst of his laughter—still rather wild despite the illness that had broken his voice—but a laughter animated, as always, by a sort of subtle complicity; and accompanying the slightly heavy but graceful gesture of goodbye from his large peasant's hand, I hear his voice slowly emitting the syllables: "Good-bye, Jean."

This feeling of brotherhood—I reencountered it in the course of numerous discussions with him, even when it came to working together. Most often, he would question me untiringly about what he thought I knew better than he, overwhelming me with the most varied questions— at times somewhat absurd. I myself made every effort to provoke, through my answers or my remarks, the blossoming of a thought that I felt to be always on the verge of awakening, and which came to light in the form of a flash of trenchant wit or of those images of which he was fond. These images were drawn from his personal memories, thus borrowed from a universe for him very familiar but which was often all the more surprising for the person he addressed, images that he would then thoroughly examine, that he would explore in all their conceivable consequences, whose many facets he would turn over in his mind with a willingness that never flagged.[1]

I still remember that he spent the last evening with me before my departure in September 1939, for what we both imagined to be a real War. But his feelings were obviously ambiguous; to the concern with which he surrounded me was mingled the excitement that he felt in representing to himself the events in which I was going to be involved. How would a man as pacifist as he knew me to be act at the moment of attack? I must admit that at the thought of this his nostrils flared ever so slightly as he showed his large teeth.

These modest memories are only worth something to the extent that they evoke what was the most natural warmth in this man, about whom it is not in the least contradictory to say that his work, devoted as it was to the anguished search for an expression at the extreme limit of the impossible, often takes on the appearance of a determined negation, while he never ceased to say "yes" to the world without any reservation or qualification. He was open to the world for better or for worse, for the most intense as for the most humble[2] and he had an appetite for apprehending it without limit as without false shame. This is borne out by his constant concern to communicate, to draw "his thought closer to that of others, of all the others,"[3] by the scrupulous attention that he manifested before the least of the people he spoke to.[4] Witness to this as well is the patient and passionate effort that he never ceased to display, above all during the mature part of his life—often at the price of an exhausting and fastidious effort at getting information—to interpret, in the light of the intuitions of his tumultuous experience, the no less tumultuous events that unfolded before his eyes. He did this without neglecting any of the aspects of these events, including those, through his education as through the influence of most of his friends, that he might have had a tendency to neglect and which emerge from what one commonly designates by the name economy.

In addition to the fact that he humbly confesses his "ignorance," he was certainly for a long time dominated by the feeling that "the world ... was for him only a tomb," by the sensation of being "lost in the passage of a cave"[5] and by the conviction that nothing remained for him but to let his "thought slowly mingle with silence."[6] But even in his writings from the mystical period, which no doubt constitute the most intense part of his work, he never ceases to cry out: "not yet!" to glance furtively but passionately at others, at this world, subject at that time to the worst upheavals, which he intuited as capable of being grasped in its entirety only as "a disaster" (of which man is perhaps the culmination),[7] but that he never gave up knowing and representing.

In fact, a whole part of Bataille's work, from "The Notion of Expenditure" to *The Accursed Share*, is devoted to that attempt at representing the world. These texts are perhaps not among the most brilliant that he wrote, and they could astound those who are used to seeing these problems approached in a more ordered and logically discursive form. But I can bear witness to the eminent place that he reserved for them in his work—to the worry that haunted him, with old age approaching, that he had not succeeded in giving to this outline the more developed form that he would have wished and which would have established, with due attention, the unity of his thought—already so remarkable—through the multiple movements of his research. I can bear witness, finally, to his stubborn will to revise, in the last years of his life, *The Accursed Share*, and to give to all those aspects of his work the true crowning that might have constituted what he himself designated as being, necessarily, a sort of essay on universal History.

This is a testimony I owe all the more for I was, from before the war and above all after 1945, one of Bataille's companions in that enterprise that unfortunately could not reach its completion—and that, no doubt, could never do so. Perhaps, among all those with whom he had ties of friendship, I appeared as one of those who, through his contacts with the world of events and things, through the competence that, quite wrongly, was attributed to him, could be of some assistance to Bataille. Might I remind one that at the time of the Stavisky affair—which is today quite forgotten, but which provoked in Bataille an intense movement of curiosity and uneasiness, coming as it did after the Nazis came to power in Germany—we spent long days at his sick bed, for he was bedridden at the time, analyzing and commenting upon the abundant and journalistic documentation that he had asked me to put together, in the hopes that we could become enlightened about the economic underpinnings of those dramatic and often incredible events? And might I remind one of his relationship with Arnaud Dandieu, the essayist of *Décadence de la Nation française* and of *Cancer américain*, who was at that time one of his colleagues at the National Library, and whom he frequented assiduously for several years? Then, later, shortly after the war, during the first years of *Critique*, there was the rediscovery in common of Keynes' and Beveridge's books, as well as his contacts with economists like François Perroux and the commentaries that he devoted to the latter's essays—the very study, to which he applied himself with conscientious patience, of works as compact as that of Colin Clark on *The Conditions of Economic Progress.*

As he emphasizes in the preface to *The Accursed Share*,[8] it certainly did not escape Bataille that to approach an interpretation of the external world—before the intervention of that "bold reversal" alone capable, ultimately, of substituting dynamic overviews "in harmony with the world" for "the stagnation of isolated ideas"—to approach such an interpretation assumes previous studies undertaken according to the rules of an insistent reason,[9] the accumulation of a documentation that could only be obtained in the company of specialists, in addition, no doubt, to a collective atmosphere of curiosity, of anxiety, and of research that implies the fairly close participation with groups more or less inspired by preoccupations of a political or economic order.

Those conditions were filled during at least two fairly long periods in Georges Bataille's life. The first is situated between 1930 and 1935—it was marked above all by Bataille's collaboration on *La Critique sociale*, and his almost daily visits with the men temporarily grouped around this journal. The second followed the creation of *Critique* and resulted in the publication of *The Accursed Share*. Between these two periods, there were long years of internal meditation, starting in 1939 with the drafting of the first lines of *Le Coupable*, a book begun "by means of an upheaval that managed to challenge everything" and that presented itself at the time as a liberation of ventures and of quests appearing from then on as having no resolution, and in which he felt he was caught.[10]

Such an oscillation in the orientation of Bataille's thought should not disguise the fact that the search to put his thought in step with the world, the fervent aspiration towards "that extreme freedom of thought that makes notions equal to the freedom of the movement of the world,"[11] occupied a growing place in his life as he progressively grew older; one might even say that he never stopped pursuing this search and this aspiration.

The steadfastness of this preoccupation is made evident if one remembers certain dates. Bataille was about to turn thirty-five when he wrote, for the journal *La Critique sociale*, "The Notion of Expenditure," and was just under fifty-two when *The Accursed Share* appeared, a book presented in its preface as being the fruit of eighteen years of work. One could thus situate around 1931 the beginning of this reflexion. In fact, it must date back even further and coincide with the period around the end of the 1920s, when, no doubt at the instigation of Alfred Metraux, he became acquainted with the theory of potlach, outlined by Mauss in his *Essai sur le don, forme archaïque de l'échange*, published in the 1925 *Année sociologique*. This discovery seemed to be at the extreme origin of the interest that he was later to show not only in ethnology but also, and to an increasing degree, in economic events, and seemed also to have arisen as an illumination that was to permit Bataille to view the world as if it were animated by a turmoil in accord with the one that never ceased to dominate his personal life.

⚜

The essential elements of this view already lie in *The Notion of Expenditure*, a dense and brilliant text, which constitutes the pivotal point of Bataille's reflexion on the world, and on man in the world.

There one finds, in the light of observations made by Mauss and other ethnologists on primitive economic institutions—in which "exchange is...treated as a sumptuous loss of objects yielded up" and in which there is thus presented, *at its foundation*, a sort of process of expenditure upon which a process of acquisition develops"—the affirmation of the "secondary character of production and acquisition with respect to expenditure." The idea of a "peaceful world true to its calculations," which would be ordered by the primordial necessity of acquiring, of producing, and of conserving, is only a "useful illusion," while the world in which we live is doomed to loss, and the very survival of societies is possible only at the price of considerable and growing unproductive expenditures. This concept—whose close relationship with personal experiences of eroticism and anguish is emphasized by Bataille, along with its relationship to that of the son, eager to squander, while remaining a victim of the avarice and the reasonable behavior of his father, even, as well, along with certain givens of psychoanalysis—this concept throws light on a large number of social, political, economic, and aesthetic phenomena. Luxury, games, spectacles, forms of worship, sexual activity (set apart from the finality of genital function), the arts, and poetry in the strict sense of the term are together so many manifestations of improductive expenditure. This concept even furnishes a first basis for interpreting the history of civilizations. "And if it is true that production and acquisition in their development and changes of form introduce a variable that must be understood in order to comprehend historical processes, they are, however, still only means subordinate to expenditure."[12]

As for man's life, it only has meaning in accordance with such a destiny for the world:

> Human life, distinct from juridical existence, existing as it does on a globe isolated in celestial space, from night to day and from one country to another—human life cannot in any way be limited to the closed systems assigned to it by reasonable conceptions. The immense travail of recklessness, discharge, and upheaval that constitutes life could be expressed by stating that life starts only with the deficit of these systems; at least what it allows in the way of order and reserve has meaning only from the moment when the ordered and reserved forces liberate and lose themselves for ends that cannot be subordinated to anything one can account for. It is only by such insubordination—even if it is impoverished—that the human race ceases to be isolated in the unconditional splendor of material things.[13]

A masterly piece of writing, in which one finds the development — expressed with a force perhaps never equalled—of a conception of man and of the world that one will see formulated in the course of Bataille's later works, whether it be in his philosophical essays or in *The Accursed Share*.

But if this "Notion of Expenditure" is presented as a harbinger of what is to come, it is also strongly marked by the circumstances presiding at its formulation, by the atmosphere in which it was conceived, and by the very tendencies of the journal in which it was to appear. The collaborators on *La Critique sociale* were for the most part members of the "Communist Democratic Circle," which brought together, beside poets and writers like Jacques Baron, Michel Leiris, and Raymond Queneau, militant members of extreme left-wing oppositional movements still marked by their theoretical Marxist background despite their break with "the party," and which were all later to follow quite diverse paths, since it was a question—if one were to mention only the most fervent—of the leader, Boris Souvarine, of Lucien Laurat, but also of J. Dantry and even of Simone Weil.

The journal, remarkable in more than one respect, was particularly so in its vigorous tone, for these heterogeneous heretics had in common the quality of being quite caustic. Is it in order to adapt himself to this violence that Bataille savagely forces the tone in certain passages of his article, or rather must one see, in that extreme furor of expression, some first attempts at the exercise of blasphematory eloquence in which he was soon to indulge during the episode of *Contre-Attaque*? It is nonetheless the case that it is difficult to find, in the work of Bataille, pieces of writing as powerful in their imprecatory violence as those that depict the bourgeois, incapable of concealing "a sordid face, a face so rapacious and lacking in nobility, so frighteningly small that all human life, upon seeing it, seems degraded," or those that evoke the meaning of Christian religion in our societies, which "wallow...in impurities indispensable to its ecstatic torments," things occurring "as though society, conscious of its own intolerable splitting, had become for a time dead drunk in order to enjoy it sadistically."

One must not forget that the importance attributed to the class struggle in "The Notion of Expenditure" reflects the discussions in which Bataille participated with his friends from *La Critique sociale*; but how did certain of these friends react to the fact that he interprets, in terms of the theory of improductive expenditure, that class struggle which broke out in an unprecedented way—since all of the modes of traditional expenditure have atrophied in bourgeois society—and in which "the living sumptuous tumult" is lost—a class struggle which thus appears as "the most grandiose form of social expenditure"? Representing revolution as the supreme form of potlach could not fail to arouse some reservations among those in charge of the journal: a preliminary note of the essay, printed at the beginning of the article, emphasized moreover that "in many respects, the author contradicts the general orientation of our thinking" and announced the imminent publication of a critical analysis of the study that, to my knowledge, was never done.

No matter what, these are aspects that one may be permitted to consider incidental to "The Notion of Expenditure," and whose divergences with certain positions adopted later by Bataille could easily be noted; they are strongly characteristic of the form taken at that time by the effervescence of his mind, but would in no way be able to diminish the fact that this crucial text is a true source from which one can already see the emergence of what Bataille would develop twenty years later in a book he designated, to several of his friends, as being the most important of his work.

*The Accursed Share* is the only book in which Georges Bataille attempted to put together a systematic exposé[14] of his vision of the world—a philosophy of nature, a philosophy of man, a philosophy of economy, a philosophy of history. It was a work, as well, from which he even attempted to draw a sort of problematic of the possible evolution of political and social problems that haunted his contemporaries toward the end of the forties.

It is always the notion of excess that is at the basis of this vision, but he endeavors this time to seek a scientific explanation for it based on improvised facts gathered from movements of energy on the surface of the globe. Certainly these facts do not suffice for "finding the key to all the problems posed by each discipline envisaging the movements of energy on the earth," but since it is a question of energy considered thus as a cosmic phenomenon, a great hypothesis is put forward: there is always excess, because the sun's rays, which are the source of growth, are given without measure. "The sun gives without ever receiving," thus there is necessarily accumulation of an energy that can only be spent in exuberance and effervescence.

Hence, as well, the modalities of life's growth, which constantly run up against limits. Certainly there are discoveries that permit growth to leap ahead, that open new spaces to the latter. But other limits do not delay in reappearing and loss becomes unavoidable.

In this history of life, man plays an eminent role in two respects. On the one hand, human technology opens up new possibilities to life as "the branch of the tree" or "the wing of the bird" did in nature; but, on the other hand, of all living beings, man is "the most apt to consume the excess of energy intensely and luxuriously." While his industry multiplies growth possibilities, he also has at his disposal "an infinite capacity to consume in pure loss." One thus rediscovers in him the ordinary rhythm of energy use in the world, characterized by "the alternation of the austerity that accumulates and of extravagance." In the same way, there are two types of men: one type is "hardly concerned with his works"—a man described by ethnologolists—while the other type is "turned towards the conservation and the fair distribution" celebrated by modern morality. Yet, in the same way the two aspects can, in turn, characterize the same man, whose expression changes "from the turbulence of night to the serious affairs of the morning."

Of these two human functions, it is consumption that permits him to be in harmony with the world: since the destiny of the universe is a "useless and infinite realization," that of man is to pursue this realization. Man becomes a summit through squandering—the most glorious operation of all and a sign of *sovereignty*.

Thus, just as Bataille's morality is properly speaking, an "over-turning" of current morality, so his economic concepts are presented as a reversal of common economic thinking. Certainly, he remains obsessed, like most of the specialists who approached these problems shortly after World War II, by the memory of the great crises of overproduction before the war, and strongly influenced by the theories that they awakened—Keynes' essays on the hypothesis of "economic maturity." And if he takes on the objective of "aligning the problem put forward in the crises with the general problem of nature," when he insists quite emphatically on "the illusion of growth possibilities offered by the acceleration of industrial development," he does not differ much from the pessimism of numerous economists of that time. But where he is innovative, where he proposes a true "Copernican change" of basic economic concepts, occurs when he perceives the fundamental difference between the economy of a separate system—where a feeling of scarcity, of necessity reigns, where problems of profit are raised and where growth can always seem possible and desirable—and that of an economy of the living masses in its entirety—where energy is always in excess and which must unceasingly destroy a surplus. Showing that the study of isolated phenomena is always an abstraction, he proposes an effort at synthesis, which was up to then without precedent, in opposition to the restricted thought of traditional economists which he compares to that "of a mechanic who changes a tire." This profound view has had some success, for one now knows the degree of attention that the term *generalized economy* has received since these lines were written.

The whole problem is to know how, at the heart of this general economy, the surplus is used. It is the use made of the excess "that is the cause of changes in structure"—in other words, of the entire history of civilizations, to which three quarters of *The Accursed Share* is devoted. A certain number of "historical givens" are successively studied there that reveal the contrast between two types of societies: the "societies based on consumption," like the Aztecs or the primitive societies given to *potlach*, and "societies based on enterprise": military societies (like Islam) or industrial ones (like modern society such as it has developed since the Reformation). A separate place is reserved for the paradoxical solution of Tibet, "a society based on religious enterprise," in which "monasticism" constitutes an original mode for expenditures of excess, a solution in isolation that, thanks to the large number of unproductive and childless monks, "stems its explosive violence *from within.*"

The choice that people of today will make regarding the mode for expending unavoidable excess—this choice will decide their future. Will they continue to "undergo" what they could "bring about," that is, to let the surplus provoke more and more catastrophic explosions instead of voluntarily "consuming" it, of consciously destroying it through ways they can choose and "agree to"?

Up to this point, Bataille's reflexions, applied to the contemporary era, and to the experiences of the use of riches that take shape there, no longer delight in the passionate reactions and rages that animate certain passages of "The Notion of Expenditure." Rather, Bataille's reflexions are those of a man whose maturity has brought him a taste for more serene judgments; at times they have even brought him the ambition—perhaps "crazy"?—of envisaging solutions that are certainly not positive in any lasting way, but at the very least, entailed moments of equilibrium capable of bringing men some respite. How different is the tone of the chapter in *The Accursed Share* devoted to luxury and poverty, from the pages where, in the article from *La Critique sociale*, the conditions governing the class struggle were described! The opinion formulated upon the Soviet—that is to say Stalinist—experience in the 1949 book contrasts with the apparently disapproving silence, with which it was surrounded in the 1933 article: not only is the judgment made that "there was no choice left," which, in sum, justifies the adopted rhythm of accumulation, corresponding to a stage in history that has simply opened a new space for growth through other ways, just as capitalism had once done, but still "communist dissidence itself" (that which contested the paths chosen by Soviet power) is accused of sharing "the general sterility of the democracies"[15] and the "collusion between the opposition and the bourgeois" is denounced. As for the most powerful capitalist society, if the fact is strongly stressed that all of its earlier behavior engaged it in an impasse, Bataille admits that it is perhaps itself on the way to glimpsing a solution by getting rid of the excess in the form of a gift, pure and simple.

Despite all of the reservations formulated, what seems to resemble a hope bathes an entire part of the last chapters of *The Accursed Share*, the hope awakened by the Marshall Plan, which could not fail to impress the theoretician of improductive expenditure, since this plan, such as it had at least initially been presented, consisted, in sum, "of using a doomed wealth in order to open up new possibilities for growth elsewhere."[16] Perhaps one finds in the pages devoted to the Marshall Plan, as in those where the Soviet experience is evoked, or yet still in the somewhat simplistic concept of the prospect of industrial development in the world, aspects that one could also qualify as being incidental to *The Accursed*

*Share.* They are certainly quite different here from those that we believe we have been able to detect in "The Notion of Expenditure." At times these latter aspects are presented in contradiction with the former, but this is because they result from the influence of events or of different readings on an extremely sensitive man—as Bataille always was; events like the Marshall initiative, which offered quite a tempting opportunity to see the theory of gift being confirmed by events, or like those of the cold war, which seemed at that time—one was on the verge of the Korean war—to give a maximum of chance to the USSR.

I am convinced that Bataille was fully conscious later on of the contingent nature of certain of these influences, and that this is one of the reasons why—not the major reason, but one of them—he so desperately wished to recommence work on *The Accursed Share* and to provide new developments for the themes exposed there.

We will never know what would have become of this new *Accursed Share* or the work that would have been its continuation, but we do know what this book, such as Bataille left it, has brought us, and it is thanks to it that we can better respond to our anguished interrogation vis-à-vis the history of the world such as it is unfolding before our eyes. Whatever one may think of certain aspects of his appraisal of Soviet or American events at the end of the 1950s, it remains the case that he saw clearly that the USSR was there as if to awaken the world, and that America, actually feeling the effect of this permanent threat, began to awaken to an awareness. He had the illumination that "paradoxical changes" could be established between these two forces and thus prove "that the contradictions of the world are not necessarily resolved by war";[17] he began to see, at last, that the growing waste of atomic and space-related expenditures of the two greatest world powers could appear one day, like a gigantic *potlach*, as though they were a means of avoiding more or less consciously, "that catastrophic expenditure of excess energy" that is war.

Thus, in *The Accursed Share*, Georges Bataille, a precursor of the theory of gift in modern economic life and of "generalized economy," was also—more than ten years before his time—the prophet of "peaceful coexistence" and of unexpected developments of the competition for expansion between the two blocs. This is a great accomplishment for a single book, and it is a legacy unexpected at the very least from a man who had for a long time forbidden himself any claim to provide a lesson. But it is nothing when compared to the development that could be implied—for the interpretation of phenomena that, in our contemporary experience, still require an explanation—by the exploitation of ideas that abound, or that begin to arise in this book, so rich and yet still so unknown, which economists and sociologists should use as a point of departure in their thinking at this midpoint of the twentieth century.

## NOTES

1. The recourse to these familiar comparisons, developed with due satisfaction, can often be found even in his written work. For example, in *La part maudite*, (39–40), in order to describe the results of pressure exerted by life in all directions, he imagines an immense crowd assembled in the hope of attending a *bullfight*: the crowd amasses inside, then grows larger outside, then climbs trees and lamp poles, just as life, after having populated "the fundamental space of the waters and the ground," takes possession of the "realm of the air."

2. In *Le Coupable*, he remarks (35): "if there is only an incomplete universe, each part is no less meaningful than the whole." And he adds, challenging the insignificance of his impressions in the train upon entering the Saint Lazare station: "I would be ashamed to seek in ecstasy a truth which, elevating me to the level of the completed universe, would withdraw the sense of a train's entrance into a station."

3. *Le Coupable*, preface, xiv (note).

4. I have seen him pursue interminable conversations with this country mailman or that village shopkeeper, whom he questioned with an untiring curiosity, but one that was full of tact and discretion.

5. *Le Coupable*, 9.

6. Ibid., preface, xiv.

7. Ibid., preface, xii.

8. *La part maudite*, preface, 14.

9. Ibid., 15.

10. *Le Coupable*, 32.

11. *La part maudite*, 14.

12. "The Notion of Expenditure," in *Visions of Excess*, trans. A. Stoekl (Minneapolis: University of Minnesota Press, 1985), 120.

13. Ibid., 128.

14. The fact that this exposé is full of detours and often labored in its layout might help some discover the truth in La Palice's statement: the movement of Bataille's thought was hardly a preparation for "discourse"—but the intensity of the unaccustomed effort that he imposed upon himself allowed him to find new and powerful images, and incomparable accents to express his vision.

15. *La part maudite*, 193.

16. *La part maudite*, 242.

17. *La part maudite*, 246.

# 6

# The Maze of Taste: On Bataille, Derrida, and Kant

*Arkady Plotnitsky*

If Bataille's confrontation with Hegel can be seen as central to his thought and writing and has become a relative commonplace (albeit a productive one), Bataille's references to Kant are only casual. I shall not, however, argue the significance of Kant in Bataille's discourse in specific (let alone textual) terms. Rather, I want to explore what can be seen as a Kantian *moment* in Bataille, as it appears within the historical and conceptual closure that, according to Derrida, defines Western philosophical discourse, or theoretical discourse, or even discourse in general. Indeed it is far from self-evident that this closure can be subsumed under the rubric of the Occident, however convenient or comfortable that demarcation might appear.

That Kant influenced Bataille is best illustrated by Bataille himself in a passing remark in "The 'Old Mole' and the Prefix *Sur* in the words *Surhomme* [Superman] and *Surrealist*": "...it was necessary to endow antinomies in general with a mechanical and abstract character, as in Kant and Hegel."[1] This coupling of Kant and Hegel is familiar to the point of triviality. It is far less trivial and far more significant, however, that this coupling and this unity are, to a considerable degree, conceived of by Bataille in terms of a historical and conceptual closure of metaphysics, the closure on which our discourse must depend, even when it is aimed at undermining the power of metaphysics and philosophy.[2] The concept of closure, furthermore, includes a crucial idea of the necessity—psychological, social, cultural, historical, perhaps even political—of metaphysical thinking. Indeed, the phrase immediately preceding the one just cited defines the philosophical closure of language: "...for human vocabulary continues everywhere to maintain throughout a faithful memory of fundamental categories" (*Visions*, 35).

With the exception of Derrida's seminal formulations, one can hardly think of a better invocation of closure: however much "philosophical usages are in question" (*Visions*, 35) and however transformed they might become, the metaphysical remnants including those left by the history of this questioning, are ineluctable in our language. It is this configuration that is powerfully explored by Derrida. The notion of closure, so conceived, is perhaps Derrida's most significant contribution to modern theoretical thought and to intellectual history in general.

It is of course true that the very concept (or category) of category is itself a Kantian, as well as an Aristotelian one. The closure begins neither with Kant (nor Aristotle, nor anyone else), nor does it end with Hegel, Bataille, or Derrida. The title of Bataille's essay (accompanied by its epigraph from Marx, metaphorically defining historical materialism: "In history as in nature decay is the laboratory of life") (*Visions*, 32) announces this closure and the proper names that demarcate it in more recent historical terms: Marx, Nietzsche, Freud, and several others as well. In doing so, Bataille's text inscribes "the historical and theoretical situation that is also our own" (*Positions*, 51), simultaneously framing it—inscribing its "parergon—between the communist and surrealist manifestos."[3]

These later parergonal structures still await an analysis at the level that their complexity and richness demand, whether we view them in a general context or see the locus of Bataille's discourse between Breton and Aragon in, as it were, the Breton/Aragon parergon. It is not that this context or (for it can hardly be subsumed under the rubric of context) this configuration can exhaust the parergon of Bataille's discourse; it can only provisionally open it. The parergon defining Bataille's discourse or, as Derrida persuasively argues, *any* parergon can neither be exhausted nor saturated. It can be neither uniquely originated, nor unequivocally closed. This is why these parergonal effects cannot be subsumed under the rubric of context, particularly *conscious* context.[4] One of my goals in this essay is to follow the *complexity* of the parergonal in the context (that is to say, *parergon*) of Bataille's discourse, specifically in relation to the question of general economy and of the major form of writing opened by Bataille.

Undoubtedly, the shadow of Hegel looms large over all this, whether in Marx, Bataille, Derrida, or in general. But Kant's shadow no less so. For, if "Hegel is always right as soon as one opens one's mouth in order to articulate meaning," he cannot be right without Kant.[5] It is this Kantian margin (or center) that I want to explore, borrowing in part my title from Bataille's "The Labyrinth." This proximity of closure might, along the way, also suggest a certain textual proximity on which I shall not insist but which cannot be ignored either.

There will be a further specificity, for my theme will be a very small but extraordinarily interesting and important portion of Kant's third critique. As in Bataille's essay cited earlier, the question of the philosophical will be situated in Kant between the question of the aesthetic (analogous to Surrealism in Bataille) and the political. It is this "left" artistic margin that will be my major concern in this essay. As Bataille's "sur" suggests, this "margin"—that is, what is marginalized and minimized within the text of philosophy—will, in the power of its efficacy, *exceed* the "center" and will thus be reinscribed as the condition of the possibility of the center. Kant already knew (or was afraid to know) that, suppressing the *excess* of knowledge that makes knowledge (i.e., philosophy) possible in the first place. My major concern however will be what Bataille manages to do with this "knowledge," for, as Derrida says, "We know this.... only now, and with a knowledge that is not a knowledge at all."[6] This is what Bataille had in mind or what we would do best to infer from his concept of un-knowledge.

In establishing his division and, a bit later, his hierarchy of the beautiful arts, Kant writes of the arts of speech (of which poetry will be then specifically assigned "the first rank"):

> The *orator*, then, promises a serious business, and in order to entertain his audience conducts it as if it were a mere *play* with ideas. The *poet* merely promises an entertaining play with ideas, and yet it has the same effect upon the understanding as if he had only intended to carry on its business. The combination and harmony of both cognitive faculties, sensibility and understanding, which cannot dispense with each other but which yet cannot well be united without constraint and mutual prejudice, must appear to be undesigned and so to be brought about by themselves; otherwise it is not *beautiful* art. Hence, all that is studied and anxious must be avoided in it, for beautiful art must be free art in a double sense. It is not a work like a mercenary employment,

the greatness of which can be judged according to a definite
standard, which can be attained or paid for, and again, though
the mind is here occupied, it feels itself thus contented and
aroused without looking to any other purpose (independent
of reward).

The orator therefore gives something which he does not
promise, viz. an entertaining play of the imagination; but he
also fails to supply what he did promise, which is indeed his
announced business, viz. the purposive occupation of the
understanding. On the other hand, the poet promises little and
announces a mere play with ideas; but he supplies something
which is worth occupying ourselves with, because he provides
in this play food for the understanding and, by the aid of imagination, gives life to his concepts. (Thus the orator on the
whole gives less, the poet more, than he promises).[7]

It might seem astonishing, but also, given the structure of closure as
delineated earlier, rather natural or logical, how much of Bataille's problematics is inscribed in this and surrounding passages in Kant. Given the
transformations of the concepts of text and history enacted by the recent
transformations of the theoretical field itself, including those in Bataille's
text, one hesitates to use the word "anticipated." These transformations,
specifically those inscribed in Bataille's text, affect our conception of what
constitutes the theoretical field and how it is constituted as much as they
affect the concepts of text and history.

There is, to begin with, the question of "economy" in its most
conventional sense, the economic question raised by Kant's conception of
beautiful art as free art (in the first sense). One might and indeed must see
it as the question of political economy as well: it is hardly useful—
"economical" or "productive"—to speak of an economy that would not be
political in the context of Bataille, even as Bataille subjects the science of
political economy and its concepts to a radical critique as a *restricted*
economy. It is a far more complex question whether, while retaining the
significance of the political and, at the same time, inscribing the general
economy as an economy of waste and expenditure, Bataille avoids a
certain idealization of *waste* as against *consumption* accounted for by a
restricted economy. The latter in Bataille manifests itself precisely at the
level of the classical science of political economy.

Beautiful art, then, "is not a work like a mercenary employment, the
greatness of which can be judged according to a definite standard, which

can be attained or paid for" (165). Derrida was perhaps the first to draw attention to these "economic" connections in Kant in "Economimesis," expanding the general concept of economy as grounding the question of genius in its relation to the question of imitation. The imitative work of genius (with respect to Nature) is an imitation, mimesis, of economy as *process*, play of forces and so on—*economimesis*—not an imitation of the product. Genius in its creation, in its *production*, imitates *how* Nature (or God) produces, not *what* is produced. Economic metaphors, including those of political economics, still permeate the *philosophical* account, the science of this "economy," expanded by Kant from a difference between beautiful art and a material ("hard") economic process, "a work like a mercenary employment," to a difference (still economic) in the occupation of the mind. Kant's "and again" is most telling in this respect: "And again, though the mind is here occupied [employed], it feels itself thus contented and aroused without looking to any other purpose (independently of reward)" (165).

Kant's *borrowing*, both negative and positive, of the economic inscriptions does not in itself constitute a problem, particularly if considered in the context of Bataille's discourse. First of all, the discourse of political economy might itself be seen, historically speaking, as *borrowing* from Kant in this respect, though it would be silly to see Kant's in turn as an original discourse in this sense. Kant must have borrowed his "mercenary" metaphors from some forms of economic and political economic discourse. There can be an original metaphor here no more than anywhere else. Second, the history of theory from Kant to Marx, Nietzsche, Freud, and Bataille demonstrates that the metaphors of economy have proved to be as theoretically *productive* as they are unavoidable. Indeed, as Bataille's discourse shows with extraordinary power, it is the economic insistence on consumption at the multiple and often interacting levels of theoretical economies—economic, political, conceptual—that is most problematic. The theoretical problem is a metaphoric loss of the economy of loss and thus of the general economy.

It is not that consumption and the pleasure of consumption are not important or theoretically and otherwise pleasurable. To reverse the configuration absolutely and to privilege expenditure unconditionally would be just as untenable. As I indicated earlier, Bataille's heavy insistence on waste and expenditure must be seen as problematic in this respect, and is "saved" only by the enormous *labyrinthine* complexity of Bataille's inscription of these concepts.

A considerable portion of the third critique might be seen as Kant's attempt at a science of this—non-economic—economy of the poet or genius, represented best by the genius of poetry, which "of all the arts...maintains the first rank." Or, closer to Bataille's terms, one might speak of economy as the science of this operation of genius, analogous to, but also different from, the sovereign operation as conceived by Bataille, requiring a major form of writing and a general rather than restricted economy as its science. Like Hegel's economy of Absolute Knowledge, the economy inscribed in Kant, being an economy of *consumption*, must still be seen as a restricted economy: the science of the operation of mastery rather than the general economy and sovereignty in Bataille.[8]

One might feel a certain uneasiness with regard to the metaphoric fusion, transfusion, or, at times, a metaphoric confusion arising in these labyrinths of "economic" inscription in Kant, Bataille, and Derrida. It is useful to keep in mind for clarity's sake that "economy" in Bataille always designates a science, a theory: in the most significant case, that of the general economy. It is a science of the sovereign operation, whereas in Derrida's reading of Kant, "economy" designates an operation, an activity of genius. In general terms, however, particularly in those of general economy, the metaphorical transfusions of that type are as productive as they are inevitable. For it is our economies as sciences or theories— accounts—that produce the economies or operation for which we want to account. The economic metaphor of *accounting* is, in turn, not accidental in this context. It is an accounting or calculation of certain operations, however endless or interminable, that we want to inscribe as calculus and accounting of the interminable and the indeterminable.

Hegel, in making the philosophy of history into the history of philosophy, already knew it quite well and was one of the first to understand the depths and labyrinths of this problem that can only be finally resolved at the level of the Absolute, that is to say, impossible knowledge. Derrida, in commenting on the transgression of Hegel enacted by Bataille's sovereignty, correctly points out the necessity of this Hegelian moment: "Not that one returns, in classical and pre-Hegelian fashion, to an ahistorical sense which would constitute a figure of the *Phenomenology of Mind*. Sovereignty transgresses the entirety of the history of meaning and the entirety of the meaning of history, and the project of knowledge which has always obscurely welded these two together" (*Writing and Difference*, 269). In his essay, Derrida also speaks of "the rigorous and subtle corridors" (254) of dialectic. Quite so, yet corridors of dialectics are not the labyrinths of the general economy. Life in the labyrinth may not be easy; it is, however, preferable to life in a more comfortable corridor. (Nobody any longer even dreams about rooms, let alone apartments or houses. Well, some do.)

That is not to say, particularly given the labyrinths of our theoretical household (in Greek, *oikonomia*, economy), that our accounting will be able to comprehend everything —"to take everything into account." That would still be an illusion, however comfortable, a dialectical corridor—that is, a restricted economy, whether political (as in Marx) or general, most general, conscious or conceptual (as in Hegel). Nobody understood this difference better than Bataille. We may think of the word difference here in either sense: a difference between two economies of accounting, restricted in general, and one between an economy and an operation that it wants to account for. The most radical difference announced by Bataille as he inscribes the general economy has to do with problematizing the possibility of an account and economy (as science or theory), *however conceived.*[9] This double (at least double) difference, therefore, this *differ-ence* if you like, will affect enormously and multiply the shape our "accounting" must take. In these regions the category of choice must seem particularly trivial.[10]

Kant's economic considerations imply a fundamental asymmetry between two economies at issue. One, "a mercenary employment," is the economy of exchange, actual or potential, including, but not exclusively, a monetary exchange. We might call it an "economic" economy. Another, a "non-economic" economy, the economy of the beautiful art and genius, is conceived above all through a radical prohibition of exchange. To be rigorous one should speak of at least three economies here, for Kant also suggests a possibility of an exchange-reward economy at the conceptual level (in the domain of understanding) as well, which the economy of the genius of the beautiful arts escapes: "and again, though the mind is here occupied, it feels itself thus contented and aroused without looking to any other purpose (independent of reward)." There is a certain purpose and reward economy in the *occupation* (employment) of the mind, but such is not the case in the employment classified as beautiful art.

This asymmetry is of fundamental significance in Kant, though it cannot be sustained on Kant's grounds, as an absolute or fundamental distinction. It is not only that the economy of beautiful art cannot be fully liberated from an exchange or reward of some sort. It must be factored in, whether we inscribe the economy of the beautiful or the

economy of beautiful art. It might include, for example, an exchange
and reward for "the mind...occupied" by a play of imagination and
feeling "thus contented and aroused without looking to any other
purpose (independently of reward)." As we have seen, however, an
*unconditional* insistence of this form of pleasurable consumption must
in turn be seen as problematic. Conditionally, this consumption and this
exchange must be taken into account. More significant is the impossibility of an "absolute" reduction of the mercenary or "economic"
economy and employment to a definite standard or (paid) reward
implied by Kant. As Bataille's analysis of expenditure suggests, no
economy of any kind can be unconditionally reduced either to an
exchange economy or an economy absolutely free of exchange. "The
Notion of Expenditure," for example, powerfully inscribes the structural
(and *structuring*) supplement of exchange.[11] Indeed, by insisting, in a
certain proximity to Nietzsche, on the *exuberance* of "exchange" and
expenditure or on the exchange of expenditures in that essay, Bataille's
text problematizes quite radically the concepts of expenditure and waste.
Exuberant, the operations involved there are always more than simply
expenditure, more than merely waste.

It does not mean that such reductions *in either direction* are not
found in theoretical practice, including in Bataille, who tends to subordinate the effects of exchange and consumption. What Bataille's analysis
demands, however, is a different inscription of the economic and its efficacy.[12] Neither the structures of rewards, including at the level of the
monetary or political economy, nor the differences between these various
economies would disappear in this inscription. How could they? Rather
they must be inscribed otherwise, in effect with an increased rigor, necessary precisely in order to account for the multiplicity and richness of these
differences. For in this enlarged difference of inscription one would no
longer be able to speak either of *one* operation or parcel operations cate-
gorically in a demarcated accountable set.

The crucial question that poses itself with regard to Bataille is
whether the difference between restricted and general economy, even
given the interaction between them, does not retain a kind of Kantian (and
thus also inescapably Hegelian) trace of absolute difference—a trace not
sufficiently erased or comprehended by Bataille. For a certain trace, given
closure, will be unavoidable. This difference concerns not only an unconditional privilege or priority of expenditure over consumption. It could be
pointed out in this context that the difference and asymmetry so inscribed
in Bataille can be seen either as the difference between an economy of

non-exchange—a non-economic economy—and an exchange economy, or as the difference between the economy of expenditure and the economy of consumption. Given Bataille's analysis of exchange (inscribed quite differently, precisely through *expenditure*) in "The Notion of Expenditure" and elsewhere, I would see the second possibility, the priority and even *idealization* of waste, as more significant in Bataille's case. A most important issue, however, is an unconditional privilege of the general economy, however inscribed, or, in general, of any economy over any other.

The labyrinth of this question is enormous and is in the end intractable. That is, in the end it cannot be mapped once and for all. What I want to do in this paper is rather to articulate the differences between Bataille and Kant, whose significance will be undiminished whatever the answer and will enable us to inscribe the difference (radical enough) from Kant and Hegel. The answer, it might be said, is important only with respect to the question of inscribing or situating Bataille's "own" text. In general theoretical terms, one might say that there is no question here. No economy of any kind might be seen so unconditionally privileged. Such is, for now at least (that is, at this particular moment in the history of theory and, of course, for specific theorists so implied), the law of the economy of the theoretical. Such is the constraint of the conditional. But then again, we cannot unconditionally separate the question of theory and the question of Bataille, particularly the question of situating Bataille's own text historically.

With the qualifications elaborated earlier, the differences between Kant and Bataille might be subsumed under two interactive rubrics: the differences in the inscriptions of the economic operation and the differences in respective sciences or accounts of the operation. It is useful to recall Bataille's own formulation of this economic problematics in *L'Expérience intérieure* before proceeding to an articulation of these differences:

> The science of relating the object to sovereign moments, in fact, is only a *general economy* which envisages the meaning of these objects in relation to each other and finally in relation to the loss of meaning. The question of this *general economy* is situated at the level of *political economy*, but the science designated by this name is only a restricted economy (restricted to commercial values). In question is the essential problem for the science dealing with the use of wealth. The

*general economy*, in the first place, makes apparent that excesses of energy are produced, and that by definition these excesses cannot be utilized. The excessive energy can only be lost without the slightest aim, consequently without any meaning. It is this useless, senseless loss that is sovereignty.[13]

Whatever differences Kant inscribes, first in the aesthetic economy (either as the economy of the beautiful or of the sublime), and secondly in the economy of the genius of beautiful art, it always remains an economy of consumption (as Kant's metaphor *taste* indicates), and, indeed, the economy of pleasurable consumption. Furthermore, in the case of the beautiful art, it remains the economy of consumption of meaning. For, as we recall, "[the poet] provides in this play [of ideas] food for the understanding" (Kant, 165). This is why one must rigorously insist on the difference between the economy of the beautiful and the economy of beautiful art; as the latter includes the former, it also exceeds the aesthetic economy of beautiful feeling by a philosophical (though still inscribed through consumption) dimension of understanding. As Kant maintains, "For beautiful art, therefore, imagination, understanding, spirit, and taste are requisite" (164).

As in Aristotle and in the tradition he initiated, after the initial demarcation of art by its difference, specifically in affecting feeling and the feeling of pleasure, the value of art will be established on the basis of philosophical criteria of one type or another. Poetry, for example, is more philosophical than history is in Aristotle or than rhetoric is in Kant. An account of this difference still remains within the domain and power of the philosophical explanation, and making poetry "more philosophical" might be necessary precisely to maintain this parergon, maintain it by identifying the difference that in part establishes its boundaries. It can be shown, however, that neither Aristotle nor Kant will be able to sustain the boundaries and parergon at issue. From within their own discourse (this is, of course, what makes the configuration so interesting), poetry and art can be shown to exceed the containment of the philosophical account in Aristotle and Kant.

The inscription of the philosophical into the poetic is, in Kant, non-trivial enough. It should be recalled that Kant's opposition (and thus a certain excess) is set between the orator and the poet rather than between the philosopher and the poet, as this opposition must be given the philosophical nature of aesthetic value in Kant. The orator, of course, also gives more than he promises, just as the poet does; "the

orator therefore gives something that he does not promise, viz. an entertaining play of imagination." There is a difference, however, indeed a
crucial difference for the orator "also fails to supply what he did promise,
which is indeed his announced business, viz. the purposive occupation of
the understanding" (165). That, according to Kant's division of intellectual
labor, will be supplied by the philosopher. The orator thus fails because
he in fact entertains, rather than conducting "a promised serious business."
The poet's (announced) entertainment, in contrast, "has the same effect
upon the understanding, as if he had only intended to carry on its business" (165), its serious, that is its philosophical, business. Beautiful art,
particularly poetry, in contrast to the experience of the beautiful, is bound
to be philosophical.

Given these corridors of the economy of taste, Kant's division of
the beautiful arts that gives poetry priority over rhetoric is inevitable,
even though both are arts of speech that are related to the mouth, the
organ of both taste and speech. This priority of voice and the hierarchies
of arts and senses it entails are exhaustively analyzed by Derrida in
"Economimesis." It might be further pointed out that the poet as
discussed in the passage at issue and the genius of the beautiful art in the
third critique in general are inscribed so as to efface in the end the material substance produced by the mouth or the phonetic substance, to
make it disappear in fully internalized play. The immediate proximity—
presence—of "voice" to "mind" finally allows one to dwell in the
absolute presence of mind and ideas. The "speech" and "voice" of
poetry become thus "the art of mind" similar to the internal self-present
speech of Husserl's transcendental phenomenology.[14] Husserl's dependence on Kant in general is, of course, huge. In the context of the
present discussion, however, Husserl writes in one of his very rare
specific references to art:

> It is naturally important, on the other hand (once again as in
> geometry, which has recently and not idly been attaching
> great value to collections of models and the like), to make
> rich use of fancy in that service of perfect clearness which we
> are here demanding, to use it in the free transformation of the
> data of fancy, but previously also to fructify it through the
> richest and best observations possible in primordial intuition;
> noting, of course, that this fructifying does not imply that
> experience as such can be the ground of validity. We can
> draw extraordinary profit from what history has to offer us,

and in still richer measure from the gifts of art and particularly of poetry. These are indeed fruits of imagination, but in respect of the originality of the new formations, of the abundance of detailed features, and the systematic continuity of the motive forces involved, they greatly excel the performances of our own fancy, and moreover, given the understanding grasp, pass through the suggestive power of the media of artistic presentation with quite special ease into perfectly clear fancies.

Hence, if anyone loves a paradox, he can really say, and say with strict truth if he will allow for the ambiguity, that the *element* which *makes up the life of phenomenology as of all eidetical science is "fiction,"* that fiction is the source whence the knowledge of "eternal truths" draws its sustenance.[15]

As the foregoing discussion would suggest, the presence of Kant here is mighty. The insistence on poetry is *particularly* revealing, though it is also necessary, given the privileged role of voice and phonetic substance in their immediate proximity to mind, the "voice that keeps silence," in Husserl. What is most interesting, however, is the question of profit or even extraordinary profit in Husserl's formulation. The philosopher "can draw extraordinary profit from what history has to offer [him], and in still richer measure from the gifts of art and particularly of poetry" (184). The philosopher's desire to consume and to take full economic advantage of both history and art (particularly poetry) is irrepressible. But it is the consumptive desire—the appetite of the philosopher—that would inscribe the philosophical into the arts in the first place in order to make it ready for philosophical consumption.

Here we might expect a burst of laughter from Bataille. First, the surrealistic Bataille would laugh at the possibility of pleasure and of the pleasure of consumption without displeasure or even without disgust— taste without dis-taste, *goût* without *dégoût*. It should be pointed out at this juncture that, as Derrida shows in "Economimesis," it is not that the economy of dis-gust goes unnoticed or is dis*counted*. It is philosophically accounted for, but is not on that account part of the economy of taste. In a singularly bad theoretical taste it is accounted for precisely as dis-gust, dis-taste, as what does not belong. A more significant issue however, in Bataille's context, is the more general conceptual or metaphoric structure of the Kantian economy and Kantian economimesis as economy and mimesis of consumption. It is this, whether in Kant or Hegel, that would be unacceptable or laughable to Bataille. "Waste and taste" might occupy separate compartments in the corridors of dialectic or philosophy in general, but they are ultimately and intimately related in the labyrinths of the general economy. That would also refer to the general economy of Bataille's own life, where the inscription of production—philosophical, sociological, artistic, or other—must have been multiply related by Bataille himself to the economy of waste, including the inscription of the difference between consummation and consumption and to the unreserved expenditure of tuberculosis, Bataille's disease, *consomption*, that consumes—that is, *wastes*—without the slightest aim, consequently without any meaning.

It must be kept in mind, however, that the general economy—as the economy of loss, waste, expenditure without reserve, and so on—and the operations it aims to account for cannot be reduced to the economy of disgust exemplified by Derrida's analysis in "Economimesis" of "disgust" and "vomiting" in Kant. The loss and expenditure enacted by Bataille's sovereign operation and inscribed in the general economy as the science of sovereignty are enormously rich and complex structures. Their inscription includes, for example, the conceptions of "gift" and "sacrifice" (analyzed at great length by Bataille) and a formidable array of other structures that must be considered with utmost rigor and precision.

"Vomiting," however, remains important in the context of general economy as an exemplification of the absolute dis-gust, something that cannot be consumed, has to be "thrown up." Or must it be? Certainly by definition, it cannot be in Kant; this is Derrida's major point in "Economimesis." In general, however, in the *general economy*, things are not so simple or restricted, threatening the Whole Kantian or the philosophical scheme of taste, and in every sense conceivable making the issue into a labyrinth—maze—populated with all sorts of monsters. The question of vomiting has, of course, its place in Bataille, a very definite place in a memorable quotation from Sade in a great and important essay, entitled, quite pertinently, "The Use Value of D. A. F. de Sade." As Bataille writes, quoting Sade:

> The process of simple appropriation is normally presented within the process of composite excretion, insofar as it is necessary for the production of an alternating rhythm, for example, in the following passage from Sade: "Verneiul makes someone shit, he eats the turd, and then he demands that someone eats his. The one who eats his shit vomits; he devours her puke. (*Visions*, 95)

The pleasures (or pain) and taste (or disgust) that take place here might be seen as monstrous enough, but they must be accounted for as what Derrida calls in "Signature Event Context" "a *structural possibility*," even if they would occur only once, and they have, in fact, certainly occurred more than once. In a certain sense, they occur all the time; not necessarily in the specific shape described by Sade, but as analogous effects of the general economy of "taste" that must incorporate "dis-taste" and "dis-gust" as its ineluctable constituent.

As Derrida shows it is only in the Kantian economy of taste as an economy of pleasurable consumption that the question of vomiting and disgust must acquire and be philosophically accounted for as having a *unique* position, from which the whole scheme might thus be deconstructed. This special position precisely allows and invites a critical scrutiny and deconstruction. Once such a deconstruction is performed and the economy of taste is re-inscribed as the general economy, "vomiting" and "disgust" become regular effects of this enriched economy, though they might under certain conditions have asymmetrical relations and be subordinated by the effects of taste and consumption. By the same token the general economy cannot be seen as only the economy of loss, waste, unreserved expenditure and so on. It can never be unconditionally separated from the restricted economy in the first place. Both "taste" and "disgust" are in fact still restricted effects of the complex labyrinth of the general economy; this, perhaps, was also Derrida's point in "Economimesis." Bataille, in the essay at issue, in inscribing this complexity, brilliantly relates Sade's passage to the question of sacrifice, communion, gift, general expenditure, and so forth, thus establishing the affects of disgust precisely as a manifestation, however extreme, of the general rather than of the exclusive, as philosophy would want to do.

It is because philosophy or traditional theory have throughout their history (with some notable exceptions, such as Sade or Nietzsche) suppressed and/or repressed the economy of expenditure that the expenditure must be brought into the foreground, but not because it has the absolute privilege over the economy of consumption. The latter economy (as science) must now be made general as well, that is, to take into account (or dis-count) and reinscribe a consumption and production as an effect of expenditure and unreserved expenditure. Since the restricted economy manifests itself, above all, at the level of the political economy, these consequences and implications *are* the value (it can no longer quite be called the use-value) of D. A. F. de Sade, the value brilliantly exposed in Bataille's "Open Letter to My Current Comrades," as his essay is subtitled. The political economy as the economy of the political must take the effects inscribed by de Sade into consideration, not an "account" perhaps.

Conversely, the economy of the sexual must take into account the effects and the very economy of the political. The relationships between these two economies should not be seen as always necessarily symmetrical. To begin, there are more than two economies involved here. The hypothesis that such economies form a *countable* set is hardly tenable, though there will certainly be multiple "set-effects" in our economic calculations, in our calculus and our accounting, of these interactions.

Derrida's extraordinary analysis of Kant in "Economimesis" depends fundamentally on Bataille's conceptions. It opens by introducing (in Bataille's sense) the concept of "economimesis" in the context of relationships between the restricted and general economies, or rather referring to Bataille's terms from infinitesimal to radical, including (as in the case of the difference between Derrida's *différance* and Hegel's *Aufhebung*) both at once.[16] As Derrida writes:

> It would appear that mimesis and oikonomia could have nothing to do with one another. The point is to demonstrate the contrary, to exhibit the systematic link between the two; but not between some particular political economy and mimesis, for the latter can accommodate itself to political systems that are different, even opposed to one another. And we are not yet defining economy as an economy of circulation (a restricted economy) or a general economy, for the whole difficulty is narrowed down here as soon as—that is the hypothesis—there is no possible opposition between these two economies. Their relation must be one neither of identity nor of contradiction but must be other. (3–4)

The two sections into which Derrida divides his essay—"Production as Mimesis" and "Exemporality"—might be seen as demarcating the problems involved along two lines or rubrics indicated earlier. The first section explores the nature or the structure of the operation, inscribing the economy of mimesis as a mimesis of the economy. The second could be seen as a critique of an attempt at the philosophical, conceptual account of both the economy of the beautiful and the economy of beautiful art. These two economies, as we recall, remain interactive in Kant, but their difference is also rigorously maintained in the third critique. Since I have considered the structure of the economic operation and the role of the difference between consumption and expenditure in some detail earlier, I would like to conclude with some remarks on the nature of the account, that is to say, precisely with the question of the general economy as science in Derrida and Bataille. It must still be kept in mind that these two issues—"operation" and "its science"—remain in a complex interaction as indicated earlier.

Derrida, in his account of the Kantian or even philosophical in general, seems in the essay at issue to stress the "desire" of the system to account for its other, specifically the system of the beautiful for the (absolute) dis-gust. The issue, clearly enough, is more general. It is the issue and account of the other of the system. The other, as the term and concept of the other, is in fact already an account of the other, and "vomit" takes in Kant a specific, privileged role in this configuration. As Derrida writes at the conclusion of "Economimesis":

> Disgust is not the symmetrical inverse of taste, the negative key to the system, except insofar as some interest sustains its excellence, like that of the mouth itself—the chemistry of the word—and prohibits the substitution of any non-oral *anal*ogue. The system therefore is interested in determining the other as its other, that is, as literary disgust.
>
> What is absolutely foreclosed is not vomit, but the possibility of a vicariousness of vomit, of its replacement by anything else—by some other unrepresentable, unnameable, unintelligible, insensible, unassimilable, obscene other which forces enjoyment and whose irrepressible violence would undo the hierarchizing authority of logocentric analogy—its power of identification....
>
> The word vomit arrests the vicariousness of disgust; it puts the thing in the mouth; it substitutes; but only, for example, oral for anal. It is determined by the system of the beautiful, "the symbol of morality," as its other. It is then for philosophy, still, an elixir, even in the quintessence of its bad taste. (25; emphasis on "anal" added)

We have seen earlier the significance of this configuration in Bataille's inscription of the interplay between consumption and expenditure, including the substitution, not by analogy only, of oral for anal. Both

Bataille and Derrida make quite apparent the folly and "naïveté" of this powerful and irrepressible desire to exclude. The latter is itself a gesture of rejection and not consumption; a rejected (repressed) rejection makes its powerful return, the return of the repressed into the structure of the philosophical (that is, consumptive) account. Derrida thus inserts in the passage just cited:

> Vicariousness would in turn be reassuring only if it substituted an identifiable term for an unrepresentable one, if it allowed one to step aside from the abyss in the direction of another place, if it were interested in some other go-around [*s'intéresse à quelque manège*]. But for that it would have to be itself and represent itself as such. Whereas it is starting from that impossibility that economimesis is constrained in its processes.
>
> This impossibility cannot be said to be some thing, something sensible or intelligible, that could fall under one or the other senses or under some concept. One cannot name it within the logocentric system—within the name—which in turn can only vomit it and vomit itself in it. One cannot even say: what is it? That would be to begin to eat it, or—what is no longer absolutely different—to vomit it. The question what is? already parleys [*arraisonne*] like a parergon, it constructs a framework which captures the energy of what is completely inassimilable and absolutely repressed. Any philosophical question already determines, concerning this other, a paregoric parergon. A paregoric remedy softens with speech; it consoles, it exhorts with the Word. As its name indicates. (25)

This question of the excluded (the most general logic of philosophy, perhaps logic itself) and paregoric remedy of parergon would, however, constitute only a part, however indispensable and however structuring, of the inscription of the general economy as science, in both Derrida and Bataille. Bataille's greatest laughter comes as he looks at the naïveté of the philosopher accounting for beautiful art. The very term beautiful would be laughable enough. Bataille's laughter would in fact be most "logical" here. The philosophical (conscious and conceptual) accounts and the *science* of philosophy (such as Hegel's *Phenomenology of Mind*, subtitled "The Science [*Wissenschaft*] of the Experience of Consciousness") are, by definition, consumptive, and thus remain a restricted economy. As Derrida notes in "From Restricted to General Economy," such a restricted philosophical economy would "pleasurably consume an absolutely close presence" (*Writing and Difference*, 273).

The philosopher, it is true, often "forgets" this pleasure of the conceptual consumption and conceptual mastery. The "forgetting" may take the form of either unconscious repressing or conscious concealment (or various combinations of both) of the knowledge of this pleasure. It has been around ever since Socrates based the difference between and opposition of philosophy and literature on the difference and opposition between truth and pleasure. Once the philosophical discourse "*pleasurably consumes,*" however, would not the framing—the parergon—that divides the philosophical and the literary or artistic be threatened in its very core? This parergon also fundamentally divides that which accounts (namely, philosophy), and the experience of the beautiful and beautiful art, that are accounted for by a philosopher. Derrida's analysis of Kant in "Economimesis" and *La vérité en peinture* suggests at least that much. Cannot, then, the third critique, an account that pleasurably consumes, be itself read as an aesthetic experience or as a work of beautiful art? The latter parergon is already to some extent violated in Kant's own text, as it is in Aristotle, by establishing the fundamentally philosophical value of the beautiful art of the highest rank, poetry. The parergonal violation inscribed in the questions just asked is of a more radical, more violent and, in theoretical terms, more fundamental nature.

First, the economy of such an "aesthetic" account, an account as beautiful art, must, according to both Bataille and Derrida, exceed the economy of consumption, that is, the restricted economy to which both philosophy and beautiful art conform in Kant. It is precisely a belief, a "naive" or "vulgar" (that is to say "philosophical") belief, in the possibility of the utilization of all intellectual energy that Bataille laughs at. For the philosopher can only believe or *claim* to take everything into his account or into his dis-count, but not "actually" do so. The economy of every account—literary, philosophical or other—is always already a general economy.

Still more significant is the question of the law or the style of a discourse in the general economy and of major writing. It would be most naive or vulgar to reverse the configuration—to reverse the parergon—and replace philosophy or theory, make literature or the "beautiful art" into a unique or ultimate genre of general economy. The latter, as we recall, still remains a science, though, to be sure, in neither a Hegelian nor a positivist sense; it is not a "positive science." But it must retain a scientific rigor in its discourse. Like Nietzsche, Bataille practiced a plural style and plural genre in his own discourse, making it both literary (in his novels or poetry) and theoretical (in his essays). But he also attempted something else in his activities related to the *Collège de Sociologie*. One must then speak of at least three genres for enacting a general economy of discourse and major form of writing. It must be pointed out that one must be rather cautious in relating the general economy and major writing in Bataille. Bataille, let us further recall, was also a librarian and the founder and editor of the journal *Critique*. Since in all of these "genres" or "styles," the social or general political economy are heavily involved, what is most at stake (*en jeu*) in the question of general economy is the law and the style of the *social* and *institutional* forms of our accounts. And this law and this style, or this genre, cannot (and in practice should not) be established once and for all, though some claim to have done so. As Derrida writes, "referring to the entire French landscape" (in 1968) where Bataille is inescapably present: "What we need, perhaps, as Nietzsche said, is a change of 'style'; and if there is style, Nietzsche reminded us, it must be *plural*" (*Margins*, 135).

Bataille, however, in Derrida's own words, "considered himself closer to Nietzsche than anyone else, to the point of identification with him" (*Writing and Difference*, 251), most of all, in the force of the impact, in the radical transformation of the "theoretical" or "literary" style, in making it *plural*. It is the maze of style and the style of a maze. "NIETZSCHE'S DOCTRINE CANNOT BE ENSLAVED. It can only be followed" (*Visions*, 184), a thought and style—*writing*—that must be entered like a labyrinth. In a brilliant little chapter "Nietzsche/Theseus" of "The Obelisk," Bataille, anticipating much of deconstruction, invokes "a derisive and enigmatic figure placed at the entrance of the labyrinth" and speaks of "the *foundation* of things that has fallen into a bottomless void. And what is fearlessly assented to no longer in a duel where the death of the hero is risked against that of the monster, in exchange for an indifferent duration—is not an isolated creature; it is the very void and vertiginous fall, it is TIME" (*Visions*, 222). No wonder that Kant, in *contemplating* the beautiful, prefers tulips in the garden to the vertiginous and even nauseating experience of the labyrinth. We must say, in all fairness to Kant, that he approaches some of this vertiginous experience in his analysis of the sublime, and thus can be seen as a precursor of both Nietzsche and Bataille (as well as Sade) in this respect. But then the whole opposition between the beautiful (the one that is framed, in a parergon) and the sublime (the one—"absolutely great"—that exceeds all parerga) collapses. It is also a collapse of the philosophical style.

It is not that in so recognizing Bataille's enormous contribution one would want to claim for Bataille, or Nietzsche, or indeed anyone, a unique significance in this transformation of the theoretical field. Rather, in an *account* that, in an absence of a better word might still be termed "historical," one would want to explore in a stratified ensemble—from Kant and Hegel, to Nietzsche, Bataille, and Derrida—what has made and still makes possible the radical transformations of the field, the transformations that make the field plural. In thinking of the theorists and practitioners of the *plural style*, one will have to refer to a landscape that can no longer be demarcated as either French or German, however important these two *land*scapes might be. Like style, if there is landscape, it must be *plural*.

## NOTES

1. In Georges Bataille, *Visions of Excess*, ed. Allan Stoekl (Minneapolis: University of Minnesota Press, 1985), 35.
2. Derrida defines the "historical and systematic unity" of this closure in *Positions*, trans. Alan Bass (Chicago: The University of Chicago Press, 1981). He writes:

> Don't you see, what has seemed necessary and urgent to me, in the historical and theoretical situation which is our own, is a general determination of the conditions for the emergence and the limits of philosophy, of metaphysics, of everything that carries it on and that it carries on. In *Of Grammatology* I simultaneously proposed everything that can be reassembled under the rubric of *logocentrism*—and I cannot pursue this any further here—along with the project of *deconstruction*. Here, there is a powerful historical and systematic unity that must be determined first if one is not to take dross for gold every time that an emergence, rupture, break, mutation, etc. is allegedly delineated. (51)

One of Derrida's major points, however, regarding this "historical and systematic unity," the point defining the closure, is that, operating at "the limits of philosophy," deconstruction does not imply an absolute and unconditional break with the language and concepts of philosophy, and the structures, such as *différance*, trace, and so on, can only be defined or rather inscribed within this closure. In fact even an absolute break is impossible, and particularly, when such a break is claimed. Deconstruction, therefore, must take place utilizing the *resources* of philosophy: "And this in no way minimizes the necessity and relative importance of certain breaks, of the appearance and definition of new structures" (24). As I shall consider below, the forms—the style—of discourse where such structures can be inscribed themselves become a crucial issue in the context of Bataille and Derrida's reading of Bataille. See also Derrida's comments on pp. 6–7 of *Positions*. As all these statements indicate, the problematic of closure permeates Derrida's project throughout.

3. The term "parergon" functions in this sense of deconstruction and reinscription of the classical notion of framing, boundaries, margins, and so on, in Derrida's analysis of Kant

in *La vérité en peinture* (Paris: Aubier-Flammarion, 1978), and "Economimesis," *Mimesis des Articulations* (Paris: Aubier-Flammarion, 1975), reprinted in English translation in *Diacritics* 11, No. 3 ( 1981), 25. The word "parergon" itself initially occurs in Section 14 of Kant's The *Critique of Judgment*, trans. J. H. Bernard (New York, Hafner Press, 1951), defining "those things that do not belong to the complete representation of the object internally as elements, but only externally as complements" (61). It thus invites the deconstruction of the whole Kantian scheme of taste.

4. See Derrida's discussion in "Signature Event Context" in *Margins of Philosophy*, trans. Alan Bass (Chicago: The University of Chicago Press, 1982), and Derrida's subsequent reply to Searle "Limited Inc., abc," *Glyph*, 2 (1977), 162–254. "Signature Event Context" was originally published in French in 1972 and then in English translation in *Glyph*, I (1976), 172–197.

5. Derrida, "From Restricted to General Economy: A Hegelianism without Reserve," *Writing and Difference*, trans. Alan Bass (Chicago: The University of Chicago Press, 1978), 263.

6. Derrida, *Of Grammatology*, trans. Gayatri C. Spivak (Baltimore: The Johns Hopkins University Press, 1976), 164.

7. Immanuel Kant, *Critique of Judgment*, trans. J. H. Bernard (New York: Hafner Press, 1951), 165–166.

8. See Derrida's analysis in "From Restricted to General Economy," *Writing and Difference*, 274–275.

9. It might in fact be seen as the major theme of Derrida's reading of both Bataille and Kant.

10. Derrida, *Writing and Difference*, 293.

11. See specifically the discussion in *Visions*, 116–129.

12. As Derrida suggests, "…we must interpret Bataille against Bataille, or rather, must interpret one stratum of his work from another" (*Writing and Difference*, 275). Derrida supplies a long and extremely important footnote to this statement, containing one of his rare, but perhaps so much more significant references to Sartre.

13. *L'Expérience intérieure* (Paris: Gallimard, 1967). Cited by Derrida in "From Restricted to General Economy," *Writing and Difference*, 270. For a general critical introduction to these issues and Bataille's major concepts see Michèle H. Richman's *Reading Georges Bataille; Beyond The Gift* (Baltimore: The Johns Hopkins University Press, 1982).

14. See Derrida's critique in *Speech and Phenomena*, trans. David Allison (Evanston: Northwestern University Press, 1973).

15. Husserl, *Ideas*, trans. W. R. Boyce Gibson (New York: Collier Books, 1972), 184.

16. See Derrida's comment in "*Différance*" (*Margins*, 14).

# 7

# On Georges Bataille:
# An Escape from Lameness?*

*Jean Borreil*

The servants of science have excluded human destiny from the world of truth, and the servants of art have renounced making a true world out of what an anxious destiny has caused them to bring forth. But for all that it is not easy to escape the necessity of attaining a real, and not a fictive, life. The servants of art can accept for their creations the fugitive existence of shadows; nevertheless they themselves must enter living into the kingdom of truth, money, glory and social rank. It is thus impossible for them to have anything other than a lame life. They often think that they are possessed by what they represent, but that which has no true existence possesses nothing; they are only truly possessed by their careers. Romanticism replaces the gods who possess from the outside with the unfortunate destiny of the poet, but through this he is far from escaping lameness; romanticism has only made misfortune into a new form of career and has made the lies of those it has not killed even more tiresome.[1]

This "lame life" to which *The Sorcerer's Apprentice* refers, this curse in the eyes of a man whose writings celebrate "the whole man," is what we would like to investigate here; this is what effectively constitutes the pivotal point of Bataille's reflexion on rationality and its reverse side. We will question, then, a "lameness" that, beyond science, art, or politics, must be overcome—the latter are all insufficient since they return humanity not to the unpredictability of "life," to its possibilities, and to its "chances," to the free play that provides man with full access to his intellectual and bodily resources, but to the small change of the "details" that wrench us from ourselves, reduce us to the small link on the chain that we are, to those "functions," necessarily partial and fetishizing, that threaten to "supplant" man, that at the very least force him *into disorder* in order to escape from the contamination that is so precisely functional.

How is it possible, then, not to be reduced to a link on the chain? How is it possible not to be *forced* into disorder, but to *choose* it? The question, answers Bataille, exceeds reason, unless it turns reason into Logos, the life of the spirit, following in this way Hermann Broch's theories, contemporaneous as they are with Bataille's text on fascism.

In the face of this rational/irrational thought, misunderstanding is unavoidable, as is the bewilderment of the reader before a work that seeks "life," only to find bewilderment—as Bataille indicates in the preface to *Sur Nietzsche* ("I admit, at the moment that I write, that a moral quest, whose object is situated beyond good, leads at first to bewilderment. Nothing assures me yet that one can overcome the test")—but at the same time which makes an explicit attempt to expose its theses in a "scholarly" form.

## DETOUR [*DIVERSION*]

Bataille's bewilderment, his reader's bewilderment; perhaps it is necessary to make a detour here in order to give them a concrete shape. This detour will remind one of questions that were pertinent once again after 1968, questions that belong to professional intellectuals outside the Party, confronted more with the embodiment of Marxism than with Marx's texts (in the end misunderstood or—what amounts to the same thing— more often repeated or "recited" than analyzed).

Lenin's theory: a split between political avant-garde and artistic avant-garde. By abandoning the classicism of what Bataille called the "readable" [*lisible*], literature divorces with politics. Let us understand by this that the golden age of the novel is over and that, in conformity with Mallarméen predictions, the reign of the "suggestion" and of "rhythm," of the "writable" [*scriptible*] begins. The latter can take several forms, developed during the war, from Dada to surrealism or to futurism/constructivism; from the linguistic attack of the Work in progress (*Finnegan's Wake*) to the indefinite scission of *The Man Without Qualities*.

In 1917 a victory displaces the status of Marx's theory: it was perceived as a theory of economy, now it has become—via Leninism—a science of revolution. Represented for the first time, the triumph of a politics defines itself as the practical realization of a theory, of a science. The result is that the victorious party and the sister parties, victorious or not, can define themselves as embodying a science, with an immediate consequence for the intellectuals outside of the Party: they aren't needed. If, indeed, one has theory and if it succeeds in political action, then there is no need for theoreticians. The word "one" would refer to intellectuals, already professional, or who will for the most part become professional. Now we see the intellectual outside of the Party confirmed in a position of exteriority. Without entering the Party, in other words, without espousing the essential elements of its theses, including the aesthetic ones—and the aesthetics of the Party, in as much as there is *one*, will more likely lean to the "readable" than to the "writeable," for the same is true in the USSR when the formal revolution of electric constructivist intensities, trapped by its own logic, falls once again (in other words, as soon as order can prevail in the *cité des arts*)—without entering the Party, the intellectual is reduced to playing minor parts and what remains for him is only... what is left, the supplement of the soul, or the decorative. Thus, 1917 inaugurates that history in which professional intellectuals become secondary to those of a Party armed with the science of the revolution and whose solidification will rapidly signify: economics as final authority, the intellectual outside of the Party (including the "revolutionary") defined by social usefulness.

Such is the situation encountered by Bataille and the Surrealists, among others; such is the situation—a modified situation but structurally the same—that a certain Sartre will encounter in the 1950s. But if the latter theorizes for a time upon the inexistence of the masses outside of the Party, the Bataille of the 1930s did not, as one knows, accept in so "rational" a manner to examine things thoroughly. This is because saving the autonomy of the masses is to save, at the same time, the autonomy of the intellectual—a way of designating oneself at the same time as an authentic spokesman: "As astonishing as this may seem," writes Bataille in "Popular Front in the Street" (in *Contre-Attaque*; May 1936, no. 1), "...one frequently notes, among militant revolutionaries, a complete lack of confidence in the spontaneous reactions of the masses. The need to organize parties has resulted in unusual habits among the so-called revolutionary agitators, who confuse the entry of the Revolution into the street with their political platforms, with their well-groomed programs, with their maneuvers in the halls of Congress. Amazingly, a distrust of the same order prevails against intellectuals. The distrust of intellectuals only apparently contradicts the one that underestimates the spontaneous movements of the masses."[2]

Bataille's question at that time is indeed to know how to situate oneself vis-à-vis the Marxism embodied by the Party, as it was after Tours and in the face of that political monopoly: a Party supported by a theory—whose well-grounded hypotheses were confirmed by the Soviet revolution— and which at the same time is the workers' party, if not that of the masses who appeared on the scene of history through the 1914–1918 war. This is a party so sure of itself, that it not only makes no call for theory, but doesn't even bother editing the complete works of Marx or Lenin and proposes contingency texts (with an eventful past) like *Gauchisme, maladie infantile du communisme* or even brochures for militants who read neither English nor German. It is an echo of the PCF's disinterest—in "Catholic" form—regarding founding texts, a disinterest that justifies the omniscience of the Party and at the same time renders it possible, in that passage of *Pour Marx* which evokes the unlocateable and dusty treasure of the Costes editions, even at the beginning of the 1960s. No demands are made by the Party on intellectuals; *a fortiori*, no orders. The only things to interest the PCF of the 1920s and 1930s, are the prestige figures—the scholars and men of letters—whose model would be the great humanist figure, Barbusse or R. Rolland. The professional intellectual who interests the PCF, then, is the one whom one will call, in the language of a certain group of the 1970s, the "democrats," the one who benefits from a social recognition sufficient enough to attract publicity without, on the one hand, appearing like a mad revolutionary, or, on the other, getting involved in political strategy, even less in the Party line—in short, the one who lends his Name to implementation. The Party actually needs him—or more precisely, only needs his name—to involve the strata of civil service intellectuals whose numbers have increased since the end of World War I. One can understand that the PCF, in these conditions, barely showed any interest in the movement of proletarian literature.

From the opposite perspective, one sees the same approach: one addresses the Party because one believes that the working class is behind it. Thus the Party is perceived as the guarantor of those who defend the great values, and the image of the elitist man is maintained: it is to a certain extent guaranteed and supported by the Party.

There remains, however, the following question, which is progressively revealed: What constitutes the realization of great values? For if the USSR is perceived as the State in which the "rational" becomes "real," then one questions the means for this rationality—a question that Gide undertakes, for example. The latter question comes to reinforce the first question, that of usefulness. A new problem will be added to the series of questions already mentioned—how can one think oneself within the framework of what is left, the decorative, in a marginal usefulness? What position is possible for intellectuals outside of utilitarian *function*? One has seen the place Bataille accords to "function." More precisely: how can one avoid distinguishing one's competence from that of men who embody Marxism—a distinction that can only pull the wool over one's eyes, since it is also true that these men at the same time present themselves as men of the masses? In more general terms: how can one take account of Marxist centrality, that "horizon" that one will later call "unsurpassable"? To this series of questions will be added the new problem of a Soviet practice barely concerned with the question of means. Until finally—from 1933 to 1934 on, when the question "how can one fight fascism?" is added to Stalinism—the series of questions becomes consolidated around this urgent point: what form of politics is possible for intellectuals in the face of German fascism? One possible answer would be that of a criticism made vis-à-vis the Enlightenment, of challenging Marxism's place within Occidental power. This is to seek the origin of the question on the side of Ideology—and then it is indeed as an Intellectual that one is implicated; in the 1930s, Herbert Marcuse would represent this form of a "Weberian" position.

Another answer (and Bataille's work in its essence adheres to this one) consists in placing oneself, not on the side of the intellectual "class," but on the contrary, against it, in a revolt against intellectuals—including those embodying Marxism—in the name of "Life" and "the whole man." Then the argument no longer revolves around the question of Marxist power, as a figure of Occidental reason, but this time, it rests on the classical inadequation between concept and reality; what the Surrealists actually say is that the Party does not correspond to its essence. In other words, they outdo orthodoxy. But the situation is more complicated, for the initial refusal of exteriority and of utility, that leads to placement entirely within political logic, and the necessity to outdo, in order to avoid being relegated to the decorative and to exist vis-à-vis the Communist machine, together lead necessarily to the denunciation of the Party. One will recognize in this the opposition between the Surrealist Revolution/political revolution in addition to the theme: it is the Surrealists who are the true revolutionaries—a politics that implies occupying the place left absent by Marxism (or, perhaps, occupying what remains). In order not to be a supplement of the soul, one must, in the process of outdoing, put a subversive thought in practice, by which the Surrealists become the true revolutionaries, without the masses.

Bataille puts in place the same system of escaping by outdoing—which gives intellectuals outside the party a space for action that escapes the logic of authorities. However (and this is no doubt the source of the "tension" of his position), note the following exception: that what is left behind, this residue, this shortfall, this soft negativity—Bataille will think it as excess, an excess constituting "the whole man," and which, at the same time, disqualifies usefulness. Once again there is the case of the literary figure: "The extreme states fell into the realm of the arts, but not without some inconvenience. Literature (fiction) was substituted for what had previously been spiritual life; poetry (the disorder of words), for real transe states. Art constitutes a small free realm outside of action, paying with its liberty for its renunciation of the real world. This is a heavy price to pay, and there are hardly any writers who don't dream of rediscovering the lost real; but to do that they must pay in the other sense: renounce freedom and serve propaganda. The artist restricting himself to fiction knows that he is not a whole man, but the same thing is true of the writer of propaganda. The realm of the arts in a sense embraces totality: the latter nevertheless escapes it no matter what" (*Sur Nietzsche*). An unvoidable lameness, where at times it is the real that is missing, at times liberty. Aesthetics holds the same place here as in all philosophies—that means of reflexion on the political and the social that speaks in the form of displacement. No doubt it is only in phantom form that literature can "designate" the whole man; it nonetheless designates it, a vanished horizon whose reflection it bespeaks, just as Engel's reading of Morgan's "primitive communism" designates this new goal: Communism. Literature? Certainly not. Only one form of literature: that of "the artist," as opposed to the "writer of propaganda"; the lameness is not of the same degree—depending on whether the real or liberty is missing. No doubt, in passing, a way of situating oneself with respect to militant literature, but above all, a way of returning literature to what it reflects in nostalgia: those "extreme states," signs of authentic spiritual life. For fiction exposes its liberty on its own, through "the disorder of words." What one must (re)discover—and which will take several denominations, and be spoken in several senses as well—is precisely this "disorder," a guarantee against "functionality" and usefulness/utilization, but this time in the real. It is to (re)discover a "prodigality," an "expenditure," excess.

Rather than examine Bataille's erotic texts or those on eroticism (both of which are too well-known), it would appear more interesting to study that theory of excess in his analyses of fascism. This is all the more the case since, in 1933–1934 and years after, what struck his contemporaries about fascism was less the routine rationality of civil service executioners, which strikes one today, than its *lumpen* quality (one has only to think of Brecht's *Arturo Ui*) and above all its irrationalism—more precisely, that return to the irrational in politics that it was.

## Nietzschean Centrality

The point of departure for Bataille's analyses is the 1930s failure known as Stalinism and fascism. The failure of socialism, together with the transformation of the ideal into a form of State that fascism permits one to analyze, lead one to believe that the fight against fascism can only be effective if it is "only one of the branches of an overall action against the State" ("On the State," found in texts in preparation for "The Psychological Structure of fascism"). To analyze fascism and to analyze Stalinism is therefore not one and the same thing—on the contrary, Bataille insists on the difference between them—but rather stems from a same reflexion upon "the form of the totalitarian State"; the insistence of a theme which is that of "The Problem of the State," the article published by Bataille in *La Critique sociale*, the review for the Democratic Communist Circle, led by Souvarine:

> In contradiction with the evolution of the 19th century, current historical tendencies appear to be propelled towards the State's constraint and hegemony. Without overestimating the ultimate value of such a perception—which could at a later point be revealed as illusory—it is evident that, in an overwhelming way, it presently dominates the confused intelligence and the divergent interpretations of politics. Certain coinciding results of fascism and bolchevism have created the general perspective of a disconcerted consciousness of history—a consciousness that, in new conditions, slowly transforms itself into irony and becomes used to considering death.

This statement marks the domination of Stalinism and bolchevism, forms of the totalitarian State: "Stalin—the cold shadow projected by this single name upon all revolutionary hope—such is the image associated with the horror of the Italian and German police, of a humanity in which cries of revolt have become politically negligible, in which these cries are nothing more than *rupture* and *unhappiness.*" It will thus be necessary to inscribe oneself within what is destroyed by these two ideologies and practices—the State and the Party—but on a different, displaced level from that implemented by the traditional left. This displacement is a third term, a non-excluded third party, which makes the displacement possible: the thought of Nietzsche, or more precisely, the reading and interpretation that Bataille makes of Nietzsche: "The refusal of classical morality is common to Marxism, to Nietzscheanism, to National Socialism. What is alone essential is the value in whose name life affirms its major rights" (*Sur Nietzsche*, Appendix). To then systematically put into question again not only Stalinism, but also Marxism which, embodied in a totalitarian State, has not only disqualified itself practically, but also theoretically: if Marxism cannot combat fascism, this is essentially because it is incapable of thinking it. Now it is important above all to think fascism, for a lucid thought is alone able to destroy the fascination that it exerts. To oppose the democratic and "rational" actions of intellectuals and leftist parties (assemblies, demonstrations) to this fascination which rests upon its refusal of classical morality, is in fact to oppose classical morality—that of the Kantian dove, that of bare hands—to force: those democratic actions appear completely ineffectual, as Bataille retraced a difficult journey in France, similar to the one made by Reich in Germany. For example, the text *"En attendant la grève générale"* insists upon this popular disarmament; it is a text written in February 1934 in which Bataille, with respect to the *Cours de Vincennes* demonstration, puts two images of the people into play: that of a popular crowd in "its impoverished majesty," an unshakable hurdle for the pale young men of the *"Action française,"* and that of a people cheated, because framed restrictively by parties and thus bereft of its own energy. "In Germany, the oldest and the most powerful organized movement of workers was brought down in a single shot, like a bull in the slaughterhouse; and here, on the courtyards full of today's pandemonium, the most threatening outcry is already nothing more than the phantom of an outcry, in the same way that those on death row are already ghosts." The "ghost of communism that haunted the world" thus returns towards nothingness; Bataille's problem will thus be to take account of those impasses of reason and of their practical failure for, even supposing that reason were right, what is ineffectual reason worth?

All this means that one must find the point through which fascist energy passes, the point where its force circulates. Now the fascists themselves have clearly designated it—even if in the form of a detour: in France, it is someone like Brasillard who sings "red and great fascism" as well as the pagan poetry of the Nazi youth; in Germany, it is Hitler himself who visits Nietzsche's sister. This spot through which energy passes is to be sought on the side of that "poetical" intensity, which can only mean this: if fascism is possible, this is because the theory of use and utilization—need, in Marxist language—does not suffice for the masses whose desires exceed rational and revolutionary programs. "The time has perhaps come where those who speak of the "struggle against fascism" should begin to understand that the concepts which, in their mind, accompany this phrase are no less childish than those of witches fighting against storms" (*The Problem of the State*).

There is a double gain here, since this theory of energy, of "the violence of despair" in the same movement qualifies anew both the excessive spontaneity of the masses and an autonomous politics of intellectuals whose central axis of reflexion is precisely energy, expenditure, excess: "It is time," writes Bataille in *The Sacred Conspiracy*, "to abandon the world of the civilized and its light. It is too late to be reasonable and educated—which has led to a life without appeal. Secretly or not, it is necessary to become completely different, or to cease being."[3]

To fight effectively against fascism assumes, then, that one leave the world of need, the world of boredom, of "stupid distress" and of that of reason in favor of the passions, alone effective: "The opium of the people in the present world is perhaps not so much religion as it is accepted boredom. Such a world is at the mercy, it must be known, of those (*fascists, to be precise*) who provide at least the semblance of an escape from boredom. Human life aspires to the passions and again encounters its exigencies (…) We are sure that strength results less from strategy than from collective exaltation, and exaltation can come only from words that touch not the reason but the passion of the masses."[4]

To refuse to have "one's wings clipped" by a rationality whose failure may be discerned in the USSR as in France, to refuse to be used, to be reduced to a state of "function," such are the conditions for freedom, such are the conditions for the fight against fascism. Here again one must return to the thought of Nietzsche; this is all the more so since fascism tries once again to take responsibility for it by distorting it, precisely by "clipping its wings," in other words by suppressing in it what is freedom: "Whether it be anti-Semitism, fascism—or socialism— there is only *use*. Nietzsche addressed *free spirits*, incapable of letting themselves be used."[5] Bataille's refusal deepens: one must emerge from use and its double perspective of need and politics, for the theory of use not only justifies the practice that embodies Marxism; it is also the theory of the fascists or the anti-Semites with respect to Nietzsche, which thus makes its definition clear: it is indeed totalitarian. What is at stake in the critique of reason: not only theory or aesthetics, but first of all effectiveness; one cannot fight against fascism with those very weapons that constitute it.

Now the problem is overturned. If fascism is a mass phenomenon, this is also because of its capacity to capture what the theories and the defenders of rationality reject: those passions that excite only in order to disappear, never solidified; those excesses, revolts, disturbances—always fading, whose trace is merely symbolic—which, however, revolutionize; these revolutions and their institutionalization are nevertheless bent on reducing the excesses, revolts, and disturbances to absence. The strength of fascism is its capacity to capture the intensity, the energy of the masses, their politics. This is the reason for its success with the lumpen proletariat. This is also the reason for Hitler's visit to Elisabeth "Judas-Foerster." This, finally, is also the reason for the Nietzschean path for thinking fascism: to tear Nietzsche away from the fascists is to understand at the same time what is being played out in fascist fascination, and Bataille's texts on fascism and on Nietzsche will then of necessity be parallel. For just as the Nazis reroute the thought of Nietzsche in order to consolidate it in its opposite, so they reroute the excess of the masses in order to consolidate it into Prussian barrack confinement. Such is the weak point of fascism, the means for thinking it out and fighting against it—and this is the origin of the reflexion on Nietzsche and the book in 1944 marking the hundredth anniversary of his birth—fascism captures this energy and reduces it to discipline. "National-Socialism is generally limited in its appeal: it calls for simple feelings, for an elementary conception of the world; to the extent that a national socialist philosophy exists, it is that of military patriotism, unaware of what it excludes, scorning what cannot be made militarily strong. Of its own accord, National-Socialism refuses to take on human interest; rather, it lends expression to German interests. Its own movement designates this: by destroying it, we destroy nothing universal, we suppress not an essential part of man, but a part that has removed itself from human totality" (in preparation for the article *Nietzsche est-il fasciste?* which appeared in *Combat*, October 20, 1944). The success of fascism is thus of the same order as that of Stalinism: it involves manipulating the energy of the masses as well as Nietzsche's texts, in favor of a politics for the party and the country. But through this—through a return to the archaism of the country and not through access to the profundity of the universal or of the whole man—it must fail. Thus fascism's capturing of energy is a way of swindling the masses, and for this reason one can and one must fight it by *reestablishing the play of excess* that it uses and confiscates in military discipline, thus "homogenizing" the heterogeneous that it had captured, reducing *essential heterogeneity* to leader worship: "the religious value of the chief is really the fundamental (if not formal) value of fascism"[6] and this religion of the chief gives the fascist militant the characteristic that distinguishes him from the soldier. Thus, from Bataille's perspective, reestablishing the play of excess amounts to fighting fascism with the weapon that appears to be the most integral to it, whereas this weapon is in fact the most foreign to it.

This position is taken in the name of the freedom of the passions. It is no longer in the name of intellectuals, but in the name of life and the possibilities that define it without closing it off, in the name of humanity. At the same time, Nietzschean thought is saved:

> Nietzsche thought, and rightly so, that one cannot define what is free. Nothing is more futile than assigning and limiting what is not yet: one must want the future, and to want it is to recognize above all the future's right not to be limited by the past, to surpass the known. Through this principle of the priority of the future over the past, upon which he insists unfailingly, Nietzsche is the man most foreign to what execrates life, by the name of death, and to what execrates dream, by the name of reaction. Nietzsche strangely designates himself as the child of the future. He himself linked this name to his expatriate existence. Our country is, in effect, the part of us that represents the past and it is upon it, and closely upon it, that Hitlerism builds its value system; it does not introduce a new value. Nothing is more foreign to Nietzsche, affirming as he does in front of the world the complete vulgarity of the Germans." (*Sur Nietzsche* Appendix)

This is why, "despite the stage props," there is the same distance between the false excess that National-Socialism offers to the masses and the excess of life, as there is between Hitler and Nietzsche: the distance "between the farmyard and the peaks of the Alps" (found in a draft of the article for *Combat*).

## ANOTHER APORETIC MOVE

For such a politics of excess, it is evident that one must emerge from the opposition Rational/Irrational, an irrelevant—and what is more—ineffective opposition. "Rationalism has most often represented human activity as reducible to the production and preservation of goods (...) it considers man's consumption of riches to be equivalent to a motor's consumption of combustible fuel: it is no longer anything but an element necessary for productive activity" (*Le Rationalisme*, in *Textes se rattachant à "La notion de dépense"*). Thus rationalism becomes another form of use; in other words, one can interpret it as a theory of servility. This is a new reason to emerge from Marxism, since, if such a conception is in fact not peculiar to the USSR, Communism, says Bataille in the same text, has nevertheless provided its most visible consequences. But to emerge from Marxism, is not, however, to negate it—it is to surpass it; thus by outdoing what, in Marx's texts, is of an economic order. A transformation of lack into excess—in other words into a generalized economy—Bataille's answer, which consists of saying that everything is production, assigns Marx to its "Newtonian" place in a discourse on generalized energy, and is itself initiated by a system of thought: this "hyperchristianity" that Bataille tries to think through from *Inner Experience* to *The Accursed Share* and whose atheist—although mystical and hyperchristian—ideas and intentions are exposed by the *Somme athéologique* from its very title onward. This is a new attempt to outdo, this time with respect to the sacred and demonstrating a will for a systematic, indeed for a scholastic account. Contrary to the servility of use, expenditure is then a force that permits one to think Romanticism, and through it, fascism. In the same way, erotic expenditure counters the boring Christian sacred: "sexual life, when considered in light of its ends, is almost entirely excess—a savage irruption towards an inaccessible summit. In its essence, it is an exhuberance opposing itself to the concern for the time to come. The Nothingness of obscenity cannot be subordinated (...) The erotic summit is not like the heroic, attained *at the price of* severe suffering. The results would appear to be unrelated to the efforts required. Chance alone seems to be decisive" (*Sur Nietzsche*, second part). Chance alone; wisdom and the rational are indeed impossible. More precisely, it is in this impossibility that Bataille's law or virtue resides and expenditure will be, as sexuality indicates it, the discourse demanding irresponsibility and inviting temptation: "Resisting temptation implies abandoning the morality of the summit, stems from the morality of decline (...) as long as a juvenile effervescence animates us, we give ourselves over to dangerous dilapidations, to all sorts of reckless possibilities" (*Sur Nietzsche*, second part). Hence this Nietzschean centrality that, as a substitute for Marxist centrality, works on two levels: negative, in order to surpass Marx; positive, in order to think both the play of possibilities and irresponsibility considered as a line of conduct. Nietzsche is indeed the one who asks us not to rediscover our childhood in a nostalgia for time past, but indeed to make ourselves children again. ["May your nobility not look backwards, but *outside*; you will be chased out of all countries; out of all the countries of your fathers and your forefathers. You will love the *country of your children* (*Kinderland*): may this love be your new nobility"; this famous fragment is quoted by Bataille in his *Memorandum* and more precisely in the third part entitled *Politics*.]

However, Nietzschean centrality cannot help but displace the points of argumentation used to surpass Marx: what is now at stake can no longer arise from scission, division, and death (as is the case with the figure of dialectical materialism), but is to be thought in the unpredictability of possibilities and of life, if not of chance; in other words, if one retranslates from the "hyperchristian," from "grace": "What is possible is actually only a chance—which one cannot accept without danger. One might as well accept a dull life, and look upon the truth of life—chance— as being a danger. Chance is a factor in rivalry, an impudence (...) The false, opaque, cunning attitude, closed as it is to any impropriety and even to any manifestation of life whatsoever—and which in general marks virility (maturity and, in particular, conversations)—is, if one looks closely, a panicky fear of chance, of game, of what is possible for man (...). To live, to demand life, to proclaim the exuberance of life, means defying self-interest."

However, once again this means that one does not emerge from Marx; through a different angle no doubt, the one that Lenin criticized so much (Lenin who, for obvious militant reasons, saw in it only an eighteenth century backwardness) whereas Marx himself caused nothing less than his "science" to rest upon it and instituted it as a founding element of the system. A founding element that, at the same time, contradicted the theory of revolution—hence the well-known controversy on the interpretation of the Marxian text.

For "Life" is certainly present in Marx's work, as designated by the names "large industry" or "bourgeoisie." And despite the "alreadys" that, punctuating the feudal period, announce and affirm in advance the established facts of the capitalist era (facts supported by past evidence), the possible is present as well: all this is part of so-called Marxist, historical theory whose form of division is, as one knows, no longer double, but triple. What is more: one may note that, in the capital phase, a generalized energetics has been substituted for the division in two, since Marx needs a logical *coup de force* for negating-denying this energetics, in other words, for implementing the scission-division in two, or, if one prefers the usual concept, dialectical materialism. One has to simply think of the status of the bourgeoisie in the *Manifesto*, which, as we know, overturns, destroys, revolutionizes, etc., in an infinite taste for orgies, an excess of life that nothing should logically break apart, if not this Hegelian offshoot, Nothingness, in other words, the proletariat (which is nothing, which is the nothing, says the *Manifesto*). We have already noted elsewhere that this assumes the stroke of magic of the "crisis" and, more recently, in analyses referring explicitly to Bataille, J.-F. Lyotard's *L'économie libidinale* sets the stage for a meeting of "little Marx and Mme Edwarda."

Thus, except by proposing a libidinal economy, one has not emerged, for all that, from aporia: in this respect it is interesting to note that when Bataille, in his turn, writes a theory of history and its fundamental periods, he uses the same figures as those necessitated by Marxian patterns: cut in three. To surpass Marxism does not mean however that one surpasses that "necessity"—or that modern "curse"—of producing a discourse of universal history and its tripartition, that of *The Accursed Share* which, in this particular case has come to be substituted for Marxist modes of production. Wouldn't one escape from the "terrorism" of the division in two only to fall once again into that of the division in three? One knows very well—to go beyond the Marxist reference and its practical effects, another *totalizing* discourse is necessary which takes account of the same problem: the birth of capitalism, or more precisely, the primitive accumulation of capital—a figure situated in Bataille's work in the "moment" of the great circulation.

For how can one be more influential than Marx? If one remembers the *Manifesto*: by a discourse of possibilities, of excess, in other words, of an energetics of productivity.  But then only capitalism, the world of productivity—as in the case of the historical, materialist Marx—remains to counter Marxist servitude, to counter the useful and need, which divide in two.

The way out is hardly obvious: there is "hyperchristianity" because only sin frees us from boredom, the ambiguous "in between" which is "problematic on the Christian side as well as on the other";  there is also hypereconomism, because only productivity permits one to surpass the theory of need.  In this sense, only the Marshall plan of *The Accursed Share* can effectively succeed Stalinism.  Is the lameness of the intellectual as inevitable as the sorcerer's stroke of magic which provokes the crisis necessary for the proletariat demonstration in the *Manifesto?*  Or is it that men are so necessarily mad...

## NOTES

* An expanded reformulation of a lecture delivered at the University of Paris VIII (then at Vincennes) in collaboration with Jacques Rancière, whom I wish to thank.

1. "The Sorcerer's Apprentice," *Visions of Excess*, trans. A. Stoekl (Minneapolis: University of Minnesota Press, 1985), 225.

2. "Popular Front in the Street," *Visions of Excess* (op. cit.), 162.

3. "The Sacred Conspiracy," *Visions of Excess* (op. cit.), 179.

4. "Popular Front in the Street," *Visions of Excess* (op. cit.), 167.

5. "Nietzsche and the Fascists," *Visions of Excess* (op. cit.), 184.

6. "The Psychological Structure of Fascism," *Visions of Excess* (op. cit.), 154.

# III. Alterity, Heterology, and Communication

# 8

# Of the Simulacrum in Georges Bataille's Communication

*Pierre Klossowski*

One who says *atheology* is concerned with *divine vacancy*, be this vacancy that of the "place" or site specifically held by the *name of God*—God guarantor of the personal self.

One who says *atheology* also says *vacancy of the self*—of the self whose vacancy is experienced in a consciousness that, since it is not in any way this self, is in itself its *vacancy*.

What becomes of consciousness without instrument?

This is still only an uncertain determination of Bataille's search, if indeed one can say of Bataille that he engages in a search: the latter always remains continuous right up to the fading of thought, even when thought is reduced to pure intensity, and thus goes beyond the death of all rational thought.

The contempt that Bataille has for the notion itself was revealed most notably in *Discussion sur le péché* with Sartre and Hyppolite in particular.[1] There, where others tried to catch him up by means of "notions," Bataille eluded them at the moment when he made evident a flagrant contradiction: he speaks and expresses himself in simulacra of notions, inasmuch as an expressed thought always implies the receptivity of the person addressed.

The simulacrum is not exactly a pseudo-notion: the latter would still serve as a reference point until it could be denounced as a false path.

The simulacrum constitutes the sign of an instantaneous state and is unable to establish the exchange between one mind and another, nor permit the passage from one thought to another. In the aforementioned "discussion" and in a conference[2] several years later, Bataille rightly denies communication because one would only ever communicate the residue of what one claims to communicate. (Hence also his suspicion about the theories of a spiritual search, in which communication would be translated into the form of a project. Project belongs to a pragmatic realm and in any case cannot reproduce anything of what has inspired it.)

The simulacrum has the advantage of claiming not to stabilize what it presents of an experience and what it says of it: far from excluding the contradictory, it naturally implies it. For if the simulacrum tricks on the notional plane, this is because it mimics faithfully that part which is incommunicable. The simulacrum is all that we know of an experience; the notion is only its residue calling forth other residues.

The simulacrum has an object entirely other from that of the intelligible communication of the notion: it is complicity, whose motives, as well, can neither be determined nor seek to be determined. Complicity is obtained through the simulacrum; understanding by means of the notion that it is from the notion nevertheless that incomprehension arises.

To "understand" the simulacrum or to be "mistaken" about it is of no consequence. The simulacrum, aiming at complicity, arouses in one who experiences it a movement that can immediately disappear. To speak of it will not in any way account for what has thus happened; a fugitive adhesion to that consciousness *without instrument* that embraces in others only what could distract, dissociate itself from the self of others in order to render that self vacant.

The recourse to the simulacrum does not however recover an absence of a real event nor what substitutes for the latter. Yet to the extent that something must happen to someone in order to be able to speak of an experience as occurring, will the simulacrum not be extended to the experience itself, as long as Bataille declares that it is necessarily lived as soon as he speaks of it, even if he later refutes himself as *subject* addressing other *subjects*, allowing only the contents of the experience to be emphasized? *Something happens* to Bataille, something he speaks of *as if it were not happening to him.* Bataille who would define it and who would draw this or that still intelligible conclusion from it. He never lays claim to, nor can he ever lay claim to a sufficiently defined expression (of experience) without referring immediately to *anguish*, to *gaiety*, to a *carefree abandon*: then he *laughs* and writes that he *died with laughter* or that he *laughed till he cried*—a state in which experience suppresses the subject. Inasmuch as Bataille was traversed by what these words inscribe, his thought was absent, nor was his intention to submit them to a meditation in the context formed by these representations. What matters for him, then, was this mode of absence, and to reconstitute it by situating its stages, in reverse, brings him to a philosophy that he necessarily refuses to put forward as such.

It is from the perspective of the simulacrum that consciousness without instrument (let us say a vacancy of the self) comes to insinuate itself in the consciousness of others; the latter, to the extent that it "postulates itself," only receives the influx of consciousness without instrument by referring to a register of notions based on the principle of contradiction, thus of the identity of the self, of things and of beings.

Here one touches upon the heart of all discussions raised by the thought of Bataille and its declarations.

The notion and notional language presuppose what Bataille calls *closed beings*. In particular, the *Discussion sur le péché* makes quite evident in Bataille's work an interference and a necessary confusion, as it were, between the notion and interdiction, between the notion *and* sin, between the notion and identity, before there was even a notion *of sin*— let us say a notion of the *loss of identity* as constitutive of sin. Thus there exists a close relationship between being of an identical nature and being able to discern between good and evil. On the other hand, when confronting his Christian and Humanist atheist interlocutors, Bataille is opposed to a "notion" of the "opening of beings" in which evil and good become indiscernible. It is evident, then, that, dependent upon the notion of identity, and specifically upon that of "sin," the opening of beings or the attack on the integrity of beings—if indeed this opening, or this attack, are only conceived under the influence of "sin"—are developed like a simulacrum of a notion. When Sartre accuses Bataille of filling the "notion of sin" with an unceasingly variable content, Bataille has this response, among others:

> I set out from notions which normally enclose certain beings
> around me and I played with them...What I have not really
> succeeded in expressing is the gaiety with which I did
> this...beginning with a certain point and, sinking into my diffi-
> culties, I found myself betrayed by language, because it is
> almost necessary to define in terms of anguish what is felt

perhaps as excessive joy and, if I expressed joy, I would
express something other than what I am feeling, because what
is felt is at a given moment a carefree abandon with respect to
anguish, and it is necessary that anguish be palpable for this
carefree abandon to be, and this abandon is at a given moment
such that it comes to the point of no longer being able to
express itself...language cannot express, for example, an
extremely simple notion, that is, the notion of a good that
would be an expenditure—a loss pure and simple. If I am
obliged, for man, to refer to being—and one can see right
away that I am introducing a difficulty—if for man at a given
moment, loss, and loss without any compensation, is a good
thing, then we cannot manage to express this idea. Language
fails, because language is made up of propositions which
cause identities to intervene and, starting from the moment
when one is forced to no longer spend for profit, but to spend
in order to spend, one can no longer maintain oneself on the
plane of identity. One is forced to open notions beyond themselves.[3]

What does it mean to open notions beyond themselves?

Or rather to what does a language respond, whose propositions
would no longer cause identities to intervene?

It is no longer to being that a language liberated from all notions
responds, abolishing itself with the identities; and, in fact, escaping from
all supreme identification (in the name of God or of gods), being is no
longer apprehended, other than as perpetually fleeing all that exists; in this
sense, the notion claimed to circumscribe being, when it did nothing but
obstruct the perspective of its flight. At last existence falls back into the
discontinuous that it had never ceased to "be."

It would seem here that Bataille's search is more or less the same as
that of Heidegger, to the extent that it would, strictly speaking, be a question of a metaphysical "preoccupation." Bataille admits to a certain parallel
progression of his meditation with Heideggerian explorations, in that the
latter takes its point of departure from the contents of experience.

The flight of being outside of existence constitutes in itself an
eternal occurrence and it is only the perspective of this flight that causes
the existent to appear as discontinuous. According to Heidegger, thought
about origins revolves around this occurrence of being: but, given that it
is powerless to sustain the perspective of flight outside of existence,

philosophy, beginning with Plato, and foregoing any strict questioning of being as being, has little by little come to dodge original questioning by explaining being on the basis of the existent. Thus, taking stock of the metaphysical situation since Nietzsche announced the advent of nihilism, Heidegger declares: *Metaphysics as metaphysics is, strictly speaking, nihilism.*[4] *It is unaware of being, and this is not because, while "thinking" being, it sets aside being as in itself thinkable, but because being excludes itself from itself* (from the existent).[5] Plato is no less "nihilistic" than Nietzsche himself, despite his effort to overcome nihilism. It is in fact the "will to power as principle of all values" that carries nihilism to its completion. The totality of the existent is henceforth the object of a one and the same will for conquest. The simplicity of Being is enshrouded in a one and the same forgetting. Thus ends Occidental metaphysics.

In this way, Heidegger denounces the situation that our world has recently attained, as having installed man in his "ontological" dereliction, a dereliction all the more fearsome since at the very same time it reveals the eternal occurrence of the flight of being and obeys a necessary curve of metaphysics. Through this denunciation, Heidegger has probed anguish as a path of return to the point of departure, be it to the interrogation point of all metaphysics worthy of this name. Taking on a sort of responsibility with regard to an "existent" unaware of itself as discontinuous and enclosed within a lack of concern for any apprehension of being as being, Heidegger sought beyond philosophy in the prophecies of the poetic spirit (Hölderlin, Nietzsche, Rilke) the return to original interrogation, right there where this spirit grasped inside of itself the flight of being as the fugitive passage of divine figures; thus he accounted for the hidden discontinuity of our existence.

Now in Bataille's work the commentary on the same apprehension is developed in quite another way. In his writing the ontological catastrophe of thought is only the reverse side of a zenith reached in what he calls sovereign moments: intoxication, laughter, erotic and sacrificial effusion, experiences characterized by an expenditure without compensation, a lavishness without measure, a destruction void of meaning, goal, and utility. Here the discontinuous becomes the motive for a revolt, a revolt in the very name of the flight of being against the existent, usefully exploited and organized for itself; this includes a revolt against philosophy, and thus also, in spite of real affinities, against the ontological preoccupation of Heidegger. "It is a professorial work whose subjugated method remains tied to results; on the contrary, what counts in my eyes is the moment of *untying*. What I teach (if it is true that...) is an intoxication, not a philosophy: I am not a philosopher, but a *saint*, perhaps a madman."[6]

In itself Heidegger's "ontological" responsibility (to the extent that it would presuppose a recuperation, hence, a metaphysical renewal, and a goal, as this "professorial work" necessarily demands it) would already be contrary to the definition that Bataille gives for sovereignty, that is, dissipation into pure loss.

It is in effect in this sense that under the pretext of developing a philosophy of non-knowledge,[7] he puts forward "*revolt* as having consciously become, through philosophy, revolt against the entire world of work and against the entire world of presupposition." The "world of work and of presupposition" is that of science "which continues to believe in the possibility of answering."

What is this revolt that philosophy has made conscious? It is entirely prefigured by Nietzsche in his criticism both of theories of knowledge and of the very act of knowing. Commenting on a maxim by Spinoza (*non ridere, non lugere, neque detestari, sed intelligere*), Nietzsche notes that the so-called serenity of the intellect requires a sort of truce between two or three contradictory impulses, while all acts of knowledge "would always depend on the behavior of these impulses among themselves, impulses that battle one another and are able to hurt one another" until "that extreme and sudden exhaustion that explains that conscious thought, especially that of the philosopher, is the most devoid of strength."[8]

To break the truce between two or three contradictory impulses within oneself in order to escape from the trickery of conscious thought—if only to become silent in exhaustion—this is what that revolt against any possibility of response amounts to in Bataille's work.

Indeed, the contents of experience that Bataille declares as being so many sovereign moments—ecstasy, anguish, laughter, erotic and sacrificial effusion—these contents together illustrate that revolt which is here only a call to the silent authority of a pathos with neither goal nor meaning, experienced as an immediate apprehension of the flight of being, and whose discontinuity exerts an incessant intimidation vis-à-vis language.

No doubt, for Bataille, these movements of pathos only present themselves as sovereign moments because they verify the discontinuous itself and are produced as ruptures of thought; however, these are contents of experience that in fact differ greatly from one another with respect to discontinuity, as soon as they become so many objects of a meditation. How could laughter, as a reaction to the sudden passage from the known to the unknown—where consciousness intervenes just as suddenly, since Bataille declares: "to laugh is to think"[9]—how could laughter be comparable to ecstasy or to erotic effusion, in spite of their "reactive" affinities in the face of a same object? How could it be comparable to ecstasy in particular since the latter would result from a group of mental operations subordinated to a goal? It is a similar difficulty that Bataille himself emphasizes and takes pleasure in lingering over, as over an enterprise beyond hope from the beginning. If these sovereign moments are so many examples of the discontinuous and of the flight of being, then as soon as mediation considers them as its object, it reconstitutes all the unsuspected stages that pathos burned in its sudden appearance—and the language of a process that is only suitable for vulgar operations[10] does nothing here but conceal the modalities of the absence of thought, under the pretext of describing them and reflecting them in consciousness, and thus seeks to lend to pathos, in itself discontinuous, the greatest continuity possible, just as it seeks to reintegrate the most being possible. Thus because (notional) language makes the study and the search for the sovereign moment contradictory, inaccessible by its sudden appearance, there where silence imposes itself, the simulacrum imposes itself at the same time. Indeed the aimed-for moments that are sovereign only retrospectively, since the search must henceforth coincide with an unpredictable movement of pathos—these moments appear by themselves as simulacra of the apprehension of the flight of being outside of existence, and thus as simulacra of the discontinuous. How can the contents of the experience of pathos keep their "sovereign" character of an expenditure tending towards pure loss, of a prodigality without measure, if the purpose of this meditation is to raise oneself up to this level through an "inner" reexperience, thus producing for oneself a "profit"? Will the authenticity of these moments—the very authenticity of wastage—not be already compromised, as soon as it is "retained" as a "value"? How, finally, would they sufficiently escape from notional language in order to be recognized only as simulacra? It is precisely the same for ecstasy, which is at the same time a content of authentic experience, and a value, since it is a sovereign moment, but which only escapes from notional language by revealing itself to be a simulacrum of death. This in a meditation that amounts to fighting with all the strength of thought against the very act of thinking. "If the death of thought is pushed to the point where it is sufficiently *dead thought*, so that it is no

longer either despairing or in anguish, then there is no longer any difference between the death of thought and ecstasy....There is, therefore,
beginning with the death of thought, a new realm open to knowledge;
based on non-knowledge, a new knowledge is possible.[11]

But: "I should from the outset insist on what generally taints this
new realm as well as the preceding one. The death of thought and
ecstasy are no less marked by trickery and profound impotence than is
the simple knowledge of the death of others. The death of thought
always fails. It is only a powerless movement. Similarly, ecstasy is
powerless. There persists in ecstasy a sort of constant consciousness of
ecstasy, placing it on the level of things proposed for ownership...it is
inevitable in the end to take it as an appropriated thing in order to make
of it an object of instruction..."

All the same, it is still a similar admission of impotence (which is an
admission of simulacrum) that gives to the movement of this search all of its
resilience and maintains it in a state of irremediable vertiginousness: neither
progression nor return upon itself, but at the same time a descent and a
movement upward in the manner of a spiral without beginning or end.

Bataille emphasizes that, in opposition to poetic creation, the
contents of experience proposed by his method for meditation *modify the
subject who practices it*,[12] and thus alters his identity. If "successful," this
method should bring about the very disappearance of the subject in order
that no instrument limit any longer, through consciousness of itself, the
sovereignty of these contents of experience.

What does this say? An existing subject, testing his discontinuity, let
us say the flight of being outside of existence, subsists as soon as his
laughter, his tears, his outpourings—in a word his pathos—are designated
by him as sovereign moments, and this living being, carried fortuitously to
the vacancy of the self, to a death of thought necessarily seeks them as
sovereign moments only based on its reintegrated self, thus based on the
servitude of identity and of the once again "closed" notion, and this, each
time it wants to teach this method of meditation. Thus it must develop
once again, on the basis of notions and identities, the proper path to open
notions and abolish identities—and of this opening and of this abolition
never be able to give anything other than the simulacrum...

*Atheology* would like to avoid the dilemma that now appears:
rational atheism is nothing other than an overturned monotheism. But
Bataille hardly believes in the sovereignty of the self proposed by atheism.
Hence only the vacancy of the self responding to the vacancy of God
would constitute the sovereign moment.

## NOTES

1. Cf. the journal *Dieu vivant*, 4th notebook, Editions du Seuil, 1945.
2. *Tel Quel*, no. 10, 1962.
3. *Discussion sur le péché*, in *Dieu vivant*, 4th notebook, 122–123.
4. Heidegger, *Nietzsche*, vol. II, Neske, ed., 1961, 343.
5. Ibid., 353.
6. Cf. *Méthode de méditation*, 218, footnote.
7. Cf. "Conférences sur le non-savoir," in *Tel Quel*, vol. 10, 11.
8. Nietzsche, *The Joyful Wisdom*, IV, aphorism 333.
9. Cf. *Méthode de méditation*, p. 213.
10. Cf. "Conférences sur le non-savoir," in *Tel Quel*, vol. 10, 15.
11. *L'expérience intérieure*, 13.
12. Cf. *Méthode de méditation*, 218-219.

# The Heterological Almanac

## Rodolphe Gasché

In a discourse that has today become dominant, the term "heterology" has acquired a status that may well serve to obliterate the rupturing effect that that notion was able to represent in Georges Bataille's practice of signification, that is, in his writing practice. It is essential to emphasize from the outset Bataille's *practice* of writing for the fundamental reason that with his *theoretical* enunciation of heterology, certainly insofar as it strives to be scientific, we do not find ourselves at the strong point of Bataille's thought. Compared to the heterological practice of Bataille's writing, his theoretical statements are rather disappointing. That, perhaps, is because he deferred providing a general overview and full explication on this matter to some later date.

Yet in no way will this reason suffice. The true reason why Bataille's formulation of a theory of heterology is so disappointing lies with his desire to present it in a thoroughly theoretical or scientific manner. Although Bataille invoked the necessity of adopting scientific discourse and its contributions in order to submit them to ends external to science on more than one occasion, such an operation is rigorous only to the extent that it obeys certain preoccupations, which I, to be brief, shall call "phantasmatic." After having outlined in the following the economy of heterology, I will try, in my turn, to "denounce" these very preoccupations that Bataille tried "provisionally to set aside—when he [...] sought to present a scientific work" (II, 302).[1] With this I have given a first reason for adopting a title that Bataille himself had discarded. The crossed-out title, "The Heterological Almanac" was to make room for "Heterological Theory of Knowledge" (II, 62).

To begin, let me examine the etymology of the word "heterology." Heterology is the discourse on the heterogeneous, or let me say, in order not to call too much upon the term "discourse," it is that which relates (*le rapport*) to the heterogeneous. The word "heterogeneous," from the Greek ἕτεροζ, is not a simple, innocent word. The first meaning of ἕτεροζ signifies the opposite term in a duality whose terms, or objects, are presumed to be known. It is seen as one or the other of two, as one member of a binary pair. A second meaning is one term from a known group in relation to several other terms of that group, but always with the connotation that this term is opposed to the others—unusual, strange, different, in short, from what should be. ἕτεροζ only signifies the *entirely other* to the extent that it represents the simple opposite in a dichotomic structure whose terms are already known. There is thus no difficulty in establishing a *relation* between a term and its opposite other, since both belong to the same group, and are known. The other in question is always already familiar, presupposed, entirely other only in a very relative way, and, consequently already dominated. Likewise, if we return to several of the "sources" from which Bataille drew the term "entirely other," for instance from E. Myerson's *De l'explication dans les sciences* (1921) one easily finds confirmation of such a limiting understanding of the heterogeneous. Indeed, for Meyerson, the entirely other, also called the irrational, is simply the opposite engendered within scientific and rational discourse—although it must be added that with Meyerson, the theoretical discourse is already understood as drawing its shape against an uncontrollable background that theory reproduces as the condition of its own possibility. The notion of the entirely other (although it enjoys a history extending back at least to Romanticism and German Idealism) is adopted as well from Rudolph Otto's *Das Heilige* as well as from *Dionysos, Mythos and Kultus* by Walter Otto. For these authors, "das ganz Andere," which Bataille quotes on several occasions, names a supreme non-human Being, derived from nothing, but from which the creation of the world, as much as the mimetic reproduction of the origi-nary event arises. This entirely other is quite near. Hence, although not known strictly speaking, this other in its very uncanniness is as familiar as the always already known opposite term of a duality which we noted with respect to the meaning of the Greek ἕτεροζ. The only distinction from the classical understanding of the structure of opposition, as well as of the heterogeneous that one can witness with these authors (Rudolph

Otto and Walter Otto), is that the excluded part of the opposition becomes valorized in a certain way. Yet it is only a reversal of sorts since, if we examine the issue more closely we must conclude that the dualism has not been broken and that the term "entirely other" is merely another word for the traditional logos, with the not insignificant distinction, however, that this word testifies to a further enrichment of the spirit who as the entirely other has reappropriated to itself that which at first had been abandoned over the course of its process of abstract self-constitution.

If, as has been noticed,[2] heterology must be thought with respect to the Hegelian *concept*, it will also be necesssary to differentiate the *entirely other*, as it functions in Bataille's text, from the homonymous notion in Hegel's writing. Indeed, it is the Hegelian notion of the *entirely other* that governs the functioning of the term in the texts of the above-mentioned authors. With Hegel, the other is always the other of the same, belonging necessarily to the movement of the exteriorization, of the alienation of the same, balanced by a return movement of the other towards the same across the different stages of the process. Thus, the opposition and its play remain within the same, the other being always in solidarity with it.

Yet with Bataille, we will have to think and/or practice a heterogeneity, which will be reducible neither to the same nor to an opposition which stems from the latter's primacy. We will then try to *delimit* the nature of heterology as well as that of the movements to which it gives rise.

## THE NEGATIVE GEOTROPISM

Let us begin with the simple opposition homogeneous/heterogeneous. It is wise to distinguish at first between three levels of homogeneity: social homogeneity (bourgeois society, state, limited exchange, etc.); personal homogeneity, the habitual homogeneity of the person; and the homogeneity of discourse (philosophic, scientific, literary, etc.). One can roughly define the homogeneity of society, of the person, and of discourse by their traits of continuity, of useful productivity, of productive expenditure. "*Homogeneity* signifies [...] commensurability of elements and consciousness of this commensurability" (I, 340). The comparability of elements presupposes their identity and the measure of their relations of identity. A "common measure," a "calculable equivalence," money, for example, guarantees the establishment of homogeneity. If "the basis of social *homogeneity* is production," the standard fixes the modalities of product exchange. Reduced to abstract and inter-changeable entities, the continuity of the homogeneous is maintained within their circulation.

The identity of products, of persons, and of facts finds its most accomplished expression in the practice of science (or of technics); its "object is to found the homogeneity of phenomena. This practice is, in a certain sense, one of the eminent functions of *homogeneity*" (I, 344). And again: "The laws founded by the sciences establish, among the different elements of an elaborated and measureable world, relations of identity" (I, 340). The bodies of society, of the person, and of homogeneous science thus guarantee, by means of different standards, an assimilation, a contin-uous appropriation of homogeneous elements, supporting and main-taining the general homogeneity of the productive sphere. This appropriation, "by means of a more or less conventional homogeneity (identity) established between the possessor and the object possessed" (II, 60) produces "a static equilibrium" (II, 59) between the two forms at stake. Production thereby becomes a function of appropriation and subordinate to it.

What is brought about in the maintenance of general homogeneity by the reduction of expenditure to productive expenditure, by the very form of accumulating productivity, by subordinating production to appropriation, by making all things identical, is nothing less than a blur-ring of the opposition interior/exterior, of the outside and the inside. This blurring is, furthermore, not innocent. Let us consider science: as it institutes homogeneity between facts science substitutes "ordered series of conceptions or ideas" (II, 60) for "exterior objects," which are *a priori* inconceivable. The movement of this substitution closely follows the Hegelian concepts of *Erinnerung* or *Verinnerlichung*, both of which denote the interiorization of the other, which is exterior only to the extent that it is always already constituted by the inside. This move-ment, which appropriates the other as the other of the same and thus as "proper" [*le propre*], erases the difference between the same and the other to the benefit of the homogeneity of the same. It furthermore masks the end-point of all appropriation, excretion, by reducing it to a positive, productive expenditure.

If the homogeneous is one pole of the simple opposition from which we began, a pole with respect to which the heterogeneous could be delimited, as we examine the heterogeneous we will soon see that the opposition cannot maintain its simplicity. In fact, the "homogeneity" of the three realms that we identified earlier betrays a certain limit. As the homogeneous establishes itself, its project of universal levelling is conditioned by a difference which it must accommodate in order to realize the static equilibrium towards which it tends.

In spite of our remark that production constitutes the basis of social homogeneity, this basis itself requires a foundation, here, the monetary standard. The latter establishes a common measure of one useful activity vis-à-vis another. It follows, in the Hegelian terms that Bataille mobilizes, that no object, including man and his activities, possesses a form "*valid in itself*" or for itself, but only "an existence *for something other than itself*" (I, 340). Reduced to a pure function, the object, the activity, man, are thus situated within homogeneous society. At first the *for something else* signifies only a relation of identity or equivalency that is itself implicated in the structure of substitution.

But homogeneity, which, it must be noted, does not embrace all of society, but only one of its parts (and is thus already limited by an exterior), functioning necessarily through the exclusion and the rejection of an unuseful part, is a "precarious form, at the mercy of violence and even of all internal dissent. It is formed spontaneously in the play of productive organization, but it must be incessantly protected against the various elements which do not profit from production or which will profit insufficiently from it or which, simply, cannot bear the restraints which *homogeneity* opposes to agitation" (I, 341). A fundamental constraint forces homogeneity's tendancy towards static equilibrium to depend on an authority foreign to the homogeneous, an authority which will have to defend the always threatened homogeneity. This function of protection is incumbent, for example, upon the state. However, the safeguarding of social homogeneity eventually demands recourse to an other that is not that of the *for something else*, not that of the equivalent or the identical within the realm of the homogeneous, and assures it a *raison d'être* that it cannot find in itself. A reason that allows it to justify itself, to found itself in a Being that is other, conferring upon it a true reality. This other, which could not possibly be of the same nature as the homogeneous and upon which the latter depends to the extent that it is bereft of an internal reason and a realistic support, to the extent that it must be able to realize the evacuations necessary to the maintenance of its equilibrium and to be able to arbitrate the dissensions which agitate it, this other, then, is the heterogeneous.

> [...] the safeguarding of homogeneity must be found in the recourse to imperative elements capable of annihilating or of reducing the different unordered elements to a rule. (I, 341/2)

Or yet still:

> This state of constant subordination of the forces of *homo-geneity*—which always depend on a *heterogeneous* element, at once fundamental and final—must be useful to a certain defi-ciency inherent in operations which they bring about. Essentially these operations are of the same nature as that of reason. (II, 229)

Finding in this "other," which is the heterogeneous, "*a raison d'être* which it [homogeneous society, R.G.] could not find in itself"—estab-lishing itself in the shadow of an imperial power that contrasts strongly with its own structure (of homogeneity), and which valid in itself, appar-ently sufficient unto itself, similar to an unbroken plenitude—one can say that "this necessity in which the *homogeneous* world is placed, of constructing the web of *homogeneity* on the basis of a heterogeneous element [...] has the value of a general law. It doesn't seem possible to begin operations that reduce what is presented to a certain common measure without having postulated in advance an irreducible element" (II, 228).

In the first place, heterology will be concerned with this inescapable and indelible relation between homogeneity and heteroge-neous elements, a relation that becomes ever more compelling as insuffi-ciencies characteristic of homogeneity are highlighted. But before developing more precisely the nature of this fundamental link, let us direct our attention for a moment to the term "heterology," or more precisely, Bataille's indecision regarding the choice of the term in ques-tion. Defining heterology "as [the] science of what is entirely other," entirely other first of all with respect to homogeneity, Bataille hesitates between several different nomenclatures.

> The term *agiology* would perhaps be more precise but it would be necessary to understand the double meaning of *agios* (analogous to the two meanings of *sacer*) as much *soiled* as *saintly*. But it is above all the term *scatology* (the science of excrement) which maintains in the present circum-stances (the specialization of the sacred) an incontestable expressive value, as the doublet of an abstract term such as heterology. (II, 61/2)

And in a crossed-out note:

> The term *heterology* related to *heterodoxy* has the advantage of opposing this form of activity to all other types of possible *orthodoxy*, but it is expedient to prefer as an esoteric term the much more concrete and expressive term of *scatology*. (II, 424)

In the course of our exposition, the reasons for Bataille's indecision will organize themselves on an implicit level, between the lines of the text, heterology, in effect, being in league with the *agios*, with heterodoxy, but above all, with scatology, which, although its meaning remains suspended, is perpetually implied. The definitive choice for the term "heterology" reflects a decision between the scientific and the esoteric—Bataille, evidently, having decided on the scientific.

If we have determined that the homogeneous must refer to an other without which it cannot weave itself as a continuous fabric, and that it is thus polarized, divided by this incontestable necessity, then this will be all the more true for the heterogeneous. The simple opposition from which we began is beginning to crumble. Let us continue to investigate for a moment the difference between the heterogeneous and the (allegedly) simple and undivided homogeneous. A first attempt at circumscription can only be negative:

> The study of *homogeneity* and of its conditions of existence leads [...] to the essential study of *heterogeneity*. It constitutes moreover the first part, in this sense that the first determination of *heterogeneity*, defined as not homogeneous, assumes a knowledge of *homogeneity* which delimits it through exclusion. (I, 343/4)

A whole series of oppositions will be required in order to determine the otherness of the heterogeneous. Whereas the homogeneous reality "presents itself with the abstract and neutral quality of strictly defined and identified objects (it is basically the specific reality of solid objects)," heterogeneous reality stems from "that of force or of collision" (I, 347). Unproductive expenditure is opposed to productive expenditure, the sacred to the profane, imperativeness and *raison d'être* to lack of being, sovereignty to subordination, a break in continuity to continuity itself, the for-itself to the for-something-else, the unintelligible to the intelligible, etc.

However, this series of oppositions is only valid to the extent that the structure of opposition itself remains intact. We have already emphasized that the homogeneous, by its very structure, could not avoid recourse to the heterogeneous, that the homogeneous was divided by this inescapable polarization. But polarization is what essentially characterizes the heterogeneous, and this not simply by its opposition to the world of the homogeneous, but as a result of a fissure that traverses it through and through.

> Heterogeneity [...] is defined as the proper realm of polarization. (II, 167)

Compared to homogeneity, which, as we have already outlined, is tainted by the heterogeneous, the realm of the latter is even more strongly marked by polarization. It is organized by a number of contradictory, mutually exclusive terms principally, the pairs high/low, pure/impure, passive/active. These dualistic oppositions divide "the entirety of the heterogeneous world and are added to the determined characteristics of *heterogeneity* like a fundamental element" (I, 350). They are *added* since "the opposition sacred and profane, or rather *heterogeneous* (strongly polarized) and *homogeneous* (weakly polarized)," is only a "subsidiary opposition" if confronted with the "fundamental, primitive opposition between *high and low*" (II, 167). What appears here already is that the heterogeneous, traversed by its strong polarizations, strong in the sense that they are *affective* polarizations, is the realm of fundamental polarization from which all oppositions take their origin, notably those of the profane and the sacred, of the homogeneous and the heterogeneous (as simple oppositions). As a site for the play of differences, the heterogeneous inscribes within itself the difference between itself and its opposite. The heterogeneous (is) rupture of continuity, a movement of scission having always already disturbed the subsidiary opposition of the heterogeneous and the homogeneous such that the latter is fissured. Thus may be explained the unavoidable referral of the homogeneous to its opposite pole.

From this point on, we must make precise—the mechanism of polarization having been put into place—the relationship of the homogeneous to the heterogeneous realm. Let us remember that in homogeneous society the function of safeguarding static equilibrium is incumbent upon the state. The state however is still a part of the structure of social homogeneity. It is not, in any immediate way, the authority of the heterogeneous in the homogeneous world. It constitutes rather an intermediary formation between homogeneous structure and the heterogeneous elements indispensable to the maintenance of order.

> The state is not itself one of the imperative elements—it is distinguished from the kings, from military leaders or from nations—but it is the result of modifications undergone by a part of homogeneous society in contact with such elements. This part constitutes an intermediary formation between the homogeneous classes and the sovereign authority from which it must borrow its obligatory character, but which only exerts its sovereignty through its intermediary. It is only with respect to this latter authority that it will be possible to envisage in what way this obligatory character is transferred to a formation which does not however constitute an existence valid in itself (heterogeneous) but simply an activity whose usefulness with respect to another part is always manifest. (I, 342)

The heterogeneous realm is deeply polarized by the distinction between high and low. These terms are psychologically overdetermined: to the low is attributed all that arises from excrement, from the miserable, from night; to the high everything aligned with the serene, the pure, the sun, etc. If the homogeneous part of society requires an opening towards heterogeneous elements, this means that it addresses itself to the high, to the sublime, to find its orient and its orientation there.

> The domination of the irreducible effervescence belongs there-fore to the part of heterogeneous society whose agitation is no longer negative like that of the miserable, but quite on the contrary, positive and imperative: the accomplished form of this part of society is designated by the name of sovereignty. (II, 222)

The heterogeneity to which the homogeneous world has recourse is of an imperative and sovereign nature. The science of the *entirely other* which heterology claims as its own thus manifests its duplicity: to the imperative, high heterogeneous corresponds a low heterogeneous that is still to be specified. From this point on, it is essential to study the relation of imperative heterogeneity to the state and to the homogeneous world as mediated by it [the state]. Situated "above *homogeneous* existence as imperative and as pure *raison d'être*" (I, 359), heterogeneity possesses an apparent independence vis-à-vis the homogeneous world. Now to the extent that the state becomes the point of suture connecting the two realms—by the very contact between the homogeneous and imperial heterogeneity—the state is subject to a "passage to an existence for *itself*" (II, 161). This is what is produced, according to Bataille, in fascism. Contrary to previous social formations (democratic, from which the state draws its present strength exclusively of homogeneity itself), the fascist state draws all its force from the outside. This outside is that of the "*heterogeneous* meaning of the leader identified with the fatherland" (ibid.). By means of "the introduction into the State of the *heterogeneous* possessor of power" an apparent identification of the state with total heterogeneous power is brought about (II, 162). Heterogeneity is concentrated in the power of the *Führer*, power "above all utilitarian judgment" (I, 350), assuming "in *all freedom* the imperative character of action—which is the particular quality of the leader" (I, 358). Thus: "The state as distinct from sovereignty can however eventually constitute the realm in which the latter is immediately exerted. The nature of the realm itself is not altered by this sudden intrusion" (II, 162). Sovereign action is composed of two sides. In the first place it consists of an "imperative negation," in an exclusion of all that is miserable and impure. It "creates [...] the positive value thanks to which it becomes possible to dispose of violent emotional reactions" (II, 163). That the world of misery may be stigmatized "as untouchable and unnameable, as *soiled* and *impure* in the strong sense of the terms" (II, 224)—this is the result of positive action, of imperative negation.

This action of exclusion and of rejection is made on the basis of a sexual overdetermination of purity which is the very domain of imperative heterogeneity:

> The imperative act of exclusion is assimilated to anal eroticism and sovereignty to sadism: this concept has the advantage of inscribing the two forms introduced here within the unity described by psychoanalysis under the name of sadistic anal tendencies. (II, 220)

Whereas anal eroticism still maintains "a body of positive and negative attitudes combined," the imperative act on the other hand, the act of exclusion, is "by definition strictly negative," "the general tendency manifests itself then in the form of a tendency towards cruelty" (II, 220/1). As cruelty towards the weak and fallen world, it is bereft of all opposite or counterpart.

> The world of sovereignty at whose heart lies royal power, appears therefore as pure, radiant and glorious, above a night charged with horrors and nightmares, at the same time as above the dull expanses of *homogeneity.* It is thus the analogue of a sun; it shines with a brightness so cruel that it is necessary to avert one's eyes. (II, 225)

Sovereign action, linked to imperial heterogeneity, proposes, by its negative function, "to *abolish* misery by depriving it of any possibility of expression, such that it might as well not be" (ibid.).

Let us now consider the second side of its action, which is in fundamental solidarity with the first. It is composed of a unifying movement, that is, of the production of a homogeneity that is in principle unlimited.

> Action is imperative: it necessarily unifies if it overcomes all of its obstacles. (II, 230)

Let us refer to Bataille's analysis of the army which is seen to be a state within the state, which "exists *for* itself, constitutes an entirety finding meaning in itself" (II, 236). Its unifying power, homogenizing in the extreme, increases with "the unification (the individualization) in the modifications of structure that characterize superior heterogeneity" that is, with the incarnation of heterogeneity in a person, in a military chief, or leader.

> The army, subject to the imperative impulse—on the basis of formless and miserable elements—organizes itself and achieves a *homogeneous* form internally, due to the negation of the disordered character of its elements: in effect, the mass formed by the army passes from a debased and feeble existence to a purified geometric order, from the amorphous state to aggressive rigidity. This negated mass, in reality, has ceased to be itself in order to become on an emotional level [...] the thing of the leader and as if a part of the leader himself. (I, 359)

The call to "attention" realizes "a sort of tropic movement (a sort of negative geotropism) raising up, not only the leader, but the entirety of men who respond, geometrically speaking, to his order, to the (geometrically) regular form of imperative sovereignty" (ibid). Geotropism: "A reaction of locomotion and of orientation of living matter under the influence of weight" (*Robert*). But the geotropism with which we are concerned is negative in that the plants, flowers (the term is primarily botanical) experience an attraction not towards the low, the earth, but towards the high, towards the sun. Geometry and negative geotropism are intimately linked, they reverberate back and forth. The fundamental relation that links homogeneity to imperative heterogeneity takes form in this way.

> The mode of heterogeneity [of the army in its initial state, R.G.] explicitly undergoes a profound alteration, managing to realize intense homogeneity without causing fundamental heterogeneity to decrease. (ibid.)

The army, whose leader is "entirely other" with respect to homogeneous existence, possesses an internal homogeneity, which, although distinct from social homogeneity, by virtue of the greatest proximity to the source of sovereign power, is an appropriate model to describe the process by which the homogeneous part of society has recourse to heterogeneous elements in order to stabilize its structure of equilibrium.

The recourse in question takes place "when the fundamental homogeneity of society (the mechanism of production) becomes disassembled by its internal contradictions" (I, 366). The intrusion of an imperative heterogeneous element into the state effects the geometric leveling of forces in agitation, thus provoking a maximum heterogeneity of the state's regulating mechanism. The state, whether or not in the person of the sovereign, becomes a repressive authority mathematically equalizing its subjects. At the same time negative geotropism is produced. If sovereignty has the "capacity to attract to itself the eventful existence that constitutes the force of royal action," then the subjects submitting themselves to the imperative decision of heterogeneity gain access to this existence "for itself" which they were lacking. They then enter into a "dazzling configuration" which lifts them to the height of the leader, and participate in some particular way, such as in the army corps, in the heterogeneous realm. Their homogeneity is less, however, when compared to that of the soldiers, for the distance that separates them from the site of heterogeny is greater. However, they can be distinguished in actual fact from what is rejected by the imperative force towards the low and outside the limits of homogeneous society. For although imperial force attracts to itself various agitated elements, it "achieves a precise partition within the agitation from which it takes its 'sovereign' flight: it separates what it attracts from an unavoidable residue that continues to form the turbulent social dregs" (II, 224).

One finds thus outlined the play of a certain reciprocity between the homogeneous and the heterogeneous world, a play, however, that in no way abolishes the two distinct regions that will henceforth mutually and decisively affect one another. We will return to this. Let us simply for the moment remember that the duality is not fundamentally upset, and that it in no way undermines the superiority of the heterogeneous. To safeguard dualism is, on the contrary, the power of the heterogeneous.

> This evidence of the profound source of power [for example, unification in a person, R.G.] maintains precisely, along with the duality of the *heterogeneous* and the *homogeneous* forms, the unconditional supremacy of the *heterogeneous* form from the point of view of the principle of sovereignty. (I, 366)

Despite all penetration of the homogeneous world by imperative heterogeneous elements, despite the relative elevation of the homogeneous part to the height of its other, the dualism and the imperial sovereignty remain intact.

## THE CORE OF SILENCE

The imperative heterogeneous region, high and pure, forms by its very intrusion into the homogeneous world the site of decisiveness whose fascinating force draws the homogeneous world into its orbit. This site is that of meaning, of "completed concentration," of the "condensation of power" (I, 362/3). It must be understood as a core.

Although our investigation of the imperative character of the heterogeneous has not yet required an account of the low heterogeneous, we must now turn our attention to it, for the sacred core, constituting the individual centre of all agglomerated society, at "the heart of human movements [,] appears as a formation of a completely distinct and even disconcerting specificity" (II, 310). It is exterior to the beings, to the persons of the homogeneous world. But if we have emphasized up to this

point the attractive character of the core in question, we will henceforth be
obliged to take into consideration the fact that it also represents the "object
of a fundamental repulsion."

> The social core is in effect taboo, that is untouchable and
> unnameable; it participates from the beginning in the nature of
> corpses, of menstrual blood or of pariahs. (II, 310)

The existence of such a core, the object of attraction and of strongly
marked repulsion, is what, according to Bataille, distinguishes human
society from animal society, characterized principally by an immediate
"interattraction."

> Everything would lead one to believe that the men of earliest
> times were united by a disgust and by a common terror, by an
> insurmountable horror turning precisely on what had primi-
> tively been the attractive center of their union. (II, 311)

It is a matter, in effect, of an interdiction whose core is as much the
scene of attraction as of repulsion. This interdiction, which concerns all
rejected objects, that is, objects of excretion whose immediate appropriation is forbidden, and which like the incest taboo in primitive societies (cf.
Levi-Strauss) founds human society in general, is in the end concerned
with the ultimate expenditure: death.

> The greatest loss of energy is death, which constitutes at once
> the ultimate end of possible expenditure and a restriction on
> social expenditure taken as a whole. (II, 332)

Or yet still:

> In effect, the very extreme behavior of human society with
> regard to corpses can be represented as opposing the human
> world to the animal world. (II, 282)

Society is formed around an interdiction placed on death and
corpses, an interdiction founded upon a "primitive disgust" that, as a
"violently *acting* force," is alone in "taking account of the clearly marked
exteriority peculiar to social things."[3] The essential exteriority of the taboo
core making it both the center of attraction and repulsion brings human

society into its orbit. Nevertheless, "the profound alteration of human life due to the action of the social core" (II, 312) is not limited to this movement. For the "essentially terrifying content around which the existence of each individual gravitates, intervenes in their relationship as an inevitable middle term" (II, 311). This core has the task of mediating immediate animal "interattraction," that is, of effecting the transformation of the repulsive into the attractive.

> It is precisely at this point that we must challenge the existence of the sacred core around which the joyful course of human communication takes shape. [...] I will show [...] that its fundamental content being what disgusts and depresses—[...] menstrual blood, the putrefaction of bodies—the active function is the transformation of depressive content into an object of exaltation—in other words the transformation of the left sacred into the right sacred—[...] the transformation of depression into tension. (II, 316/7)

The core is thus a core of mediation and transformation occurring in the region of heterogeneity which brings the homogeneous world into relation with the imperative heterogeneous world. It is, in fact, an operation *in* the heterogeneous which we now see to be double, divided between a low or left heterogeneous and a high or right heterogeneous.

> On the whole, what is left involves repulsion and what is right, attraction. This in no way means, however, that the different sacred objects are divisible into left and right objects and, in fact, within the realm each object has a left aspect and a right aspect, one being possibly more important than the other. Yet it must be added that the relatively left or right aspect of the given object is mobile. (II, 330)

During the transformation, whose definitive site is the sacred core, the changing of the high/low, right/left aspects does not occur in just any direction; as with politics, there is only a transmutation from the left to the right. The internal activity of the core consists therefore of a transformation from the low heterogeneous to the high, pure, and imperative heterogeneous. Everything that represents pure loss, and which thus menaces the integrity of the community, or of the individual, that is, menaces their homogeneous structure, is changed by means of this mutation which is to be understood as the constitution of a barrier, of a partition, of an obstacle that divides the object in question from within. Once divided, its left part is repressed and its right part gains access to the realm of the higher heterogeneous.[4] The low heterogeneous embraces in the first place every-thing linked to death, the ultimate representative of unconditional loss. The setting up of the dividing line or the operation of transformation will therefore produce a primordial valorization of life as it avoids, at the same time, a contagious circulation of free energies.

> If a middle term that participates in the nature of death inter-feres in a movement communicating exuberance and joy, it is only to the extent that the very dark repulsive core around which all agitation gravitates has made out of the category of death the principle of life, out of the fall the principle of upwelling. (II, 317)

Preserving absence within presence, the repulsive within the attrac-tive, death within life, the attractive founds itself abyssally.[5] The core, in which mediation and transformation take place, is constituted at first as an absence of core, as a vertiginous abyss of destruction, to the extent that it arises from death. For this reason, Bataille speaks of it as of a "region of silence," as a site before speech and human society, a site inseparable from its function of mediation, and which cannot be thought as occurring after the fact. A "core of violent silence" (II, 319), it is the scene of an originary transfusion of life and death, of nature and culture. It belongs neither to one side nor to another. It is already presupposed in the attrac-tiveness of filth. This becomes obvious when Bataille speaks of the unavoidable  necessity of a mediation within eroticism between a man and a woman.

> The most important point here is that a region of silence is introduced between a man and a woman and is imposed upon them in a way which bewitches them. Their relations are thus mediated, humanized in the most profound way [...].
> Between two beings whose movements are comprised of an overflowing life, the theme of reciprocal repulsion, bearing on sexual parts, is present as a mediator, as a catalyst building the power of communication [...]. (II, 318)

"Empty of meaning" without the intervention of a sacred core, of a region of silence, the relations between lovers would have nothing human about them. Attraction through what inspires horror is its inevitable condition. In this site, the interdiction, and its transgression, becomes thus a sudden appearance of meaning, of language, of communication, etc. But of what meaning is it really a question?

> Common human relations appear immediately and easily to be unbearable. It seems to me that it is only to the extent that a silence heavy with a certain tragic horror weighs upon life that the latter is profoundly human. (II, 318)

This core of violent silence produces a tragic meaning, ruptured meaning, meaning that assumed scissiparity; in other words, a meaning that is in league with death, with the death of meaning.

It is only here that one can understand why this site of mediation, of transmutation, is equally the region in which the *separation* of the repulsive from the attractive, of life from death is produced. What we have seen to be true of repulsion, that its entry "into the field of consciousness would not have been straightforwardly possible" (II, 239), is no less the case for attraction. All transformation of the low heterogeneous into the high heterogeneous can only be registered against a background of ruptured silence. Indeed, the pure and imperative heterogeneous sublates the tragic into itself. The region of heterogeneity, after having subjected all the overflowing, destruction, and dilapidation of the low heterogeneous, draws from this excessive agitation the resources that allow it to withdraw into and constitute itself as a full meaning whose plenitude is a function of the interdependence of the imperative heterogeneous and the homogeneous sphere. Now that we have revealed the dualism that divides the heterogeneous as well as the homogeneous, we are in a position to consider the ensuing subservience of the low heterogeneous to the high heterogeneous, as well as the mobilization of the latter by the homogeneous region.

If "the heterogeneous is what is agitated" (I,637), then in its site it is the scene of separation, of the emergence within its own realm of what will breach/broach [*entamera*] all self-possessedness, that is to say, for example, of what will come into opposition under the rubric passivity/activity.

> The heterogeneous realm is a perfect example of a moving realm and its agitation creates within limits that are its own, oppositions that can be as strong as, and from a certain

perspective, even stronger than those that separate the
entirety of heterogeneous elements from the profane realm.
(II, 227)

The mobility of the heterogeneous region thus gives rise to a polarization by which it itself becomes affected. Yet, the pole of the sovereign
heterogeneous only takes up the act of separation, the mobility of scissiparity that is at the base of the heterogeneous, to invest it with a sadistic
desire for purity, plenitude, and existence. It is a movement that paradoxically tends towards the suppression of mobility in the fixity of unshaken
meaning, or power. This appropriation, that functions as the arresting of
agitation within the proper [*le propre*], rejecting the impure to the extent of
its very annihilation, is however only founded upon repressed mobility.
Heterogeneous sovereignty, the only one able to claim existence,
"demands agitated passion, felicitous or unfelicitous, for the heterogeneous world" (II, 228). It is only by resuming within itself the agitated
world, by gaining support from what is rejected, that the imperative
heterogeneous can constitute itself. "Since all that is *agitated* belongs to
the *heterogeneous* world, only the elements of this agitated world will be
able to furnish the portion of necessary violence" (II, 222) of the sovereign.
And yet again: "The sovereign realizes all possible activity based on the
profound agitation of the mobile world" (II, 224).[6]

The region of heterogeneity, site of mobility, of tumult, of agitation,
of separation, producing its own polarization into low and high,
condenses itself, thus uncoupling the high pole from the low, all activity
that reduces to silence, and condemns to passivity the low pole, from
which, however, it draws its substance and subsistance. The act of
resuming, of lifting up mobility into a fixed pole denatures the tragic
rupture of the agitated, and displaces it towards the generation of a luminous meaning. Hence the absence of meaning and passivity of the low.

The *high* element of polarization is called *active* with respect to
the *low* element because in the first place it is the high that
excludes the low [...] Thus the *low* element is presented at first
as passive. (II, 167)

Compared to the decisive cruelty of sovereignty, low heterogeneity
sees itself condemned to passivity. The first is characterized by "the force
of *heterogeneity* most contrary to that of the paltry" (II, 224). This usurped
force, as it were, does not exhaust itself only in the rejection of paltry

forms, but brings about as well the affective displacements essential to the survival of sovereignty; in other words, it undertakes by its very force the transformation of repulsion into attraction.

> The necessity of the displacement is itself in keeping with the strictly passive character of the elements upon which it bases its production. The generally inferior forces have against them not only the homogeneous part but the superior elements of the heterogeneous part: they are thus the object of an excessive oppression to which, in their own right, they can only oppose a passive resistance, given that, by definition, they are amorphous and undirected. (II, 163/4)

Low heterogeneity, "the naked and unlimited form of undifferentiated *heterogeneity*" (I, 360), lacks force (a force that is, at least in a certain way, foreign to its nature) because the paltry forms of heterogeneity have "an absence as their origin." They are quite simply incapable of "assuming with sufficient force the imperative act of excluding the abject (which constitute the basis of collective existence)" (II, 219). All of this combines to characterize them as passive in the aftermath which cuts, excludes low heterogeneity.

Let us now reconsider the relation between the homogeneous and the heterogeneous by taking account of the fissure that runs through the heterogeneous realm. Clearly, the "two *heterogeneous* worlds, royal and miserable, must be represented as belonging to a realm radically separated from the homogeneous world" (II, 227). The reasons for this have appeared in preceding passages. We have seen the dependence of the homogeneous world with respect to imperative heterogeneous authority, the irrevocable necessity of an opening of the homogeneous to the intrusion of heterogeneous elements, on the basis of inner divergences, lack of a *raison d'être*, etc. The structure of the homogeneous realm, constituted by an exchange of current measurable and identifiable values between abstract subjects, requires, by means of the standard, an authority that supports it, around which homogeneous society can completely order itself. The infringement of this heterogeneous kernel upon the homogeneous region profoundly alters its structure. The homogeneous region calls forth what by definition it excludes.

> The rejection of paltry forms alone has a constant fundamental value for homogeneous society [...]; but due to the

fact that the act of exclusion of the paltry forms necessarily associates the *homogeneous* forms and the imperative forms, the latter can no longer be purely and simply rejected. *Homogeneous* society in fact uses the free imperative forces against the elements which are the most incompatible to it and when it must choose from within the realm that it has excluded the very object of its activity (existence *for itself* at whose service it must necessarily be placed), the choice cannot fail to fall on forces whose practice has shown that they in principle acted in the most favourable direction.  (I, 353)

The mobilization of the pure heterogeneous used to eliminate the low, confers on the homogeneous world its *raison d'être*, since it cannot find within itself the force of exclusion required for the maintenance of its structure, but finds this force exclusively in the plenitude of the decisiveness of noble and elevated elements.  Two complex complementary movements begin their play.  First, homogeneity, resorting to heterogeneous forces in order to resolve its internal irreconcilable differences, not only takes on a founding plenitude through association with these forces—by assimilating them or by becoming similar to them—but it also renders these same forces subservient by putting them in its service, by reducing them to its own ends.  Second, the operation of excluding paltry forms undertaken by imperative heterogeneity makes it akin to the homogeneous formation.  This is what ultimately renders the connection of the two worlds possible.

Imperative *heterogeneity* not only represents a form differentiated from vague *heterogeneity*: it supposes in addition the structural modification of the two parts, *homogeneous* and *heterogeneous*, in contact with one another.  On the one hand, the homogeneous formation closely allied to royal authority, the State, borrows from this authority its imperative character and seems to gain access to existence *for itself*, by realizing the cold and stripped-bare necessity [devoir-être] of the entirety of homogeneous society.  But the State is in reality only the abstract, degraded form of living necessity [devoir-être] required as effective attraction and as royal authority: it is only vague homogeneity having become restricted.  On the other hand, this mode of intermediate formation that characterizes the State penetrates in turn imperative existence: but in the course of this introjection, the very form of homogeneity becomes, this time in reality, existence *for itself* by negating itself: it is absorbed in heterogeneity and is destroyed as being strictly homogeneous due to the fact that, having become negation of the principle of utility, it refuses all subordination. (I, 334; cf as well I, 637/8)

It is thus thorough penetration of the imperative realm and of the homogeneous world which, tending toward the erasure of their own peculiar structures, provokes their mutual assimilation. It remains nevertheless the case that the two realms do not become identical, for whatever may be the modification of the heterogeneous in the direction of the homogeneous, sovereign power retains its unconditional quality.

Let us consider once again the relation of the low heterogeneous to the noble and elevated heterogeneous in order to complete the complex network of the heterological space constituted in our present approach.

Despite the overall play between the homogeneous region and the imperative heterogeneous elements, this play remains precarious and carries within it "a promise of imbalance and of ultimate disaster" (II, 225).

It would obviously be necessary to evoke here what Bataille develops as a mythological anthropology, an anthropology that supports to a large extent the necessity of such a fall. Let us however only advance some indispensable propositions on the basis of which this anthology is constructed. The human being from the mythological perspective that Bataille gives it, is conceived "as a sort of waste product," as a "deviation of nature," but of a formless nature, torn between conflicting alternatives and creating conflict. As excrement, man is "flagrant heterology [...] with respect to the world that gave rise to him." Separated from nature, from a nature in itself profoundly divided, unable to reassemble himself under any concept, man, as waste product, assumes the heterological practice of which he is only the most pronounced exponent:

> It is rupture, heterogeny in all its forms, the incapacity to ever draw together what has been separated by an inconceivable violence, that seems to have engendered not only man, but his relationship with nature. (II, 117)

No sinking into the homogeneous world—"under the intoxicating torpor of reason" (II, 223) and under the rule of power—would be able in the end to succeed in extirpating what is essentially subversive in man's heterological nature, in the scissiparity of his being. Against "the comic right of belonging to oneself" (II, 212/3) in the illusion of a for-itself closed in on itself, will sooner or later be opposed "the intimate harmony between life and its violent destruction, that is to say, tragic existence" (II, 247). Proof of this is the persistence and the perseverence of the low heterogeneous world, notwithstanding its indefinite exclusion by the homogeneous region and the superior part of the heterogeneous which depend not only on its rejection, but which draw from this rejection their force and their power. The power that always appears as strongly individualized, satisfying the desire to guarantee things, uniting in it the high heterogeneous forms such as sacred force and military power, must be designated "as a fatal alteration" of the "overall movement" requiring tragedy in communal life (II, 342/3). The institutionalization of power implies "the *alteration* and the *alienation* of the free sacred activity to which it lends its force" (II, 345). If it is indeed crime: separation, rejection, putting to death, etc. that is at the origin of the sacred, its transformation into the right, glorious, pure, unshakeable, and untouchable sacred eventually also calls for the death of the sovereign, this being all the more so since he tends through his cruel decisiveness to circumvent any threat he might fear. The power that, despite its criminal origin, "is the only force seeking blindly to eliminate crime from the earth," will necessarily attract to itself the movement that will lead to its fall.

> At the center of human agitation there is the crime that engenders sacred, left and untouchable things. These impure sacred things themselves engender an awesome force, sacred as well but right and glorious; but this personalized force is still submitted to the threat of crime. For the renewal of crime is necessary to the intense movement that is produced at the center of human groups. It is crime that essentially constitutes the tragic act and it goes without saying that it involves one day or another the criminal himself, the violent one, in death. (II, 346)

The transformation of the left sacred into the right sacred is only the work of imperative heterology to the extent that the transmutation is usurped in order to establish the definitive stability of power. In addition, the changing of the low heterogeneous into the high heterogeneous obeys the internal "logic" of heterology according to which heterological practice renews its flight by means of the vertiginous precipitation of the high, to which it had at first given birth.

Given the activity of the upper heterogeneous and of the homogeneous world, the paltry world of the low heterogeneous appears to be marked by passivity. An activity peculiar to the low world could only be engendered on the basis of a double movement. In the first place:

> ...*power* finds its source in the putting into play of sacred things; it is exhausted due to the fact that it tends to empty sacred things of their criminal content. Thus it promotes the rationalism from which it dies and little by little loses the strength to take on both the religious and military character that is essential to it. (II, 346/7)

It is from the inevitable *rapprochement* of the homogeneous and imperative heterogeneous worlds—despite the efforts of power to preserve what is unconditional—that the situation favoring the fall will arise.

In the second place, it will be necessary to envisage a passage from the world of paltry forms to activity, "to a form of conscious activity" (I, 368). Subversion will come to oppose the imperative forms of action.

> These subversive forms are none other than the lower forms transformed in view of the fight against sovereign forms. The necessity peculiar to subversive forms demands that what is low become high, that what is high become low, and it is in this requirement that the nature of subversion is expressed. (I, 368)

Subversion, understood as restoring the movement altered and arrested by high heterogeny, gives vigor once again to the free mobility of opposite terms: "What is high will become low." Subversion will realize the "impossible" transformation of the right sacred into the left sacred! And this by means of an inverse process to that whereby low agitation is usurped by the imperative heterological elements—and not only through their fall, disintegration, or precipitation. The first gesture, which would result in a "destructive negation," assumes the function of the cruel and positive action peculiar to the individualized nature of imperative power with an end, although mimicking a simple reversal of power whose direction would merely have changed (nothing is less certain in fact than the outcome of destructive negation which always risks becoming fixed in the meaning of imperative forms), but which nevertheless differs essentially from it. The insistence on the individual (or institutional) character of high heterogeneous power (cf. below), an individuality that is opposed, through its concentration of action in a site or in a person, to the passivity of the vague heterogeneous, will now permit one to envisage an agent and a different *topos* for subversive action. When destructive negation is adopted by agitated plurality, high forms are taken over with the goal of using them against their own intentions.

> Plurality is only found again in the passive expanses of nature or of misery, when the reactions are purely negative or destructive [...]. (II, 230)

This agitated plurality stands not only in simple opposition to individualized sovereignty, but is also the space in which imperative function is expended, a feature by which it radically breaks with the oppositional structure.

> 'Neither God nor masters' signifies existence as value, but an existence excluding all exercise of sovereignty. (II, 176)

Existence as "permanent decomposition," that is to say, governed by the tragic principle, is the space wherein subversion attracts by their fall, and reinscribes the imperative forms, the fixity of the imperative heterogeneous in monumental immobility, in order to make them the object of its operations.

Thus a space of agitation takes shape on whose basis one must rethink the status of the contradictory terms whose circuitous relations developed up to now will be seen to be modified. Let us take for example the opposition attraction/repulsion.[7] In what one calls opposition there is in general a hierarchy: one term either dominates the other or sublates it in a dialectical movement. With Bataille, however, we learn that hierarchy is itself only one of "the forms and not [...] [the] founding of *heterogeneity*" (I, 357). It is an essential (this word is quite appropriate here) characteristic of superior heterogeneity. It will be necessary then to see what, in the movement between the two poles of the heterogeneous, constitutes the superiority of one term vis-à-vis the other.

The core of silence at the heart of social agitation is the site where the difference between attraction and repulsion is produced, as well as that of their reciprocal transformation.

> There is at times an attraction, at times a repulsion, and all objects of repulsion can become in certain circumstances an object of attraction or vice versa. (I, 347)

This core is also the site of the transformation of the left sacred into the right sacred. But, as long as we restrict ourselves to considering that space of production wherein the opposing couples are generated, the core of violent silence, nothing explains why one of its terms becomes definitely superior. The core of transformation which is the site of the subversive movement only raises one term in order to make it fall unceasingly into its opposite. Yet the heterogeneous realm stretching between the two poles is precisely the region that escapes this principle.

> If one represents schematically the subversion of a society, the words oppressor and oppressed do not designate the entirety of the oppressors and the oppressed (which necessarily corresponds to the social whole) but only those oppressors or oppressed for whom each imposed oppression is not compensated in principle by an equivalent experienced oppression—and vice versa. The movements of attraction and repulsion that found the subversion are situated then in the interior of the heterogeneous region (which alone escapes from the principle of compensation). (II, 217)

This passage necessitates the following remarks: that the heterogeneous realm is a realm strongly polarized by the fact that the oppositions that characterize it are not equal (as in the homogeneous region); that there is therefore an oppressive hierarchy; that the attraction and repulsion are not identical. One will remember that the low heterogeneous is defined by its weak capacity for repulsion which is why it is rejected by the superior forms that violently engage in exclusion to the benefit of attraction; a benefit that only reveals itself to be possible by lighting more or less definitively upon a pure heterogeneous form.

> Heterogeneity has as its foundation an attraction; that attraction is more or less strong and, in addition, it tends to get lost

if the object of substitution is not distinguishable by a fixed
demarcation. (II, 433)

High and low heterogeneity, the two fixed poles, the strong polarization, thus bear witness to an arresting of movement. The necessity leading
to this stagnation having become apparent, there is no longer any need to
dwell on it. What however is revealed here is that the entire play of oppositions between the homogeneous on the one hand, and the high and low
heterogeneous on the other, combine in a figure in which the terms are in
solidarity. From this perspective, none of the terms are capable of
producing a rupture that would cause the system of developed relations to
be shaken.

It will be necessary, then, to come back to that core of silence in
which separation, the rupture of continuity, and the translation of the
engendered opposing couples into their opposites takes place. It is within
this core that one must think the compensatory movement which exists in
solidarity with a movement of uninterrupted rupture occurring between
attraction and repulsion, as a movement of the constant transgression of
limits. But, on the other hand, a wanton violence that agitates the core's
movements, an outrageous violence that comes from a certain outside,
produces the blockage of the rending and the closing of which the core is
the site.

To the core of repulsion and attraction that constitutes social
animation there is added a formation which is derived from it
but which is exterior to it. (II, 342)

This formation is that of stabilization, of fixation, of the demarcation
of the high with respect to the low, an effect of the high heterogeneous,
which can only be thought through its connection with the homogeneous
world. This is also a fixation of the low, based on the couple homoge-
neous/imperative heterogeneous, in its passivity and envisaged annihilation. With respect to the homogeneous world, which functions as the
dividing line that cuts through the heterogeneous realm engendering a high
and a low, the *entirely other* represented by the heterogeneous compared
to the homogeneous, is thus always already a heterogeneous that is
mastered, enslaved, put into service. Thus it doesn't really matter if it is a
question of the high or the low heterogeneous.

However the sacred, at least a certain sacred—the other having
been altered by the fixing of its poles on a definitive and stable

meaning—is by its very nature "neither high nor low" (II, 167). The movements of attraction and repulsion of which it is the site are not in any way privileged. There is a compensation between the two opposed movements, but no static equilibrium. For the separation into polarized terms and their mutual transformation, excretion and assimilation, attraction and repulsion, only become possible given a conception of the heterogeneous as what is rejected, expulsed and separated. Assimilation, attraction obey a movement of expenditure, or originary rupture in which these are only the terms required to be able to reiterate expenditure indefinitely, the projection out of the self.

Hegel, speaking of the attractive and repulsive force, of the different unity and plurality respectively, criticized their fixing as absolute qualities. Pure things of thought, of understanding, they are equal to one another, differing only in direction. Since each of the directions can only be understood as the effect of the contrary force, direction is an empty relation, defined by the fixing of one of these forces. But on the other hand, fixing upon a single one of these forces that defines the direction of its movements disturbs the nature of their reciprocity and their equivalence. There follows the sublation of their opposition without which they lose their intelligibility. Having a meaning/direction [sens] only in reference to each other, they cease to exist as soon as one of these forces assumes the right to define its own meaning. But on the contrary as equivalent, in their mutual equilibrium, they are nothing, existing only insofar as they are opposited.[8]

The two opposite forces only have meaning in their unity, in their sublation, in their annihilation: as magnitudes they are incommensurable.

> Just as one can hardly say that time is greater than space, so one can hardly say that a force of attraction is greater than a force of repulsion. They can no more emerge from an equilibrium than can those entities which they presently are: Unity and Plurality.[9]

It is readily apparent that Hegel's critique of fixation is taken up again by Bataille: his whole endeavor testifies to this. But is the sacred core of silence nothing more than the site of annihilation occurring in the indifferentiation of the polarizations which it causes to emerge in order to transform them into their opposites? Certainly not, for, by its very violence, this core puts together in order to rip apart again, attracts in order to repulse, assimilates in order to excrete. Wouldn't it therefore

simply be the opposite of the wanton assimilation—a function of the
superior heterogeneous, bringing to it the negative feature of expenditure, of nonsense? Thus Bataille's position would simply reverse Hegel,
where he would eventually inscribe himself, only on the other side. It is
not easy to settle the question once and for all. It remains undecidable
because such a reversal certainly is produced. What appears to reinscribe
this reversal as the first gesture in a future displacement, in a movement
thwarting the logic of the Hegelian system, this we will leave suspended
for the moment.

Suspended as "the impossible," this reinscription could only take
place through the deliberate rejection of all mastery, sovereignty, and
sense (or nonsense) engendered by such a reversal or any type of sublation [*Aufhebung*] whatsoever. It would only be produced in a repetitive
structure no longer dominated by either sense or non-sense, in a structure
that would cause the fixing in the pure or abstract negative to be irretrievably and helplessly aborted.

It would be difficult to situate this gesture in the statements
surrounding the heterogeneous by asking them this question which is,
moreover, inevitably philosophical.

## THE DOWNFALL

The impossibility in question results from the nature of theoretical
and/or philosophical discourse. Indeed the movement of transgression
can only be read in the practice of Bataille's writing.[10] The texts on
heterology only bear its trace surreptitiously.[11] The "heterological theory of
knowledge" envisaged by Bataille is doubled by his declaration of its
impossibility. This is a work of deconstruction, important certainly, but
taking place initially solely on the theoretical level, as its negative double.

Heterology's borrowings from the exact sciences—more precisely,
the link with scientific empiricism—will therefore be problematic. On
several occasions, Bataille has himself underlined a certain link tracing
heterology back to the French sociology of Durkheim and Mauss. This is a
direct link which, moreover, is not without criticism. Freudian psychoanalysis, dialectical materialism, etc. must also be mentioned. The notions
and the facts that will become the material and the conceptual apparatus
for the heterological discourse are all borrowed from sciences established
already. It must be noted, however, that Bataille lays more stress on the
facts than on the notions put forward by these sciences.

In addition, it will be necessary with Bataille to oppose philosophical
development "to the real development that belongs even more to life than

to discursive thought," the real development belonging to the realm of the representation of the individual and its existence (II, 304). That the object of representation might be a particular individual, an individual made particular, a fragment of a fragmented world, will have decisive consequences for the status of the material, for the entirety of facts, in which these facts will remain just as much particular, subject to no domination by any universal principle that would lift them up to the height of its unity. The space of representation of the particularized, by means of facts devoid of any unity of meaning, is, indeed, as the notion of "real development" suggests, of "mythological" or "phantasmatic" nature. There are, however, "constant links" (for example between shit and men), and heterological exposition will not be able to ignore them. It is not only facilitated by them, on the contrary, the observable empirical reactions "have a great indicative value from a theoretical viewpoint" (II, 70/1) if they arise from a realm of affects that touches "the entirely other," the expulsed and the rejected. Let us then turn to the links established between heterology on the one hand, and the theoretical and the empirical on the other hand.

It is quite surprising that Bataille often translates the German term "*das ganz Andere*" as "foreign body." Highlighting in *La valeur d'usage de D.A.F. de Sade* the two contradictory movements of excretion and appropriation (doubling the division of social facts into the religious and the profane) he writes:

> ...the object of the activity [excretory, R.G.] [...] is found each time treated as a foreign body (*das ganz Andere*); in other words, it can just as well be expulsed following a brutal rupture as reabsorbed through the desire to put one's body and mind entirely in a more or less violent state of expulsion (or projection). The notion of the (heterogeneous) *foreign body* permits one to note the elementary *subjective* identity between types of excrement [...] and everything that can be seen as sacred, divine, or marvelous. (II, 58/9) (*Visions*, 94)

We will return at the appropriate moment to this translation of the completely other by "foreign body." Let us retain for the time being only the identification of the foreign body with the heterogeneous. The expulsion of the heterogeneous can be motivated by two different intentions. Excrement is presented "as the result of a heterogeneity and can be developed in the sense of greater and greater heterogeneity" (II

59/60): heterogeneity incommensurable to the homogeneity established by the body with, as its final goal, the conservation of the latter, or else, a sign of a "brutal rupture" already presupposing a final rupture of the expulsing body. In the first case, the act of assimilation is reduced to the appropriation of homogeneous bodies and excretion becomes a subsidiary function of assimilation. In the second case, "the process of a simple appropriation is presented normally within the composite process of excretion, as necessary to the production of an alternating rhythm" (II, 59). Here, the appropriation is a function of excretion, a process that consists of introjecting foreign and heterogeneous bodies in order to later reject them. On first sight, it seems that it is only a question of a difference internal to the function of mediation. But:

> Excretion is not simply a middle term between two appropria-tions just as decay is not simply a middle term between the grain and the ear of wheat. The inability to consider in this latter case decay as an end in itself is the result not precisely of the human viewpoint but of the specifically intellectual view-point (to the extent that this viewpoint is in practice subordi-nate to a process of appropriation). The human viewpoint, independent of official declarations, in other words as it results from, among other things, the analysis of dreams, on the contrary represents appropriation as a means of excretion. (II, 65) (*Visions*, 99)

It is important to distinguish between "middle term" and "means." Excretion is not a middle term—it is neither the term nor the site of a mediation, neither middle, nor center, and supports no dialectic whatso-ever that might arise from appropriation and excretion. Rather, excretion must be understood as an end in itself. Appropriation thus becomes the means to assure expenditure only to the extent that it is a question, where excretion predominates, of assimilating the expulsed in the interest of the greatest expenditure. The site of excretion or of excorporation thus proves itself to be the site of a non-identity, of a repeated rupture. What is here envisaged corresponds to a rejection of the very possibility of homogeneous enclosure, breached in the series: assimilation → excre-tion → assimilation, and in the other, connected series: excretion → assimilation → excretion. As regards the two complementary series, notwithstanding the predominance of excretion as an end in itself in the latter, one can without considerable difficulty find examples of them in "objectified nature." But such an effort only bears witness to an attempt to assimilate, in scientific or philosophic discourse, elements that are irreducible both *de jure* and *de facto*. The enterprise, too easy, encountering no obstacle, has as its goal to situate the unknown, the basic irrationality of an unlimited expenditure, into relation with the objectified, homogenized known.

> It would be too easy to find in objective nature a large number of phenomena that in a crude way correspond to the human model of excretion and appropriation, in order to attain *once again* the notion of the unity of being, for example, in a dialectical form. One can attain it more generally through animals, plants, matter, nature, and being, without meeting really consistent obstacles. Nevertheless, it can already be indicated that as one moves away from man, the opposition loses its importance to the point where it is only a superimposed form that one obviously could not have discovered in the facts considered if it had not been borrowed from a different order of facts. (II, 64) (*Visions*, 98)

Thus, finding once again in nature the two connected series (let us say however that science will have difficulty in admitting the second) which reconnect the realm of human facts to one that is immediately objectified, the sharpness of the importance of the opposition tends to be effaced, as is the priority granted to assimilation with respect to excretion, as well as its opposite. The question of theoretical discourse imposes itself here.

We have already underlined the tendency inherent in science towards the homogenization of the world by means of identification and measure.

> In intellectual development, the site of incorporation becomes a site of identity that is never lost through the hierarchy of series of facts: it is through the establishment of a relationship of identity between the apparently irreducible elements that human intelligence appropriates them to the benefit of industrial activity. (II, 424)

Now it is precisely the assimilation of facts, excretion and appropriation, for example, that is easy when scientific reference is made to the always already objectified realm. Yet, the facility of this assimilation which

is the sign of a hurried effacement of the decisive character of the so-
called opposition, is criticized not only by heterology but by science
itself.  The easiness of such a reduction is even more awkward for
science than the difficulties that could counter the project of homogenization.  Not only a symptom "of the unconscious obstination brought
to defections and outlets," but a sign of the unhealthy "obstination of the
will seeking to represent to itself in spite of everything [...] a homogeneous and servile world" (II, 64), the difficulties encountered in homogenization bear witness to the desire to represent at all costs, without
respite and without anything remaining, the order of the heterogeneous.
Science certainly aims to *once again* attain unity.  But it also aims to
think and to represent the other.  Here lies the paradox of science.
Wanting to grasp at any price the other as other, it however only leads to
its own homogenization, its objectification, which necessarily makes of
the other, the other of the same.

Added to this is an aspect no less decisive for scientific and philosophic practice.  If one grants that the work of science is of a homogenizing, assimilating nature, then one must recognize that it must lead
sooner or later to a terminal phase in the direction of excretion.  What, at
this moment, will find itself expulsed from the theoretical system, will
represent the unassimilable, "the operation's irreducible waste products"
(II, 61).  This process of excretion corresponds to what one could call
theoretical *production*, whose function consists at first in the rejection of
the irreducible.  But here, for science or philosophy, whose principal
activity is of an appropriative nature, this excretion is, as in restricted
economy, only a middle term permitting a new assimilation of the
expulsed.  This is all the more true for philosophy since it is haunted by
the idea of universal and totalizing appropriation.

> The interest of philosophy resides in the fact that, in opposi-
> tion to science or common sense, it must positively envisage
> the waste products of intellectual appropriation.  (II, 61)
> (*Visions*, 96)

The process of reappropriating philosophy's undigested waste
products is made possible by the fact that it doesn't produce just any
waste product, but "total waste products."  Total waste products are
those unassimilable elements that have already been sufficiently homogenized to lend themselves to a new assimilation.  Philosophy "most
often only envisages these waste products in abstract forms of totality

(nothingness, infinity, the absolute) to which it itself cannot give a positive content."

> ...It can thus freely proceed in speculations that more or less have as a goal, all things considered, the *sufficient* identification of an endless world with a finite world, an unknowable (noumenal) world with the known (phenomenal) world. (II, 61) (*Visions*, 96)

The philosophy of totalization and interiorization, tracing the other upon the same, excretes waste products such as the universal system, the abstract forms of totality. As such these forms are immediately recuperable: the products of assimilation put into circulation—abstract substitutes for the irreducible—are reassimilated at the end of their course. Moreover, as abstract products, and "abstract" means "isolated," arising from no connection, from no mediation, for "if such a connection is impossible, the element envisaged remains in practice unreal and can only be objectified in an abstract way" (II, 64), they are necessarily the object of a rejection.

In response to the paradox that consists in desiring homogenization and at the same time in wanting to think the other as other, a practice or production (which is not excretion in the strong sense of the term) with reappropriation arises such that the effort at monopolizing the non-assimilable may be incessantly repeated. Hence the rumination, the perpetual repeating of the objectification of the non-objectifiable, the sign of which is abstraction.

This is equally true, although to a lesser extent, for scientific and empirical practice. It can only take into consideration heterogeneous objects, facts, or reactions insofar as they are objectified. Bataille gives the following definition of objectivity:

> Scientific data—in other words, the result of appropriation— alone retain an immediate and appreciable character, since immediate objectivity is defined by the possibilities of intellectual appropriation. (II, 63) (*Visions*, 98)

Objectivity is an obstacle only to the extent that it allows appropriation. It is the alienated counterpart of an interiority. It is also what is real, that which can be capable of being grasped as a sensible or intelligible object.[12]

Philosophy and science are thus unable to take account of the heterogeneous: "out of principle itself, science cannot know *heterogeneous* elements as such" (I, 344).

> The heterogeneous is even resolutely placed outside the reach
> of scientific knowledge, which by definition is only applicable
> to homogeneous elements. Above all, heterology is opposed
> to any philosophical system. (II, 62) (*Visions*, 97)

Here, where the objectivity of heterogeneous elements, products of philosophy and science, has only "one purely theoretical interest since it is possible to attain it only on the condition that one envisage the *waste products* in the total form of the infinite obtained by negation," a purely theoretical interest, moreover always in suspense, never really attained, since objective heterogeneity has "the defect of being able to be envisaged only in an abstract form" (II, 63), we will be able to once again raise the problem of the relation of heterology to empiricism. This is all the more so since one "must recognize the depth of the empiricist intention beneath the naïveté of certain of its historical expressions. It is the *dream* of a thought purely *heterological* at its source. A *pure* thought of *pure* difference. Empiricism is its philosophical name, its pretention or its metaphysical modesty."[13] Denouncing the limits inherent to the empirical sciences, Bataille postulates the necessity

> of constituting a knowledge of the *non explicable difference*,
> which supposes the immediate access of intelligence to matter
> predating intellectual reduction. (I, 345)

This comes very close to the desire for the "*pure* thought of *pure* difference." Likewise, there is the privilege accorded by Bataille to the subjective and to the concrete, evident in the following sentence:

> [T]he subjective heterogeneity of particular elements is, in prac-
> tice, alone concrete. (II, 63) (*Visions*, 98)

Inevitably, then, the question of these signifiers, of their organizing role in Bataille's text, but above all the meaning of the term practice is asked. It would also be necessary to evoke the concept, inherited from Mauss, of "total phenomenon," of "total social fact." An explanation of these terms not being possible here, let us simply say that the heterogeneous difference envisaged by Bataille could not be pure, facticity having been shaken in the purity of its difference, its irreducible positivity, no less than in the abstraction of its concept.

Let us reconsider then the link between heterology and empirical science. This relationship is undeniable, the detour through science is unavoidable, but how does it operate?

> When one says that heterology scientifically considers questions of heterogeneity, one does not mean that heterology is, in the usual sense of such a formula, the science of the heterogeneous. (II, 62) ( *Visions*, 96)

Heterology cannot be the science of the heterogeneous in the first place, because it has no object in the traditional sense. The heterogeneous element of which heterology would be the "science" is only a space. "This element itself remains undefinable and can only be fixed by negations" (II, 63). This is true in the same way for foreign bodies: fecal excremental matter, ghosts, unlimited time and space. Its "specific character [...] can only be fixed by negations such as the absence of all common measure, irrationality, etc." (ibid.). The heterogeneous element is free of specificity, it is impossible to classify it as a species. Having no properties, the heterogeneous element lacks the very characteristic, the specific nature of all (homogeneous) objects of science. The non-assimilation that distinguishes it results from its opposition to all classification. Yet, if something cannot be appropriated by science (or philosophy) this something remains unreal. Irreality would thus be a characteristic of the heterogeneous. Another of its features is the absence of all objectivity.

> It must even be added that there is no way of placing such elements in the immediate objective human domain, in the sense that the pure and simple objectification of their specific character would lead to their incorporation in a homogeneous intellectual system, in other words, to a hypocritical cancellation of the excremental character. (II, 63) ( *Visions*, 98)

The heterogeneous element (as foreign body and space) is characterized by the impossibility of any mediating apprehension bringing it into the immediacy of the objective human realm.[14]

Refusing all empirical and scientific circumscription, is the heterogeneous element the pure transcendental? Or is it a thing in itself as a theoretical construction indispensable to the intelligence of empirical things? Is it the object of knowledge of an immediate intuition? Is it a simple theoretical fiction?

The transcendental object does indeed intervene, but in an unsuspected way. Like Nothingness, the infinite, totality, etc., it is a total waste product, a sign of philosophy's powerlessness to grasp the entirely other as other. The transcendental object itself could thus belong to heterology, but solely to the extent that the thing in itself, the transcendental, would be a product of the paradox internal to philosophy and science.

> ...the intellectual process automatically limits itself by producing of its own accord its own waste products, thus liberating in a disordered way the heterogeneous excremental element. Heterology merely takes up again, consciously and resolutely, this terminal process which up until now has been seen as the abortion and the shame of human thought. (II, 63) (*Visions*, 97)

Clearly heterology has no object before the appropriating operation of philosophy (or of science) which unavoidably produces, in its waste products, bodies foreign to its homogeneous structure. It is only by scientific and philosophic practice that something like the heterogeneous springs forth. The desire of the intellectual process, which motivates its homogenizing appropriation, can only produce the heterogeneous in a disordered way as it interminably gathers its excrement in the hope of digesting it in the long run. Heterology is founded upon this waste product, progressively removing its abstract character, making it play the leading role in the spectacle of expenditure.

Whatever Bataille might have said about anthropology—mythological, that is to say phantasmatic anthropology, defining the *anthropos* by its primordial function of excretion—it is difficult not to see that this anthropology, with its decisive traits, is itself the undigested (undigestible) product of philosophy and science. For heterology does not only gather together into itself the diverse waste products of theoretical discourses, it takes up again the "terminal process," the process that leads these discourses to the limit of their possibilities. Their internal operations, as they inevitably bear witness to this function of rejection, of expulsion, and despite all efforts at obliteration and obnubilation, open a space of which they are ignorant, an unmastered and unmasterable space, which is written as an element of *downfall*, of loss, and of expenditure.

Mythological anthropology is only a staging of this, moreover a derisory one, which may always collapse in its turn.

Resuming the internal movement of theoretical discourses, pushing them to their limit, heterology, which proves here to be already like a practice, "*leads to the complete reversal of the philosophical process which ceases to be the instrument of appropriation, and now serves excretion; it introduces the demand for the violent gratifications implied by social life*" (II, 63) (*Visions*, 97). The relationship of heterology to science (and to philosophy) is then at least double. As it recovers its waste products and precipitates it toward its limits, heterology irrevocably inscribes theoretical discourse within the space of a *downfall.*

> Only, on the one hand, the process of limitation, and, on the other, the study of the violently alternating reactions of antagonism (expulsion) and love (reabsorption) obtained by positing the heterogeneous element, lie within the province of heterology as science. (II, 63) (*Visions*, 97)

The violent alternation of what could still appear as a fact is to the same degree the alteration of the fact itself. Having value and meaning only within the limits of the homogeneous field, it undergoes in the heterogeneous a decisive displacement. Being a waste product, and hence non-objectifiable, unintelligible, unreal, etc., it becomes a non-fact, devoid of any determination, even an abstract one that would permit its incorporation, though ephemeral, into theoretical discourse. The very essence of the altered fact is affected and violently torn apart by its opposite. The fact thus becomes impure and, because impure and soiled, becomes "a non-explicable difference." It implies immediate knowledge of this difference, however, but solely to the extent that the impure difference of the foreign body ruptures the intact body, breaks open its homogeneity. The difference is undecidable because the rejected body, the foreign body, its external existence, cannot be distinguished from the now ruptured intact body, invalidating all possible determination. The difference can thus be seen as the product of intrusion or of expulsion. It is the impure difference of life and death. Consider the juxtaposition of the two following sentences:

> Thus it is that, in the presence of death, what remains of life only subsists *outside of itself.*

And:

> It seems to me that the decisive element in the attitude towards
> the dead is the fact that the dead man is a *socius*, that is to say
> that it is very difficult to distinguish him from oneself. (II, 287)

After considering philosophy and science as realms traversed by the
heterogeneous, it remains to briefly consider two other regions and their
relation with heterology. They are religion and poetry.

If philosophy is indeed forced to "positively" envisage the "waste
products of intellectual appropriation," it is yet powerless to give them "a
positive content."

> Only an intellectual elaboration in a religious form can, in its
> periods of autonomous development, put forward the waste
> products of appropriative thought as the definitively heteroge-
> neous (sacred) object of speculation. (II, 61) (*Visions*, 96)

Notwithstanding the difference between philosophical speculation,
tending to tirelessly recapture its total waste products, and religious speculation, keeping the exteriority of the heterogeneous outside, the split
brought about between the left sacred and the right sacred leads unavoidably to a progressive homogenization of the upper sacred realm, leaving
intact only the lower sacred, such that God ultimately becomes "the
simple (paternal) sign of universal homogeneity" (ibid.). If religion institutes a definitive heterogeneous, it will only be that of the low heterogeneous indefinitely submitted to an upper strongly homogenized
heterogeneous. Let us note with Bataille the difference between
heterology and religion which channels and regularizes social projection:

> Religion differs [...] from a practical and theoretical *heterology*
> (even though both are equally concerned with sacred or excre-
> mental facts), not only in that the former excludes the scientific
> rigor proper to the latter [...] but also in that, under normal
> conditions, it betrays the needs that it was not only supposed
> to regulate, but satisfy. (II, 62/3) (*Visions*, 96–97)

One must remember here that the sacred, the object of religion, is not
simply the heterogeneous, any more than are the total waste products of
science or of philosophy, if such a simple heterogeneous were to exist at
all. The heterogeneous is in league with the sacred, as it is with the

unconscious of psychoanalysis, but they both are only "restricted forms with respect to heterology" (I, 344/5).

> ...it is possible to say that the heterogeneous world is constituted, to a large extent, by the sacred world and that reactions analogous to those that sacred things provoke reveal those of heterogeneous things which are not strictly speaking regarded as sacred. (I, 346)

With regard to poetry, it seems to retain great value "as a method of mental projection in that it permits access to an entirely heterogeneous world." Yet, even freed, protected from the great systems of appropriation, it is engaged solely "in the path of a total poetic conception of the world, leading necessarily to an aesthetic homogeneity." It nevertheless conserves, in one single feature, a heterogeneous character in "the practical unreality of the heterogeneous elements that it puts into play" (II, 62), an unreality that is opposed to the objectification of the world through science and philosophy. The unreality in question equally serves to guarantee the duration of heterogeneity, to establish it as a superior reality. Thus, it merges in its practice with Hegelian negativity, with pure Nothingness that negates itself. The practical unreality of poetry is thus not to be taken for an unreal practice energized by a theoretical definition of reality by theoretical discourses. The first fastens on to duration; the second is unconditional expenditure.

Comparing science/philosophy (which, despite its tendency and its desire for homogeneity, leads to total waste products), religion (doing without any scientific procedure, pushing the dichotomy between homogeneity and heterogeneity so as to produce definitively heterogeneous waste products that it channels towards the low), and poetry (hesitating between unreal practice and practical unreality, establishing a sublime heterogeneous realm devoted to eternity), we see several traits that mark heterological theory. It is characterized by the rigorous opposition between the two regions. It considers the waste products in what makes them definitive and irretrievable. It is scientific to a certain extent, and contributes to the practical satisfaction of heterogeneous projection.

## INSIGNIFICANT PRACTICE

Heterology is necessarily practical.[15] Historical urgencies (the fight against fascism and the opposition to surrealist aestheticism) have deeply reinforced this characteristic. Still, political configurations do not begin to explain Bataille's insistence on practice. In order to do this we must turn to "theoretical" considerations.

If heterology claims to a certain extent to be theoretical, if the traversal of theoretical discourse is imperative, this is principally due to a possibility that opens as a gap in scientific or philosophical discourse, out of the contradiction to which these discourses lead by progressing towards a gradual homogenization of the world. This contradiction results from the fact that philosophy and science want to capture the other as other, while reducing it necessarily to the same, to the other of the same. Overwhelmed in the face of this contradiction, the theoretical discourses only have a single outlet, the rejection of what does not allow itself to be assimilated by means of a repression, of a denial or even by infinitely turning over the total waste product. It is here that the practice of heterology takes off, by causing the always failed regression towards the homogeneous to abort, by opposing to speculative procedure one that is *other,* practical. Still, practice is only the reverse side, congenital to and in solidarity with the theoretical, an other that is consequently restrained. It will then be necessary to attempt to "think" in heterological practice some-thing that escapes at least "by a bit" from the classical dichotomy. The privileged example of heterological practice is laughter.

> *As soon as the effort at rational comprehension ends in contra-diction, the practice of intellectual scatology requires the excre-tion of unassimilable elements,* which is another way of stating vulgarly that a burst of laughter is the only imaginable and definitively terminal result—and not the means—of philosoph-ical speculation. (II, 64) (*Visions,* 99)

A strange practice is laughter, setting itself strongly apart from tech-nical and from what one has come to call political practice. Why does laughter take on a value here of heterogeneous practice? It is in no way a question of "attributing an exceptional importance to a *secondary* process like laughter" writes Bataille in a scratched-out note. Laughter only assumes the power of rupture through "the only outlet imaginable," an outlet that manifests itself at the moment when theoretical procedure no longer has at its disposal anything other than evacuation as a means for safeguarding homogeneity menaced by contradiction. Rational discourse speaks of "the heterogeneous elements in so symbolic and so abstract a way that the act of envisaging them no longer even involves a simple phenomenon of practical clearing like laughter" (II, 425). And, for good reason, for the evacuation that intellectual scatology brings about only consists in the temporary elimination of total waste products with the hope of recuperating them in good time. The expulsion is only temporary and conditional. Laughter laughs at intellectual scatology, at its congenital constipation and at its incapacity to resolve contradiction except by rejection, at its obstinacy in maintaining at any price a homogeneity, shaken from the outside of the excluded other. It laughs at the fact that there is homogeneity only by means of an evacuation that thwarts homogenization in its very project. But above all, laughter laughs at the function of evacuation as a means, of its reduction to a middle term between two appropriations. It is in this that laughter, eluding the function of mediation, becomes "definitively terminal and not the means of speculative philosophy." It settles the question of both contradiction and rejection by setting an uncrossable limit to the solution of contraries and to their eventual reconciliation.

Laughter is a practice that stands out against the opposition theoretical/practical: its heterological aspect stems from the fact that it in no way merges with either of these terms. It is of the same nature as that with which theoretical discourse/classical practice has nothing to do and, consequently, is like the other irretrievable by these discourses. As practice, laughter belongs to excluded objects and shares the right of impure things to belong to the heterological realm.

> ...one must indicate that a reaction as *insignificant* as a burst of laughter derives from the extremely vague and distant character of the intellectual domain, and that it suffices to go from a speculation resting on abstract facts to a practice whose mechanism is not different, but which immediately reaches concrete heterogeneity, in order to arrive at ecstatic trances and orgasm. (II, 64/5) ( *Visions,* 99)

Insignificant, laughter bursts outside of the intellectual realm, at its edges, pushing it back into vagueness, provoking its escape, its fall. But insignificance characterizes heterological practice as well, which becomes in this way an act irreducible and unassimilable to meaning, insignificant like all that is expulsed by rational comprehension, in order that the latter can be guaranteed a significance in its homogeneous world. This insignificance, however, only takes its capacity for rupture from its opposition to meaning and that, eventually, is only one more negative characteristic by which the heterogeneous distinguishes itself.

Laughter as heterological practice is only a *secondary* practice; its mechanism is not different from speculation in its dealing with abstract facts. Yet it immediately attains concrete heterogeneity. Abstract facts are the unassimilable elements of science provisionally set aside. Laughter doubles the speculative range, but—it is this that characterizes laughter and heterological practice (in general)—it is *added* to the unassimilable, to the irreducible as a supplementary heterogeneous. Heterological practice, even there where it manifests itself through secondary acts—it can never hope to take shape in a purely, originarily heterogeneous practice—is heterogeneous only at the price of repeating the unassimilable of philosophy and of science, denying itself in this respect all efforts at comprehension, of intellection, in splitting, in adding itself to the already heterogeneous. If there is heterological practice, it will not be in the production of *immediately* heterogeneous actions but by a movement that eventually causes the reserve of what is irrecuperable to comprehension to overflow. This movement of adding the heterogeneous to the already rejected, is what must be understood as heterological practice, and not the acts conceived according to their content, a content always motivated by their opposition. Heterological practice consists thus in the unlimited multiplication of acts and of heterogeneous things, in the extension of the space of contradiction, in the violent opening of the uncrossable gap through the production of deliberately squandered gestures. Here, heterological practice—by its very insignificance, by the very accumulation of the irreducible (not in its contents, which always become the abstract object, and thus that of an eventual reappropriation)—as movement of unproductive expenditures, signifies not only a saturation of the heterogeneous (of its space)—a laughable saturation—but rupture, separation, abyssal deepening of contradiction, until any effort at mediation on the part of theoretical discourses is rendered ridiculous.

But this is true as well of what is conventionally called practice. Heterological practice is only such to the extent that it is added without distinction, without desire for *Aufhebung*, to abject things, to the extent that it refuses the power of domination, of mastery over that to which it has been added. If Bataille writes that heterogeneous impulses towards a determined social milieu "are *in practice* identified through heterology with man's *raison d'être*" (II, 66), then one must remark that the relation established between a certain anthropology and the heterogeneous impulses is the result of a *practical* identification.

This implies two things: first, that the identification is an adding of one heterogeneous to another, that it is a heterological identification and not deduced or implied in any philosophical sense; second, that anthropology, man's *raison d'être*, is a representation of a heterological nature, resulting not from rational comprehension, but from a practice of heterological representation. The space that is hereby opened is one in which acts are disseminated, a space of representations that can be identified from a heterological point of view (because they are added), but which are irreducible to one another, none having the privilege of setting itself up as a middle term.

The impulses, however, have a telos, an end: the phase of excretion. Thus, they can contribute to the multiplication, to the proliferation of things, of facts, of heterogeneous acts. But the end necessarily implies the subordination of violent impulses to a useful goal.

> ...they [the impulses, R.G.] can find, through the historical movements by means of which humanity spends its own strength freely and limitlessly, both total gratification and use in the very sense of general conscious benefit. (II, 66) (*Visions*, 100)

The general interest in question, a conscious interest, must inevitably channel the free discharging of impulses into a useful goal. Subjugated immediately by the interest that hangs over the social Revolution for example, the excretory impulses find their limit, their sense, and are thus reduced to means; means that, as Bataille has remarked, can always be subjugated to superior forms, fixing the heterogeneous reaction in imperative forms. Thus, the Revolution, regardless of its tendency toward an overflow, catastrophy, and gestural profusion, is not a pure heterological practice. There can be no pure heterological practices any more than there can be purely heterogeneous facts.

The "reality of this ulterior interest" which, as a general conscious interest, intimately affects the heterological practice of the Revolution, obliterating "the sacrificial character of a Revolution" by remaining "profoundly unconscious" (II, 66/7), is however "the practical *raison d'être*"—practical in the heterological sense. Utilitarian and possibly usurious interest serves precisely as a springboard for heterological excessiveness which suspends, if only for a more or less short moment, all utilitarian motivation.

> The revolutionary impulse of the proletarian masses is, moreover, sometimes openly treated as sacred, and that is why it is

possible to use the word *Revolution* entirely stripped of its utilitarian meaning without, however, giving it an idealist meaning.
(II, 67) (*Visions*, 100)

It is through the pertinence of its excessiveness and of the non-
recuperable violence that escapes on all sides from being grasped by any
utility, even after the fact, that revolutionary practice can be heterological.
Although the revolution is only a possibility in light of a future interest
which gives it a meaning after the fact, there remains a residue that eludes
all recuperation. If this interest, limiting heterological practice in its violent
effervescence, is its requisite condition, this is because heterological practice cannot last: it only manifests itself in opening [*l'effraction*], in violation
[*l'infraction*], becoming lost, at the moment of its eruption.

Refusing to be grasped, practical heterology can become an object of
science no more than can the always ambiguous heterogeneous things.
Heterological theory, as well, can only be added in the end, as a practice
to other heterological practices, as one practice among others that nevertheless draws attention for a moment to its decisive character. Entering
into excremental configuration it loses its value as discourse.

Like general economy,[16] heterology is not the loss of meaning, but a
"relation to the loss of meaning." It gains access to this loss, after having
described the effects of heterology, by becoming in turn such an effect. In
this way, it loses its meaning, that is, as a "science" dealing with the various
forms of the heterogeneous, but, in the midst of these senseless forms, it
retains meaning as an effect.

## FOREIGN BODIES

The movement of loss inherent to heterological discourse proves to
be inevitable from the moment that one reconsiders the heterological practice of laughter from another perspective. Given the primordial place that
the excretory processes occupy in human existence, nothing prevents one
from putting laughter in contact with defecation. With laughter, then, it is
a matter of liberating a discharge through the buccal orifice, through the
organ of language.

But in laughter excretion ceases to be positively material: it
becomes ideological in this sense that the excremental object
of spasmodic contraction is only an image and not a certain
quantity of sperm, urine, blood or feces. This image can be

that of one of the excrements listed or that of one of the exterior organs. (II, 71)

Laughter laughs at what is expulsed and doubles the excretory act. But contrary to anal defecation there is ideological excretion on the level of language and of discourse. In this case, its heterological character stems from the fact that it is the transgression of discourse, of language itself, beyond its articulation. Relating to an image, or liberating an image of loss, laughter opposes discourse from its tangible side: the image and unarticulated sound of laughter being what resists its substitution by transparent language. Laughter bursts language by introducing into it both the image, as body or tangible representation, and a practice that transgresses articulated sonority towards the bursting of sound itself. To laugh at the effort of rational comprehension which must result in contradiction as it rejects any unassimilable elements for the benefit of homogeneity is to ruin the homogeneous order of words in a heterological practice that doesn't insist on a positivity of its own. If heterological theory, the science of the *entirely other*, is the elaboration of an excremental constellation and the production of an entirely other with respect to (and in) theoretical/philosophical discourse, then this "science," arising necessarily from the rational order, despite the modification that the latter will have undergone, is an evacuation of heterology in itself which must remain unavoidably foreign to all scientificity. A foreign body, heterology *in* heterological *theory* is not only the subservient object of theoretical discourse, but also the rejection of any comprehensive, rational, ordered project; in brief, the explosion of the concept of heterological theory itself.

There is therefore a rejection of discourse, of the theoretical, of the logical, of articulated language, heterological theory ruining itself, beyond language, among heterogeneous facts, practices, things. Or yet still: treating itself as a foreign body, as a completely other, heterological theory (or heterological knowledge), laughing at itself as at an ordered group of "words introduced in a certain way into sentences that exclude them" (II, 72), transgresses the limit of the theoretical—which still kept it above what it, in a "general over-view," claimed to express—in order to fall on the side of the irreducible. As its "own" waste product.

Let us return to the translation of the notion of *das ganz Andere* by foreign body. The foreign body is first of all a body, a body *outside of itself*, yet barely distinct from the body proper. It is a body that doubles the body proper, sticking to this body like a shadow or a mask. This foreign body is nothing less than the *socius*, that is, death. The impure body only acts as foreign body to the extent that it is outside, that its introjection into the homogeneous body is forbidden. It seems to me that a *rapprochement* with certain of Freud's remarks is possible at this juncture, treating the symptom as a foreign body in the self,[17] as well as the causative trauma of the hysterical phenomenon.

> The causal relation between causative psychic trauma and the hysterical phenomenon is not such that the trauma would set off the symptom as an *agent provocateur*, the symptom which would then persist in an independent fashion. Rather, we must affirm that psychic trauma, or rather its memory, acts in the manner of a foreign body that remains an active agent long after its penetration.[18]

Memory is here the reminiscence of an originary scene linked to castration as a representative of death.[19] The primitive scene acts like a foreign body due to the fact that the self forbids it access to consciousness, eliminating all possibility for its discharge through abreaction, through *Usur*, which would ruin the body in its propriety. No real relief through the authority of the self proves possible. Each overture towards the foreign body, be it through introjection, or through projection outside of the self towards it, only ruins the body in the space of death or of its representation. The relation between body proper/foreign body is thus distinguished from that between the same and the Hegelian other. The brutal expulsion of the foreign body in the desire for a reabsorption after the fact is replaced, in Bataille, by a desire to provoke an irreparable rupture of the body proper, to become a foreign body itself. The intrusion of the foreign body into the homogeneous sphere has two effects: there is the weakening, in analytical terms, of the homogeneous by the heterogeneous; the adaptation by means of conciliatory forms to parts foreign to the self, arising from the internal world, without the self ceasing its effort at repression; added to this is a homogenization of the foreign body introduced through the forms that it is forced to take, in order to be able to valorize its rights against the power of the homogeneous.

The foreign body calls forth by this very aspect of intrusion, of introjection—all the more if one takes into account the polarization that marks the heterogeneous realm—an astronomic metaphoric that we will try to measure to the full extent of what is possible. It is, in effect, a question of the fall of the meteor, foreign body *par excellence*. Speaking of what makes a king a king, that is, a heterogeneous body, Bataille writes:

> The designation has literally fallen from the sky. The one whom it has marked with its seal is comparable to a meteor fallen in the middle of a field, among other stones of a similar appearance. Nothing will allow one to say that the meteor, and the meteor alone, has not fallen from the sky. It is true that the royal person, once naked, can in no way be distinguished from other human bodies. But "the grace of God," the grace of heaven, has chosen among others that one body called king. This is why no body is more radically foreign to the mass comprising the people. (II, 223)

What is a meteor first of all? In philosophical literature which it has not ceased to haunt, the meteor has the status of a singular object, doubly determined as having fallen from the sky and yet being only one stone among others.

Since Aristotle, meteors are bodies comprised of an imperfect mixture. "Miniatures of lightning" according to Descartes, meteors, far from being true stars, are only the result of terrestrial phenomena, of exhalations that, condensing themselves, become inflamed and fall back to earth. Thus, their matter is not necessarily of an invariable nature, but on the contrary:

> (they are) all the more (variable) since there are exhalations of several different natures. I don't believe it impossible that the clouds that shape them sometimes produce a matter that, according to the color and the consistency that it has, will seem made of milk, or blood or flesh, or else that by burning itself becomes such that one takes it for iron or for stones (...).[20]

For Schelling, the adoration of meteorites is the sign of a surpassing of astral religion. It marks the becoming telluric of the spiritual star. The fall of the star is a violent act, a fall headfirst, a sort of decapitation of the high. Consequently, it is a bloody fall:

> One sees that they (the meteors, R.G.) are actually hurled headfirst in that continual flaring up and abating which is peculiar to them during the fall. That this struggle is no less fierce

than that, in which the organic and the inorganic first separated, proves the irrefutable fact that, apart from actual rocks, there have fallen not only plant-like masses, but also masses which are like gelatin, indeed hæmogenic masses, legitimate products of an organic rupture or dismemberment.[21]

Banned from the celestial constellation, expulsed from the homogeneous world, the foreign body of the star (exhalation or spiritual projection) falls from the vault of the sky like a disaster, headfirst, throat cut, becoming once again matter among matter. But, however, bearing significant traces of the fall that will distinguish it from the other stones among which it falls: blood, impure body, sacred body. In effect, if one considers the etymology of the word meteor, the latter designates at the same time suspension, elevation, and fall. The foreign bodies of meteors, heterogeneous elements, expulsed and reintroduced into the homogeneous world, belonging to both regions at the same time, "are comparable, in their unreasoned movement, to the trails of fire that would unquestionably lift life up into their wake" (II, 230). Their disastrous effect is welcomed into the homogeneous world only to the extent that it cannot do without such a lifting up, such a *raison d'être*, such a sovereign authority that, when adapted to this world, confers meaning upon it. With the exception of the reservation that this foreign body be a fallen body, that it only be distinguished thus in a minimal though significant fashion from the rest of the homogeneous world, the latter "submits itself to fascinating *decisiveness* with the exception of decisions just as daring," and enters into the orbit of this fallen star (II, 230).

The heterogeneous region is defined "as the realm proper of polarization," of strong polarization, compared to the weakly polarized homogeneous realm. The meteor, descended from the sky, dragging its head, is a foreign body that has turned on itself. πολεῖν, to turn, is the etymological root of the word polarization. It is as a partially homogenized heterogeneous body that it makes the homogeneous world turn in its orbit. Through its agitation it causes the world to be dependent, by polarizing it. It is a world that, without this dependence (πέλω) on a terrifying heterogeneous force (πελώριος) would dissolve into Nothingness. But the celestial axis (πόλος) that traverses the tellurian world with its luminous ray is diffracted in the homogeneous milieu until it is extinguished.

Polarization: a term of physics—a particular modification of luminous rays by virtue of which, once reflected or refracted, they become incapable of being reflected or of being refracted again in certain directions. (*Littré*)

In polarization through simple refraction, the luminous ray "is no longer reflected and is extinguished, thereby affirming the character of polarization," as the *Littré* further states. It is this that takes place during the progressive homogenization of the heterogeneous element, provoking in this way the "promise of unbalance and of final disaster" (II, 225).

With polarization we also open, using the word's reference to the celestial axis, the pages of the almanac, the calendar that fixes the regular and constant relation of the terrestrial world with the celestial world. Indeed πόλοζ means in Ionian Greek, the sun dial, configured as a round disk with a vertical pin whose shadow indicated the time. The almanac, on the other hand, published annually, following the path of the sun, turning on itself in its orbit, periodically cancelling itself out, contains all the days of the year and information about the constellations of the sky and the stars. The *Littré* gives us the following etymology:

> This word is quite ancient; it is found, with the meaning we attach to it in *Eusebius* (...) in the form ἀλμεναχα (...) M. Lenormant proposes an Egyptian etymology: in Coptic *al* means calculation and *men* memory, from which one was able to create the composite word *almeneg*, calculation for memory. It is difficult to go beyond the word such as it was given by *Eusebius*. Egyptian etymology has a certain probability. The following have also been indicated: the article *al* and the Hebrew *manach*, to count; the article *al* and the Latin *manachus*, a circle traced on a solar dial and being used to indicate the shadow for each month.

Whatever the relevance of these etymologies, the links of the almanac to polarization are rather obvious. But it also follows that the almanac is an instrument of calculation, a means of prediction and fore-sight regarding the celestial influences on the tellurian world: a means to mastery, if necessary, of their disastrous effects. It is an instrument in the service of homogeneity.

This, then, explains Bataille's refusal, the title, *The Heterological Almanac* crossed-out in favor of another, *Heterological Theory of Knowledge*. Yet, it is in the chapter thus titled that Bataille has negated all scientific possibility for knowledge of the heterogeneous, thereby postulating the impossible calculation of its occurrence. The initial title proved insufficient—all the more so since the heterogeneous excludes all chronology (II, 440). But that is not all: the polarization of the heterogeneous realm from high to low, from light to dark, implies the almanac's insufficient account of the relation sustained by "heterology and night" (ibid.), of the times when meteors fall—meteors whose movements escape all calculation.

What authorizes us to revalorize this title, except that it had been crossed-out? In the first place, the *rapprochement* of the two terms "almanac" and "heterological" provides that the heterological almanac could not be a simple almanac. In fact it could only be a question of an almanac affected by the heterological theory of knowledge, of an almanac that will procure no knowledge in the strict sense of the word, an almanac whose base will no longer be calculation and mastering foresight.

A common almanac not only contains all the days, holidays and lunar cycles, but also a good number of strange facts: places, people, events. Heterology, as science, is not a proper science. What is included under this name could only be the (in principle) unlimited group of heterogeneous effects, incongruous with respect to one another. As we have seen, neither religion, nor poetry, nor philosophy and science produce a pure heterogeneous. But although a pure heterogeneous by definition cannot exist, the sacred, the unreal, the total waste product, are, despite their ambiguity, aspects of the heterogeneous. In the final reckoning, for we must indeed make our impossible calculation, heterology, as a science, is itself only an effect of the heterogeneous, connected to it without however merging with it. Would the heterological almanac, then, not be that book that collects within itself the divided-up space of the heterogeneous and that finally loses itself in it, crossing itself out as a book, as a treatise on heterology, expending in this way its title as it gathers up within itself the *scattered nature* of the heterogeneous?

The almanac, however, followed the movements of the sun like a sundial, tracing with the shadow of the pivot piercing the circular plaque, the hours and months of the year; an operation that pulls down the sun onto a horizontal plane, into the low region of the shadow. This pulling down, a rotation of the vertical onto a horizontal plane of projection, results in the annulment of the sun's luminous force, the extinction of its fires against the vertical pivot. The shadow of the pivot, the pivot pivoting on itself, is the trace of writing, the heterological almanac, its space. Out of the extinction of the solar foyer, out of the opening of the solar ray ruptured by the raised stylus, the blackness of the shadow or of the ink presents the multiple figures of a fallen sun. The sun, in effect, is "the only object of literary description." The writer "believes he is obliged to play a role in relation to the sun" (II, 140). Dazzling and blinding, the writer is charged with a heterogeneous character: being projected onto the excremental constellation, onto the order of suns in decomposition, the writer inscribes himself within that heterogeneous book which is the heterological almanac.

Thus the phantasmatic[22] fabric comes into view, in which a term such as heterology is inscribed, a term whose character every scientific or philosophic formalization would unavoidably alter. By putting this term to work within the homogeneous order of concepts, the product of this work would, at best, be useful.

## NOTES

1. We are quoting from the *Complete Works* of Georges Bataille, published by Gallimard in Paris. The Roman numerals designate the volume, the Arabic numbers the pages.

2. Cf. J. Kristeva, "Bataille, l'expérience et la pratique," in *Bataille*, coll. 10/18, Paris 1973, 34.

3. A reference made by Bataille to E. Durkheim, in particular to *Règles de la méthode sociologique*, P.U.F.

4. This transformation was analyzed by Bataille particularly in the pages about the country village, an analysis that was part of the courses held at the "Collège de sociologie."

5. The bar inevitably erases this abyss.

6. One could refer here to the text *En effet la vie humaine...*(II, 163/4) in which Bataille demonstrates that imperative heterogeneity lives at least in part from the affective charges to which it is subject by means of a displacement.

7. However we could just as well have provided the following dichotomic terms: excretion/assimilation, ebb/flow, centripetal force, centrifugal force, etc.

8. Hegel, *Jenenser Logik, Metaphysik und Naturphilosophie*, Hambourg 1967, p. I/3.

9. Ibid., p. 23.

10. With this reading, all philosophical questions collapse as well.

11. For example, in what one might take to be a certain importance of philosophical or scientific discourse, or an insufficient rigor in Bataille's exposition.

12. "If one defines real exterior objects, it is necessary to introduce at the same time the possibility for a relation of scientific appropriation" (11, 64).

13. J. Derrida, *L'Écriture et la Différence*, Paris, Seuil, 1967, 224.

14. The subjectivity advocated by Bataille proves itself to be incomprehensible to the immediacy challenged here.

15. Cf. J. Kristeva, op. cit.

16. Cf. J. Derrida, op. cit., 397.

17. S. Freud, *Gesammelte Werke*, Frankfurt a. M., Fischer, vol. XIV, p. 125.

18. Ibid., vol. I, p. 85.

19. Ibid., vol. XIV, p. 160.

20. R. Descartes, *Oeuvres Philosophiques*, Paris, Garnier, 1963, vol. I, 745.

21. Schelling, *Philosophie der Mythologie*, Darmstadt, 1966, vol. II, 360.

22. We are preparing, in a work now underway, a more developed elucidation of the relationship between philosophy and phantasm, a work that attempts to produce an inscription of Hegelian phenomenology in a phantasmatic weave, exceeding it on all sides, and whose scene would be the text of Georges Bataille.

# 10

# *Bataille and Communication:* Savoir, Non-Savoir, Glissement, Rire

*Joseph Libertson*

*It is human error to constantly translate the incompleteable character of the real, and, therefore, of truth. Knowledge which would measure up to its object, if this object were incompleteable, would develop in all directions. It would be, in its entirety, an immense architecture in demolition and under construction at the same time, barely coordinated, never from top to bottom. Once things are represented in this way, it is gratifying to be man.* Le Coupable

A multiplicity of dual oppositions structures Bataille's system. These oppositions are individually developed according to a stable, repeated configuration. The specificity of Bataille's categories, considered as a factor governing their substitutive invocations and multiple contexts, is perceptible only as a function of this specialized configuration of opposition. The purpose of this essay will be to describe certain structures of opposition found in Bataille's text, in the context of their relation to that zone of his system that may be termed "knowledge."

On a most basic level, the Bataillean opposition may be described as a confrontation of two terms which places in question the ontological status of the space designated by their proximity. The terms, whose immediate relation is given as non-toleration, will be further articulated by Bataille according to a model of compressed intimacy or contiguity whose violence will be described as a *mise en jeu*. This *mise en jeu* is simultaneously a *mise en question*. For instance, the terms "continuity" and "discontinuity" will designate a concept of ipseity whose radical closure is in question. The terms "prohibition" and "transgression" will describe, with their complement "dépense," a concept of "escape from closure" whose possibility or accomplishment is in question. The terms "savoir" and "non-savoir" will designate a mode of cognition whose status as a reification is in question. These oppositions, along with such others as "sacred/profane," "poetry/prosaism," "sovereignty/servility," "individual/ community," etc. will describe in their totality a meditation upon the ontological problem of an ineluctable closure which is always given as "in question." The category "uncertain closure," as it is applied to the general problem of subjectivity in Bataille's texts, will be given many names. The most basic, and the most often repeated, of these names will be "*la communication.*" This name will stand for a subjectivity defined (through a repeated structure of opposition) as a *mise en jeu.*

The procedure that develops the *mise en jeu* from a basic opposition has a characteristic form in Bataille's text. Its first term designates a form of closure, and is invoked as an ineluctable fact by Bataille. Invariably, its introduction is accompanied by a negative value judgment. Within the context of the basic ontological integrity of a subject, this term will be "separation," "isolation," or "discontinuity."

In a perceptual or intentional context, the term will be "homogeneity," or, later, "the profane vision" or simply "savoir." In the context of subjectivity, the term will be "prohibition." In every case, the term "closure" will have the status of a form of integrity whose ostensible non-violence is derived from an evacuation of a form of violence. Thus, discontinuity is invoked as an opposition to the violence of continuity, considered as a destructive economy of life and death. Prohibition is invoked as an opposition to transgression, considered as an excess that threatens a subject's integrity. Homogeneity is invoked as an evacuation of heterogeneity, considered as an affective function of subjectivity that would compromise the effectiveness of a cognitive form of reification. The primary term of non-violence or integrity is judged negatively, but is always invoked as an inevitability. No alternative will be offered for the closure which is "discontinuity": "nous sommes des êtres discontinus." The articulation of discontinuity with the concept of a struggle for survival will introduce the relation "utility," in the intentional context of homogeneity or knowledge, and no alternative will be offered for this relation: "notre seul possible est le travail."[1] The same articulation will establish the imposition of the *interdit* as an integral function of subjectivity, and again no alternative will be offered.[2] Closure, even though defined as contingent, is ineluctable.

The second term of the Bataillean opposition, whose initial predicate is "violence" or "escape from closure," will be invoked as a violence against which integrity is directed. This violence will be judged positively by Bataille, and will be accorded a relative primacy over integrity or closure, in two basic ways. In the first place, the primary term "opposition to violence" is shown to *presuppose* the term to which it is opposed. The reification of homogeneity will presuppose the heterogeneity it reduces.[3] Discontinuity, as a moment in an economy of life and death, will presuppose that economy in its basic definition as "individual life" or "mortal life."[4] Prohibition will presuppose transgression through its very opposition to the latter.[5] Secondly, and much more importantly, the term "non-violence" is shown to partake of, participate in, or be animated by the violence to which it is opposed. Discontinuity, which devotes its energy to a struggle for survival which opposes the violence of continuity, must derive that energy from life itself which is defined as a continuity of energy transcending the life span of the isolated being.[6] Prohibition, defined as a comportment that aggressively outlaws transgression, thereby participates in the violence of that very transgression.[7] Prohibition prepares transgression, calls to transgression as its complement and violent end. "The taboo is there to be violated."[8] Homogeneity, given as a reaction that banishes the affective possibility of heterogeneity, is further defined as itself an affective reaction, and thus ultimately an "intense" vision, a partial, incomplete reduction that is radically conditioned by the heterogeneity it reduces.[9] Thus, the force that opposes violence is *itself* shown to be a form of violence.

That the two terms of each Bataillean opposition condition each other to the point of mutual contamination does not lessen the force of their opposition. Discontinuity may be constituted by continuity, but must comport itself in radical opposition to the latter, because of the presence of survival as a necessity. Homogeneity may be defined as "heterogeneity-reduced," and prohibition may ultimately be defined as a form of transgression; but these terms are violently opposed, and the axis of their opposition is the relation "utility," whose own foundation is the problematic of discontinuity and survival. Indeed, the specificity of Bataille's dialectic is its sacrifice of a term of synthesis, in favor of a space of tense contamination in which two modes of being invade each other, contaminate each other, compromise each other, while paradoxically retaining the integrity of their opposition.

The space of this contamination is the actual locus of Bataillean "violence," and has a strict priority over the ostensible "violence" of the second term of each opposition (heterogeneity, continuity, transgression, etc.). The triumph of the initial term of violence over the term of closure or non-violence would be the synthesis Bataille will not accept. The refusal of such a synthesis will take, in his texts, the form of a series of terms that are invoked to designate a violent contamination. Within the early system "homogeneity/heterogeneity," this term was the model of "tension" or "intensity" which ultimately designated homogeneity. In the later context of discontinuity, several new terms will be derived for this purpose, chief among them the *glissement*, which describes a subjectivity trapped between two modes of being which constitute it simultaneously;[10] the *impossible*, which designates an ipseity whose closure is both absolute and uncertain;[11] *inachèvement* and the *effort d'autonomie*, which also designate this problematic closure;[12] the *mise en jeu*, etc. Within the context of prohibition and transgression, a simultaneity of fear and desire as motivations of both these comportments will be introduced as an index of their mutual conditioning:[13] the category "impossibility" will reappear to function as the "condition of possibility" of an effective or accomplished transgression; *dépense* will be carefully defined as a *mise en jeu* without resolution or destruction,[14] etc.

In Bataille's text, closure is always ineluctable, as is a violence that threatens and conditions closure. The intensity of a problematic closure is human violence, for Bataille: the violence of an isolation from which there is no escape, but to which an imminent and inescapable destruction is always intimately present. In the absence of a possibility of resolution to this problematic closure, the generalized concept of isolation and its "other" will have the character of an exigency and a paradox, in Bataille's text. This exigency will be called "la communication." Its multiple forms include a discontinuous being that *must* escape its limits, and which *cannot* escape its limits; a subject who *must* deny the constraint of the *interdit*, but whose transgression *cannot* be other than a maintenance of prohibition, upon the model of a *mise en jeu*; an intersubjectivity that *must* abolish alterity, but which *cannot* function as other than a mutual impenetrability. The paradigm for these and many other forms of "communication," in Bataille's thought, may be perceived in a discontinuity that *contains more than it can contain.*

### Dire la communication

It is in the failure of questioning that we laugh. (*Sur Nietzsche*)

Transgression is given by Bataille as an activity, upon the model of an exigency: a giving-in, a pre-voluntary form of *dépense* as *mise en jeu.* But it is also defined as a revelation or form of cognition. The knowledge that the *interdit* "is not imposed from outside" "appears to us in anguish, at the moment when it is still at work, and when we yield nevertheless to the impulse that it opposes" (E, 43). This awareness, to which all forms of cognition whose foundation and protection is the *interdit* itself would be blind ("science," "knowledge," the "profane world of things"), is an awareness of the fact of "communication" considered as *experience.* The problem of knowledge in Bataille's system is introduced by the question: "What may be said about the fact of communication, as it is apprehended in the act of transgression?" How may communication be thought, within the context of a *mise en jeu* of the *interdit?* Or, as Maurice Blanchot writes,

> (H)ow could thought, supposing that it were affirmed there for an instant, ever return from such an *atteinte* and bring back from it, if not a new knowledge, at least, from the distance of a memory, what would be required to maintain itself under its guardianship?[15]

Against the background of Bataille's categories, the problem posed by Blanchot is extremely complex. Since discontinuity is animated by continuity, and biologically constituted by (an intercellular and environmental) "communication," and since knowledge is initially defined as (a profane) non-communication, the question of knowledge becomes: How may communication's anti-communication communicate (itself)? The verbs "return," "bring back," and "guard" suggest an immediate escape-from and evacuation-of the violence of communication; and we know that an evacuation will make communication impossible. It appears that a knowledge of communication will of necessity be a reification; that discontinuity's project of transitively speaking (thinking) its own inner experience of communication can only be related to that experience as a falsification, a profane knowledge "gained." The only sign of escape from this apparent aporia may be perceived in Blanchot's phrase, "supposing that it were affirmed there for an instant." Does thought affirm itself originarily in the domain of communication? Is thought, like discontinuity or the *interdit*, an affirmation immediately solidary with the term it opposes? Is knowledge a communication that opposes communication?

### NON-SAVOIR AS IMMINENCE

Knowledge is always given by Bataille as subjectivity's inescapable proximity to the existent, a mediation as ineluctable as the instinct of an animal. Though the predicate of this mediation is "servility" in Bataille's text, the absence of an alternative to servility will always be stipulated by him. "Just as the summit is only inaccessible in the end, so decline is from the beginning unavoidable" (SN, 57). The structure that supplants such an alternative will be a conditioning articulation of the *interdit* and transgression, applied to knowledge. This articulation will have the name *non-savoir*.

> I have seen at the end that the idea of communication itself leaves naked—not knowing anything. Whatever it may be— failing a positive revelation within me, present at the extreme—I can provide it with neither a justification nor an end. I remain in intolerable non-knowledge....(IE, 12).

A thinking subject intends the "idea of communication," *within the context* of a reification defined as the primacy of the *interdit*, according to the model of an intense, paradoxical failure of reification—*non-savoir*— whose ontological predicates are "nudity" and "intolerability." This impossible failure of an ineluctable reification is founded by Bataille's prior descriptions of ipseity as a problematic closure. The following paragraph directly relates this closure to *non-savoir*, by means of a complex, strategic pseudo-diachrony:

> Anguish assumes the desire to communicate—that is, to lose myself—but not complete resolve: anguish is evidence of my fear of communicating, of losing myself. Anguish is given in the theme of knowledge itself: as *ipse*, through knowledge, I would like to be everything, therefore to communicate, to

lose myself, however to remain *ipse*. The subject (me, *ipse*) and the object (in part undefined, as long as it is not entirely grasped) are presented for communication, before it takes place. The subject wants to take hold of the object in order to possess it...but the subject can only lose itself: the nonsense of the will to know appears, nonsense of all possible, making *ipse* know that it is going to lose itself and knowledge with it. As long as *ipse* perseveres in its will to know and to be *ipse*, anguish lasts, but if *ipse* abandons itself and knowledge with it, if it gives itself up to non-knowledge in this abandon, then rapture begins. In rapture, my existence finds a sense once again, but the sense is referred immediately to *ipse*; it becomes my rapture, a rapture that I *ipse* possess, giving satisfaction to my will to be everything. As soon as I emerge from it, communication, the loss of myself cease; I have ceased to abandon myself—I remain there, but with a new knowledge.

    The movement begins again starting from there...(IE, 53,54)

Through the extreme difficulty of the above paragraph, Bataille's concept of knowledge asserts itself, profoundly conditioned by the logic of discontinuity and continuity as communication.

    (I) Anguish, the moment of coincidence of fear and desire, or fear conditioned and constituted by desire, characterized the moment of transgression. But it also characterized the moment of imposition of the *interdit*. Univocal as its function may be with regard to the sacred and profane worlds, the *interdit* is imposed in a manner that calls to the sacred world and has the status of an "accord" with the violence of the sacred. The *interdit* is imposed in order to be transgressed. It now becomes evident that the function of the knowing subject, under the *aegis* of the *interdit*, is conditioned by the same complexity. This subject, according to a formula repeatedly used by Bataille, "veut être tout"—"wants to be all"—wants to be the universe. But this desire is motivated by the discontinuous need to survive in an integral form: to remain *ipse*, identity to self, integrity.

    The <u>uncertain</u> opposition of autonomy to transcendence puts being in a <u>position which slips</u>: each being ipse—at the same time that it encloses itself in autonomy, and for this very

> reason—wants to become the whole of transcendence: in the
> first place, the whole of the composition from which it has
> begun....(IE, 85; I underline)

The "will for autonomy" (ibid.) becomes "will to be all," since the limit case of autonomy is the absence of alterity. To be all is to leave nothing outside. But the position hides a logical *glissement*. To want to be all is to want to abolish the limits of the things in the world. This abolition of exteriority is continuity: being without limits. To want to be all is to want to lose the limit of one's particularity, and at the same time to want to enclose all within the limit of one's particularity, to want to communicate utterly with the transcendence of All, but to do so by making of All the integral discontinuity of Self. The model according to which this primary objectality functions is that of anguish (fear–desire). Discontinuity fears the transcendence constitutive of objects (continuity) and wishes to engulf all objects with Self (discontinuity). But this wish to be transcendence implies loss of isolation (separation, discontinuity), hence a certain dissolution into continuity. To remain *ipse* is not commensurable with the desire to transcend isolation. But for the discontinuous being, the two desires cannot but coincide rigorously. Hence anguish is the originary relation of *ipse* to the object, and this relation immediately envisages discontinuity's limits.

> Human life is linked to lucidity—which is not given from
> without, acquired in opposite conditions—a lucidity comprised
> of unceasing contestations of itself, dissolving ultimately into
> laughter (into non-knowledge). Lucidity, contestation, cannot
> fail to attain the consciousness of limits—where the results
> vacillate, where being is the putting into question of oneself.
> (C, 347)

Lucidity is constituted by anguish, as contestation of Self in the desire to be All. Its results must "vacillate," since its project is paradoxical. The act that objectifies is simultaneously an antiobjectification, a contestation of ipseity. Denis Hollier aptly speaks of this moment in the context of a wordplay on "penser" and "dépenser": "Thought that awakens thus awakens against itself...Through awakening, thought retracts: it spends itself (se dépense[16]). Human life, then, "links itself" with lucidity, in the context of its "effort for autonomy." Lucidity "cannot fail" to become a consciousness of limits, since it was from the beginning such a consciousness: a *dé-penser*.

(2) "dissolving into laughter (into non-knowledge)": knowledge leads to the limit, because knowledge as a willful comportment is motivated by a relation to the limit. Just as the *interdit* called for transgression, through an intimate accord hidden within its illusory opposition, knowledge calls to *non-savoir* as its violent complement, its hidden condition, its silent end. "The non-essence of the will to know arises": it is not reason that motivates the desire to know—no more than it was reason that instituted the *interdit*. The desire to know is violent—is *violence*: the violence *of* discontinuity as *glissement*, as *mise en jeu*. It is an exigency conditioned by survival and by death. It leads, through its privileged illusion of objectivity and the possession of truth, inexorably to its limit. The experience of this limit is *non-savoir*. As the *rire*, it is the dissolution of lucidity. It is the greater violence toward which lucidity's violence (contestation) leads, as *dépense* and transgression were the greater violence approached by discontinuity and the *interdit*. The *rire* conditions the project of knowledge itself. The project is its own potential dissolution: an inevitable dissolution that becomes imminent dissolution.

*Angoisse* gives way to *ravissement*, as *savoir* leads to *non-savoir*. The phrase "non-sens de la volonté de savoir," "non-sens de tout possible" introduces this quasi-temporal, logical progression from violence to greater violence. Knowledge leads, through a certain apprehension of the illusory nature of the "possible," to a violent awareness of the fact that discontinuous man is the im-possible. The moment of *non-savoir* is equivalent to and solidary with the im-possible. The negative prefix of each term is the *condition* of the concept it modifies (contaminates). *Non-savoir* as the experience of limits is the condition for the dependent, temporary, illusory moment which is knowledge. The *impossible* is also the experience of limits ("which cannot avoid its limits, and cannot hold to them either" (C, 261)), and is the condition for the illusion of the possible (utility, survival, accomplishment).

Anguish gives way to *ravissement*, having prepared it, called for it, as the *interdit* gives way to transgression in paradoxical solidarity with it. What is the temporality of this progression?

(3) "letting *ipse* know that it will lose itself and knowledge with it": the phrase "will lose itself" indicates a movement toward loss that cannot be stopped, and a knowledge of the inexorability of that movement. This is the temporality of discontinuity: the temporality of the exigency as imminent violence, a violence that never arrives as pure destruction, but which forever threatens, in the form of the im-possible coincidence of destruction and limits. The last phrases of Bataille's demonstration, in

their feigned temporality of simple succession, mime, through the optic of the im-possible, this perpetual imminence:

> If *ipse* abandons itself and knowledge with it, if it gives itself up to non-knowledge in this abandon, then rapture begins. In rapture, my existence finds a sense once again, but the sense is referred immediately to *ipse*, it becomes *my* rapture…(IE, 53)

The im-possible is represented here by the verbs "to abandon itself" and "to give itself." *Not* to be able to abandon self is the being of discontinuity. But this being is also the experience of the perpetual *exigency* of that impossible abandon. The meaning recovered in *rapture*, which "aussitôt"—immediately, or "always already"—refers itself to *ipse*—is the impossible: impossible limits, impossible destruction. "Aussitôt" is precisely a prolongation, a continuation, of "will lose itself": incessant imminence combined with incessant closure. "As soon as I emerge from it, communication, the loss of myself cease; I have ceased to abandon myself…" (IE, 53). The return, the end of loss of self, the end of communication, is the end within the beginning of this movement of knowledge. The coincidence of the end and the beginning in a perpetual imminence is the *impossible*. *Rapture* always "commence," always begins, is always beginning, or about to begin. Its beginning is always deferred by the immediacy of its relation to *ipse*. The movement of this beginning may perhaps be described by a formula invoked by Michel Foucault (in "Préface à la transgression")[17] for the description of the relation of transgression to the Limit: a "spiral which no simple infraction can exhaust" (35). Or the "aussitôt" of *rapture's* relation to *ipse* may parallel Foucault's "line which…[aussitôt] closes up behind it in a wave of extremely short duration." In both cases, a kind of imminence describes the impossible, which is *non-savoir*: what Philippe Sollers has aptly called "logic and agony of logic".[18] *Non-savoir* is the impossible. *Ipse*, as discontinuity, is the impossible. *Savoir*, as "will to be everything," is the impossible. "The movement begins again starting from there…." Knowledge as the impossible is "an immense architecture being demolished and constructed at the same time" (C, 279). It is a movement that begins, ends, and begins again, even as it begins.

## LOGOS AND "INACHÈVEMENT"

The contemporary student of Bataille confronts a critical tradition whose appearance followed Bataille's death. This tradition, rooted in an awareness of the misunderstandings that classified Bataille as a "mystic" during his lifetime, has declared with urgent sympathy the immediate relevance of Bataille's thought to contemporary philosophical issues. Simultaneously, it has attributed to his categories a radical, violently subversive opposition to the categories of a "traditional" discourse. Such an attribution, while proximate to the exuberance of Bataille's texts (often to the extent of a disturbing mimicry of the philosopher's own procedures), creates serious difficulties in interpretation. One such difficulty is the imposition of a duality "tradition/subversion" which is governed by a nonproblematized reading of the opposition *"interdit/transgression."* According to this reading, the term "tradition" is understood with a univocity not characteristic of "prohibition" in Bataille's text. The term "subversion" is granted an efficacy never accorded to "transgression" by Bataille. Within this context, a historical epistemology, whose limits were clearly given as ineluctable by Bataille, has been called "consciousness comfortably established, trained, the heavy tranquility where the Occidental man has chosen to withdraw."[19] Elsewhere, it has been mistakenly said of a "communication" correctly perceived as the *exigency* of a "leaving of oneself," that "it is accomplished upon a backdrop of destruction and death," that it is an "access to the summit beyond all words" whose condition of possibility is a subject who would "reject all concern for the future...by devoting itself to pure expenditure."[20] Elsewhere still, it has been said that against the background of classical oppositions that were never "true oppositions, that is total and radical oppositions," "Bataille thinks the absolute opposition"; that this "radicalization" of the "instrument of metaphysics" renders it "an instrument of subversion, of destruction of traditional discourse."[21] The concept "dépense," read by the same author as an "unconditional loss," is termed "the sacrifice of the very meaning of restricted exchange, in a word the dilapidation of the proper, of cleanliness/ownness [propreté] and of property."[22] These statements, among others, refer to a thinker for whom "the putting into question remains characteristic of the isolated being" (C, 436); for whom *dépense* "does not kill but soils" (SN, 46); for whom "sacrifice is comprised of a mixture of anguish and frenzy" (PM, 106); for whom "the sacrificer is divine only with reticence" (ibid., 105); for whom "human nature cannot reject the concern for the future *as such*" (SN, 54). The notion of a defiant, efficacious subversion, applied to Bataille's theoretical practice, may not be coherently posited within the context of his multiple demonstrations that "the decline is from the outset inevitable" (SN, 57), that "our only possible is work" (C, 241). A perception of "communication" as exigency is not possible within the terms of a logic of accomplishment or efficacy. Such a logic cannot perceive the structure *"inachèvement"* which renders the *logos* itself an architecture whose demolition is its very construction; a transgression defined as a failure to destroy ipseity; *a non-savoir* repeatedly defined as a problematic reification. Such a logic, above all, cannot perceive the governing function of the *mise en jeu* which informs the following, fundamental Bataillean concept of philosophy in its historicity:

> Only philosophy takes on a strange dignity given that it assumes an infinite putting into question. It does not merit an unquestionable prestige because of its results, but only because it responds to man's aspiration requiring the putting into question of all that is...its entire value is in the absence of rest that it maintains. (C, 374–375)

## RIRE

Jacques Derrida, who sees traditional philosophy as a set of concepts whose historical primacy as a mode of thought allows no radical contemporary "escape," is a uniquely equipped reader of Bataille. His concept of "deconstruction" of Western "metaphysics" through a careful and interminable displacement of concepts manifests, in general, a deliberate indifference to any *telos* of revolutionary escape from classical "constraints." For Derrida, philosophy is its own deconstruction, and its exemplary tension results from its continual "solicitation" of its own limits. This rigorously sustained point of view forms the background of his brilliant essay on Bataille.[23] Nevertheless, there are problems in Derrida's reading of Bataille—problems that refer us once again to the violent structure of conditioning we have been discussing in Bataille's thought.

"From Restricted to General Economy: A Hegelianism without Reserve" is an analysis of Bataille's attitude toward Hegel, and concomitantly a discussion of the relation of Bataille's thought to traditional philosophy. Developing a painstaking articulation of Hegelian "mastery" and Bataillean *"souveraineté,"* Derrida describes what he sees as the effect of Bataille's central categories on the classical philosophical discourse. It is this sector of his essay that interests us here.

We have seen above (C, 347) that for Bataille, thought leads inevitably to *non-savoir*, which may take the form of a certain burst of laughter: "lucidity made of incessant contestations itself, ultimately dissolving in laughter (in non-knowledge)." This laughter represents the moment of the impossible and of communication, as we have seen. "Essentially, it is from *communication* that laughter proceeds" (C, 390). The structure of this laughter is that of transgression, the interior experience, or communication, in the human sense: the anguish of discontinuity at the extreme of the possible, faced with the limit, and aware that this situation is the impossible. Now, for Derrida, the *rire* is an interruption of the philosophical discourse. It originates with Bataille as reader of that discourse. The *rire* is the modality of Bataille's reading of philosophy. It is the functioning of his concepts as an interruption of philosophy's repression. In the case of Hegel, Bataille's *rire* appears when the Master's embrace of death is adequated with a philosophical need to continue living: "Burst of laughter from Bataille. Through a ruse of life, that is, of reason, life has thus stayed alive" (WD, 255). The *rire* interrupts the conservative, profane motivation of thought. But what is laughable? For Derrida's Bataille,

> What is laughable, is the submission to the self-evidence of meaning, to the force of this imperative: that there must be meaning, that nothing must be definitively lost in death, or further, that death should receive the signification of "abstract negativity," that a work must always be possible which, because it defers enjoyment, confers meaning, seriousness, and truth upon the "putting at stake." This submission is the essence and element of philosophy...(WD, 256–257)

We have seen the imperative of this submission before: it is the imperative of survival, the necessity that founds the profane world. However, we have also seen that this imperative takes its energy from, and is utterly conditioned by, the very *desire* which is its supposed opposite: continuity, the desire for a questioning with no answer, desire for violent loss. This is "the *strength* of this imperative." Derrida, who is thinking in terms of an opposition between mastery and sovereignty, does not bring into play this desire at the heart of knowledge's "submission"; but at the same time, in the context of servility, his terminology refers to it, in the phrase, "confers meaning, seriousness and truth upon the *putting at stake*." A certain awareness of the *putting at stake*, of the infinite contestation which is its own constitution, rests at the heart of knowledge. The *putting at stake* (and we note here the problematic passive-active transitivity of anguish) *precedes*, logically, the conferring of meaning. What Derrida describes in the context of submission is this precedence of the *putting at stake*, a precedence which "aussitiôt"—immediately or "always

already"—conditions and problematizes the transitivity of the verb
"confer." Our reading of Bataille has shown us that this transitivity is
already violent, already conditioned by desire, already a *putting at stake*
even as it seems to be the opposite. The conferring of meaning and seriousness is already the affirmation of contestation. [Derrida explicitly maintains this point of view in the context of his declaration that "Bataille took
Hegel and absolute knowledge seriously" (WD, 253). Bataille's *rire*, even
in its derision, takes its force from the taking-seriously of what it solicits.
We are here questioning the absence of this problematic on the side of
Hegelian mastery.] This structure enables us to see the difficulty of
Derrida's last sentence, "This submission is the essence and the element of
philosophy," in relation to Bataille's insistence that "it responds to man's
aspiration requiring the putting into question of all that is," and that "its
entire value is in the absence of rest that it maintains" (C, 374–375). In
Bataille's eyes, the *rire* would not be an interruption of the servility of
knowledge, but rather an anguish at the heart of that servility, an anguish
that immediately compromises the very term of servility. Again, in the
temporality of discontinuity, the *rire* would not supervene, but would
condition submission from the beginning. Philosophy would be, not only
the *risible*, but the *rire* itself. "Laughter is thought" (EI, 213). "It is in the
failure of questioning that we laugh" (SN, 63). Can this mutual conditioning
be suspended momentarily, for the sake of argument, on the grounds that
the opposition is more pertinent than the solidarity of the terms? Bataille's
system does not allow us to think so, and neither do the resonances of
Derrida's terms. To "the strength of that imperative" may be justly added
another phrase: "that there must always be possible a work that, because it
defers enjoyment, confers meaning…" The reader of this formula can
hardly fail to be reminded of transgression which "maintains the taboo in
order to take pleasure in it," nor can he fail to perceive the preparation of
transgression inherent in work's deferring of pleasure—in a word, the transgression inherent in work.

  This problematic of conditioning, which erodes the concept of
*souveraineté* as an opposition to the (Hegelian) discourse of reason,
causes a hesitation in Derrida's positing of the *rire* as interruption; a hesitation that ends in an open contradiction, as a comparison of the two
following quotations demonstrates:

> <u>Far from interrupting</u> dialectics, history, and the movement of
> meaning, sovereignty provides the economy of reason with its
> element, its milieu, its unlimiting boundaries of non-sense.
> (WD, 260–261)

> In sacrificing meaning, sovereignty submerges the possibility of discourse: <u>not simply by means of an interruption</u>, a caesura, or an interior wounding of discourse (an abstract negativity), but, <u>through such an opening</u>, by means of an irruption suddenly uncovering the limit of discourse and the beyond of absolute knowledge. (WD, 261, I underline)

The correctness of Derrida's first sentence is exactly the condition of the wrongness of the second. Sovereignty (laughter, transgression, communication: the impossible) does not interrupt the dialectic; in "giving it its element," sovereignty silently conditions and takes part in the constitution of the dialectic. Sovereignty is far more than its difference with regard to mastery: it is an exigency so pervasive that, beyond the pseudo-opposition of its status as "not-mastery," it is *part of* mastery. Derrida's radical separation of the two concepts causes the "hyperbole" of the second sentence, an exaggeration of the power and efficacy of sovereignty which in turn causes an almost symmetrical misuse of every term involved: (1) Sovereignty does not sacrifice meaning, but constitutes it in its violence, as the desire inherent in *savoir*, (2) Sovereignty does not destroy the possibility of the discourse of reason: it contributes integrally to that very possibility, which is at the same time violence, the *impossible* of reason; (3) Sovereignty is not an interruption, or an eruption of the discovery of the limit, but the constant, silent awareness of the limit which constitutes discourse—an awareness that occupies the movement of reason itself.

This contradictory problematic of interruption is accompanied, throughout Derrida's essay, by a contradictory hesitation with regard to the problem of loss, sacrifice, or consumation of meaning. Here, as elsewhere in the text of contemporary Bataille studies, the problem concerns the violent efficacy of Bataille's thought, considered as a subversive strategy. Derrida writes, at one point:

> Sovereignty must still sacrifice [mastery] and, thus, the presentation of the meaning of death. For meaning, when lost to discourse, is absolutely destroyed and consumed. (WD, 261)

And several pages later:

> Sovereignty is the impossible, therefore it is not, it is—Bataille writes this word in italics—"this loss." The writing of sovereignty places discourse in relation to absolute non-discourse.

Like general economy, it is not the loss of meaning, but, as
we have just read, the "relation to this loss of meaning."
(WD, 270)

Is sovereignty the sacrifice of meaning as absolute destruction, or is it the
*impossible*, a certain incessant *relation* to the (impossible or imminent)
destruction of meaning? Jacques Derrida hesitates between the two alternatives, but Bataille's text makes clear that only the second is an option. The
sacrifice of meaning is precisely the experience of the *impossibility* of the
destruction of meaning, exactly as the sacrifice of a human being, for the
sacrificer, is the experience of the impossibility of destroying ipseity.
Derrida's second sentence resolves the difficulty of his first sentence.
Sovereignty is precisely a perpetual *relation* to the loss of meaning—a loss
that never occurs—within the project of conferring meaning itself—a
project that contains, and is in a sense aware of, that relation. The relation
of knowledge to its own greatest danger—loss of meaning—within knowledge itself—is the impossible. Derrida has understood the importance of
the impossible as a conditioning factor in Bataille's thought, but he has not
appreciated the immense extent of the impossible's influence on all the
major moments of Bataille's demonstrations. Derrida sees that the impossible conditions sovereignty, but he does not appear to realize that it conditions knowledge as well. It may be that this prior condition escapes him
because he is committed to the idea of an adversary relation between
Bataille and "traditional" thought, in which Bataille's position is that of the
subvertor of a repressive structure. How could such a formulation perceive
knowledge itself as the impossible?

Concomitant to this problem is another contradiction. Derrida notes
that "one could even abstract from Bataille's writing an entire zone
throughout which sovereignty remains inside a classical philosophy of the
*subject*, and above all, inside the *voluntarism* which Heidegger has
shown still to be confused, in Hegel and Nietzsche, with the essence of
metaphysics" (WD, 267). But Derrida's own vision of the *rire* and of
*souveraineté* as subversions requires him to read Bataille precisely on this
level he claims to reject, as the following sentence shows:
"[Mastery]…becomes sovereign when it ceases to fear failure and is lost as
the absolute victim of its own sacrifice" (WD, 265). The radical voluntarism of this formula is exactly the opposite of sovereignty as we have
seen it in Bataille's text. The specificity of the sacrifice is, firstly, that the
subject does *not* stop fearing failure—("sacrifice is comprised of a mixture
of anguish and frenzy" (PM, 106), and, secondly, that the sacrificer does

not, cannot lose himself as the victim of the sacrifice. The entire weight of the sacrifice and of sovereignty consists in their status as pre-voluntary conditions, problematizations of the concept of will.

## GLISSEMENT

The voluntarism of a derisive subversion of tradition's submission is repeated by a final difficulty in Derrida's text. This difficulty centers on his reading of the *glissement* in Bataille, and concerns language, one of the major zones of "communication" in Bataille's system. The *glissement*, initially a description of dis-continuity itself (in conjunction with such terms as *inachèvement, impossible, effort d'autonomie*), and in general the sign for the concept "problematic closure" in Bataille's text, is read by Derrida as the context of a strategic subversion of the integrity of an "old language":

> Since it is a certain sliding that is in question, as we have seen, what must be found, no less than the word, is the point, the place in a pattern at which a word drawn from the old language will start, by virtue of having been placed there and by virtue of having received such an impulsion, to slide and to make the entire discourse slide. A certain strategic twist must be imprinted upon language; and this strategic twist, with a violent and sliding, furtive movement must inflect the old corpus in order to relate its syntax and its lexicon to major silence. (WD, 264)

The strategic placing of words allows the *glissement* to follow its own violent course toward the destruction of concepts and meaning:

> This writing...folds itself in order to link up with classical concepts—insofar as they are inevitable...in such a way that these concepts, through a certain twist, apparently obey their habitual laws; but they do so while relating themselves, at a certain point, to the moment of sovereignty, to the absolute loss of their meaning, to expenditure without reserve, to what can no longer even be called negativity or loss of meaning except on its philosophical side; thus they relate themselves to a nonmeaning which is beyond absolute meaning, beyond the closure or the horizon of absolute knowledge. (WD, 267-268)

Ultimately, the "destruction of discourse" is "an endless and baseless substitution whose only rule is the sovereign affirmation of the play outside meaning," "a kind of potlach of signs that burns, consumes, and wastes words in the gay affirmation of death: a sacrifice and a challenge" (WD, 274).

The model of the "*glissement calculé*," robbing concepts of their meaning, destroying by incessant substitution the discourse itself, is significantly resumed by an apparently casual simile which is in reality essential: "a kind of potlach of signs." The voluntarism of Derrida's formulations does indeed rejoin that of potlatch, but in a way that endangers his entire argument. For the specificity of potlatch in Bataille's system is its subordination of destruction (of goods, and even of human beings) to an acquisition of societal *rank*. A chief who destroys goods in the name of another is defying his rival in order to achieve an advantage over him. "(W)hat is appropriated in destruction is the prestige that it gives to the (individual or group) destroyer, which he acquires as a good and which determines his rank" (PM, 118). Potlatch is a ritual that, while closely similar to the violence of the sacrifice, is nevertheless fundamentally compromised by its desire for gain—what Bataille calls its "mobilization of the useless." This compromise is the result of the voluntarism of potlatch. It superimposes a calculation on what cannot be calculated: the glissement which constitutes the violence of the sacrifice. Derrida's words are well chosen: "a sacrifice and a challenge."

Derrida, while not explicitly suggesting that Bataille "makes words slide," nevertheless superimposes, in his concept of a "sovereign writing," the mastery of the subject over the uncertainty of language, in formulas like "imprint upon language," "strategic twist," and "calculated slippage." This last, in the system of Bataille's categories, is not an option. The *glissement* is very precisely that which cannot be calculated. It is the end of calculation, the violence of calculation's impossibility. This points up the hidden truth of Derrida's argument, a truth so often explicitly stated in Derrida's work, but strangely latent in his reading of Bataille. The fact that a word "drawn from the old language" "begins to slide," "and to make the entire discourse slide," is, ultimately, what *already* happens in the discourse of reason. The fact that the classical concepts, while appearing to function predictably, relate themselves "at a certain point to the moment of sovereignty, to the absolute loss of their meaning" is, according to the temporal model of savoir and *non-savoir*, the very nature of the discourse of reason itself. The "destruction of discourse" in the form, among others, of "an endless and baseless substitution," *is* the discourse. The discourse is its own interminably imminent destruction, as we have seen Bataille insist. The *glissement* of a *mot glissant* is the movement of *meaning* itself.

Hidden within a paragraph of Derrida's introduction to his reading of Bataille is an exemplary, Bataillean vision of philosophy itself:

> (T)he <u>impossible</u> meditated by Bataille will always have this form: how, after having exhausted the discourse of philosophy, can one inscribe in the lexicon and syntax of a language, our language, which was also the language of philosophy, that which nevertheless exceeds the opposition of concepts governed by this communal logic? Necessary and impossible, this excess had to fold discourse into strange shapes. (WD, 252–253)

How may philosophy, after having "always already" exhausted the resources of its questions in its incessant movement toward the closure of utility (the profane world), inscribe (to control again) the force of those contestations in its profane language? How may communication, after having exhausted its force in the struggle to silence itself, resuscitate that force in order to silence it again? The movement of this excess within a continual closure is philosophy itself, and the strangely contorted discourse Derrida refers to is the *logos*. "Necessary and impossible": these words describe, for Bataille, the imperative of reason itself. The *logos* is the impossible.

## COMMUNICATION

> In my view nothing is more embarrassing than success. (*Le Coupable*)

An underestimation of the violence of thought in its historicity, combined with a strategic, highly sympathetic overestimation of the violent efficacy of Bataille's thought, falsifies in Jacques Derrida's essay the central tension in Bataille's system. The terms of Bataille's oppositions condition each other so intimately that pure servility, and pure destruction, are radically compromised. Equally compromised is the will of the thinking subject, since the conditions of knowledge and *non-savoir* are pre-voluntary. The *glissement* knows no calculation; it *captivates*: "as long as this slipping away wasn't graspable, it was captivating; it was so to the ultimate degree of tension" (IE, 126). It is not a voluntary subversion that interests Bataille. It is rather the dissolution of will in a ubiquitous, imminent subversion at the tense center of thought itself. The form of this perpetual imminence, too often misunderstood by Bataille's readers, is a *logos* conceived as *communication*:

> What one doesn't usually see while speaking: that discourse, even negating its own value, doesn't assume only him who engages in it, but him who listens to it...I find in myself nothing, which is not even more than myself, at the disposal of my fellow being. And this movement of my thought which flees from me—not only can I not avoid it, but there is no moment so secret that it doesn't animate me. Thus I speak— everything in me gives itself to others. (IE, 128–129)

"Ma pensée qui me fuit"—my thought which flees me—and "everything in me gives itself to others"—these are the essential characteristics of the *logos* for Bataille. Passivity at the seat of will, loss in the heart of isolation, paradoxical generosity beyond survival.

What is the thinker's exigency, finally, for Bataille himself? We could agree with Jacques Derrida's formulation of the *impossible* as a project of inscription of excess within a philosophical language, as long as we inter- preted that formulation in Bataillean terms, for philosophy itself. But we cannot agree with its voluntarism, if it applies to Bataille. For Bataille's ulti- mate stance before the dilemma of thought is not a project, but an anguished, entirely ambiguous *question*:

> Will I let my thought slowly—slyly, and tricking as little as possible—mingle with silence? (C, 242)

"Slyly, *and* tricking as little as possible"—the thinker's exigency is a loss beyond calculation, situated in the heart of calculation itself. If the *logos* is an edifice whose demolition is its very architecture, the communication of a subject whose dissolution is the condition of his very integrity, then we may prefer to Derrida's logic of inscription this formula by Michel Foucault:

> Would it be of any help, in any case, to argue...that we must find a language for the transgressive which would be what dialectics was, in an earlier time, for contradiction? Our efforts

are undoubtedly better spent in trying to speak of this experience and in making it speak from the depths where language
fails, from precisely the place where words fail it, where the
subject who speaks has just vanished...." (LCP, 40)

But our preference for Foucault's formula is predicated on an underlining
of the verbs "to try" and "to make speak," with their ultimate imperative
movement; and on an understanding that the vanishing subject speaks as
he vanishes, in an unending imminence which is that of Bataille's
question.*

* The attempt to delimit a critical tradition or tendency, of recent birth and
of complex proportions, requires a concomitant attempt to take a distance
from the procedures of that tendency. Such an exigency is integral to the
project of the above essay and may be perceived in the outward gravity of
its discursive procedures. The author has chosen to avoid, in his argument,
a certain exuberance characteristic of many Bataille studies. He has done
so in accordance with the requirements of his questions. These questions
point to a sector of the Bataillean text that, in his opinion, has remained
opaque to a contemporary critical tendency. The gravity of their elaboration, rooted in a concern for intelligibility, is also intended as the movement
of an exuberance of a different kind.

## NOTES

1. *Le Coupable* (Gallimard, 1944), 241. References to this book, as well as references
to *Sur Nietzsche* (1945), and "La Structure psychologique du fascisme" (1933–1934), will
follow the pagination of volumes I, V, and VI of Bataille's *Oeuvres complètes* (Gallimard,
1969–1973). [Editor's note: I have used my translation of *L'Expérience intérieure* for this
article. Pagination from this text refers to *Inner Experience*, trans. L. Boldt, Albany: SUNY
Press, 1988). The following abbreviations will be used: C (*Le Coupable*); IE (*Inner
Experience*); SN (*Sur Nietzsche*); E (*L'Erotisme*, 10/18, 1970); PM (*La Part maudite*, Minuit
"Points," 1967); LM (*La Littérature et le mal*, Gallimard "Idées," 1972).]
   2. E, 47; LM, 240.
   3. "La Structure psychologique...," I, 343–344.
   4. PM, 62.
   5. LM, 240; E, 34.
   6. PM, 62.
   7. E, 71; E, 76.
   8. E, 71.
   9. "La Structure psychologique...," I, 359.
   10. IE, 111.
   11. C, 241, 261.

12. C, 263, 266, 376.

13. E, 20, 45–46, 51, 75–76; SN, 54; PM, 105–106, etc.

14. PM, 76; E, 23, etc.

15. "L'Expérience-limite," *NRF.* 118 (août 1962), 591.

16. D. Hollier, "Le Matérialisme dualiste de Georges Bataille," *Tel Quel* 25, 43.

17. M. Foucault, "Préface à la transgression," *Critique* 195–196, 1963, 754–755.

18. P. Sollers, "De Grandes irrégularités du langage," *Critique* 195–196, 796.

19. P. Sollers, "Le Toit," *L'Ecriture et l'expérience des limites*, Seuil, 1968, 106.

20. J-M Rey, "La Mise en jeu," *L'Arc* 32, 1967, 21.

21. R. Gasché, "L'Avorton de la pensée," *L'Arc* 44, 1971, 25.

22. Ibid., 11.

23. J. Derrida, *Writing and Difference*, trans. A. Bass (Chicago: University of Chicago Press, 1978) 251–278.

# IV. Inner Experience and the Subject

# 11

# Bataille's Erotic Writings and the Return of the Subject

**Paul Smith**

A couple of years after the appearance of Levi-Strauss' *Structures élémentaires de la parenté* in 1949, Georges Bataille began to work on his "*L'histoire de l'érotisme*," an attempt to provide the theoretical background and justification for his erotic writings.[1] "L'histoire de l'érotisme" makes extensive use of Levi-Strauss' work, perhaps because this first document of structuralist thought was readily discernible for its propinquity to Hegel's philosophy and so was assimilable to Bataille's thought at that time. But attractive and relevant as Levi-Strauss' work might have been to Bataille, he had some reservations about the dialectic between nature and culture that marks the foundations of structuralism; it is in relation to the character of the erotic and of eroticism in general that Bataille takes up the challenge of such a dialectic.

For Bataille the erotic is specifically the point of tension between the animal body and the civilized body; man's erotic drives constitute a kind of wedge driven between the opposing demands of animality and humanity. This conception of the place of the erotic, exhaustively worked by de Sade, is hardly very original, but it nonetheless pervades Bataille's work on eroticism and his erotic writings. By dint of existing between nature and culture, erotic energy is, according to Bataille, not part of that dialectic which governs human society. It therefore represents the area of transgression available to each individual subject within the structures of society. Indeed, Bataille even suggests that a definition of eroticism can be arrived at by considering it as the desire to change any given condition: it is "a revolt, a refusal of the proposed condition"[2] and makes eroticism the point of instability in the nature/culture opposition.

Levi-Strauss had set the tone for all future structuralist thought by stressing the rigid, continual, and exclusive imbrication of nature and culture. What is most notably excluded because of this dialectic is any but the most abstract and summary recognition of the life of the individual—thus structuralism's claim to be announcing the death of man. The effect of the structuralist commitment is to see the individual as an abstract bridge between the natural and the cultural. Some later structuralist thinkers like Kristeva or Lacan have questioned this abstraction of the life of the individual; Bataille, however, seems to have been aware of its dangers from the beginning. He assumes that the nature/culture distinction disregards the individual's inner life, or "the inner experience which men communally have"[3] and about which he wrote at length.[4] This interior experience therefore acts as the locus for a battle against the agents of systematic thought[5] who turn the individual into "a lie"[6] by establishing him as a legalistic and fixed entity.

At the time of writing *L'histoire de l'érotisme*, Bataille was caught on the wave of an intellectual life that was beginning to meld phenomenology, traditional philosophy, and structuralism. At that time his concern with the individual subject was somewhat unorthodox. Thus it is that we find that many of Bataille's comments about the paradoxical (that is to say, anti-orthodox) nature of the individual's actual lived experience are confined to footnotes, *brouillons*, *ébauches*, and *annexes*. However in the erotic writing itself his conviction that the erotic is the privileged agent of the interior life is quite apparent. The erotic explicitly disrupts the abstract or legalistic wholeness, the assumed plenitude of the individual. The erotic dismantles the controlled and fixed existence of any notion of the completeness of the individual. For example, the anticipatory boudoir scenes of *Divinus Deus* describe "a bottle [that] was waiting in a bucket and *my face was deformed* in the crystal of the glasses."[7] The plenary presentation of the subject is thus shattered by the transgressive experience of the erotic. The logical end point of this alteration in the representation of the subject is brought about in the mention of that urge familiar to all readers of Bataille—the urge for death or disappearance within the passes of the erotic. Charlotte d'Ingerville in *Divinus Deus*, for example, expresses her erotic urge as the desire to "be nothing more than a dust that no-one would recognize" and Pierre remarks in turn that "she seemed determined to disappear."[8] All the bodily effluxes that are essential aspects of sexuality in Bataille's texts point in the same direction. They represent the desire to empty the body of its wholeness. Pierre's mother finds erotic release in rolling around in the woods and pissing in her clothes and on the ground. When Charlotte describes a similar experience it is for her "as if life abandoned her."[9] In the opening scenes of *Le Bleu du Ciel*, the odors of those bodily effluxes are specifically the odor of death, the corrupted body, and they emanate from the dilapidated and failing body of Dirty.[10]

On one level this exhaustion of the body is obviously part of Bataille's whole paradoxical project of expressing the mystical vitality of the interior life: the body functions through *aphanisis*, making toward the desired transcendence of rational existence. On another level, however, it can be taken as a profoundly indicative metaphor of Bataille's relation to the structuralists. The destruction of the notion of the fixed subject has become crucial to later structuralists or 'post-structuralists' and I dare say that many of the researches now being carried out in relation to the subject will return to Bataille for indicators. The trend has already been started by the late Roland Barthes. His theory of the orgasmic text that disrupts our fixed view of the subject's plenitude led him to express in his last book, *La Chambre Claire*, his own view of the interior life. For him it is specifically a life outside of all intellectual systemization—especially of the structuralist variety.[11] Leaning heavily on both Bataille and Barthes is the work of Jean Louis Schefer which talks of "the interior body," that part of our lived existence upon which our paradoxical experiences are marked.[12] These writers and others like Jean Francois Lyotard or Luce Irigaray have taken up Bataille's hint that theoretical constructions of the subject such as those which punctuate the history of structuralism actually concern no one (that is, they can serve no individual lived experience). Coming after an era of heavily systematized thinking these writers are exploring Bataille's notion that "man's only truth, glimpsed at last, is to be a supplication without response"[13] or, at least, a supplication to which an abstract theory of the subject cannot respond.

## NOTES

1. "L'histoire de l'érotisme," *Oeuvres Complètes* t. VIII. Paris, 1976, is an unfinished text, arising out of Bataille's notes for *La Phénoménologie Erotique*. It provides the elements for the complete work, *L'Erotisme*, Paris, 1957. The textual editors reproduce

Bataille's notes for *La Phénoménologie Erotique*, made in 1939. Most of the material of those notes is present in the 1951 "L'histoire de l'érotisme" but Levi-Strauss is, obviously, a new introduction to the 1951 text. In *L'Erotisme* Bataille has re-written his thoughts on Levi-Strauss to produce a new chapter, "L'énigme de l'inceste," 219-244.

    2. *Oeuvres Complètes*, t.VIII, 66.

    3. *Oeuvres Complètes*, t.IV, Paris, 1971, 396.

    4. "L'expérience intérieure" is the title of an essay to be found in *Oeuvres Complètes*, t.V, 7–189, and the phrase is a continual motif throughout Bataille's writings.

    5. See for example Althusser's *Lenin and Philosophy and other essays*, London, 1971, and Levi-Strauss's *Anthropologie Structurale*, Paris, 1958. A rigorous and provocative critique of structuralist notions of the subject can be found in Stephen Heath's excellent article, "The Turn of the Subject," *Ciné-Tracts*, no. 8., 32–48.

    6. *Oeuvres Complètes*, t.VIII, 497.

    7. *Oeuvres Complètes*, t.IV, 300, my italics.

    8. Ibid., 284.

    9. Ibid., 290.

    10. *Oeuvres Complètes*, t.III, Paris, 1911, 385–391.

    11. See especially Barthes's *Le Plaisir du Texte*, Paris, 1973, and *La Chambre Claire*, Paris, 1980. See, too, my forthcoming article in *Sub-Stance*, "We Always Fail—Roland Barthes' Last Writings."

    12. A good introduction to Schefer's work and its peculiarities is *L'Homme ordinaire du cinéma*, Paris, 1980.

    13. *Oeuvres Complètes*, t.V, Paris, 1973, 25.

# Bataille, Experience and Practice

**Julia Kristeva**

> At one time it increased so as to be a single One out of
> Many; at another time again it grew apart so as to be Many
> out of One.  Empedocles
> *Experience, its authority, its method cannot be distin-*
> *guished from contestation.*  Bataille

It is clear today, at a time when our culture is no longer the only center of the world, that since the bourgeois Revolution, the essential adventure of literature has been to take up again, dissolve, and displace Christian ideology and the art that is inseparable from it.  In general, this attempt consists of stressing the moment of negation contained in Christianity, but a moment that is sublimated when Christianity *unites* the subject with supreme theological authority; it consists of stressing rupture, dissolution, and death by means of a problematic that is at once funereal, macabre, and "decadent" (as one will say at the end of the twenty-first century while investing this term with the pride of those who undermine) or else by means of a dissolution of the fabric of language itself—the last guarantee of unity.  All of this work remains, however, the reverse side of monotheistic (humanistic, substantialist, or directly transcendental) authority—this side of it, as long as the unity that this work opposes is suddenly, and by a gesture of repression, dismissed, not seen, set aside. Negativity's attack on Christian ideology and art continues, but it does not acknowledge that a *thetic moment, a stasis,* an ephemeral pause is the condition for its renewal. As if this affirmative moment frightened that negativity, and as if, rather than attacking this affirmative moment, this negativity preferred to leave it in abeyance, *intact,* elsewhere, for others.

## THE THETIC MOMENT OF PROCESS {PROCÈS]

One will understand how a literature built upon this principle finds refuge in a tomblike enclosure, one of dissolution and death; the only thetic moments that it can represent are merely detached substances, isolated from the process of fragmentation, and *fetishes,* since this race towards dislocation will pause only for desire centered upon an object that is either a bodily fragment or a fragment of language. The fetishization of the fragmented body or of verbal components, indeed of the "text," is thus the reverse side, an accomplice to the negativism that attacks the unity of the subject without emerging from it in natural and social process [*procès*].

This negativism only remains intra-subjective and intra-unitary, the reverse side of the monology (and the mono-theism) to which it adheres and imagines it can fight, as long as it is unable to postulate—in order to expend—the *affirmative* moment in the process creating meaning at all levels of the semiotic system, in other words in the *economy of the subject* and in the *content* of the message (in its historical, ideological meaning).

Now to side-step this affirmative moment amounts to side-stepping the possibility *of a meaning,* that is, of a logic, of a knowledge and, by extension, of a practice inasmuch as the meaning, the logic, and the practice imply *the moment* of pause. Consequently, the texts that obey this movement [those that side-step] are no longer art in the sense of a practice that guarantees that subjects are put in contact or "communicate" (according to Bataille)—subjects that, in the presence of an (ideological) meaning and the fading of this meaning, find themselves to be at once universal and next to nothing, in a "probability" (writes Bataille) of reciprocal relations that form the unstable and fragile coherence of a free social group.

By side-stepping the thetic phase of the subject and the affirmation of a meaning, of a knowledge, of an ideology to be dissolved, negativist and fetishist texts are therefore doomed to abandon that function of art which is to create a "communal probability." If they thus assume for themselves the right and the advantage of unveiling unspoken logic and of debunking the inner workings of bourgeois Christian art having henceforth become stagnant, frozen, and repetitive, such modernist texts abdicate the relationship with others, with the group, with the social community. Since negativism and fetishism are subjective and necessarily elitist, they address themselves to the closed *self*, but if they do enunciate objective laws that the self has repressed, they don't cause it to cross the threshold of its relationship to the group. Now it is precisely on this threshold that metaphysics is reconstituted, that the unity fought against is reinstated and that the subjects, lucid though they may have become about their internal mechanism (thanks to psychoanalysis and the negative-fetishist avant-garde), become opaque once again, servants of oppressive laws, of technical reproduction, and of positivist saturation right to social conformism.

Within the perspective of the avant-garde literary adventure, Bataille is perhaps the only one, with Joyce, not to have modestly or disdainfully renounced this thetic moment of the process producing meaning that creates the subject as subject of knowledge and as social subject. In our opinion, Bataille's work seems to revolve around this precise moment. It is following the completion of Christianity, and its affirmative moments, postulating the subject and knowledge, thus creating an opening for society as well as modern philosophy—that Bataille affirms a new practice. His approach is thus situated vis-à-vis the closure of Christian idealism, rather than its ignorance or its avoidance. If he finds the authoritative clarification of this idealism in Hegel's work, he attacks it based on Hegel and by following the same path in reverse. Hegel suppresses negativity by means of the concept and absolute knowledge. Bataille rediscovers negativity in that repressed moment of absolute knowledge that is immediate experience.

He rehabilitates the tangible and human activity of the *self* but only in order to denounce the illusions it fosters. He insists upon the unity of the human spirit,[1] but in order to rediscover the sacrifice therein and the "self—for death." He proclaims love and fusion, but for their relatedness to death.

One can resume the movement of this negativity that says "yes," or the movement of this "yes" open to negativity in the following way: "I" who speak, speak from within logic and therefore can only affirm. Let us remember Frege's demonstration, that there can be no negative judgment.[2] But this discursive affirmation is laid out upon a flux of negativity that exceeds it and that is extra-discursive, a current of nature and society (that of others) where the "self" is only vertigo, "hearth," "dance," where knowledge is not but where the heterogeneous is unleashed. The problem is to *speak*, thus to *affirm*, this pre-discursive materiality; to bring the awakening and the lucidity of the speaking subject to the movement preceding discourse and the subject; to cause this heterogeneity to pass over to a problematic community is the only possible link through which the community can become constituted, to cause the subject to submit to that flux, empty of intellectual content, that exceeds it, but nonetheless requires it.

The affirmation necessitates a "convergence," a "coordination," a "cohesion," a "coherent whole": "I place myself in such a perspective that I perceive these opposite possibilities as becoming coordinated. I don't attempt to reduce them, but I make every effort to grasp, beyond each possibility negating another, an ultimate possibility of con-vergence."[3] "I have sacrificed everything in the search for a point of view from which the unity of the human spirit may emerge."[4] "I wanted nothing other than to search for cohesion within the diversity of described phenomena."[5]

Now the coherent, unary subject is put into play by a violent hetero-geneity—the material force that breaks its coherence. "A character of dance and of decomposing agility…situated this flame 'outside of me.' And as everything mingles in a dance, so there was nothing which didn't go there to become consumed. I was thrown into this hearth, nothing remained of me but this hearth. In its entirety, the hearth itself was a streaming outside of me."[6]

To know this "streaming outside of the self," to affirm this "flame," is impossible for the "absolute knowledge" that constitutes itself precisely because heterogeneity is assumed in an opaque atomic subject. Hegel's dreariness stems from the fact that he forgets this heterogeneity, that he buries himself in absolute knowledge and in activity (work), in "balance and harmony," in other words in the reconstitution of God: "Hegel, at the moment when the system closed, believed himself for two years to be going mad: perhaps he was afraid of accepting evil—which the system justifies and renders necessary…perhaps even his various bouts of sadness took shape in the more profound horror of being God."[7]

Thus one doesn't have to resort to absolute knowledge in order to bear witness to heterogeneity exceeding the discursive subject. All systematicity, therefore all knowledge, is incapable of grasping the move-ment of this excess, of witnessing its arbitrariness. Absolute knowledge itself, while it is not a systematizing *techné*, to the extent that it abstracts the unity of the system (and thus of the subject) and tends to justify and thus include the heterogeneous in this unity, is a limit to be crossed. It is part of the mysticism that Bataille traverses precisely in order to pass to the other side. Mysticism, idealist dialectics, and scientific concatenation undergo, in Bataille's work, an analogous criticism because he sees their complicity as arising from their repression or justification of the "arbitrary" and of "life," of the violence of biological and social heterogeneity, of the animality and of the social aggressivity of man: "Thought that doesn't limit this arbitrariness to what it is, is mystical."[8] "There is a mysticism that is opposed at times to that approbation of life right to death...But the opposition isn't necessary."[9]

If one doesn't try to grasp this heterogeneous reality but to submit to it, the fact remains that one must submit to it through discourse. It is a "discursive real" that will display heterogeneity and affirm its negativity. But discourse is not to be confused with this heterogeneity. It is only when other "operations" pass through "the discursive real" that the latter ceases to be simply a discursive real, and witnesses heterogeneous reality. Bataille insists on the fact that the operations of heterogeneity are not discursive operations even if they pass through language; it is a matter of a "non-discursive"[10] experience, but one that assumes discourse and makes use of it.

Language is only a support for ruptures. It serves in order that the blank spots, the breaks in meaning be inscribed: "A feeling introduced by a sentence. I forgot the sentence: it was accompanied by a perceptible change, like a releasing hook, severing the ties."[11]

The weakness of Christianity in this context, according to Bataille, is that it was unable to free the non-discursive operations from discourse itself, that it confused *experience* with *discourse*, and that it reduced experience to the possibilities of discourse, possibilities that it broadly surpasses even if this confusion has permitted a much greater softening of the discursive register than is the case in other cultures. "The projection of the point, in Christianity, is attempted before the mind has at its disposal its inner movements, before it has become free of discourse. It is only the rough projection, from which one attempts to attain non-discursive experience."[12]

Thus Bataille successively dismisses mysticism, absolute knowledge, the discursive real. To propose what, in maximum proximity to the heterogeneous?

*Laughter*: fading of meaning and only possibility for communication. To laugh at knowledge, at fear, at the self, therefore at any stasis taken on and passed through.

*Eroticism*: "the affirmation of life right to death." In other words the affirmation of continuity, of fusion, of union, by means of separation and discontinuity. Community and reproduction are its points of departure since they are the essential moments of the subject, links indispensable to its testing [*procès*]: "the fundamental sense of reproduction is in no less way the key to eroticism."[13] Bataille takes on, therefore, what society advocates as perpetuation of its continuity, in order to introduce into this social security lock what it represses but what constitutes it: separation and death. That death is invisible outside of reproduction and filiation; that their struggle is indeed the truth of social relations: this is what Bataille reveals through the mechanical monotony of social reproduction. Reproduction is not only socially necessary, but it is the element indispensable to eroticism; it is the linkage that resists the violence of death, the logical principle assuring the "passage from discontinuity to continuity," without which there is no contradiction. What is sought then is not to abolish filiation, the *One* or mastery; it is to recognize them as moments indispensable to the "putting-into-play that surpasses them, in order to find through them an adequation of the subject with the *movement* (the "flux," the "flame") of nature and of society. It is only in this way, by maintaining and representing the thetic phase which the process [*procès*] exceeds, that this phase is not only experienced like a frightening taboo, but becomes the site where desire is articulated. "The taboo, observed other than in terror, no longer possesses the counterpart of desire that is its profound meaning."[14] The thetic-affirmative phase, maintained and opened in the heterogeneity that dissolves it, is no longer law, commandment, unity; it is called desire. In what we could call other "semiotic systems" and notably in the Orient, Bataille specifies that the subject can attain extra-discursive heterogeneity without resorting to desire. (In this sense, Artaud is perhaps more "oriental" than Bataille.) But in the Christian West, which has hypostasized the unary subject and repressed its heterogeneity by imposing such dominant and envied figures as those of the Stoic Sage, of the Head of State, to bring desire to light once again means attacking the reserves of social power. Power, in our society, is constituted by repressing the desire which is its "counterpart." To bring desire to light once again is not an end in itself, but from Bataille's perspective, serves to closely examine the foundations of this power, of this taboo, of the saturations that block and prevent the traversal of discourse and knowledge; this bringing desire to light again aims for the mobility of experience, in which *ipseity* is lost. A reading of Hegel and Bataille shows how desire, for the philosopher, arises on the path leading to the constitution of unity, while for Bataille, desire is, on the contrary, the path to its consummation, its annihilation.

## HEGELIAN DESIRE

In Hegel's work, desire (*Begierde*) is a moment constituting the notion of *consciousness of self*: it is, then, a particularization and concretization of negativity; a representation both of its most differentiated and most suppressed movement, it is a *completed* dialectics. Consciousness of self begins to become articulated when one loses the object—the other—in relation to which it is postulated and which is "simple and independent substance," founding sense certainty. Consciousness of self negates this object in order to return to its self and only loses it as simple substance in order to realize its own unity with itself. Desire is the negation of the object in its alterity or as "independent life" and its introduction into the knowing subject; it is the assumption of alterity, the suppression of difference (that of certainty and of consciousness); it is the resolution of differences, "the universal resolution," the "fluidity of differences." If this movement constitutes life, the consciousness of self follows the same path with respect to life as a "movement of distinct figures" or "process" [*processus*]; and only has meaning with respect to vital fluidity.[15]

Let us note that this course of desire is marked by paranoia: consciousness of self is constituted through the suppression of the other or of the Other and desire is this suppression itself; having always been on the path to desire, "consciousness of self" becomes its other without, however, abandoning it. The movement of scission is perpetuated and it is the very essence of the consciousness of self corresponding to desire. But once again, this scission is subordinated to the unity of self in the presence of the spirit. Desire is the agent of this unity, or let us say that it is the agent of unification through the negativization of the object. It is the deviation of negativity towards the becoming—One, the indispensable moment unifying the schizoid haze into an identity, though it be infinitely divisible and fluid. Hegel articulates a truth here about the subject, that Lacan later made explicit: the subject is necessarily paranoid, following the drive of desire that sublimates and unifies the schizoid rupture into a quest for objects. Paranoia is thus not only the condition for all subjects—one only becomes a subject by accepting, even if temporarily, the paranoid unity suppressing the other—but this unity exists in immediate proximity to the fragmentation that one could call schizoid; it camouflages its secret, all the while drawing energy from the latter. If the "fluidity of differences" constitutes *the unity* of the consciousness of self, it menaces it as well, for with respect to this fluidity alone, there is no longer a place for any *unity*, any desire, any subservience [*Unterwerfung*] to life; on the contrary, what determines this division is death, rupture, the inorganic, and separation without unifying fluidity.

On this level, as in the entirety of its path, the Hegelian dialectic begins by dissolving the immediate unity given to sense certainty; but after having noted the moments of its division, of its splitting in half and of its mediation with respect to the other, the path comes back to the same, fills it with the other, and consolidates it. Theology is sideswiped by philosophy, but in order to become reconstituted again on good grounds. The "Self" is divided and doubted in order to become reunified in the unity of the "Consciousness of self." Therein lies the ambiguity of idealist dialectics; it postulated the division, the movement, and the process [*procès*], but dismisses them with the same gesture in the name of a superior metaphysical and repressive truth that will become the "Consciousness of self" and its correlative on the judicial level—the State. It is moreover in its "state" form, in the unitary and unifying, centralized and mastered sense, that Hegel will greet even the French Revolution and its Constitution; the metaphor of the sun represents the fulfillment of the reasoning subject, of the One, of the bourgeois State.[16]

As if, having sensed the fragmentation of the Self and its negative link with the elements of material and social continuity, idealist dialectics automatically arrogated to itself one of the most lucid visions of the loss of subjective metaphysical and political unity. But anxious to reestablish this unity, riveted to it and proceeding with it in mind and with it as its point of departure, it concludes the movement of negativity in this very unity. *Desire* is the notion that remains the most accurate representation of this telescoping of negativity in unity.

Bataille reexamines this unified subject and takes it in a reverse direction, through desire and without "middle term" to the moment of immediate experience that it has forgotten. But he is sure that one would not be able to grasp this "immediate experience" dismissed by Hegel, without first encountering the enticement of the unity of knowledge to which it logically leads. To encounter the taboo through desire is, in Bataille's work, to return to immediate experience, after the latter has acknowledged its movement within the "Idea" and within "absolute knowledge." Eroticism and desire once again introduce the subject—

fulfilled and completed by "absolute knowledge"—into the immediacy of the heterogeneous, without intermediary, without mediation and which, on this condition only, causes the enticement of unity to dissolve. It is to a completed "self" that the heterogeneous appears in the form of desire and eroticism at the moment when desire exhausts the "self." "If it is possible for others, for Orientals whose imagination does not burn at the names of Theresa, Heloise, Isolde, to abandon themselves to empty infinity *with no other desire*, we cannot conceive of ultimate collapse in a way other than in love. At this price alone, it seems to me, I gain access to the extreme limit of what is possible and if not, something still is missing from the path in which I can't help but burn everything—right up to the exhaustion of human strength."[17]

In this path in which everything is burned, it is above all the initial affirmation of a subject, *ipse*, that is lost in the unknown. *Ipse* that knows and for this reason remains separated from the whole and is extinguished through desire. Since eroticism implies fusion, it does not conserve *ipse*: fusion is more accurately its recasting, through desire and the other, also through the continuity implied by filiation: "in fusion, neither *ipse* nor the whole subsist. It is the annihilation of everything which is not the ultimate 'unknown,' the abyss into which one has sunk."[18]

Thus, *desire and eroticism* are, along with *laughter*, the means for leaving *ipseity* and attaining an immediate communication: eroticism is "the refusal of the will to withdraw into oneself."[19] Such a communication is only possible on the condition that one suppress entirely the patience of the logical concept, which defers and leads to a servile "I." The "I" affirmed only in order to disappear through eroticism and desire is the only "sovereign I": sovereignty, which in essence is possibility for non-discursive communication, passes through the affirmation of the paranoid "I" which is the "I" of desire. Sovereignty is a return to the heterogeneous by traversing, through the desire that reestablishes continuity, the stasis of the knowing "I." One must give strong emphasis to this moment in Bataille's work: desire and the heterogeneity to which it leads do not constitute a "this side of" of knowledge and its unary subject but their traversal; carnal organicity, erotic orgies, and obscenity exist only as contradictions, as struggles, between the violent materiality external to the subject, and the affirmed authority of this very subject. "Nothing is tragic for the animal, which doesn't fall into the trap of the *self*."[20] "Violent thought alone coincides with the fading of thought."[21] "The experiences of heterogeneity would be better called "meditation" if this word didn't have a "pious sense."[22] Bataille also proposes to call it "comic operation" because the comic is precisely what maintains an ephemeral appearance of sense in non-sense.

The process [*procès*] thus attained by this positivity of reason maintained, is the process [*procès*] of nature itself. However, experience doesn't consist of becoming mingled with nature through delirium or poetry. While it touches upon both of them, experience is missing both from desire and poetry, through *meditation*. Experience is played out in nature but, through the refusal that is meditation, it goes further than nature: "Poetic delirium has its place *in* nature. It justifies nature, accepts its embellishment. Refusal belongs to clear consciousness, taking stock of what is happening.

The clear distinction between all possibilities, the ability to proceed to the most distant point arises from calm attention. The unbridled play of the self, the act of going beyond anything given, demands not only this infinite laughter, but this slow meditation (mad, but through excess).

(…)

Release withdraws one from play—as does excessive attention.

(…)

I approach poetry, but in order to be absent from it."[23]

## THEME, FICTION

The *theme* is what, in the discursive systems, best represents that thetic moment around which the process [*procès*] momentarily crystallizes; in this way *the theme* is in league with *laughter*, with *desire*, and with *eroticism*. We reach here Bataille's literary choice: the transposition of the "sovereign operation" in language demands a *literature*, not a philosophy or a knowledge; more precisely it demands a *literature of themes* that is inevitably tragic and comic at the same time. Thus poetry is excluded from the sovereign operation; even if it "expresses within the realm of words a great squandering of energy," it fails to attain violence since, by abandoning the *theme*, it abandons the affirmative-thetic moment with respect to which the contradiction of non-related energies is measured:

> If one suppresses the theme, if one grants at the same time that rhythm has little interest, then a hecatomb of words without god or *raison d'être* is for man a major way of affirming, through an effusion bereft of meaning, a sovereignty which apparently *nothing can touch*.

The moment when poetry renounces the theme and meaning permits, from the viewpoint of meditation, the rupture that is opposed to the humiliated stammerings of ascesis. But since it becomes a game without rules, and in the impossibility of determining violent effects, since it lacks a theme, the exercise of *modern* poetry is subordinate, in its turn, to *possibility*.[24]

Poetry without a theme, as well as laughter, sacrifice, and eroticism, remain "minor examples of sovereignty," "children at home."

This literature of sovereign themes cannot be a novel taking itself seriously either, for the latter, even in the case of Proust's work, is an attempt at mastery: "an effort to bind time, to know it."[25]

The sovereign subject can only be someone who *represents* experiences of ruptures: his *themes* evoke a radical heterogeneity. His practice: to write the themes of eroticism, of sacrifice, of social and subjective rupture. This series of themes will resemble the erotic novel or the philosophical essay—it matters little; what is important, is that the violence of thought be introduced there where thought loses itself.

*L'impossible, L'Abbé C., Histoire de l'Oeil, Le Petit, Ma mère, Anus solaire,* and *Madame Edwarda* all affirm the themes of eroticism in order to dissolve them, through a rupture of the "characters" and of logical sense.

The erotic theme is a semantic contradiction: the erotic situation is a reunion of opposites: "On the level where things are in play, each element constantly changes into its opposite. God suddenly takes on 'a horrible grandeur.' Or poetry slips into embellishment. With each of my efforts to grasp the object of my expectations, the latter changes into its opposite."[26] If the same logical movement were maintained in poetry, it would lead to the negation of poetry.

The theoretical writings like *Inner Experience, Eroticism, Guilty, The Accursed Share,* and the anthropological or political studies, both link and dissolve the themes of ideological, religious, or scientific systems.

These two sides of Bataille's written production proceed by affirming theoretical, conceptual, and representational positions. But they negativize and relativize these affirmations. Since it is affirmative, Bataille's thought denounces itself, because it denounces thought in its very form: "What counts, in the type of thought that I am introducing, is never affirmation."[27]

But at the same time, these affirmations are indispensable and indestructible, like thought in Frege's writing: "I felt remorse that it was impossible for me to annul my affirmations."[28] "Alone in the night, I remained reading, overcome by that feeling of impotence."[29] Impotence is the measure of the difficulty provoked when one traverses affirmation: the thetic.

One will understand here that in Bataille's work, it is not a question of *thought*, of *writing*, or of *discourse*, in the formalist sense of all these terms. It is a question of the *experience* that is always a contradiction between the *presence* of the subject and its *loss*, between thought and its expenditure, between linkage (logos) and its separation. If it requires a subject and discourse as its thetic phase, it opens them towards the *operations* that the subject and discourse do not exhaust but for which the subject and discourse are necessary conditions. One will say that Bataille's books are not language but rather eroticism, jouissance, sacrifice, expenditure; but that at the same time, jouissance, sacrifice, do not exist without the unary authority of the subject and language. No doubt this is what upsets the norms of our society's "code for love," a society that has severed knowledge from jouissance and which loses them when, sporadically, they happen to contaminate one another. It is in this severance and through it that power is installed as oppressive force: the subject who knows (who "knows" mathematics, economics, finance) exercises a power that mingles with state power and tends more and more to be substituted for it. As for jouissance, one reserves the dark rooms, the alcoves and the corridors of religion for it. The operation attempted by Bataille erases this *severance* and makes a *contradiction* of it. For jouissance to be that of a subject, it must contain the authority of knowledge in which the subject is fulfilled; and jointly, in order that knowledge not be an exercise of power but the operation of a subject, the latter must discover in its logic, the jouissance that constitutes it. The term *eroticism* summarizes these two movements. But who, in capitalist society—where subjects are reduced to relationships of production—can bring about this eroticization of knowledge and this knowledge of eroticism? Not the scholar, not the master, not the decorative artist: they are all caught by action or by its inanity, but fail to attain contradiction.

The subject who is actually in a position today to bring about this "sovereign operation" must be someone who possesses knowledge (philosophy and science), can expose its themes and confront them with a non-discursive operation. This gesture implies a possible eroticization of knowledge and of discourse, since they are open to heterogeneity; the possibility of maintaining contradiction: one designates this possibility by the name of fiction.

The *writer* of this *fiction* is, then, this subject that cannot be localized; as the subject of reason it is focused, but constantly divided into multiple fissures by the eruption of the drive that is not symbolized, that separates and rearticulates logical structures.

Creating fissures in a logical authority that continues to be maintained can lead right to linguistic dislocation, as in the case of Artaud. One can add linguistic subversion to ideological subversion as Joyce has done. Bataille does not always touch verbal structure: this is perhaps a limitation of his experience that has the advantage, however, of making it more communicable. But he is in profound solidarity with Joyce in his subversion, through fiction, of the "great semiotic units" of ideology and knowledge. As is the case with Joyce and his negative "wake" (*Finnegan's Wake*), he is in a constant alertness: "I feel on the contrary as though I am alertness itself, since, on the level of the requirement of thought, I am in the state of the hunted animal."[30] Like Joyce, he introduces this alertness into what is repressively separated from it: sexuality which has, in this way, become jouissance. The fact is that the writer is not just the only subject in our culture for whom language is a heterogeneous contradiction not repressed by social censure; he is also the only subject for whom "signifieds," "ideational contents," and "themes" are also heterogeneous contradictions, and it is for this reason that they are "fictions," in other words, it is for this reason that they bear a truth that symbolic and/or social censure has not been able to repress.

We find ourselves here at a crucial moment in the functioning of the "sovereign subject." He is the one for whom the tale, in other words, the representation of a series of events, is not an "objective story" (in the sense that the scholar, having separated knowledge from jouissance, intends it) but a narration, a *fiction.* What does this mean?

Psychoanalysis is constituted, as one knows, by the art of listening to tales, since it finds in this the most archaic form of formulating the subject's experience in a discursive way. Today one contends that it is at the time of Oedipus that the first tale was formulated as an attempt to reconstruct and to formulate the past experience of the individual, as an attempt to master this experience. This means that narrative structure takes up elements occurring earlier and organizes them, by mediating them through language, of course, but structurally, through *desire* for the respective poles of the family structure. The tale, then, is the semiotic structure that corresponds to the unification of the subject in its Oedipal relation through the desire and the castration articulated within it. This structure, over-determined by familial triangulation, takes up once again and translates, in higher semiotic systems, the free energies remaining outside of the first symbolizations in addition to unconscious representations.

Fiction, however, borrowing as it does the path of the tale, reiterates the constitution of the subject in Oedipus as desiring and castrated subject. But, contrary to "objective," "historic," or simply fictive tales that can be blind to their cause and simply repeat this cause without realizing it, the "sovereign operation" consists in "meditating" upon the Oedipal cause of fiction and thus of the desiring–reciting subject. It consists, as does Bataille's work, *of representing through themes*—and thus not only of introducing "poetically," through rupture and the modifications of linguistic structure—what the Oedipalization of the subject has repressed; it consists, then, of representing "free energies," circulating through the body of the subject itself or towards the fragmented bodies of social partners (parents or others). In this sense, the sovereign operation consists of traversing Oedipus by *representing* Oedipus and what exceeds it. But if Oedipus is the constitution of the unary subject as knowing subject, the sovereign operation consists of traversing Oedipus by means of an Oedipus surmounted by Orestes. In these fictional tales, through the maintenance of theme, of lucidity, and of "meditation" as means of *representing* pre-Oedipal free energies, Bataille confronts Orestes with Oedipus and puts them into reciprocal and infinite reflection. The traversal of Oedipus is not its lifting, but its knowledge. The fictional *theme*, by its very *structure*, represents the *economy* of this knowledge of transgression; the theme is a signified (unified representation) which is not *one* but which contains a *semantic multiplicity* at the same time that it is supported by a *multiplicity of drives* for which it is the focal point. In this sense, all fictional themes and all fiction share the economy of a traversal of Oedipus. But Bataille leads this operation to its moment of sovereignty to the extent that he makes it explicit through the *contents* of the theme. What the fictional theme represents is not immaterial; it meditates upon the "limit points" of expenditure, of sacrifice, of eroticism leading to utter loss. These are states passing by way of the mother and the desire for her but, far from becoming fixated upon her and, even less, from sublimating her, they pass through her and dirty her; in other words, they discover in her the body of the woman who—finally—is not that of the reassuring progenitor with whom one can identify.

## JOUISSANCE

The tale, then, is a structure whose economy is desire. This is what distinguishes it from poetry whose economy, according to Bataille, is that of a "discrediting." In other words, poetic language is a violent eruption of negativity in discourse, a negativity that denounces all unities and destroys the subject by destroying logic; it sinks into "night." This negativity without stasis is a rejection, a destruction that has turned away from all objects, in the void, without desire: "Putting everything into question grew out of the exasperation of a desire, that couldn't be directed to the void."[31]

Artaud's poetic experience is close to that economy of rejection that is confused with "nature" and its "night": schizophrenia. Attached to this paranoid side, desire on the contrary leads the subject through the night of its loss, so that it bears witness to this in the form of fiction. In the desire that forms the fictive, negativity is centered in themes (characters, situation, ideological fragments); it is withdrawn from the nature from which it emerges and is given back to active man. On the other hand, "Putting something into question without desire is a formal, indifferent act. One could not say of this act: 'The same is true for man'."[32] Desire is figurative; it represents human relationships. But, for inner experience, desire is not an end in itself. If there is a means for surpassing poetic night, it is necessary that desiring figuration be surpassed in its turn. Inner experience is only there to make negativity into something other than desire: a jouissance. Jouissance is the traversal of representation and of the desire that emerges from the night of drives, thanks to the *maintenance of logic*. "Dazzled by a thousand figures consisting of anxiety, impatience, love. Now my desire has only one object: what lies beyond those thousand figures and night."[33] Returning to night by means of a desiring figuration, jouissance abandons desire: "But in night, desire lies [*ment*] and, in this way, night ceases to appear as its object."[34] Bataille's novels are only the setting for desire in order to release a burst of laughter: nonsense, loss, in other words, jouissance? If the tale follows the logic of desire, the tale—destroyed by a fully meditated eroticism—exposes jouissance.

The sovereign subject is one that knows itself as subject to the extent that it knows the Oedipal limit; it doesn't surpass it without postulating it as a *limit* and not as an end in itself: this is what Bataille's novels demonstrate, novels that are inseparable from his theoretical positions and give them their real values. One will understand, then, that such a sovereign subject, the subject of erotic fiction or of the eroticization of knowledge, is only sovereign to the extent that it has no power (in the sense of an exercise of strength). Like the fictional theme whose unity is always plural and fading, or like the contradiction, charged with eroticism, that confronts the presence of the subject with its loss in the heterogeneous, the sovereign subject refuses all positions, all fixations. This trans-Oedipus, as opposed to an anti-Oedipus, only takes on a position in order to engage in revolt: "sovereignty is revolt, it is not the exercise of power. Authentic sovereignty refuses..."[35] It does not provoke, as does the Greek Orestes, the installation of new laws; but it refuses the old ones, reflects them infinitely, shows the fiction that founds them and that they repress. If this trans-Oedipus is an Orestes, it does not forget that it has been an Oedipus and consequently refuses the new law by means of a new fiction.

For Bataille, to be Orestes is to be the result of a play [*jeu*], a play that is impossible without the authority of the law that is the self. "I am the result of a play [*jeu*], which, if I were not, would not be, which could not be."[36]

Bataille designates this experience as being "inner." But, since it is the site where power is contested, a site constituting the subject who is not the subject of power (as it has been thought and lived by society and, in particular, by Occidental society), but a free, contesting subject, this experience has impacts that surpass, to a great extent, what is "inner."

On the theoretical level, the sovereign subject of inner experience founds the possibility for a new subject who, without renouncing the subject of knowledge—whose fulfillment Marx and Hegel showed by completing its negativity in the Concept or the Revolution—returns to the latter its heterogeneous negativity at the same time as its jouissance.

On the historical level, the fact that it has been possible to think such a subject marks the end of a historical era that is fulfilled by capitalism. Shaken by social conflicts, revolutions, the claims for irrationality (from drugs to madness, claims that are in the process of being recognized and accepted), capitalism is making its way towards an *other* society that will be the achievement of a *new* subject. "The inner experience" of the "sovereign subject" is one of the symptoms of this revolution of the subject. Thus it must be thought of as an indispensable complement to the social practice of men, a practice whose meaning and objectives it is already modifying.

From within this perspective, we will now examine the relationship of *experience* (jouissance and/or meditation) such as it is understood by Bataille who, in transforming Hegel, stands in relation to him, and to *practice* such as it is understood by dialectical materialism in its over-turning of Hegel.

## IMMEDIACY "IN THE BACK" OR IN THE BURST EYE

In *L'Erotisme*, Bataille writes: "In the mind of Hegel, what is immediate is bad, and Hegel surely would have linked what I will call experience to the immediate." By this declaration, Bataille indicates that, if the term experience is a Hegelian concept, the sense that it has for Bataille is distinct from the Hegelian sense by the emphasis placed on *immediacy*.

"This *dialectical* movement, which consciousness exercises on itself and which affects both its knowledge and its object, is precisely what is called *experience* [*Erfahrung*]. Hegel distinguishes the moment when the object immediately appears to consciousness, which is only a pure apprehension, from the moment of true experience when a new object is constituted from this first one, and this through the return of consciousness to itself, through 'our own intervention.' It shows up here like this: Since what first appeared as the object sinks for consciousness to the level of its way of knowing it, and since the in-itself becomes a *being-for-consciousness* of the in-itself, the latter is now the new object. Herewith a new pattern of consciousness comes on the scene as well, the essence of which is something different from what it was at the preceding stage."[37]

A first mysterious movement, that of "immediate certitude" when the object appears, is distinguished from the moment when consciousness truly realizes *experience*; this constitutes the second moment when immediate certitude will be introduced into the presence of consciousness through the *turning about* of the latter and ("behind its back, so to speak" writes Hegel).[38] We will know nothing of this first movement of the object's appearance, except that its essence is negative, but to isolate it in its negativity, without linking it to what follows, would be to reduce experience to nothingness.

Thus, it seems that one moment of experience is recognized as assuming the annihilation of consciousness, of its presence, and of its metaphysical unity. But, by not recognizing any objective material authority, structured logically and independently of the laws of consciousness, idealist dialectics cannot specify the objective, material relationships whose conflictive nature engenders the "sense certainty" *before* the latter becomes an object of knowledge. Experience is thus always that of a *knowledge* that, while it is not that of science in the technical sense of the term but of the theological science of an absolute knowledge, relies on the same thinking subject: that of consciousness present to itself and retaining from the heterogeneity that undermines it, [and shapes it (*la travaille*)], only the impression of void, of nothingness, of lack "behind its back, so to speak."

Bataille, on the contrary, closely examines this first moment of immediate apparition and assigns to the latter what is essential to experience. But, far from leaving it like an indeterminate nothing, like a simple negation of consciousness and of the presence of the subject,[39] he designates its concrete and material determinations. Bataille specifies in these theoretical writings that this moment of immediacy referred to by Hegel is the moment of specularization, it is the eye that sees a desired object; the first object apprehended is apprehended as—"spectacle."[40]

> I said earlier of the position of the point that starting from it, the mind is an eye. Experience from that moment onward has an optical perspective in that one distinguishes within it a perceived object from a perceiving subject, just as a spectacle is different from a mirror. The apparatus of vision (the physical apparatus) occupies moreover in this case the greatest place. It is a spectator, it is eyes which seek out the point, or at least, in this operation, visual existence is condensed in the eyes. This character does not cease if night falls. What is thereby found in deep obscurity is *a keen desire to see* when, in the face of this desire, everything slips away.[41]

If inner experience consists of introducing knowledge into immediacy, it is in order that knowledge traverse vision, spectacle, representation. Inner experience is a backwards traversal of specularization as initial moment in the constitution of the subject. Far from becoming fixated in knowledge, the "self" in inner experience demonstrates that what Hegel was striving for through "absolute knowledge" (identity of the practical idea and the theoretical idea) is an impossible knowledge. Why? Because in requiring a traversal of "seeing" it cannot know [savoir] any fixed object, but rather sees in the place of the object only a "catastrophe," a contradiction, a struggle that can be neither localized nor identified.

> This object, chaos of light and of shadow, is *catastrophe*. I perceive it as object; my thought, however, shapes it according to its image, at the same time that it is its reflection. Perceiving it, my thought itself sinks into annihilation as into a fall in which a cry is emitted. Something immense, exorbitant, is liberated in all directions with a noise of a catastrophe; this emerges from an unreal, infinite void, at the same time loses

itself in it with the shock of a blinding flash. In a crash of telescoping trains, a window breaking while causing death is the expression of this all powerful, imperative, and already annihilated irruption.[42]

One must return to what is this side of specularization and take it up again in an immediate catastrophic "seeing." Not to relegate the immediate "to the back" of spectacle, but to traverse it in a representation maintained as a rupture of all identification, of all identity, of all specularization, thus as a ruining of representation itself: "it was necessary that the contemplated object make of me this mirror of redirected light, that I had become, for night to offer itself to my thirst."[43]

Sovereign fiction is precisely the representation of concrete operations (sexual, mortal, social) that exceed specularization and its subject—the subject of [*sa-voir*]. It is a necessary condition for knowledge to be maintained and traversed, and for the process [*procès*] of meaning grasped by representation and knowledge—"the unknown"—to be represented in the theme of representation. Sovereign fiction represents a spectacle whose economy contradicts representation and spectacle: sovereign fiction is the representation of an unknown non-knowledge. The subject is there, but without knowing itself ideally, it sees itself in it, represents itself in it: "I become *ipse*" "unknown to myself." It is only as *ipse*, thus maintained as subject, affirmed and present in language, that it frees itself as individuality, narcissism, center of specularization and that it can enter into a communication. As the other, it is the condition for recognizing the unknown: "In it, I communicate with the unknown."

What is important in this gesture by Bataille is not that it designated the specular essence of the idea and of the subject present to itself in experience. Heidegger did it several years later in his commentary on the notion of experience in Hegel's work (1942–1943).[44] Bataille's gesture does more than simply specify what Hegel does not say with respect to the presence of *being*, something phenomenology does; neither does it simply grasp the Hegelian system on the basis of its fulfillment in "the absolute idea" (which already surpasses the phenomenological attitude) in order to reveal "the highest contradiction" contained in the latter.

Nor does Bataille simply carry out the gesture of formalism (peculiar to poetry, to literary theory and, indeed, to psychoanalysis) that consists both of replacing *representation* by language and of rupturing representation by putting language into play. When he speaks of the "discursive real" Bataille knows that what appears as image is language, but he doesn't stop at this complicity—(image–language); he seeks what produces, and in this sense precedes or exceeds, the two accomplices (image–language): he seeks in the economy of meaning, the passage of drives putting the subject to death, through desire for the forbidden others. The tale will represent, then, these operations, dangerous for representation and for language.

Bataille's gesture makes explicit the objective, concrete determination of the specular essence peculiar to the present-knowing subject. This determination resides: 1) in the constitution of the symbolic function and more particularly in the constitution of language and narration; 2) in drive-related investments of the natural and social continuity in which the individual operates and which specularization begins to censure. For Bataille, the truth of the subject does not consist in saying that it is present, nor even less in saying that it is always disseminated. The truth of the subject consists in fiction (in the sense of a doubly contradictory representation, as we have already suggested). It will make use, then, of language to show concrete operations in which the sexual taboos constitutive of repression and/or of knowledge are transgressed. If the subject is specular, it is because it *speaks* and because it *observes sexual taboos*. It is thus by the *pluralization* of the word and by the *transgression* of taboos, but always in the word and by maintaining these taboos, that the subject can abandon the site of specular Master and encounter its "unknown" source. Eroticism in discourse and *a fortiori* in the discourse of knowledge or in philosophical discourse: therein lies the condition for a materialist and dialectical attitude with respect to the subject. A *materialist* attitude because it provides its material, bodily, social and language-related conditions, conditions of which the presence of the subject is unaware. A *dialectical* attitude because it preserves for the subject the position of "contesting sovereignty," a sovereignty that can be fixed neither in a mastery nor in an absence, but refuses, negates, transforms the order of things, and hence, transforms reality.

Thus, as we have said, it is in *fiction* and not in *knowledge* and in its *concept*, that experience finds its adequation. Hegel foresaw a moment surpassing the position, the presence, and the limit through the movement of consciousness itself, left to its own drives; however, if a beyond is then attained by this "drive-related experience," it is always internal to consciousness, such that thought disturbs the absence of thought and upsets inertia. But for Hegel, this path is necessarily fixed as a series of progressions and can lead only to the *adequation of the concept with the object, of the object with the concept*. On the contrary, Bataille's inner experience, which in this sense brings to mind Sade, breaks open the finality of this progression, not to arrest it, but to dismantle the drive-desire and the tale that speaks them.

All tales are a story of the eye; the telling of experience is the story of its rupture.

## ON THE DIALECTICAL AND MATERIALIST CONCEPT OF PRACTICE

Subordinated to the "drive for the Good" "the practical Idea" (*Praktischen Idee*) is found in the Hegelian *Science of Logic* to be like a clearly stated theoretical idea, receiving "its individuality" or its contents from the "outside."[45] This drive for the Good differentiates it essentially from Bataillean experience of which Bataille writes: "I imagine that it is bad to give it superior goals."[46] However, the practical Idea is not unrelated to Bataillean experience. Like Bataillean experience, the practical Idea is a return to exteriority from the onset of knowledge, but, contrary to it, this return does not know itself as such; the Hegelian practical Idea is still missing an "active subject." Now it is precisely an active subject in process [*en procès*] that Bataillean experience calls for.

Marxism inherits from Hegel an ambiguity with respect to the "active subject" within the concept of *practice*. Classical Marxism does not bring out the "active subject" of practice and slips toward a concept of practice that resembles a practice without a subject. It is only Maoism that surpasses this limited concept of practice by accentuating "personal experience."

Dialectical materialism accentuates "tangible human activity" by opposing it to the Idealist "intuition" that would be an immediate apprehension of the object. This gesture of Marx in the *Theses on Feuerbach* extracts the notion of "immediate apprehension" of the object from its subjective confinement in a consciousness closed upon itself, and invests it in a negativity that, however, is not that of the "active subject" that Hegel speaks of and that Bataille calls for. Thus, by getting rid of Feuerbach's subjectivism, Marx introduces an objectivization of the immediate apprehension of reality, but this objectivization does not concern the subject itself; it develops in the relations of production, in what is exterior to the subject. In other words, even if subjective authority necessarily becomes objective and negative in practice, there is no one to think this objectivization. The subject of such a practice does not know itself as active subject; consequently, it remains secretly in league with the Feuerbachian subject.

In an analogous way, Lenin only accentuates the exteriority of practice with respect to logic, in order to postulate that it is practice that founds
the Hegelian "syllogism of action" and not the contrary. "Practice above
(theoretical) knowledge, for it is the dignity not only of the universal but
also of the immediate real."[47]

Marxist theory thus rehabilitates immediate experience but does not
notice the teleology of practical action indicated by the Good, and does
not develop the economy of the "highest contradiction"[48] that will be put in
place with the introduction of the Concept in the practical Idea. It does
not arise from what Hegel calls "the practical concept," which, according
to him culminates in an "impenetrable" "atomic" subjectivity, not exclusively individual—the "generality and knowledge" of its own alterity that is
objectivity: "a practical, objective concept, *determining in itself and for
itself,* and that, as a *person, is an impenetrable, atomic subjectivity* (n.s.)
but that, at the same time, far from being an individuality exclusive of all
the others, is, for itself, generality and knowledge and has as object, in its
other, its own objectivity."[49]

Marxism has not developed Hegel's "practical concept" on a materialist ground. Lenin emphasizes the external determination of practice, *but
side-steps its impact for the subject,* an impact implied by the Hegelian
"concept" even if it blocked the subject from the authority of knowledge
itself.

Mao Tse-tung takes up again these commentaries by Lenin vis-à-vis
Hegel in his essay "On Practice" and accentuates personal and immediate
experience as material characteristics essential to practice. If he postulates
"the activity of production" as decisive for all practical activity, then he
adds to the register of practices: *the class struggle, political life, scientific
and aesthetic activity.* The practical moment is represented according to
"overturned" Hegelian logic. It is a question of an "apprehension" of
"external and approximate relations," of an "exteriority." Only *the repetition of phenomena* within the objective continuity of social practice
produces the qualitative leap that is the emergence of the concept establishing internal relations. Mao insists upon two aspects of practice; it is
*personal* and it requires an "*immediate experience.*" To directly know
such a phenomenon or such a group of phenomena, one must participate
*personally* in the practical struggle that aims to transform reality, to transform this phenomenon or that group of phenomena, for it is the only way
of entering into contact with the latter as appearances; it is also the only
means of discovering the essence of the phenomenon, of that group of
phenomena and of understanding them. "All authentic knowledge is the

outcome of immediate experience."[50]  "One who negates sensation, who
negates direct experience, who negates personal participation in the practice destined to transform reality is not a materialist."[51]

This emphasis on "direct and personal experience," perhaps the
most insistent in Marxist theory, tends to make manifest a conscious
subjectivity that, due to this fact, has become the site of the "highest
contradiction." It is a question of a subjectivity that Hegel postulates in the
"practical concept"; impenetrable, atomic, non-individual, bringing about a
general knowledge. Maoism involves and produces such a subjectivity, a
subjectivity that becomes the motivation for the practice of social transformation and revolution.

One of Mao's essential contributions to the theory and practice of
dialectical materialism consists of the rediscovery, within its framework of
such a subjectivity.

One could not however forget that the "practical concept" that
completes the Hegelian edifice and is transmitted as overturned in
dialectical materialism, contains moments preceding it in the spiral of its
formulation. The "immediate experience" of reality enclosed by practice
and transmitted to knowledge integrates the time of the *Erfahrung*, the
time of the meaningful apprehension of the heterogeneous object, by
relegating it to a position "behind its back." But let us try to think of a
subject that does not follow this Hegelian prescription leading the latter
right to the unity of absolute knowledge: what would happen if a
subject, traversing and dissolving this totality that culminates in the "practical concept," did not become resigned to hiding immediate experience
"behind its back," but rather brought out the rupture of the subject and of
the object that accompanies it and which is the problematic condition for
the entire course of the Idea? Such a subject—and we have said that it is
the subject of fiction—will no longer be taken for the "impenetrable and
atomic" subject of the "practical concept," but will constitute the
condition for its renewal.

Mao distinguishes clearly between the two moments of idealist
dialectics that mechanistic materialism and the dogmatism of Marxism
tended to crush. The triple movement that he postulates: practice-truth-
practice[52] implies that between the three phases there is a difference in
status between the "apprehended objects" and the "consciousnesses" that
apprehended them. The emergence of the *true object* in practice is thus
to be distinguished from its *scientific knowledge* which will provide scientific truth, in order to lead to another *practical test*. The moment of practice is indissolubly linked to that of true scientific knowledge, but is

distinguished from it. What becomes of this moment? Science can describe how the Chinese Communist Party during the 1930s had a specific practice, consisting of certain concrete and real steps and certain concrete analyses of the economic and political situation, that permitted it to grasp the new object, the peasantry, as the striking force of the revolution in order to subsequently produce its theoretical underpinnings, as Mao did in his study on the class struggle in China.

But a complementary epistemological question remains: is there a particular status of the *subject at the moment of practice* and which differs from the status *of the theorizing subject?* Marxist theory, which is not a theory of the subject, does not provide an answer to this question. It is content with discerning between objective economic determinations and the logical unfolding of practice, with evoking, then, its conditions and its structure, not inter-subjective and intra-subjective dynamics. We have already underlined dialectical materialism's abandonment of the negativity traversing the subject, and the historical justifications for this abandonment.[53]

However, practice, in whatever form it takes, dissolves the compactness [*compacité*] and the self-presence of the subject. Practice puts the subject into contact, thus into a negative relationship with objects and other subjects of the social milieu which it contradicts (whether or not this contradiction is antagonistic). In order to be situated, then, in an exteriority vis-à-vis the subject, the contradiction internal to social relationships ex-centers the subject itself, and articulates it as a site of passage, a non-site where opposite tendencies struggle: needs, desires, drives whose moments of stasis (thetic moments, representations) are just as much linked to affective (parental, love) relations as to class conflicts. In ex-centering the subject, rejection confronts the subject's destruction with the structures of the natural world and of social relations, collides with these structures, and drives them away. Thus, rejection implies the annihilation of what was formerly an objectivity. At the same time, a linking, symbolic, ideological, and thus positivizing component intervenes ("we intervene," writes Hegel) in order to constitute, in language, the new object that the rejecting "subject" produces through the objective process of rejection. Practice contains, as fundamental moment, the heterogeneous contradiction—a struggle of the subject put in process [*mis en procès*] by a natural or social and not yet symbolized outside, with former moments of stasis, in other words, with systems of representation that defer and delay the violence of that rejection.

As drive-related rejection confronts historical and social processes [*processus*], not only is the transformation of these very structures realized, but also the recasting of the subjective-symbolic structuration, the reconstitution of the knowing subjective unity with the new object that it has discovered in the social process [*processus*].

## THE FICTION OF PRACTICE

By its explicit intentions and by the requirement of its logic, by the race to death—implicit jouissance—whose silhouette can never be discerned too far behind the contradictions the subject confronts in its struggle, revolutionary practice emphasizes this moment of the subject put in process [*mis en procès*]: it must be suppressed as subjective unity in the beginning and as living being in the end, if the objective law of the struggle demands it.

But in order to do this, and as if paradoxically, the subject of social practice hypostasizes *the thetic moment of rejection*, the moment of "paranoia." A dilated, swollen, tenacious "self," armed with ideological and theoretical assurance, fights in representation the former moments of stasis that resist rejection. Having joined the course of historical processes in action, the process of meaning professes to be an agent in the representation of a "Self," that of revolutionarism which doesn't need to know and even less to deeply examine the mechanism of negativity that destroys it or reunites it. Objectively, this "impenetrable and atomic self" is the unit by which negativity invades the social scene.

By repressing "the activity of the senses" or "immediate experience" to the extent that it destroys this "Self," Hegel's "practical concept," or the "practice" of dialectical materialism borne by such a "Self," is doomed to a mechanical repetition of action without modifying the real, material and meaningful, objective and subjective order of things. Since it fixes an opaque reality in an atomic and nullified subjectivity, such a "practice" blocks the very process of the practice aimed at "transforming the *subjective and objective* process [*procès*]."[54] However, by rehabilitating certain aspects of sensual human experience, and in particular its external material determination, dialectical materialism takes the path of what one could call *the practical analysis* of the "impenetrable" and "atomic" subject, bearer of the practical concept. Dialectical materialism is aware that this impenetrable subject is the logical and historical condition for action, that its thetic phase is in league with ethical teleology; it makes use of this information and, engaged in the movement of social revolution, does not analyze it discursively, does not criticize it, does not put it into play.

It is henceforth incumbent upon the signifying operations— whether "sovereign," verbal, or other—to make practical analysis, which dissolves the impenetrable and atomic subject, enter *discourse*.   In the present historical period, this practical analysis, which is brought about as an effective, unspoken component in the social practice governed by contradictory relationships between atomic subjects, necessarily needs, therefore, to find *language*, and to be realized in it as *fiction*, in order that the atomic "self," assured of the justice of its battle, be penetrated by the acting negativity of the process [*procès*], right to paranoid enclosure itself and without sparing its reassuring logic.   Lacking such a fictional verbal realization, practice—including revolutionary practice—exploits and isolates negativity outside of units that are *moïques*, verbal, organizational, state-related, etc; and, by consolidating them, installs symbolic as well as real oppression.   Bataille, who became interested in the causes and the logic of fascism, certainly saw in fiction—which represents and meditates upon limit-experiences and challenges specular and narcissistic unity from language right to ideology—the discreet, yet so profound and upsetting, means for struggle against oppressive unity and against its reverse side, exuberant or macabre nihilism.

Bataille's operation explores precisely the moment constitutive of practice which consists of postulating and destroying the unity of the subject in a process [*procès*] that postulates and displaces *theses*.   It is this moment that he designates by the name of *experience*, and that is, in its way, an overturning of Hegelian *Erfahrung*.   Fiction-experience exposes the moment of strength peculiar to all practice and, in doing so, it speaks—Bataille would say "communicates"—with all the subjects who, in different domains, pass through this problematic moment of practice, even if they return from it, in order to leave it "behind their back."

To conclude, we will say: as long as social practice dismisses rather than absorbs experience, fiction is the only means to reexamine and to thus analyze the teleology of practice.   The fiction of experience constitutes the condition for renewing practice since, by cutting the social chain, experience is beyond the site [*est le hors lieu*] of its expenditure.

The role of fiction as experience, in Bataille's sense, is thus to lift, in whatever society, the repression weighing upon the moment of struggle between process [*procès*] and thesis, a particularly threatening moment dissolving social and subjective relationships but guaranteeing in this very way its renewal.   Thus it answers to an expectation buried in the communal representation of practice, an expectation that makes itself felt most intensely at historical moments when the displacement grows greater and deeper between social practice itself and the representation it is given by the dominant ideology.

## NOTES

1. *L'Erotisme*, 10.
2. Cf. "La négation," *Ecrits logiques et philosophiques* (Paris: Ed. du Seuil, 1971).
3. *L'Erotisme*, 49.
4. Ibid., 10.
5. Ibid.
6. *Inner Experience*, trans. L. Boldt (Albany: SUNY Press, 1988), 127.
7. "Hegel," in *Inner Experience*, 110.
8. *Méthode de méditation*, 232.
9. *L'Erotisme*, 8.
10. *Inner Experience*, 119.
11. "Orestie," *Oeuvres Complètes*, vol. III, 204.
12. *Inner Experience*, 119.
13. *L'Erotisme*, 17.
14. Ibid., 42.
15. "The simple 'I' is this genus or the simple universal, for which the differences are *not* differences only by its being the *negative essence* of shaped independent moments; and self-consciousness is thus certain of itself only by superceding this other that presents itself to self-consciousness as an independent life; self-consciousness is Desire. Certain of the nothingness of this other, it explicitly affirms that this nothingness is *for it* the truth of the other; it destroys the independent object and thereby gives itself certainty of itself as a *true* certainty, a certainty which has become explicit for self-consciousness itself *in an objective manner*." Hegel, *The Phenomenology of Spirit*, trans. A. Miller (Oxford: Clarendon Press, 1977), 109.
16. "Ever since the sun has been in the firmament and that the planets turn around it, one has not seen man placed upside down, that is founded upon the idea and building reality upon it. Anaxagorus was the first to say that 'meaning' governs the world, but that it is only now that it has come to recognize that thought must govern spiritual reality. This was then a superb dawning. All thinking beings have celebrated this period. A sublime emotion reigned at that time; the enthusiasm of the mind made the world shiver as if at that moment alone, one had arrived at the true synthesis of the divine with the world." Hegel, *Leçons sur la philosophie de l'histoire* (Vrin, 1937), 215.
17. *Inner Experience*, 120 (italics mine).
18. Ibid., 115–116.
19. *L'Erotisme*, 29.
20. *Inner Experience*, 73.
21. *Méthode de méditation*, 232.
22. Ibid., 219.
23. "Etre Oreste," *O.C.*, vol. II, 219.
24. *Méthode de méditation*, 220.
25. *Inner Experience*, 137.
26. "Etre Oreste," *O.C.*, vol. II, 219.
27. *Méthode de méditation*, 231.
28. Orestie, *O.C.*, vol. III, 205.
29. Ibid.
30. *Méthode de méditation*, 234.
31. *O.C.*, vol. II, 222.

32. Ibid.

33. Ibid.

34. Ibid.

35. *Méthode de méditation*, 221.

36. "Etre Oreste," *O.C.*, vol. III, 217.

37. Hegel, *Phenomenology*, 56.

38. Hegel, *Phénoménologie de l'esprit*, t. 1, 77.

39. An attitude that Hegel denounces as being a "scepticism that finishes by the abstraction of the Nothing or with the void" (Ibid., 70).

40. *Inner Experience*, 124.

41. "First digression on ecstasy before an object: the point" (*sic*), in *Inner Experience*, 124.

42. "Death is in a sense an imposture," in *Inner Experience*, 73–74.

43. *Inner Experience*, 124.

44. "Hegel et son concept de l'experience," Cf. *Chemins qui ne mènent nulle part* (Paris: Gallimard, 1962).

45. *La Science de la logique*, vol. II (Ed. Auber), 498.

46. *Méthode de méditation*, 228.

47. *Cahiers dialectiques*, O.C., vol. 38, 203.

48. Hegel, *Science de la logique*, vol. II, 549.

49. Ibid.

50. *Quatres essais philosophiques*. Editions en langues etrangères 1967, 9.

51. Ibid., 10.

52. To be linked to Bataille's three-part distinction, with respect to inner experience: operation–authority–expiation of authority.

53. Cf. "Le sujet en procès" appearing in vol. I *Artaud* (10/18).

54. Mao Tse-tung, op. cit., 23.

# 13

# Bataille and Science: Introduction to Inner Experience

*Jean-Louis Baudry*

*At the extreme point of reflexion, it would appear that scientific givens have value to the extent that they make any definitive image of the universe impossible. The ruin to which science has subjected, and continues to subject, fixed concepts, constitutes its grandeur, and more specifically, its truth.* Le Coupable

*This is no doubt difficult, but man only arrives at the most charged notion of burning possibilities in direct opposition to common sense, by opposing scientific givens to common sense.* Inner Experience

*...science only advances where it may and calmly, leaving, through a lack of means, the decisive problems unresolved.* Inner Experience

The expression "inner experience" has raised interpretive difficulties, if not renewed misconceptions, and despite Bataille's attempt to clear up the most prominent misunderstandings, he himself may appear to maintain an ambiguity or an intended imprecision in meaning surrounding this term. "I had," he writes, "previously designated the sovereign operation by the name inner experience or extreme limit of the possible. I now designate it by the name *meditation*. Changing the word indicates the nuisance of employing any word whatsoever (sovereign operation is of all words the most fastidious: comic operation would be less misleading); I prefer meditation, but it has a pious connotation." It is true that the expression "inner experience," attracted by the space of the book whose title it forms, seems to have suffered from received language, from deliberate non-discursivity (though it summons the discursivity it negates), from the intentionally allusive (although insistent) character given to this book.

However, if one gives some thought to the development of Bataille's thought in its entirety, one will notice that the hollowness that this or any other expression must designate appears fairly soon, and that Bataille doesn't cease specifying its range and affirming its necessity in relation to a constant reflexion on knowledge, the place that it occupies in the global system of society, and, more specifically, in relation to a constant reflexion on science. It is by virtue of this reflexion that inner experience finds, among other things, its strong point, that its requirement is revealed and that its specific determinations are elucidated.

If, in Bataille's work, thought never leads to a global and systematic exposé, and this for the very reason that all systems are put into play by means of an overall practice with which it, as system, could not comply, everything is linked nevertheless. It seemed useful to retrace, therefore, among other possible paths, the one that links Bataille's reflexion on science with "inner experience." This is all the more the case since we hope that this path, by dialectically circumscribing the requirement that inner experience must meet, can help to remove from this experience the cheap and tattered spiritualist finery with which one tries incessantly to misrepresent it.

It is precisely in order to fight against the implicit spiritualism, the idealism and the moral confusion sustained by the Surrealists that Bataille sets off, in *The Use Value of D. A. F. de Sade*, the opposition heterogeneous/homogeneous, an opposition that corresponds to a new development of his thought and to a theoretical reinforcement.

Bataille recognizes in all individual or social organisms two contradictory and complementary movements: one of appropriation; the other of rejection, of expulsion. The latter concerns the heterogeneous elements—

elements one would find difficult to define to the extent that any definition would bring the heterogeneous back to a process of homogenization, a first difficulty, that announces, moreover, the complex relationship between Bataille and language. One can say, however, that the heterogeneous is characterized by the alterity, the negation and the alteration it determines in the homogeneous that, unlike the heterogeneous, can indeed be defined. Nevertheless, Bataille attempts to approach the heterogeneous by taking up once again the categories of sacred and profane used by the French School of Sociology. For example, he enumerates concrete forms of the heterogeneous: "Sexual activity, whether perverted or not; the behavior of one sex before the other; defecation; urination; death and the cult of cadavers (above all, insofar as it involves the stinking decomposition of bodies); the different taboos; ritual cannibalism; the sacrifice of animal-gods; homophagia; the laughter of exclusion; sobbing (which, in general has death as its object); religious ecstasy; the identical attitude toward shit, gods, and cadavers; terror that so often accompanies involuntary defecation; the custom of exchanging brilliant, lubricious, painted and jewelled women; gambling; heedless expenditure and certain fanciful uses of money, etc. ...together present a common character in that the object of the activity (excrement, shameful parts, cadavers, etc. ...) is found each time treated as a foreign body (*das ganz Anderes*); in other words, it can just as well be expelled following a brutal rupture, as reabsorbed through the desire to put one's body and mind entirely in a more or less violent state of expulsion (or projection). The notion of the (heterogeneous) *foreign body* permits one to note the elementary subjective identity between types of excrement (sperm, menstrual blood, urine, fecal matter) and everything that can be seen as sacred, divine or marvelous" (*Visions of Excess*, 94).

One notices at first that by causing the entirely other—*das ganz Andere*—to intervene, this enumeration indeed appears to be inscribed in a conception that is dialectical, but differentiated however from that of Hegel to the extent that it implies a divergence, an irreconcilable opposition. It is not the other; it is the *entirely* other. As a matter of fact the notion of foreign body introduces a rupture into the principle of identity. The foreign body—this is also the reason for its expulsion—erodes any accepted identity. Much later, in *Eroticism*, Bataille provides an exemplary description of the action of the heterogeneous. "We can easily imagine the surprise of one who...would discover without being seen the amorous transports of a woman whose distinctive character would have struck him. He would see a sickness, analogous to a dog in heat.

As if a bitch in heat had been substituted for the personality of one who received guests with such dignity...It is even an understatement to speak of sickness. For the time being, the personality is *dead.* Its death, for the moment, makes way for the bitch, who profits from the silence surrounding *the dead woman's absence."* On the other hand, the foreign body makes one think of the partial object and of the drives with which it is associated. It is distinct from it to the extent that it is applied to the social body.

But the simple opposition homogeneous/heterogeneous is insufficient. The fact is that the heterogeneous is itself undermined by an opposition; it is constantly exposed to the action of homogenization. In other words, negativity can never be delimited; it does not have its own unity. The negative aspect is constantly hollowed out, divided. Homogeneous and heterogeneous are not only opposed to one another in contradiction, but they are defined with respect to contradiction. The homogeneous is defined by the tendency to suppress contradiction or to refuse it, to become blind to it, for the heterogeneous is its exasperation point. One can immediately see the interest that the homogeneous/ heterogeneous opposition holds for political analysis and the application that results from it in order to determine the mechanisms of ideological integration as well as to situate revolutionary action in all of its aspects. Bataille himself will make use of it in order to analyze the fascist phenomenon.

Bataille thus calls the science of the heterogeneous *heterology,* but this in order to immediately recognize that heterology has an impossible status. In effect science (and moreover philosophy as well) only develop by establishing identities, by bringing the other back to the same. How then would it be possible to establish a science of what would never allow itself to be reduced to identity and whose mere presence gives a laughable if not illusory character to the identical? Science and philosophy do indeed belong to homogenizing authorities. "When one says that heterology envisages the questions of heterogeneity in a scientific manner, one doesn't mean by this that heterology is, in the usual sense of such a formula, the science of the heterogeneous. The heterogeneous is even resolutely placed outside of scientific knowledge which, by definition, is only applicable to homogeneous elements. Above all, heterology is opposed to any homogeneous representation of the world, in other words, to any philosophical system." Philosophy and science moreover do not have the same position nor the same function in the process of general homogenization. The role of philosophy is to homogenize the unassimilated residue of science; it attempts to recuperate the outside excluded from science and, as it were, to erase the dangerous limits, were they to be recognized, of knowledge.

Furthermore, as we have implied by speaking of alteration, heterogeneous elements escape objectivization. Since it is decidedly concrete, the heterogeneous element *affects the subject,* and the omission of this factor would destroy its specificity. This is indeed why it could also not be submitted to the objectifying operation conducted by science.

*Heterology* is, then, marked by an impossible existence. It sets as its goal a rigorous knowledge of the laws of the heterogeneous, but the heterogeneous eludes objectivization and the identification necessary to formulate laws. "Science," writes Bataille, "cannot know heterogeneous elements as such." Inaccessible to science, they are excluded by science. How, then, would it be possible to approach the heterogeneous realm, to constitute its field, to present a knowledge of it that is different, irreducible to scientific knowledge, a knowledge negating itself in its terms, to the extent that it participates in the heterology of the elements it studies? A methodological concern traverses the entire work of Bataille: to account for, to expose, and to build a *knowledge* of what is by nature inaccessible to knowledge. To measure up to the requirements of the heterogeneous, a heterogeneous doomed to silence but which, if kept silent, would become the accomplice of repressive homogenization. All of Bataille's practice in writing, in its various forms, in its successive corrections and resumptions, aims to respond to the existence of the heterogeneous by recognizing that the discursivity of homogenizing thought has its rights, to which it will not submit. Thus it will maintain at all costs and in its entirety the place of non-mutilated reality.

The term heterology presents, then, a value that is symptomatic. It designates the contradiction that animates Bataille's thought, the contradiction between a demand for rigor and the impossibility, for him, of sacrificing the elements that escape this rigour; the impossibility, then, of becoming satisfied with the limits imposed (through reason, through the contradictions of language, of thought). In *Conférences sur le non-savoir,* Bataille expresses very well this heterogeneous movement characterizing his practice: "Those who have followed the exposition of my thought must have grasped that it was in a fundamental way a perpetual revolt against itself."

The notion of the heterogeneous, such as Bataille conceives it, seems indeed to result from the convergence of Hegel's phenomenology, as the role of negativity is defined in it; of psychoanalysis, in the discovery of drives, of their objects, in the theory of repression that presents analogies with the definition of the heterogeneous as excluded; and finally, of Maussian anthropology.  It is to a great extent in relation to Mauss's work that Bataille will be led, on the occasion of the founding of the *Collège de Sociologie*, to specify even further his position with respect to science and to formulate the requirement of a method that allows for what he often calls "lived experience."  As a matter of fact, Bataille integrates the discoveries of the French School of Sociology but displaces them from their site and transforms their field of application.  One already sees this in the relationship between sacred/profane and heterogeneous/homogeneous.  Bataille recognizes, on the other hand, that the notion of the sacred and the distinction between the pure sacred and the impure sacred have a decisive importance in the development of thought.  One finds therein the whole group of heterogeneous elements enumerated by Bataille and, subsequently, the "divine function"[1] at work in inner experience—in what links it to the sexual putting into play of bodies; one therefore also finds the contradiction that hollows out the heterogeneous, a contradiction that Christianity has attempted to reduce. In the same way, it is on the basis of the economy of sacrifice that Bataille develops his concept of communication, just as the existence of potlach will permit Bataille to think the contradictory relationship between work and non-productive expenditure, between the role of loss, and consummation as regulatory system bound to desire.  But the concepts of "total social phenomena" and of "total provision" seem to us to have a total and decisive influence upon the conception of a generalized economy.  It is probable that Maussian sociology in its traversal of the different strata of social reality, in its ambition to establish relations between the different forms of social activity, imposes upon Bataille this requirement of a generalized theory, of a related conceptual mechanism by means of which all individual and social activity will be put in accord with all of the others.  In *Eroticism*, Bataille will once again take up Levi-Strauss's definition of the total social phenomenon which is "endowed with a meaning at once social and religious, magical and economical, utilitarian and sentimental, juridical and moral."  Sociology of this period transforms the modes of thought inherited from the development of the sciences of nature and modifies the system for organizing facts.  It breaks open the imperviousness of the different strata of the social whole that philosophy as specialized activity (political economy, law, history of religions, etc.) attempts to preserve.

However if sociology indeed shakes the edifice partitioned by the various orientations of knowledge, as science, it would not be able to reflect upon its own position. On this point, one grasps the importance of the slippage that Bataille effects from the sacred/profane relationship that allowed scientific activity to preserve the illusion of occupying a neutral site, of being in the position of inaccessible observer, sheltered from all contagion, to that of homogeneous/heterogeneous that reinstates science within the whole of social practices, that forces it to situate its own function and the repression that constitutes it, since it participates in homogenization.

But there is more. When social anthropology constitutes its object through the relation of the profane to the sacred, it is doomed to a contradiction, if not even to a partial incomprehension of its object. The fact is that the sacred, its functioning in rites, magic, religion, its relationship to death and to sex, together have the effect of putting the subject into play, and one knows that the subject is really revealed only to the glance of that which alters it. But this is a subject to which sociology as science would not be able to gain access since the object that it studies can only be totally revealed through the alteration of the subject that produces it—a requirement that sociology could not allow without destroying the objectivity that sustains it as science and, consequently without destroying itself. During the sessions of the *Collège de Sociologie*, Bataille will insist upon this aporia internal to sociology (and that justifies in his eyes the very existence of this College in its differential relationship with official sociology). He will linger over this theme in *Eroticism*, showing for example with respect to the Kinsey report, no matter what the interest of its theories, moreover, that one must choose between the totality of the object studied—but to the extent that it alters the subject, it is suppressed as object—and the objectivity of science which in this case gains access to an incomplete object and thus contradicts its scientific ambition. A contradiction that strikes at the very heart of sociology and that Bataille makes evident in a note to *The Sorcerer's Apprentice*: "Sociology itself, in fact, has difficulty avoiding the critique of pure science to the extent that it is a phenomenon of dissociation. If the social fact represents by itself the totality of existence, and if science is only a fragmentary activity, then the science that envisages the social fact cannot attain its object if that object, to the extent that it is attained, becomes the negation of science's principles" (*Visions of Excess*, 233).

It is necessary to stress Bataille's methodological intentions and the importance that he accords to the totality of the real; a methodological position that is obviously an extension of the ideological struggle that he leads against a society that mutilates and that survives in proportion to what it excludes.

By suspending the question of the subject to which it, as such, could not accord primacy, science becomes the accomplice of the theological concept of the subject. It is through the same conspiracy that complicity is established between silence on the subject and the full subject of philosophy and religion. Philosophy and religion border upon science and it is obviously through the same concern to envisage a non-mutilated "real" that Bataille will intensify his questioning of science through a reflexion upon the implications of philosophy and religion. The expanse of the domain to which Bataille directs his questioning responds term for term, in other words, to the range of the different fields of human practice subject to an exclusion. It is the extent to which the subject has been excluded, as altered subject, as the subject of sex, as the divided subject, that Bataille is forced to intensify his questions. Bataille's *forced* displacement across the different realms of knowledge will be the source of the difficulties emerging at the *Collège de Sociologie*, and the disharmony between Caillois, Leiris, and Bataille. "We must choose," writes Leiris, "and if we claim kinship with sociological science such as it has been constituted by men like Durkheim, Mauss, and Robert Hertz, we cannot dispense with conforming to its methods." Bataille, noting this disharmony, will comment that it is not possible to make an abstraction of the subject—"one of the most accepted results of man, to discover what he really is, is no doubt the absence of any unity of being." Long before publishing *Eroticism* Bataille writes: "Two beings communicate in the first phase through their hidden wounds. There is no deeper communication; two beings are lost in a convulsion that binds them. But they communicate only by losing a part of themselves. Communication links them through wounds by which their unity, their integrity is dissipated in fever." A designation of sex that perforates the closed envelope of the Cartesian subject guaranteeing the privileged isolation of science. Hence the contradictory status of social anthropology which postulates, as object, what it, as science, must exclude: "Initiations, sacrifices and festivals represent so many moments of loss and communication between individuals. Circumcisions and orgies are sufficient evidence that there is more than one link between the wounds of sex and the wounds of ritual; added to this is the fact that the erotic world itself has taken care to designate the act in which it is carried out as sacrifice, to designate the resolution of this act as a 'little death'." Thus it is that Bataille sees himself obliged to come back endlessly to a methodological reflexion. "The domain of sociology is the domain and indeed the only domain of life's crucial decisions," he writes. But as well: "Can sociology be presented as a science analogous to others—

sociology a science like biology and astro-physics?" "I have stressed and will continue to stress the fact that the phenomena that I am attempting to describe are experienced by us...Even more: I consider it a decisive act in the development of man to recognize what the heart of our existence really is. In other words, I believe that there is nothing more important for man than to recognize himself as dedicated, bound to what inspires the most horror in him, to what provokes the greatest disgust."

Psychoanalysis has responded to the question of whether or not it is possible to know an object that eludes objectivity—to the extent that the mere observation of it results in an alteration-irruption-disappearance of the knowing subject—psychoanalysis has responded to this question, if not under the conditions peculiar to science, at least according to certain modalities permitting the transmission of the facts considered: "Psychoanalysts," writes Bataille, "are reduced to a sort of distortion peculiar to the principle of science: their method is only communicated through a *subjective* experience: all psychoanalysts must first be psycho-analyzed, since objective knowledge is clearly insufficient...From this the fact necessarily ensues that only psychoanalysts could recognize the value of psychoanalytical givens. However none of this is the case: psychoanalysis and its distortion have caused *objective* givens, quite generally and sufficiently known, to circulate." It is probable that Bataille's analytical experience at that time had an influence upon his methodological orientation and that through this experience, Bataille was convinced that it was necessary to conceive of another method, well suited to other criteria, in order to gain experience of another object: the heterogeneous subject, the subject of the heterogeneous. In any case it is thanks, in large measure, to the breakthrough made possible by psychoanalysis that it becomes possible to question science about its practice. "I am forced to insist upon an obviously denatured character, obviously exterior to the general mentality of experiences belonging to minds deeply debased by certain objective types of knowledge. Not only have Leiris and I acquired the essential principles of psychoanalysis (both of us have been psychoanalyzed) but we have been fairly influ-enced by what French sociology in particular has taught us. In these conditions, our lived experiences can be considered to a certain extent as *fabricated*. It will be easy for me to show that such an alteration, that such fabrication was necessary for us to become aware of the essentially repugnant character of sacred things."

A "beyond science" takes shape, then, that is not a renunciation of science but a transformation, a mutation of scientific givens. Bataille's contribution in this domain is to have reintegrated science—which claims to be autonomous—within the entire group of practices belonging to the social body by situating it within general economy. Bataille's theoretical activity is played out on the borders of science, in a constantly held relationship that provides his work with a reference point and a foundation.

On this point Bataille is forced to take a detour through prehistory. For it is not enough to note the silent existence of the subject in scientific practice and to conceive of an external field [*un hors-champ*] that puts the subject in question for science; even more, one must consider the conditions under which the subject appears and its determinations as a specific mode of matter—reflexion upon this reveals that these determinations of the subject have traversed history while constituting it and being constituted through it. Bataille will reflect deeply on the *passage from animal to man*: "What interests *us* in the most ancient carved stone, is that it opens up the world designated by *us*. It is the first object that refers in a privileged way to that universal subject that has at all times made up the human whole. From the outset it heralds that whole, associated with it, with which it is endlessly associated. It is the object that heralds the subject, that heralds the *I*, that heralds...the *us*." Following in this respect the Hegelian procedure, he sees in work the first indication of man's appearance, of the subject's appearance. But the work that specifies man as economic subject is itself integrated within an economic determination, the economy of desire—something that Hegel saw clearly, and that Bataille conceptualizes as relating to work as taboo, the realm of the taboo. Work and taboo are linked through a reciprocal relationship. They affirm one another by negating themselves reciprocally. But if work is protected by the barrier of the taboo from the field of desire, it is indeed because the productions of desire are already inscribed in the economic base of work, both as negative investments putting in danger the production and the system of distribution and exchanges, and as positive investments. If work, the production of the slave, is conditioned, according to Hegel, by a renunciation of definitive desire, which, in short, is absolute for Bataille, there could never be a definitive renunciation; this is the case for the simple reason, among others, that the desire that disorders also introduces an ordering in the realm of productive work—the ordering through excess that allows one, by means of an improductive expenditure of the "accursed share," to reduce an accumulation of goods whose excess would present a deadly danger for society, which could no longer guarantee its control.[2] From this perspective, as well, desire is an integral component within the infrastructure since the deadly excess of desire offsets the deadly excess of the production of goods. If work indeed puts aside the desire that threatens it, desire, in seizing upon the product of work, permits it to reproduce itself.

Work, as negation of animality, is protected by the barrier of the taboo from animality maintained, the "other" animality that is no longer "natural" animality, but the wandering and obsessing animality of sex that was isolated by work and made fascinating by the taboo. A changed animality emerges from the negation of animality. But in this way, work and taboo will occupy different places as the subject is engendered; they define stratified functions of the subject, or of subjects that are differentiated though inseparable. Work, which naturally negates-transforms givens, engenders the humanity-subject. The taboo is both particular and universal. It is addressed to everyone with the exception of no one. There is no humanity without work, but there is no man without taboo. Work engenders the subject, but the taboo founds him. It founds him, torn between the necessity of the work that engenders him, and the transgression of the taboo as a crossing of the limit, where he loses himself by nonetheless gaining access to the other animality that defines him.

This relationship of the taboo to its transgression, that proposes the subject as riveted to its loss, as possessed by what is beyond its limit [*son hors-limite*] and as once again linked precisely to the functioning of desire, forces one to postulate the subject as belonging to a universal real, and to consider the form of osmosis that is established between them. The importance of the role of a general economy, which does not allow desire to become established as something outside of the real [*comme hors réel*], founded upon a transcendental lack within the subject's being, becomes clear. For Bataille, desire is inserted within an economy, upon the two sides of the subject, to the extent that it is historical humanity and limit of humanity. On the one hand desire is linked to the production of riches that is obsessed by it, and on the other, it is bound to what Bataille calls, perhaps cautiously, and no doubt as a trap laid for philosophy: being.

To grasp the content Bataille gives to this concept—philosophy's poorest concept according to Hegel—it would be necessary to reread it in its entirety; particularly where it is placed in a concrete situation—in his novels. For being is never given in itself; it is in fact never given, if not by chance and in the form of the loss of the one to whom it is given. This is what we were saying: it can only be thought in the form of transmutation, exchange, movement—in an economy; a transfusion between organizations that expand, that open up, that are lost and then reconstituted.

Actually, it is a communication or a "slippage" putting in play what is established as continuity and discontinuity with respect to being. Bataille only ever considers being as a composition (cf. *The Labyrinth*; it is in this sense that his position is materialist)—a composition whose elements are dissociated—a test of being's continuity; or are grouped together in new formations—a discontinuity of being in individual beings. One indeed notices here the Lucretian side of Bataille's materialism—a description of the various states of matter; and its Engelsian side—their liaison and their reciprocal engendering. "Each element capable of being isolated from the universe always appears like a particle susceptible of entering into the composition of a group that transcends it. Being is always a group of particles whose relative autonomies are maintained" (*Inner Experience*, 85).

Being appears to us to be the fundamental notion that permits a coherent reading of Bataille's thought. It is Bataille's richest concept to the extent that it irrigates his principal concepts, which all designate a practical concept as well: communication, slippage, sovereignty, chance, expenditure, laying bare, etc. One might say, however, that this is not a concept; the individual being that I am cannot conceive of it or define it. It can only be put into play by what puts me into play as an individual being. It could, then, only be affected at the point where individual being is opened up and succumbs, "a woman beneath her dress, a god at the throat of a sacrificed animal." "Being," writes Bataille, "is 'ungraspable'—it is only grasped in error; the error is not only grasped in this case, but is the condition of thought."

In this way Bataille introduces a major difficulty in the gnoseological problem. For if the continuity of being, based on its composite forms, can, if necessary, be deduced through reason, it is only accessible through a singular experience, the experience of an individual being who, in the passage to continuity, must affirm his individuality in order to be able to negate himself as such. An experience which is itself that of the contradiction inherent in the existence of the subject, as a limit of the discontinuity absorbed by continuity. But this is a contradiction that science would be unable to postulate, since it eliminates its subject and maintains itself based on a rational universal that precedes the existence of the individual. "As regards the continuity of being," writes Bataille, "I restrict myself to saying that it is not, in my opinion, knowable, but we are able to experience it in random forms which can in part be contested. Negative experience is, in my view, alone worthy of attention, and this experience is rich." This negative experience is that through which the subject is put to the test, is experienced as subject, as this particular subject, but by negating itself, *being negated*.

Enveloped by the passage from discontinuity to the continuity of being "which," as Bataille puts it, "is barely imaginable without sex," the relationship of the taboo to its transgression is found to be related to the moment when the subject dissolves, affirms itself but as limit, ruptured by what negates it. Transgression opens one to the continuity of being; it is the experience of rupture, of a discontinuous being that fails, situated, as it is, in its orifices, its sex. It is means of approach by which discontinuous being is undone and dies in a brief crisis or a definitive decomposition as it gains access to continuity. "What is always at stake in eroticism is a dissociation of constituted forms." "Being actually divides itself—its unity is broken in the first instants of sexual crisis." Transgression is the unbearable putting to the test by which the subject grasps itself as the fugitive result of differentiated and contradictory forms of matter. As active operational negativity, it postulates the real subject in the complexity of the mechanisms that constitute it, at the intersection of social production and reproduction conditioned by taboo and transgression and the economy of drives running up against the biological and against the representatives of desire. Transgression responds to that moment where the subject emerges from the taboo; it is the test by which the subject emerges for what it is, inseparable from an "experience of limits" as Sollers puts it. Thus work engenders the subject, the taboo founds it, but transgression, one might say, produces it when contradiction is actualized.

One is now in a position to understand why, for science, the position of the subject—traced by the taboo and emerging from its transgression in the thrust of desire—cannot be exposed. Science, resulting from the realm of work, can only be developed within the delineated realm of the taboo where desire is diverted and the subject—the subject laid bare by transgression—is buried. Science, threatened with its own destruction, cannot return to the subject producing it. "If we produce scientific work, in effect," writes Bataille, "we are envisaging objects as being external to ourselves as subjects. The scholar himself becomes, in science, an object external to the subject who alone produces scientific work (but who couldn't produce it if he weren't first negated as subject)." "The taboo at first did the work of science: it distanced its object, which it banned from our consciousness; at the same time it caused the movement of fright, which resulted in the taboo, to elude our consciousness— at least our clear consciousness. But the rejection of the disturbing object and of the disturbance was necessary to the undisturbed clarity of the world of activity, of the objective world. Without the taboo, without the primacy of the taboo, man would not be able to reach the distinct and clear consciousness upon which science is founded."

The taboo and its transgression are indeed complementary to the opposition homogeneous/heterogeneous. Homogenizing science excludes but is not able to envisage what it excludes nor the experience that is implied in what it excludes. It is not able to pass through the taboo and cannot speak of what falls under the power of the taboo, or can only speak of it from the outside by reestablishing as object what fulfills the function of subject. Science, belonging to the world of work made possible by the taboo, is incapable of gaining access to the position of subject inasmuch as it emerges from the contradictory relationship of the taboo and its transgression. Science maintains itself by excluding the subject from which it profits, which it exploits in the investments of desires. At the same time it is unaware of the place where its different fields are dialectized, a place that is only thinkable when one recognizes the producing subject and history as putting the subject to the test. Thus, when it makes man its object of knowledge, it reduces him to the level of things. This is indeed why eroticism, which can only be grasped in an experience that alters the subject and puts it in question, has in this sense a test value and marks the limit of scientific activity. Science can only realize a reductive movement that will result in a humanistic overinvestment, leading in its accomplished scientific form to rationalism. Passing from the study of nature to the requirement of an exclusive rationality, it eliminates as well, then, the dialectical authority of the knowledge's process, of the subject internal to this testing process, of the investments of desires that pass into this testing process. However it will be necessary to rely on the constitution of a transcendental subject. This is a subject that guarantees the validity of science since it isolates itself from the articulated whole of different practices—practices that can be thought only through the recognition of the real subject, taken in the whole of its drives and of its relationship, and that of its drives, to social practices.

Thus science originates in the specialized activity of all human practices and their cohesion. It abandons them to philosophy which, participating as well in homogenization, reinforces exclusion and appears to envisage totality only at the level of what one must necessarily regard as repression. "This search for a coherent whole," writes Bataille in the preface to *Eroticism,* "is what opposes my effort to those of science. Science studies a separate question. It accumulates specialized works. I believe that eroticism has a sense for man that scientific procedure cannot attain. Eroticism can only be envisaged if, when one envisages it, one envisages man...I have sacrificed everything to the search for a point of view from which the unity of the human spirit emerges." After Hegel, he defines his enterprise, and the concern for totality that it reveals—a will to leave nothing aside—as an anthropology, but unlike Hegel, as a ruptured anthropology, thus marking the impossibility of a totalization.

The delimitation of science, the aim of what it excludes and which founds its possibility, together determine a beyond-science whose scope and approach Bataille tries to define by the designation inner experience. If he can vary its terms according to the principal orientation of the chosen "experience" (the subject put to the test in "divine function," application, laying bare, etc.), in *Eroticism*, where he postulates the specificity and the necessity of inner experience with respect to science, its means of expression do not change. Bataille affirms with inner experience the existence of an "other" with respect to science—as practice of the subject producing science—and with respect to the mode of knowledge, to the formulation of a method. In this domain of the other with respect to science, an other which Bataille is the first to rigorously think through in its entirety, it is no longer possible to oppose theory and practice, knowledge and the alteration of the knowing subject, knowledge and the practice of the desiring subject whose overflowing drowns knowledge in a non-knowledge. "No one can both know, and not be destroyed" writes Bataille in *The Accursed Share*.

The term "experience" is meant to take account of this internal and necessary relationship and is thus chosen in a privileged way by Bataille, whereas "inner" introduces what opposes it to the objectivity-exteriority of scientific procedure. Inner indeed specifies the outside of the outside peculiar to scientific procedure. "I insist upon it," writes Bataille. "If at times I speak the language of a man of science, this is only at a surface level—the scholar speaks about the outside like an anatomist about the brain." He even emphasizes that one necessarily has recourse to the objective givens guaranteeing the validity of experience. By raising the problematics of the heterogeneous, of what is excluded by science and therefore by the subject, Bataille does not question either science or its validity in the name of some sort of transcendental experience; he marks its limits and, by establishing an unprecedented conceptual whole, which indirectly takes on the givens of individual sciences, history, the history of work and religions, he succeeds in showing how these limits were established, and to what necessity they responded. But Bataille always intervenes at the point where scientific activity stops without knowing that it has run up against a wall. Bataille writes:

> To begin with, I cannot arbitrarily rule out my own access to
> the knowledge brought about by the impersonal method. My
> experience always assumes knowledge of the objects that it
> puts into play (in eroticism, it is at least a question of bodies,
> and in religion, of the stabilized forms without which there
> would be no religious practice). These bodies are only given
> to us within the perspective in which they have historically
> taken on their meaning (their erotic value). We cannot sepa-
> rate their experience from those objective forms and from their
> external quality arising from their historical appearance. These
> precise forms which come to us from all sides are not only
> unable to oppose the *inner experience* that responds to them,
> but they help it to emerge from the fortuitousness that charac-
> terizes the individual.

As opposed to science, inner experience postulates the subject, but as
opposed to philosophy which uses the subject to guarantee being, inner
experience postulates the subject as resulting from being (from a certain
form of matter), but in postulating the subject, it also postulates the
moment of its negation.

Through inner experience, both a method and a field are defined,
whose intent, in itself contradictory (linked to science, to knowledge, but
putting science and knowledge into question, remaining inaccessible to
them), is determined to expose the movement of contradiction. A field
that is inseparable from its exposition, from the movement by which it is
expressed, which is also inseparable from its method, from its counter-
method, discovered or reinvented by Bataille in the very test of inner experience. A method inconceivable outside of a practice of the subject, a
practice of limits that allows the subject to put itself in question. "My
method or perhaps my absence of method is my life."

"There is," writes Bataille in the preface to the second edition of
*L'Impossible*, "a double perspective vis-à-vis the human species: on the
one hand, that of violent pleasure, of horror and of death—exactly that of
poetry—and, in the opposite sense, that of science and of the real world of
utility. Only the useful, the real have a serious character: truth has rights
over us. It even has every right over us. Yet we can, and we even must
answer to *something* that, not being God, is more powerful than all rights:
that *impossible* to which we only gain access by forgetting the truth of all
those rights, by accepting disappearance."

## NOTES

1. We call "divine function" the subject's specific test of its own limits, in which God is at the same time negated and put into play, in what he implies. For example, one can get an idea of this testing from the following statement by Bataille: "God is not the limit of man, but the limit of man is divine. In other words, man is divine in the experience of his limits." (*Le Coupable*)

2. In *Hegel, l'Homme et l'Histoire*, Bataille specifies that the opposition between the Master and the Slave, which responds in Hegel's work to a logical presentation, can be experienced by the same individual subject. In this way, he introduces a contradiction internal to the subject which is the work of desire—an interrupted dialectic through which the displacement of mastery into sovereignty, an entirely different matter, is brought about.

# V. *Histoire de l'oeil* and Bataille's Fiction

# 14

# ...And a Truth For a Truth: Barthes On Bataille

**Michael Halley**

Metaphor/metonymy: Like a sorcerer's wand, the concept raises the possibility of a writing, above all if it is coupled: here, he says, lies the power to say something.

In his reading of George Bataille's short novel *Histoire de l'oeil*, Roland Barthes argues that its erotic component is an exclusively rhetorical phenomenon occasioned by odd metonymical convergences of two distinct and autonomous, in fact parallel, metaphorical chains. The novel's referentiality is entirely intertextual; no recourse to any a-textual concept of the erotic is acknowledged, this despite the fact that Bataille's novel verges on the pornographic in its description of perverse sexual practices.

In opposition to Barthes one could maintain that the novel does in fact demonstrate via its narrative *voice* the theory of eroticism which Bataille elaborates in his study *l'Erotisme*. By reading Barthes' text closely I try to elucidate how he has succeeded in stripping Bataille's text of its symbolic capability, its capacity for describing and manifesting in language the idea of the erotic. My attempt is to restore Bataille's text, to return to it what Barthes' formalizing strategy has taken from it.

❧

In *Sade Fourier Loyola* Roland Barthes writes:

> Sade is an "erotic" author, one says incessantly. But what is
> eroticism? It is always nothing but a word [*parole*], since its
> practices can only be coded if they are known, that is spoken.
> Now our society never articulates an erotic practice, only
> desires, preambles, contexts, suggestions, ambiguous sublima-
> tions such that for us eroticism can only be defined by a
> perpetually allusive word [*parole*].[1]

Eroticism, then, names a code for which there exists no key. Erotic
describes a behavior that is always absent, profoundly hidden, impene-
trably repressed. Barthes does not deny the reality of the practice of
eroticism, rather he doubts the capacity of language to capture or even
approach it. Erotic writing cannot succeed in evoking its referent
because that referent, eroticism itself, defies representation. Barthes'
disqualification of the purely erotic from the scene of writing can be
viewed in the context of his indiscriminate rejection of thematic criticism,
his refusal to see in literature a mirroring of human activity, the expression of man's experience in the world. Once a theme is subjected to a
written code it is irretrievably abandoned, hopelessly subsumed by the
formal proliferation of semantic structures which replaces it without ever
recording it. What is true for Barthes' conception of literature is equally
true for his literary criticism. He too replaces one item for another. The
critical text is a reinscription, a rewriting of the literary text and each of
these can generate meaning only from within, via the juxtaposition and
interaction of its constitutive elements: letters, words, grammatical
arrangements, and rhetorical tactics. Each text operates autonomously,
and excludes the other. Barthes' reading of George Bataille's short novel
*Histoire de l'oeil* provides a revealing example of this phenomenon of
exclusion.

For Bataille, there does exist an erotic truth beyond the coded
language of infinitely deferred referentiality. It is directly accessible in
"inner experience," and Bataille's scriptural task is entirely dedicated to
communicating it. To retrieve the erotic requires at once unspeakable self-
violation and unthinkable societal transgression: One must be willing to
confront the fascinating, vertiginous conjunction of "la reproduction et la
mort,"[2] to entertain the convergence of sex and death, to admit their
singular, specularly interchangeable nature. In *l'Erotisme* Bataille
supports his thesis by invoking the radical loss of consciousness which

occurs at the moment of orgasm. In *Histoire de l'oeil* he goes further, presents an illustration, the detailed account of the death by strangulation of a Spanish priest who, in passing from life to death, experiences sexual intercourse for the first time, and simultaneously renounces his vocation. The action transpires at the end of Bataille's book.  Three traveling companions, the narrator, a woman named Simone, and Sir Edmond, an Englishman, have fled to Spain where, in Seville, they decide to visit the church of Don Juan.  Simone enters the confessional and encounters a young blond Spanish priest.  What she confesses is that she is masturbating as she talks to him, and she asks the priest if he is masturbating as well. She crosses over the partition which separates them to find out. She seizes his erect penis and sucks it in her mouth.  Sir Edmond arrives with a golden chalice and ciborium used for the celebration of the mass, and he forces the priest to urinate in the chalice and then to drink his urine. Afterwards, Simone masturbates him so that his semen spurts on the ciborium. What follows is the scene of his erotic death: "Get on your feet," Sir Edmond commands, "you're going to fuck this girl."[3] Don Aminando, the priest, is thrown to the ground where Sir Edmond and narrator pin him down:

> Simone removed her dress and squatted on the belly of this singular martyr, her cunt next to his flabby cock.
>
> "Now," continued Sir Edmond, "squeeze his throat, the pipe just behind the adam's apple: a strong, gradual pressure."
>
> Simone squeezed, a dreadful shudder ran through that mute, fully immobilized body, and the cock stood on end.  I took it into my hands and had no trouble fitting it into Simone's vulva, while she continued to squeeze the throat.
>
> The utterly intoxicated girl kept wrenching the big cock in and out with her buttocks, atop the body whose muscles were cracking in our formidable strangleholds.
>
> At last, she squeezed so resolutely that an even more violent thrill shot through her victim, and she felt the come shooting inside her cunt.  Now she let go, collapsing backwards in a tempest of joy.
>
> Simone lay on the floor, her belly up, her thigh still smeared by the dead man's sperm which had trickled from her vulva.[4]

Barthes never mentions this scene, or even the existence of Don Aminando in his reading of *Histoire de l'oeil*, a reading that pretends to account for, to isolate and define the erotic component in Bataille's text. That this passage may have left him cold and unaffected is conceivable, but even so he is unjustified in ignoring it altogether. Bataille is overtly attempting a thematic presentation of the erotic, a direct evocation in language of an idea, namely that the erotic occurs in the experience of death, and to the extent that the reader participates in, internalizes the dying priest's ecstatic terror he or she gains direct access to it. Barthes refuses to read these lines which are intended to actualize a conception of the erotic which Bataille has theoretically elaborated elsewhere (in *l'Erotisme* and *l'Expérience intérieure* for example). He ignores the evidence of Bataille's text, simply skips over it in his effort to neutralize the erotic within an irremediably formal system of self-deferring references.

The word eroticism thus detached from its referent, Bataille's narration becomes an empty sign that serves to articulate an inflationary economy of empty semantic proliferation. What is Barthes denying, by denying Don Aminando and his erotic death? In the "Preface" to the *Phenomenology of Mind*, Hegel exhorts his reader to stand firm in the face of irreality [*jene Unwirklichkeit*], the vertiginous moment that constitutes the act of dying for the self-reflective, thinking subject. To conceive, to accept, and to welcome one's own death even as it encroaches onto and eclipses consciousness is a purely philosophical stance. To incarnate the true in one's life is to hold close to the dead [*das Tote festzuhalten*], to inhabit the irreality of that presence. The reader is asked to attempt the impossible, to pursue the irreal, that is to remain conscious at the moment when consciousness is irreparably lost, to keep on seeing as vision is extinguished. Similarly Bataille asks his reader to see what Don Aminando sees at the moment of his ejaculatory death, to experience the erotic as it occurs in the life of the dying priest.

Barthes, who refuses Bataille, refuses Hegel as well. He has never read Hegel, has been content to let others relate the text to him, just as he relates the *Histoire de l'oeil to* his reader without ever treating it directly: "And if I hadn't read Hegel...the book which I haven't read and which is often told to me before I have the time to read it, this book exists for the same reason as the other...Aren't we free enough to receive a text *hors de toute lettre?*"[5] This is precisely the liberty he grants himself with regard to Bataille's text. *Histoire de l'oeil* (the story of Don Aminando's eye) which he has not read exists all the same for him (au même titre) as he presents it in his own text. Barthes is rejecting the text of Hegel and the text of Bataille for an understandable reason. He abhors their inherent and essential violence: Barthes' aversion to and sublimation of "the violent act" is categorical: In *Roland Barthes par Roland Barthes* he writes, "In all violence he (me/Barthes) could not help perceiving, bizarrely, a literary kernel...the illustration of a *stéréotype pathétique*...which made him experience a feeling for violence that he comes to know on no other occasion: a sort of severity (a pure clerk's reaction, no doubt)."[6]

If Barthes cannot accept the violence in Bataille's text, how then does he manage to read it? *Histoire de l'oeil* is the story of an object. It recounts what happens to the eye. What happens is exclusively rhetorical: *Histoire de l'oeil* functions metaphorically. "[A] term, the Eye, is *varied* through a certain number of substitute objects standing in a strict relationship to it: they are similar (since they are all globular) and at the same time dissimilar (they are all called something different)." The eye serves as the "matrice"[8] for a system of metaphorical representations. The first of these, formed by a process of analogous substitution,[9] is the egg. "It is a double variation, affecting both form (*oeil* and *oeuf* share one sound and vary in the other) and content (although absolutely distinct, the two objects are globular and white)." Roundness and whiteness thus established will define the measure for further metaphorical proliferation: "that of the saucer of milk, for example, used in Simone and the narrator's first piece of sex play." Here a pearly attribute manifests itself in the developmental history of the eye, and it in turn leads to further analogical extension, eggs (*oeufs*) as they refer to animals' testicles. Eye, egg, plate, eggs, "This completes the sphere of metaphor within which the whole of *Story of the Eye* moves ..."

Barthes's next move is to reapply the technique he has just elucidated. He has identified one metaphorical chain, and by analogy (seemingly the law of both Bataille's romanesque creation and Barthes' critical tactic) he constitutes another which runs parallel to the first. Transparent liquid determines the model for the second proliferation. Tears, urine, and sperm are included. After describing the genesis and structure of these metaphorical chains Barthes proceeds to ask whether they exhibit a determinate beginning, whether "the metaphor does have a generative term." The word "generative" is intended to be read literally and in the masculine. Barthes wants to know whether the metaphors are sexually grounded, whether the proliferation of analogous forms is initiated by a phallic thrust ("the sexual").[10] He thinks not, and for two distinct reasons. First, the metaphorically conceived representations are never phallic in dimension (unless what we have here is a "round phallicism"). Secondly, at the end of the work Bataille meticulously accounts for the sources of all the metaphors he has chosen.[11] *Histoire de l'oeil* then, freed (in Barthes' view) from phallocentrism, constitutes a "perfectly round metaphor." It takes its own spherical form as its model, and its domain is precisely identified with its spatial configuration. Here, in the perfectly round metaphor, individual manifestations, incarnations, themselves round, circle endlessly: "each of its terms is always the signifier of an other term...without it being possible ever to break the chain."

Barthes elaborates "the critical consequences" of this remarkably efficient and self-serving system: "*Story of the Eye* is not a deep work. Everything in it is on the surface; there is no hierarchy...it is circular and explicit, with no secret reference." Only "a formal criticism" can even begin to approach the formally proliferated metaphor, spheres revolving in a sphere, which constitutes this text, a text that leaves not even the slightest vestige of a transcendental referent, an a-textual element (a concept) which, from its privileged position hors-texte, can orchestrate and ultimately explain all purely textual machinations.

A question lingers. How and where does the erotic appear? Formal criticism is invoked to regulate formal literature. What space can be left open for love and death within the spiraling texts? Barthes responds by recalling the apparently insignificant transparent liquid sequence which he has installed parallel to the dominant and ontologically functional eye-like proliferation. (That this latter formalizes itself spherically while the former propagates itself in a straight line never keeps Barthes from asserting their parallelism. The apparent inconsistency isn't a problem for him.)[12] Barthes argues that the erotic occurs in Bataille's text when a term belonging to one metaphorical chain deserts camp and is made to signify in the other. "[B]reak an egg," "put out an eye," "they eye sucked like a breast," "drinking my left eye between her lips." Barthes defines this practice as metonymy and he concludes: "Of course one can imagine other definitions of eroticism than linguistic ones (as Bataille himself showed)" yet in *Histoire de l'oeil* at least, "we shall probably concede that Bataille's eroticism is essentially metonymic," an intertextual play of rhetorical tropes.

This figuration of the erotic reflects favorably on its definition in *Sade Fourier Loyola* as "a perpetually allusive word [*parole*]," in fact doubly so. Not only is the signifying chain itself semantically empty, but it is besieged with unexpected, unpredictable, inexplicably odd metonymic convergences which must be nonetheless, or in Barthes' view, all the more acknowledged. Has Barthes succeeded in reducing Bataille's text to a play in and about language? The question must remain an open one so long as the absolute exclusion from his own text of Don Aminando's death scene remains unexplained. One cannot help but wonder if Barthes himself is collaborating in the sabotage of his own reading. To maintain that eroticism in *Histoire de l'oeil* is linguistically based, and then to suppress the one passage in the book where Bataille portrays in living language[13] his intuition that eroticism is constituted by the experience of death in sex, sex in death, seems almost too awkward, too compromising, too blatant a falsification to accept at face value. Barthes even supplies key self-incriminating statements, his never having read Hegel, his refusal to accommodate violence in consciousness. What is going on?

To find out we must return to the passage Barthes has omitted. Here, the "eye," which has been circulating throughout the novel in much the manner Barthes suggests, manifests itself one final time: Simone feels Don Aminando ejaculate inside of her and she "collapses backward in a tempest of joy." At the next narrative *point de repère* the dead priest is alluded to objectively as lying on the floor. The "inner experience" of eroticism is never shown and never seen. What Don Aminando has encountered is not directly accessible to the reader. We can now understand why Barthes never grants autonomous power to the eye. It renders nothing visible, bespeaks a radical absence in sense of perception. But this absence, which Barthes traces as a non-representational transparency throughout the novel, an absence that he valorized as such, in fact symbolizes an immediate and overpowering presence. The transparent, invisible eyeball, Don Aminando seeing what we cannot see, apprehends and comprehends all. Emerson has given his voice to this experience:

> Standing on the bare ground—my head bathed by the blithe air, and uplifted into infinite space—all mean egotism vanishes. I become a transparent eye-ball. I am nothing. I see all...I am glad to the brink of fear.[14]

Transparent vision, its absence in sensual representation, coincides with visionary transcendence. This is the experience to which Hegel is alluding when he talks of holding close to death, watching it appear in a consciousness which it eliminates, and this is Don Aminando's experience as well. He dies in generation, his ejaculation marks the moment of his death, and his eyeball, which has seen the unseeable, remains, a transparent globe in Bataille's text. Simone demands that Sir Edmond pluck it from the head of the dead priest and give it to her. He does so, and she proceeds to embrace it, placing it first in her "cul" and then in her "chair." What she has shared with the priest, his erotic death, she now repeats symbolically with his eyeball, the transparent globe that represents transparency itself, the invisible nature of inner experience. Such is the eye which proliferates itself as an absence throughout the novel: The eye which has seen what will never again be seen with the eye. The eye which maintains the experience of death, dead itself in representation. It is the formal repetition of that irreal event.

Bataille's *Histoire de l'oeil* is the story of a symbol, not a metaphor. Barthes has been fooled, but understandably so. Symbols usually refer to presences, real existences; they symbolize something. But Bataille's transparent globe symbolized no thing, a pure ex-istent absence, the experience of irreality, the maintenance of life; sexual reproduction in death; an event which entails the extinction of all things sensual. The eye as symbol in Bataille's text symbolizes that irreality, invisible to the naked eye. Hence it appears as an empty metaphor. Nothing itself, one would never expect it to lead to a dialectical other, the perfect plenitude of inner experience, the unseen scene of life in death, death in life, that which is beyond mere vision, not bereft of it. Barthes has taken the eye for what he has mistaken it to be, an empty sign, and thus he uses it, proliferating its emptiness throughout his text. His mistake is not so much to have misread Bataille's text, but not to have read it through to the end, to its culmination in the death of Don Aminando, and the subsequent evocation of his transparent eyeball. What then does Barthes refuse, by refusing to finish Bataille's story?

In a lecture entitled "Flaubert et le travail du style,"[15] which Barthes delivered at Wellesley College on October 30, 1967, and which appears in print in a much shorter form as "Flaubert et la phrase," in the *Nouveaux essais critiques*, Barthes cites the linguists Robinet and Chomsky to support his claim that sentences can be extended indefinitely: Strictly speaking, "Nothing obliges one to close a sentence," he says, "nothing obliges one not to increase it." He then quotes a linguist whose name he cannot remember: "Each of us, ultimately, only ever speaks in his whole life a single sentence that death alone comes to interrupt." He characterizes this affirmation as being "profoundly metaphysical." Its suggestion terrifies him. Language, verbal communication, the seemingly endless proliferation of signs, ends in death. Barthes is not prepared for such a confrontation. So, he neglects to finish Bataille's text, to follow the self-perpetuating metaphor of the eye to its ultimate conclusion, there to discover its symbolic function: to direct consciousness beyond re-presentation, semantic perpetuation, to its end point, its telos, a culminating (and initiatory) absence.

Formalism is dedicated to the elaboration of absence in the empty presence of the word. Its commitment to textuality is significant. Given its emphasis on close reading, the scrutiny of forms as they appear on the page, it is ironic that formalism never valorizes the presence of absence itself which inevitably begins just where the written trace lets off. The (ir)reality of the blank page never poses a problem for the formalist critic who chooses to discount it, to ignore it, just as Barthes chooses to ignore the conclusion of Bataille's *Histoire de l'oeil* in an erotic death from which the symbolically transparent eye emerges. Barthes of course sees right through it and back to the metaphorical transparencies (eyes, eggs, testicles) which have preceded it. The absence of presence is the theme of a story—Bataille's, Hegel's—that Barthes would just as soon skip.

## NOTES

1. *Sade Fourier Loyola*, le Seuil, 31–32.
2. *l'Erotisme*, Editions de minuit, 19.
3. *Madame Edwarda, Le mort, Histoire de l'oeil.* Union generale, 164.
4. Ibid, 165.
5. *Roland Barthes par Roland Barthes*, le Seuil, 104. I thank Professor Mehlman of Boston University for this reference.
6. Ibid., 162–163.
7. "The Metaphor of the Eye," trans. J. A. Underwood, in *Story of the Eye*, trans. Joachim Neugroschel (London: Marion Boyars, 1979), 119–127. In the course of two pages of my manuscript I make numerous references to this text. Rather than cite each one individually I encourage the reader to study the remarkable essay in its entirety.
8. "Matrice"; Barthes uses this word to characterize the eye's capacity for grounding an extensive series of analogous substitutions. "An organ which, in woman, contains the product of conception right to its birth," says Littré. Barthes's attempts to exclude female sexuality are comprehensive, both here and throughout his oeuvre. Nonetheless, its tell-tale signs continue to crop up and to confound his efforts.
9. For an enlightening study of the mechanism of metaphorical proliferation via analogical substitution, read J. Derrida's "Economimesis" in *Mimesis: des articulations.* In regard to the metaphorical capacity of the color white, read his "Mythologie blanche," in *Marges.*
10. In *Sur Racine* Barthes's refusal to admit a specifically feminine generative force is similarly categorical. He goes to great lengths to signal Hippolite as the "personnage exemplaire" in *Phèdre*, and to emasculate la mer/mère, the force ultimately responsible for his

demise. For a reading of this conceptually significant homonym, see C. Mauron on *Phèdre* in *l'Inconscient dans l'oeuvre et dans la vie de Racine*.

11.  Barthes here assumes, without the slightest trace of a justification, that Bataille is telling the truth about the factors in his childhood from which the "metaphors" of the text emerged.  Even if this were true at the biographical level, the question of whether the events and the "metaphors" are in fact related or whether Bataille merely thinks they are remains wide open.  Why does Barthes become such a docile reader at this moment?

12.  The fact that the two metaphorical chains cannot be graphically conceived as parallel indicates that a falsification is occurring in the critical discourse.  The author is attempting to make ends meet or in this case, to keep them from meeting, at all costs.

13.  Bataille's language in itself is not "living."  He recounts an episode, but the reader who reads what Bataille has written reads more than what is printed on the page.  What cannot be represented in the word itself can be recouped in the reading experience.

14.  Ralph Waldo Emerson in "Nature," *Collected Essays*, fourth series.

15.  I am indebted to Charles Holladay, a senior at Boston University, for calling my attention to this lecture which is recorded on tape and available at the Geddes Language Laboratory at Boston University.  I have transcribed the quotations from the tape into writing.

# 15

# On the Eye of Legibility: Illegibility in Georges Bataille's Story of the Eye

*Mikhal H. Popowski*

## INTRODUCTION

"The eye is an egg" says Simone, one of the characters in *Story of the Eye*. The analogical network into which the verb "to be" (explicit or inferred) is integrated gives an iconic dimension to the narrative text. Thus, on the verbal level, the images are determined either by metaphorical processes or by the verb "to be" itself. Arising from the operation of metaphorization in the analogical mode, phrases like "the eye is an egg" are themselves also metaphors. They are therefore part of the process producing meaning that, working within the intratextual analogical combination, allows a certain indetermination to appear. In fact, by means of this particular combination, the narrative text provides the reader with a group of intratextual images lifted from the cultural code and the "real" code.

An image has "…in a certain way" the particular quality of being "the boundary of meaning." (R. Barthes "La Rhétorique de l'image" *Communications*, 19, 1964)

The *Story of the Eye* is, as it were, the result of an associative glance directed at "things": a glance that determines the referential links of signs with things: a glance that overlaps and distinguishes units of what is "real" according to particular modes; an analytical and synthetic glance whose dynamics generate text and generate forms but not meaning. Meaning resides here in the form, and everything else is fundamentally "neutral" because semantically "open." We will attempt therefore to show how (a) the thematics of the eye emit, through intratextual processes, the possibility of an opening of meaning which is nothing other than its own neutralization, (b) how this neutralization is responsible for a displacement of cultural units and cultural phenomena, and (c) how this displacement or de-production of the cultural and therefore the conceptual sphere forges an illegibility[1] that is nothing other than the legibility of the narrative text.

## SIMULTANEITY OF THE GLANCE AND THE WORD, OR THE "GLANCE-WORD"

A profound relationship exists between the image and the production-reception of discourse: not that the image still precedes or follows discourse as one could perhaps assume is the case in pictorial art, but that the discourse and the image are produced and perceived simultaneously.

> What can be said from this moment on, is that *mutation* always results from a displacement, from something "moved" within the system of guarantees. It is as though the sudden superimposition of several forms of outline and non-congruent links within a single ideological space, had the effect of *permitting* objects to be *viewed*, objects that had up to then remained *invisible*, since their status vis-à-vis the dominant ideology at that given point was that of the *strange*. It is as though the appearance of these objects had set off *a crisis within the system of guarantees* (which usually define the admissibility and inadmissibility of objects) and, as a result, had set off a weakening of ideological resistance at this point. (H. Thomas, *Remarques*, 92, our italics)

Within the realm of de-production, image and discourse correspond, since they operate simultaneously; such that if there is image it is because there is discourse and vice versa (we call "de-production" the operation by which a certain state of things is undone, be it linguistic, conceptual, or other). The production of strange and hybrid images is the effect of the word's operation or even the effect, if one considers metaphor, of a "glance" directed at language, which is the recipient of a reality of things, of a given cultural reality.

> ...a first type of relations is precisely one which introduced this reflexion, and which puts into play the vision of the world, the cosmology, the entirety of concepts that together organize a society at a given moment in its history, and the iconic models (on *two levels—optical and thematic*) formulated by this entirety...(M. Rio, *Le dit et le vu*, 57–58)

Using metaphor and its impact on the text's production as a point of departure, the "glance" is the basis upon which the tale rests. It is up to the "glance-word" to be responsible for a de-production of values (macro-structure) and linguistic signs. This word belongs to a producing subject who is a sort of catalyst transforming the fragmented nature of language into a compact unit from which emerge not only new textual situations, but new images and linguistic situations as well.

From the macro-structural perspective, the glance plays a generative role. Raising the very possibility of modalities such as "seeing" and "understanding," it makes concepts both develop and disappear. Thus it is that, from an intratextual point of view on the level of verbal structure, the "seeing" takes on a thematic consistency, guiding the entire text. Now if we connect these two levels of structure, we will say that the "seeing" acts not only as a generator and as a thematic, but that it is the indication of a praxis of writing within the narrative text.

> Not to read, is, here, to ignore the formal necessity of Bataille's text, to ignore its own fragmentation, its relationship to the narratives whose adventure cannot simply be juxtaposed with aphorisms or with "philosophical" discourses which erase their signifiers in favour of their signified contents...Bataille's writing, in its major instance, does not tolerate the distinction of form and content. (J. Derrida, "From Restricted to General Economy," 267)

We therefore propose on the one hand to determine the way in which the thematics of the glance work intratextually and, on the other, to determine the various distributions of the units linked to the thematics.

To determine the thematics of the eye or the modality of "seeing" is to reveal a highly important dimension of *Story of the Eye* and it is consequently to indicate just as fundamental a relationship between the "opaque" portion of the text on the productive level and its illegibility on the receptive level. It is to join, then, the moment of the text's production to that of its reception.

## BIOLOGICAL SEEING AND PHENOMENOLOGICAL SEEING

The thematics of the glance are directed by the textual unit "eye," noticeable by its frequency in the text. By definition the eye is the organ of vision: it permits viewing. Biological seeing and phenomenological seeing are metaphorically united: one sees the world, one sees "things" as one understands the world and things. The eye is thus both the eye of organic vision and the eye of conceptual vision. It introduces a double thematic channel: on the one hand, pertaining to the "sensorial"; on the other, pertaining to "reflexivity," thus becoming the organ and/or the way of learning about reality.

Syntaxico-semantic distribution of the unit "eye"

In the text, the unit "eye" occupies several places. It even occupies the entire space if one judges it by its frequent occurrence, its thematic force, its analogical relations, and its position with respect to the concept of meaning.

Yet, as we shall see, depending on its place in the syntagmatic chain, the "eye" indicates a textual "spatialization," itself generating meaning. Let us examine once again the notion of spatialization as it is used by Y. Lotman:

> The fictional text is considered to be a secondary system working upon the primary system of language and shaping a given socio-cultural reality. According to Lotman, spatial relations are what play a leading role in this activity. The fictional text makes use of "a language of spatial relations" such as interior/exterior, near/far, high/low...in order to symbolize non-spatial relations such as good/bad, protected/endangered, free/enclosed etc...Now, if such a language forms the constituent elements of the text as model for the world, then the model of its description is well obliged to take account of it. This Lotmanian analytical model describes the text, therefore, as a semantic space subdivided into two disjointed parts. Between the two parts, there is a boundary characterized by impermeability. (R. Warning, *Pour une pragmatique*, 334)

Thus, we now propose to concern ourselves with the distribution of the unit "eye" as it is generative of spatialization and, by implication, of meaning.

The eye facing itself

In determining its various intratextual distributions, the eye indicates (1) an effect of intratextual spatialization, and (2) an iconic intratextual effect. The first spatial manifestation of the unit "eye" is that of a face-to-face confrontation, a linear trace in which the unit refers to itself as if from one point to the other of a straight line.

> ...planted herself before me; and, with her eyes fixed on me...(10) [*s'installa devant moi, <u>sans me quitter des yeux</u>*.] (71)[2]

> ...allowed me to stare at hypnotically...(22) [*me laissait <u>regarder comme en hypnose</u>*.] (81)

> ...if we chanced to notice one another...we could not help reddening when our eyes met in a silent and murky interrogation. (35) [*si <u>nous nous apercevions</u>, nous ne pouvions <u>nous voir</u> sans rougir avec une interrogation trouble <u>dans les yeux</u>*.] (93)

The "eye" referring to itself is the eye of equivalence. It marks a spatial linearity which is immediately completed by a temporal pause. "The eye within the eye" is not only the eye that goes from the same to the same (equivalence) but is also that which, at this precise moment, ceases to see, arresting the function of "seeing" in the fixity of its open glance. "The eye within the eye" is a unique figure: it is the eye of retention, the eye of interruption, the eye of hypnosis, the eye centered on itself, returning to itself in a movement of closure and rupture.

> The open eyes were more irritating than anything else. (43) [*Surtout les yeux ouverts la crispaient*.] (99)

> ...those eyes, extraordinarily, did not close. (43) [...*il sembla surprenant que les yeux ne se fermassent pas*.] (99)

> Marcelle gaped at this spectacle...then she said to me without even looking at me...(16) [*Marcelle regardait fixement...elle me dit sans voir*.] (77)

Simone, for her part, no longer viewed the hot, acrid come...
without seeing it...(22) [*Simone de son côté ne regardait plus
que le foutre, sans voir en même temps.*] (81/82)

...her...body...as beautiful as her fixed stare. (27)  [*son corps
était aussi beau que son regard fixe.*] (86)

...their eyes gaped with unrestrained joy. (27) [*le regard rendu
fixe par une joie immodérée...*] (86)

...I felt I could see her eyes, aglow in the darkness peer back
constantly...at this breaking point of my body...(30) [*il me
semblait que ses yeux se tournaient dans la nuit vers ce point
de rupture de mon corps.*] (88)
etc....

When the eye looks at the eye, it triggers fixity. The staring eye para-
lyzes the stared-at eye and immobilizing (itself), it arrests at once everything
that falls into its field. Such that, fixing a particular point, in this case itself, it
erases the surrounding space and elements and reduces at one and the
same time a whole field of recognition. This limitation of the field exterior
to the fixed upon point is also a limitation of knowledge, a reduction of
plurality and dynamics, an obstruction imposed upon spatial circumscription, a blinding of the glance. The eye is thus simultaneously the organ of
"seeing" [*voir*] and of "knowing" [*savoir*] and that of their impossibility.
Only reflexivity, an operation that leads from the same to the same, is still
possible. But, since the distance from the same to the same is above all the
reduction of the distance inherent in knowing, if one stops to consider this
proposition, one will see that legibility and illegibility deeply infiltrate one
another in the thematics of the text. Participating in the ocular function as a
function of cognition/knowledge [*connaissance*] and recognition/re-cogni-
tion [*re-connaissance*], illegibility is at this precise point the result of the
eye's being blinded, the moment where the eye, lost in fixity, reduces the
entirety of neighboring elements and, in so doing, breaks their virtual recognition [re-connaissance]. There exists, then, an ocular function, but its
operational possibilities are obviously severely reduced by the phenomenon of reflexivity, the eye remaining centered upon itself. Now, if we turn
once again to the analogical network, reconsidering therefore the system of
equivalences and associations, we will see that it perpetuates this face-to-
face confrontation of the eye:

...and fix her wide eyes on the white eggs. (33) [...*afin de fixer sur les oeufs ses yeux grands ouverts.*] (91)

"The eye within the eye" or "the eye" in the egg—the same fixity of fixation is maintained in the same linearity, proceeding indifferently from one point to the other, when the two points are, in this context, equivalent signs. In reflexivity, the workings of the unit "eye" are not dynamic, if by this term one understands a possible situational modification by the passage from one unit to another, from one class of units to another. Ocular retention, linked to ocular stagnation, is also a semantic retention: since distance and movement are missing (from one another), the eye looks at itself looking, right to infinity.

> Now isn't it precisely such writing *en abyme* that thematic criticism—and no doubt criticism as such—can never, to the letter, account for?
> The abyss will never have the glint of a phenomenon because it becomes black. Or white. The one and/or the other in the squaring of writing. (J. Derrida, *The double session*, 265)

As the center of an eminent and enormous stagnation, the eye retains meaning because, in the process of retention, it seizes upon and eliminates the virtuality or the movement by which meaning could take place. Since meaning demands a relationship of different units, a relationship abolished in this context, there results a glance which leads nowhere if not to itself. The neutrality of meaning—its neutralization—is signified by the metaphor of the "ocular opening": the open eyes are, paradoxically, eyes limited to a self-functioning or, on the semantic level, to a tautology. Thus, when the eye looks at itself looking, it can know nothing of what is looked at—its inability to move corresponding, therefore, to an immobilization not only of the meaning of the unit "eye," but of the meaning of the discourse that includes it, such that there exists a close relationship between the thematics of the eye and the problematics of illegibility. We could even say that one is the metaphor for the other. It happens, then, that the eye knows one thing and one thing only: it knows that it sees, it knows that its seeing is caught in an infinitely reflected reflexion or, what is more—to make the formula more radical— it knows the abyss of its reflexion. The eye shimmers with and sends back the non-finite which, in its turn, reflects [*reflète*] and sends back [*réfléchit*] the same image or even the silent identity of the image. There is, then, a pun between "to know" [*savoir*] and "to see oneself" [(*se*) *voir*]. "To know" [*savoir*] "to see that" [*voir ça*]. To see the indefinite pronoun. To see the eye. The adequation between one eye and the other is precise, perfect, total. Fulfilled, it can only say itself. It reflects, then, like an echo from signifier to signifier, from signified to signified, from sign to sign.

If analogy had already prepared the way for the regrouping of signs, it is then up to the eye to complete the process, when the latter proceeds towards the silence of signs. Fading (away) (in the presence of) meaning, words lose their possible meaning as if, faced with the split in language, there were only one solution: silence. This is the crisis of signs. If silence can still be considered as the bearer of information and/or meaning, it is only to the extent that it is informative of itself. Illegibility resides precisely in this silence.

> For with respect to that which can only be seen and heard, which is never confirmed by another organ and is the object of Forgetting in memory, of an Unimaginable in imagination, of an Unthinkable in thought—what else can one do, other than speak of it? Language is itself the ultimate double which expresses all doubles—the highest of simulacra. (G. Deleuze, *The Logic of Sense*, 284)

"[*sous*]"-"[*à*]"

The presence in the clause of "[*sous*]" and of the preposition "[*à*]" signals an apparent rupture in the immobility of the adequation. The face-to-face confrontation of the units is displaced towards a "this side of" and/or a "beyond," towards a high and/or towards a low that imply a filtering of meaning into the text, a gap in intratextual opacity. Since the metaphor of the eye comes into play within the space of the text—spatiality—the straight line and the symmetry proceeding right to infinity, are together replaced by the spatio-semantic strata that displace the stakes of the unit "eye."

> Dumbstruck, as though about to see Marcelle bleed and fall dead in the window frame, we remained standing under the strange, nearly motionless apparition. (26) [*Atterrés comme si Marcelle devait <u>sous nos yeux</u> tomber morte dans l'embrasure, nous restions debout au-dessous de cette apparition immobile.*] (85)

...all that remained before us was an empty...window... showing our aching eyes. (24) [*Il ne resta devant nous qu'une fenêtre vide...ouvrant <u>à nos yeux las</u>*...] (86)

...Marcelle could come only by drenching herself...with a spurt of urine that was limpid and even illuminated for me...(28) [*Marcelle en effet ne pouvait jouir sans s'inonder... d'urine claire et même <u>à mes yeux lumineux</u>*...] (87)

...the rear wheel vanished indefinitely to my eyes. (30) [*Le pneu arrière de la cycliste disparaissait <u>à mes yeux</u>*...] (88)

...a "half-sucked egg" was shipwrecked before our very eyes. This incident was so extraordinarily meaningful to Simone that...(34) [*Un oeuf à demi-gobé...fit naufrage <u>sous nos yeux</u>, et cet incident eut pour Simone un sens extrême.*] (91)

...the burning urine streamed out from under the eye down to the thighs below...(67) [*L'urine ruisselait <u>sous l'oeil</u> sur la cuisse la plus basse.*] (116)

The preposition [*à*] and the morphemes [*sous, au-dessous*] create in their turn a phenomenon of textual spatialization. They are used in either a literal sense, or in a metaphorical form, especially when it is a question of the preposition. "[*Ouvrant à nos yeux*]," "[*et même à mes yeux*]," and "[*disparaissait à mes yeux*]" are segments whose value or semantic content differ.

"Showing our aching eyes [*ouvrant à nos yeux*]" = to open before [*devant*] the eyes, or simply to open the eyes—the segment re-enacts the face-to-face confrontation of eyes, the reflexive equivalence, the straight line.

"for me [*à mes yeux*] = a renewal of the relationship between "to see" [*voir*] and "to know" [*savoir*]. To see for oneself.

"vanished to [*à*] my eyes" = a renewal of the blinding of the eye. Re-cognition annulled.

If the morphemes [*sous/au-dessous*] indicate an apparent literal meaning producing a double spatial level (eye = point of reference, sous = lower space); the preposition "*à*" on the whole takes up again and completes the preceding conditions relative to the face-to-face confrontation of the eye. It appears, then, that within the thematics of the glance, including the relationship of the modalities of "seeing" and "knowing," the unit "eye" serves somehow as a zero point—a level zero—from which the spatial evaluation results. In the context of the problematics of meaning, this unit is presented as the point of departure for meaning. Now, if "knowing" or meaning were from the outset annulled and/or impossible within the reflexive position of the points on the straight line, or of the face-to-face confrontation, and even if one could still hope that they reappear in the context of "gradations"—thanks to the introduction of the signs "*à*" and "*sous*"—we have no alternative but to note the failure of knowledge and meaning—even their massive failure—outside of the eye. Spatial gradation doesn't lead to the realization of a meaning any more than does the straight line.

> A certain strategic twist must be imprinted upon language; and this strategic twist, with a violent and sliding, furtive movement must inflect the old corpus in order to relate its syntax and its lexicon to major silence. (J. Derrida, "From Restricted to General Economy," 264)

> Who will ever know what it is to know nothing? (G. Bataille, *Le Petit*, 22)

## THEMATIC LEGIBILITY AND ILLEGIBILITY

One can see that spatialization accentuates the wall of opacity that seems to characterize the meaning of the text. The latter is removed not simply through the workings of textual structuration, nor through that of its discourse, nor through that of a referential and cultural de-production; but through the convergence of all of these phenomena in and towards the thematics of the eye. The illegibility is therefore intratextual: let us take this to mean that it is to a great degree part of the problematics of the text. Placed by and on the level of the thematics of the eye, illegibility corresponds to a blinding.

> ...the contrary impulses overtaking us in this circumstance neutralized one another, leaving us blind [*nous laissant aveugles*] and, as it were, very remote from anything we touched, in a world where gestures have no carrying power, like voices in a space that is absolutely soundless. (44)

A blinding of the glance, of the eye and an impossibility for knowing and for recognition; the text speaks, thus, of its own rupture with meaning, with the concept of meaning. It implicitly speaks its insufficiency, its want; the failure of its culmination and of its closure. It cannot be a question, then, of textual polysemia nor even, as Barthes says:

> ...of a (limited) dissemination of meanings, sprinkled like gold dust upon the surface of the text. (R. Barthes, *S/Z*, 7)

but of an atrophy of meaning concurrent both on the intratextual, verbal level and the macrotextual, extratextual level. If it were possible to learn about the text's language, we would be quite obliged to recognize that the latter runs up against obstacles linked in a profound way to the thematics of the text. Since illegibility is a part of this thematics, it raises both the problem of the reception of the text's material and that of its production. The illegibility is thus at the threshold of legibility. To recognize its status is to begin to decipher the text. Hence the textual circularity, a circularity endlessly taken up again at different levels of the text.

> I stretched out in the grass, my skull on a large, flat rock and my eyes staring straight up at the Milky Way...that open crack at the summit of the sky, apparently made of ammoniacal vapours shining in the immensity (in empty space, where they burst forth absurdly like a rooster's crow in total silence), a broken egg, a broken eye, or my own dazzled skull weighing down the rock *bouncing symmetrical images back to infinity.* [*en renvoyaient à l'infini les images symétriques.*] (42)

## PARAMETERS OF ILLEGIBILITY

If we then attempt to situate the notion of illegibility, we see that it is an integral part of the narrative text, either as an operation upsetting linguistic units, or as a de-production of cultural and ideological authority, explicit or not, or finally as an intratextual problematics directly linked to the thematics of the eye or of the glance and to modalities such as "seeing" and "knowing."

### Illegibility and "Crisis"

Illegibility is, so to speak, both the moment and the result of a "crisis," if by this term one understands an effort or an effect, whether concerted, theoretical, or well thought-out, that fractures and/or transforms a systematic domain. In *Story of the Eye*, this fracture is at least triple: on the one hand, it affects cultural authorities and givens, then linguistic givens, and finally, crosses the intratextual thematic channel. It signals therefore the moment when cultural, ideological, and linguistic units are transformed on a systematic level.

### Simultaneity of legibility and illegibility

This fracture through crisis raises a first problem. It is indeed important to know its coefficient in order to determine what its possibilities for communication still are. In other words, it is important to know the degree of crisis. For, judging by the cultural and linguistic deformations and, assuming that the tale is and remains at the very least legible, we must note that, all in all, the fracture is partial and therefore that a whole group of linguistic and cultural signs still resonate with meaning. Hence a certain complexity:

What does complexity mean?

> Here the term does not simply mean an empirical complication in interactions and interrelations; it means that the interactions and interrelations inherently bear a principle of theoretical and logical complexity, since one must consider organization and disorganization, complementarity and antagonism together, instead of separating them and purely and simply opposing them. Complexity, according to our concept, is what forces us to associate notions that should apparently be mutually exclusive, in what is at once a complementary, concurrent and antagonistic fashion. (E. Morin, *Pour une crisologie*, 154)

Thus, not only is there legibility, but there is, simultaneously, illegibility. Is it possible to split the two notions or, as we are inclined to believe, do illegibility and legibility become joined in such a way that legibility becomes illegibility, its necessary, antagonistic, and simultaneous complement?

Illegibility and legibility seem to take part in a same movement: (1) on the discursive level, when units such as those of the analogical network—at once legible and illegible—bear and lose their meaning, their referent, thus raising in the context of a certain systematic homogeneity, the problem of the narrative text's meaning; (2) on the thematic level, when the modality of "seeing" bears and loses that of "knowing," carrying with it an entire spatial intratextual play; (3) when, finally, illegibility itself becomes, on the level of production, the very phenomenon of legibility.

Since illegibility is, then, the threshold of legibility or, rather, since legibility is situated at the threshold of illegibility, the two terms converge in a same time and a same text. The fundamental ambiguity of *Story of the Eye*, its complexity vis-à-vis meaning, is above all the quasi-geometric result of the simultaneity of the two converging and concurrent phenomena. The fact is that the text's "crisis" is such that it expresses a time of transformation that is both intratextual (the moments of "coincidence" and of "simultaneity" that provoke the blinding) and extratextual: the gestation time of the text. Such that the narrative text is itself what marks this crisis, the latter being precisely what one can read from and in the text.

Raised in this way, the problematics of legibility and illegibility become, then, not only a problem of reception, but a problem of production. In the process of production, the "crisis" resulted from a renewed questioning of culturalo-ideological givens, be it from a disturbance of the homogeneity of the system including them. On the level of discourse and deep structure, the crisis took an analogical form, thus expressing the "upsetting" of signs. It is a matter, then, of grouping the two elements together and of noting that if there is "crisis" and if we read "crisis," the latter is fundamentally linked to a disturbance of the system(s) governing their organization, their meaning.

> The idea of disturbance is the first to cause the concept of crisis to emerge. This idea is actually two-sided. On the one hand, it can indeed be the occurrence, the accident, the *external disturbance* that triggers the crisis...
>
> But most interesting are not disturbances causing the crisis, *but the disturbances arising from processes that are apparently non-disturbing*. Often, these processes appear to be the too large or too rapid growth of one value or of one variable vis-à-vis others: (...) When one considers these types of processes in systematic terms, one sees that *quantitative growth creates a phenomenon of overloading: the system becomes incapable of resolving the problems that it had resolved short of certain thresholds*. (E. Morin, ibid., 155, our italics)

The disturbances make themselves felt at first in the text and through it. In this sense, they take part in the process of textual production either as their origin (macro-structure), or as their component (verbal structure and deep structure). They invalidate the system (the systems) through a movement or a choice of valorizations different from the known and determinable system of valorizations. As a result, they provoke the emergence of units or variables that displace the organization and the meaning of preceding systems. We encounter these variables again in the analogical textual network. The "eye," the "egg" etc....create a phenomenon of overloading that is the signal or the intratextual coefficient of a rupture with preceding systems.

The problematics of legibility/illegibility lie within the jurisdiction of production. But since this is the case, and given that the text is itself the indication and the result of crisis, we must note that the text's reception is a coordinate of its production. The reception thus cannot avoid taking into consideration the deviations introduced through production. Now if, as we have suggested, the text is the moment and the indication of a crisis, then this produces two immediate consequences: on the one hand, the text is not the re-production of an extratextual "reality"—real acts and events—but the production and the manifestation of an intratextual "reality" that decides its mode of reception; on the other hand, since the text is the result of a macro-structural de-production (cultural and ideological values) it processes its own coefficient of illegibility such that reception can henceforth no longer be a simple linear operation, or an operation of re-cognition. In this case, it is no longer possible to present the full details of legibility in terms of what immediately corresponds to an extratextual reality. At the moment of its reception and its production, the text is a potential "reality," a transformation, a re-construction. Thus it marks a time of rupture that is more or less intense, and therefore more or less perceptible. Result: if it is still possible to speak of legibility in *Story of the Eye*, this is because the notion is included in both discursive and narrative practice, and in the very thematics of the text; be it in its illegibility.

### Illegibility or the reader's failed expectations

There can be no doubt that the reader of *Story of the Eye* is a "situated" reader. Today this is almost a truism. However, to say that the reader is situated means that he carries with him interpretation schemes taken up by knowledge and experience, themselves established in and by a given socio-cultural context. As such, the reader approaches and will always approach a text—of any nature—with this so-called "cultural" baggage that he "applies" implicitly to the reading of the text. It would appear, then, that what is at stake in the narrative text, from a pragmatic point of view, is situated, as we have attempted to show, not simply on the level of the text's enunciation, of its verbal production; not simply on the level of the organization of these givens, separated or re-separated from the cultural reality assimilated by the reader, but on the level of the reader himself to the extent that he puts into play cultural practices learned or integrated. Thus there exists what we could now call a reader's "expectation," determined by his knowledge and his experience. The legibility is no longer restricted to the text, but enlarged to encompass the entire context of production and reception. In this sense, the illegibility corresponds to a failed expectation for the reader, to a weakness of the respondent or of the response or perhaps even to an excess. Whatever may be the determining factor, it situates (is situated in) a site that cannot be introduced into the system that forms the reader's expectation (that the reader's expectation forms), be they the cultural pigeonholes and the learning experiences of the same type as the latter. Intratextual illegibility puts to the test the ways in which the reader could appropriate the text's meaning. It creates play, this being "a"/"some" play between the cultural mass that the reader represents and that which is implanted in and by the text. This play is in a certain way omnipresent in each text, but depending on the relative strength of its coefficient, its divergence will be more or less great and its reception more or less articulated.

> As a result, when one defines fictional discourse with the help of the opposition between the internal situation of enunciation and the external situation of reception, one must not lose sight of the fact that this operation functions necessarily within a transcendant historical situation and that the fiction is related pragmatically only within this historical situation encompassing the two others. (R. Warning, *Pour une pragmatique*, 331)

Status of illegibility in *Story of the Eye*

Thus it is necessary henceforth to circumscribe legibility and illegibility within a sector that goes from production to reception, whereas neither one nor the other are *ever entirely* true to the image of cultural givens. One could enlarge the context and suggest that each text is the bearer of its own illegibility. But then in what way is *Story of the Eye* different from other texts? In this way: *Story of the Eye* bears the mark of its illegibility in that it makes its own status out of it. Illegibility is thus no longer only the general characteristic of production, but its particular status at all levels of textual production and manifestation. Thus it happens, strangely, that the reading and therefore the reception of *Story of the Eye* necessitates taking on illegibility as an immediate component of legibility. This means that if one were to try to discover the meaning of the narrative text, one would be forced to pass through the channel and the thematics of illegibility as governing legibility. In other words, *Story of the Eye* leads one to intuit that legibility is no longer a phenomenon grasped directly, nor is it a positive phenomenon either, but that it is—in this context—something grasped negatively and indirectly such that, still within the same context, one could say that the legibility and the illegibility of the text are closely united (hence the complexity), that they are both complementary and antagonistic, and that one cannot qualify the text at the moment of its reception as being simply positive or negative because one must from the present moment envisage the two terms in their respective correspondence and harmony. This means, then, that one can no longer speak of legibility OR of illegibility, but rather of legibility AND illegibility.

The important thing in this case is that the reader can be compensated for the lack in his knowledge only if he accepts to play the game of the text and consequently to read it and un-read it [*le délire*] in a simultaneous movement. The perspective changes, then, to the extent that the narrative text is no longer unidimensional but bi-dimensional at the very least. Now, what characterizes this double dimension is that it situates its two poles at extremities that are opposed in current logic such that, if one takes up the metaphor of the eye again, one will say that one must look in both directions at the same time, and even more, in opposite directions. This is a textual strabism. Hence the illegibility.

Conclusion

It is thus no longer possible to situate the reader outside of the circuit of production. The reader is only a potential receiver loaded with an accumulation of knowledge and who can only be sensitive to the text if he confronts it directly, in other words if he is willing, given his knowledge and his various learning experiences, to penetrate the play of the text. This means that the problematics of reception within the framework of pragmatics cannot situate the reader in an abstract outside, in a zone outside of the text, or even within the text; but rather in a place—a sort of close conjunction—where the reader-receiver, drawn to read the text, will be in one way or another bound to grasp the movement by which the text is made legible, be it the precise moment when *Story of the Eye* speaks its own paradox, namely the complementarity, the simultaneity of legibility and illegibility.

It is impossible to avoid the problematics of legibility/illegibility: all texts lead to it, in general, implicitly; in the case of *Story of the Eye*, this is done explicitly because it is understood that the very notion of illegibility is an integral part of the textual thematics, an integral part of its discourse, an integral part of the text itself.

## TRANSLATOR'S NOTES

1. Throughout the text, I have translated Popowski's terms "lisibilité/illisibilité" as "legible/illegible." I have chosen this translation over the alternate terms "readable/ unreadable" in order to foreground what Popowski suggests is the near inscrutability or impenetrability characterizing *Story of the Eye's* reception, effects caused by the disruptions and displacements of cultural semantic units whose crisis Popowski attributes, among other things, to ocular stagnation and retention.

2. In order to convey more clearly the author's arguments about textual spatialization and iconic effects of the eye, I have included, in italics, the French quotations from *Histoire de l'oeil*, underlining what the author had chosen to italicize. The English translations are those of Joachim Neugroschel. *Story of the Eye*. London: Marion Boyars, 1979.

## REFERENCES

Georges Bataille, *Le Petit*, J. J. Pauvert, 1971.

Roland Barthes, "Rhétorique de l'image" in *Communications*, 19, 1964.

Roland Barthes, *S/Z*. trans. R. Miller. New York: Hill and Wang, 1974.

Gille Deleuze, *The Logic of Sense*. trans. M. Lester. New York: Columbia University Press, 1990.

Jacques Derrida, "From Restricted to General Economy: A Hegelianism without Reserve" in *Writing and Difference*, trans. A. Bass. Chicago: University of Chicago Press, 1978.

Jacques Derrida, "The double session II" in *Dissemination*. trans. B. Johnson. Chicago: University of Chicago Press, 1981.

Edgar Morin, "Pour une crisologie" in *Communications*, 25, 1976.

Michel Rio, "Le dit et le vu" in *Communications*, 29, 1978.

Herbert Thomas, "Remarques pour une théorie générale des idéologies" in *Cahiers pour l'analyse*, 9, 1968.

Rainer Warning, "Pour une pragmatique du discours fictionnel" in *Poétique*, 39, 1979.

# 16

# Transgression and the Avant-Garde: *Bataille's* Histoire de l'oeil

**Susan Rubin Suleiman**

*One can find everything in a text, provided one is irrespectful toward it.*
Umberto Eco

Mainly, this essay will be about reading. Specifically, it will be about different ways of reading literary pornography, as exemplified by one of the great works of the twentieth century belonging to that genre. In order to understand what is at stake in this enterprise (my discussion is not meant to be purely academic), we must take a few steps back and look more fully at the figure of Georges Bataille.

At the time of his death in 1962 (at age sixty-five), Bataille was known to a rather limited public—in France, that is; outside France, he was almost totally unknown. The French public knew him as the editor of a small but influential journal, *Critique*, which he had founded after the war and to which he contributed regularly (his first article, in the inaugural issue, was on Henry Miller), and as the author of a few books of essays—notably a study on eroticism, a volume on modern literature and evil, and a volume of philosophical fragments on what he called "the inner experience," to which Jean-Paul Sartre had devoted a long and rather negative review when it was first published in 1943.[1]

Some readers knew Bataille as the author of two novels with scabrous subjects: *L'Abbé C.* (1950), which deals with the sexual and political torments of a priest during the French Resistance; and *Le Bleu du ciel* (1957), which deals with the sexual and political torments of a Parisian intellectual during the mid-1930s (it was written in 1935). Finally, to the intellectual elite, Bataille was also known as the author of *Histoire de l'oeil* (*Story of the Eye*) and *Madame Edwarda*, short pornographic novels that had appeared in extremely limited editions under two different pen names.

*Histoire de l'oeil*, first published in 1928, occupies the privileged position of liminary text in Bataille's *Oeuvres Complètes*;[2] but like *Madame Edwarda* (1941), it never appeared under Bataille's own signature during his lifetime. This is one indication of the pornographic status of these texts, at least in a legal and sociological sense—a good place to start if one wants to define pornography. A pseudonymous author cannot be prosecuted, especially if his work appears in a very limited edition and bears a false place of publication.[3] Although in our permissive days such prudence may be deemed unnecessary, one does well to recall that only a few years before Bataille's death the Editions J-J. Pauvert were brought to trial in Paris and heavily fined for publishing the works of Sade.[4]

By a remarkable turn of cultural history, in the space of a few years Bataille became one of the central references, a veritable culture hero, of the French literary and philosophical avant-garde.[5] In the decade following his death, his work elicited major essays by Roland Barthes, Julia Kristeva, Jacques Derrida, Philippe Sollers, Maurice Blanchot, and Michel Foucault, to mention only those who subsequently became culture heroes in their own right, in France and elsewhere. In fact, Bataille's writings functioned as a major intertext in the theories of cultural subversion and of (literary) textuality that were being elaborated around the *Tel Quel* group during the years immediately preceding and following the explosion of May 1968.

In 1970 the prestigious publishing house Gallimard began publishing his complete works (which now run to twelve volumes), with a preface by Foucault that began: "It is well known now: Bataille is one of the most important writers of his century."[6] In 1972 the *Tel Quel* group organized a *décade de Cerisy* devoted to Bataille and Antonin Artaud; in his opening remarks, Sollers stated flatly that no worthwhile thought could take place after 1968 that did not take account of—indeed, that was not in some way determined by—the thought of Artaud and Bataille, touching on sexuality, knowledge, the family, speech and writing, representation, madness; in short, on every subject worth thinking about.[7] No wonder that Susan Sontag, with her usual intuition for significant intellectual trends on the Continent, devoted a long essay chiefly to Bataille as early as 1967.

The obvious question is why Bataille's work should have been felt so deeply to correspond to a certain notion of textual and cultural modernity. It was not only, as some might think, a matter of promoting to a central place that which had been marginal—one of the characteristic gestures of any avant-garde. The French literary and philosophical avant-garde of the 1960s and 1970s found in Bataille's work an *exemplariness* that went far beyond a mere desire for paradox. But it will not be enough to suggest or even analyze the reasons for this correspondence; it will also be necessary to criticize them, in the radical, epistemological sense: to make decisive, to separate, to choose. For we are not dealing with some safely distant question of cultural or literary history. The question of Bataille's relation to the problematics of modernity is contemporary; it concerns *us*. This is nowhere more evident than in his practice of literary pornography.

## PORNOGRAPHY AS TEXTUALITY

In her essay "The Pornographic Imagination" (1967), which remains one of the rare attempts to analyze the relations between pornography and modern writing, Susan Sontag stated that "books like those of Bataille [she was referring to *Histoire de l'oeil* and *Madame Edwarda*] could not have been written except for that agonized reappraisal of the nature of literature which has been preoccupying literary Europe for more than half a century."[8] Pornography, as practiced by a writer like Bataille, was one of the ways in which modern art fulfilled its task of "making forays into and taking up positions on the frontier of consciousness," one of the manifestations of the modern artist's constantly renewed attempt to "advance further in the dialectic of outrage," to make his work "repulsive, obscure, inaccessible; in short, to give what is, or seems to be, *not* wanted" (p. 45).

By situating Bataille's pornographic fiction in the French tradition— or, more exactly, antitradition—of transgressive writing, a tradition whose founding father was Sade, Sontag manifested her own allegiance to the adversary values of the European avant-gardes of this century. For of course the avant-garde of the 1960s was not first in our century to valorize an aesthetics of transgression. That process had begun much earlier, with the Futurists and Dada, and was consolidated by the Surrealists via their own reading of Sade and Lautreamont. It was the Surrealists, too, who placed eroticism at the center of their preoccupations with cultural subversion. But it was in the 1960s that the potential for a metaphoric equivalence between the violation of *sexual* taboos and the violation of *discursive* norms that we associate with the theory of textuality became fully elaborated. It is here that both Bataille's practice as a writer and his thought as a philosopher became a central reference.

Philippe Sollers, in a long essay devoted to Bataille's book on eroticism (the essay appeared in *Tel Quel* in 1967), suggested that all of modern literature, from Sade's *Juliette* to Bataille's *Histoire de l'oeil*, was haunted by the idea of a "bodily writing" (*écriture corporelle*), to the point that the body had become "the fundamental referent of [modern literature's] violations of discourse."[9] Derrida, in an essay on Bataille published in the same year, suggested that the transgression of rules of discourse implies the transgression of law in general, since discourse exists only by positing the norm and value of meaning, and meaning in turn is the founding element of legality.[10] Already in 1963, in an essay devoted to *Histoire de l'oeil*, Barthes had explicitly stated: "The transgression of values, which is the declared principle of eroticism, has its counterpart—perhaps even its foundation—in a technical transgression of the forms of language."[11]

The importance of this idea—which suggests that the transgressive content of a work of fiction, and of pornographic fiction in particular, must be read primarily as a metaphor for the transgressive use of language effected by modern writing—cannot be overestimated. What we see here is the transfer (or, to use a very Bataillean term, the "sliding," *glissement*) of the notion of transgression from the realm of experience—whose equivalent, in fiction, is representation—to the realm of words, with a corresponding shift in the roles and importance accorded to the signifier and the signified. The signified becomes the vehicle of the metaphor, whose tenor—or as Barthes puts it, whose foundation—is the signifier: the sexually scandalous scenes of *Histoire de l'oeil* are there to "signify" Bataille's linguistically scandalous verbal combinations, not vice versa.

To fully appreciate the importance of this shift, we must briefly consider Bataille's own notion of transgression. For Bataille, transgression was an "inner experience" in which an individual—or, in the case of certain ritualized transgressions such as sacrifice or collective celebration (*la fête*), a community—exceeded the bounds of rational, everyday behavior, which is constrained by considerations of profit, productivity, and self-preservation. The experience of transgression is indissociable from the consciousness of the constraint or prohibition it violates; indeed, it is precisely by and through its transgression that the force of a prohibition becomes fully realized.

The characteristic feeling accompanying transgression is one of intense pleasure (at the exceeding of boundaries) *and* of intense anguish (at the full realization of the force of those boundaries). Nowhere is this contradictory, heterogeneous combination of pleasure and anguish more acutely present than in the inner experience of eroticism, insofar as the latter involves the practice of sexual "perversions" opposed to "normal," reproductive sexual activity. In eroticism, as in any transgressive experience, the limits of the self become unstable, "sliding." Rationalized exchange and productivity—or, in this case, reproductivity—become subordinated to unlimited, nonproductive expenditure; purposeful action, or work, becomes subordinated to free play; the self-preserving husbandry of everyday life becomes subordinated to the excessive, quasi-mystical state we associate with religious ecstasy and generally with the realm of the sacred.

These ideas were already present in Bataille's 1933 essay "La Notion de dépense" ("The Notion of Expenditure"). They were developed and refined in his later works, in particular in *L'Erotisme* (1957), which presents a theory of eroticism in the historical and cultural perspective of transgressive practices in general.

What theorists of textuality like Barthes, Derrida, and Sollers accomplished was to transfer, or perhaps more specifically to extend, Bataille's notion of transgression to modern writing—to *écriture*. For *écriture*, in the sense in which they used that term, is precisely that element of discursive practice which exceeds the traditional boundaries of meaning, of unity, of representation; and just as for Bataille the experience of transgression was indissociable from a consciousness of the boundaries it violated, so the practice of *écriture* was indissociable from a consciousness of the discursive and logical rules, the system of prohibitions and exclusions that made meaning, unity, and representation possible but that the play of *écriture* constantly subverted.[12]

It now becomes clear why Bataille's writing, read in a particular way, could function as a central reference and as an exemplary enterprise for the French theorists of modernity of the 1960s and 1970s. His theoretical texts provided a set of concepts or "key words" whose applicability extended from the realm of cultural and individual experience to the realm of writing: expenditure, transgression, boundary, excess, heterogeneity, sovereignty—this last being a key term in Bataille's vocabulary, whose implications, as Derrida brilliantly demonstrated, are the very opposite of Hegel's term "mastery." Mastery is linked to work, and above all to the affirmation and preservation of meaning; sovereignty, by contrast, is precisely that which enables an individual to expose himself to play, to risk, to the destruction or "consummation" of meaning.[13]

Accompanying and complementing the theoretical texts, Bataille's pornographic fictions provided metaphoric equivalents for his key concepts, as well as a locus for their elaboration: the eroticized female body. Finally, Bataille's writing practice, tending toward the fragmentary and the incomplete, provided the example of a writing that (as Derrida put it) "will be called *écriture* because it exceeds the logos (of meaning, of mastery, of presence)"; the sovereignty of the Bataillean text, as of all *écriture*, resides in the text's "commentary on its absence of meaning."[14]

As I say, what is involved here is a particular reading of Bataille—a very powerful reading that has (or had) at least two advantages: first, it is integrative, allowing the commentator to consider all of Bataille's varied writings as part of a single artistic and intellectual quest. In this integrative view, the pornographic narratives Bataille did not sign with his own name or did not publish even under a pseudonym during his lifetime become as much a part of Bataille's signature as any of his other writings; thus, Julia Kristeva noted in her 1972 essay on Bataille that "Bataille's novels are inseparable from his theoretical positions and give them their real value."[15] Maurice Blanchot, in a similar way, began one of his essays by stating that central to an understanding of Bataille's thought are not only his theoretical works but also "the books he published under a name other than his own," whose "power of truth is incomparable."[16]

The other advantage of this kind of reading—let us call it the "textual" reading—is that it is generalizable: Bataille's varied writings are seen as parts of a single enterprise, and that enterprise becomes emblematic of modern transgressive writing in general.

If there is one thing, however, that the theorists of textuality have taught us, it is that no reading is innocent. Every reading is an interpretation, and every interpretation is an appropriation of a text for its own purposes. Every interpretation has its blind spot, which I like to think of not only as the spot or place from which the interpreter cannot "see" his or her own misreading of a text, but also as the spot or place *in* a text from which the interpreter averts his or her gaze.

What is the spot in Bataille's text from which the powerful textual reading averts its gaze? To answer that question, it is necessary to turn to an *other* reading, one that has its own significant blind spot but that nevertheless has the advantage of making us see Bataille—as well as the theory of textuality in whose service he was so powerfully enrolled—in a new, problematic light: I refer to the recent feminist reading of Bataille's pornographic fiction and of his theory of eroticism and transgression.

## PORNOGRAPHY AS "REALITY"

I know at least two versions of the feminist reading, which complement rather than contradict each other. In the United States, Andrea Dworkin has discussed *Histoire de l'oeil* in the context of a political attack on pornography. In France, Anne-Marie Dardigna has discussed Bataille in a sophisticated analysis of the modern (male) erotic imagination.[17] What Dworkin and Dardigna both succeed in doing, albeit in different ways and with different degrees of persuasiveness (I find Dardigna's detailed readings more persuasive than Dworkin's), is to focus our attention on that from which the textual reading averts its gaze: the representational or fantasmatic content of Bataille's (and other modern writers') "pornographic imagination," and the political (in the sense of sexual politics) implications of that content. I stated earlier that the textual critics considered Bataille's pornographic narratives inseparable from his other writings. At the same time, it is striking to note how very few have devoted any kind of sustained analysis to these narratives. Blanchot and Kristeva insist on the importance of the pornographic novels but then go on to more general and abstract considerations. Sollers writes thirty pages of close commentary on *L'Erotisme* but devotes only a few (extremely intelligent ones, it is true) to a work of fiction, *Ma Mère*.[18] Derrida at no point explicitly mentions Bataille's novels.

As for Barthes, his essay on *Histoire de l'oeil* remains one of the most interesting—as well as one of the rare—detailed commentaries on that text. The whole thrust of Barthes's analysis, however, is to bracket the representational content of the fiction and to insist on the play of metaphoric and metonymic transformations (egg-eye-testicle, milk-urine-sperm, etc.) that underlie and ultimately determine the surface progression of the narrative. It is only at the end, in a comment I have already quoted, that Barthes makes explicit mention of the transgressive content of the story of *Histoire de l' oeil*—but he does *that* only in order to affirm the primacy of Bataille's linguistic violations over the sexual and cultural violations that the narrative represents.[19]

No doubt this averting of the gaze by textual critics is due more to their general suspicion and critique of representation in art, and in narrative fiction in particular, than to sexual timidity, or what the French call *pudeur*. Nevertheless, it seems not insignificant that in their pursuit of the metaphoric equivalences between textual violation and the violation of bodies, what they passed over was precisely the *view* of the body and of the body's generally hidden organs, which were displayed and verbally designated on almost every page of Bataille's pornographic texts.[20]

"But let us leave the scene and the characters. The drama is first of all textual." This remark by Derrida (which I am quoting slightly out of context, for Derrida was not referring to Bataille's fiction but to the "story" of Bataille's relationship to Hegel)[21] sums up, I think, the strategy—and the symptomatic swerve away from representation—that characterizes the textual reading of Bataille. What characterizes Dworkin's reading is exactly the opposite. I am going to concentrate on hers rather than on Dardigna's, because it is more concise and also a lot simpler, allowing me to make my point by exaggeration, as it were. I am calling this reading not thematic but "ultrathematic," for reasons that will become evident.

Here is how Dworkin begins her discussion of *Histoire de l'oeil*:

> The story is told by a narrator in the first person. He grew up alone and was frightened of the sexual. When he was sixteen he met Simone, the same age. Three days after they met they were alone at her villa. Simone was wearing a black pinafore. She wore black silk stockings. He wanted to pick up her pinafore from behind to see her cunt, the word he considers the most beautiful one for vagina. There was a saucer of milk in a hallway for the cat. Simone put the saucer on a bench and sat down on it. He was transfixed. He was erect. He lay down at her feet. She stayed still. He saw her cunt in the milk. They were both overwhelmed.[22]

And so on for seven more pages of deadpan summary, detailing Simone's and the narrator's sexual exploits, which culminate in the rape and murder of a priest in a church in Seville, followed by their embarking on a schooner from Gibraltar to sail to further adventures. By means of this unwavering attention to "the scene and the characters," Dworkin flattens Bataille's narrative into a piece of pulp pornography. *Histoire de l'oeil* becomes, in the space of her summary, indistinguishable from novels with titles like *I Love a Laddie* or *Whip Chick* (which she summarizes in exactly the same way), or the photograph in *Hustler* magazine entitled "Beaver Hunters," showing a spread-eagled naked woman tied to a Jeep, the trophy of two gun-carrying male hunters (Dworkin describes and analyzes this photograph and the accompanying caption in detail, pp. 25–30).

In effect, Dworkin recontextualizes Bataille's novel, or in more technical terms relocates it in what Gerard Genette would call a new "architexte," a new generic category.[23] This was precisely the kind of reading, or misreading, that Susan Sontag foresaw and tried to ward off, when she insisted that Bataille's novels had to be read in the context of European avant-garde writing: "lacking that context," she wrote, the novels "must prove almost unassimilable for English and American readers—except as mere pornography, inexplicably fancy trash" (Sontag, p. 44).

Now the interesting thing is that Dworkin has read Sontag—but she refuses to "buy" Sontag's argument. In the analysis that follows her summary of *Histoire de l'oeil,* she seems to be replying to Sontag, and indirectly to Barthes as well, whose essay Sontag had evidently read although she didn't refer to it explicitly. Where Sontag, following Barthes, admired Bataille's "spatial principle of organization," which consists in "the obscene playing with or defiling" of a limited number of objects (chief among them being the eye of the title), Dworkin merely notes, sarcastically that "high-class symbols are...essential to high-class pornography: eggs, eyes, hard-boiled, soft-boiled..." (p. 75). Where Sontag saw the power of Bataille's writing in its dark view of sexuality, "as something beyond good and evil, beyond love, beyond sanity; as a resource for ordeal and for breaking through the limits of consciousness" (p. 58), and above all in the fact that "Bataille understood more clearly than any other writer I know of that what pornography is really about, ultimately, isn't sex but death" (p. 60), Dworkin replies:

The intellectual claim made for the work is that Bataille has revealed a sexual secret: the authentic nexus between sex and death....But in fact, Bataille has obscured more than he has uncovered. He has obscured the meaning of force in sex. He has obscured the fact that there is no male conception of sex without force as the essential dynamic....The grand conceptions—death, angst—cover the grand truth: that force leading to death is what men most secretly, most deeply, and most truly value in sex. (p. 176)

Obviously the crucial words here are "male" and "men." What Sontag saw as the revelation of a troubling truth about human sexuality, Dworkin diagnoses as the particular truth of *male* desire, or the male imagination of sex, in our culture.

Now I am going to embark on a series of spiraling "Yes, but's."

Yes—politically, I find Dworkin's argument important, in the same way that Kate Millett's argument in *Sexual Politics* was important. There is something in our culture that endorses and reinforces violence against women, as any daily newspaper will confirm; and this violence seems to be inextricable from very old, deeply ingrained, essentially masculine attitudes toward sex.

But—rhetorically, as a reading of Bataille, or even as a reading of a single work by Bataille (for Dworkin claims no general knowledge of Bataille's *oeuvre*), Dworkin's pages on *Histoire de l'oeil* are by any standard less than satisfying. If the textual critics avert their gaze from representation, Dworkin cannot take her eyes off it. She is so intent on looking at "the scene and the characters" that she never sees the frame. I am using "frame" here as a shorthand for all those aspects of a fictional narrative that designate it, directly or indirectly, as constructed, invented, filtered through a specific medium: in short, as a *text* rather than as life itself. Not unlike those consumers of pornography who skip the descriptions to get to the "good parts," Dworkin reads too quickly: she devours the text in order to get to its "core," or (to change metaphors) she traverses it without attention to its shape or the grain of its surface.

Where the text says: "I stood for some time before her, without moving, the blood rushing to my head and trembling while she looked at my stiff prick make a bulge in my knee-pants," Dworkin reads: "He was transfixed. He was erect." Where the text says: "Then I lay down at her feet without her having moved and, for the first time, I saw her 'pink and black' flesh cooling itself in the white milk," [24] Dworkins reads: "He lay down at her feet. She stayed still. He saw her cunt in the milk."

As you notice, I have not chosen anodyne sentences as my examples. Bataille's text is without a doubt pornographic.[25] But certainly one thing that contributes to its effect—even to its pornographic effect—is the contrast one feels between the long, sinuous, grammatically "exquisite" sentences (which in French appear even more so because of the use of the past historic tense [*passé simple*] and the imperfect subjunctive, indices of classical literary narration) and the explicitly sexual, obscene words ("stiff prick") that crash through the structure of the syntax, as Simone's transgressive behavior crashes through the stillness of a summer afternoon.[26] In the second sentence the text avoids naming Simone's sexual part explicitly, using instead a periphrasis set off by quotation marks, which suggest a literary or pictorial allusion: "her 'pink and black' flesh" ("sa chair 'rose et noire'"). The allusion is to Baudelaire's famous verses about Lola de Valence, who was also represented in a famous painting by Manet:

> Mais on voit scintiller en Lola de Valence
> Le charme inattendu d'un bijou rose et noir

> But one sees scintillating in Lola de Valence
> The unexpected charm of a pink and black jewel.

In Baudelaire's poem, there is a "displacement upward" (to use Freud's phrase) from the woman's genitals to the jewel she wears or possesses. This displacement is founded on both a metaphoric and a metonymic equation between genitals and jewel (Lola's sex is "like" a jewel and is surrounded by jewels)—a very nice coup, rhetorically speaking. Bataille does Baudelaire one better, however. He characteristically displaces things downward, for "sa chair rose et noire" (which here clearly refers to the lower part of Simone's body) could also refer to a woman's face, with the adjective "noire" having slid over, in both cases, from hair to flesh by means of a transgressive metonymy: flesh cannot, literally or logically, be both pink and black, but one can have pink flesh framed by black hair—as in Proust's recurrent descriptions of Albertine's face, for example; or as in the narrator's view here of Simone's genitals framed by black pubic hair.[27]

Bataille's implicit equation of face with genitals—which, as in Baudelaire's poem, can be read both metaphorically and metonymically—is much more shocking and violent, especially if it is read as metaphor, than Baudelaire's equation of jewel with genitals.[28] This rhetorical violence, whose milder manifestation is the metonymic sliding of the adjective *noire* (pink *and* black flesh?), is consonant with the transgressive behavior represented in the scene. Without losing sight of the scene, we must remark (and our remark will be a great deal closer to Barthes than to Dworkin) how closely the language of the text "repeats" or "doubles" the content of its representation.

Yes, but. Dworkin, responding to my reading, would no doubt accuse it, and me, of a culpable formalism. She is obviously aware of the language of the text, even in English translation, but the argument of her book—that pornography is harmful to women because of the scenes or images it represents—requires that she consider Bataille's language as mere ornament, and as a dangerous ornament, since it "stylizes the violence and denies its meaning to women" (Dworkin, p. 176).

Yes, but. Dworkin's argument also obliges her to see, in every book she reads, simply more of the same thing. This prevents her from noticing differences that might lead to a more significant questioning— and a more persuasive critique—of Bataille's text. For example, Dworkin writes about the character of Simone that "she exists in the male frame-work: the sadistic whore whose sexuality is murderous and insatiable... She is a prototypical figure in the male imagination, the woman who is sexual because her sexuality is male in its values, in its violence. She is the male idea of a woman let loose" (p. 176). It may be true that Simone's sexuality is male; but if so, then it is precisely the nature of male sexuality that is figured in Bataille's text as problematic. Simone is presented throughout the novel as a sister soul of the narrator, who in true Bataillean fashion is never more tormentedly aware of the Law than when he is transgressing it. Neither she nor the narrator fits the descrip-tion of "sadistic whore." The significant thing about Simone is precisely that she is not a whore, but a "young girl from a good family," a virginal-looking adolescent who, like the narrator himself, experiences sex as profoundly scandalous (from Greek *skandalon*: trap, snare, stumbling block).[29]

Just as she is not a whore, Simone is not sadistic in Sade's sense: the Sadean hero, or heroine, puts a premium on transgression, but transgres-sion in Sade occurs when a sovereign subject defies an external Law. In Bataille, the Law is internalized; the drama of transgression occurs *within* the subject. (He did not have a Catholic childhood for nothing.)

It is also the case that in Bataille's fiction the privileged locus of this drama is the female body. Bataille's internally divided subject is, emblem-atically, a woman: Simone, Madame Edwarda, Marie in *Le Mort*, the narrator's mother in *Ma mère*, Eponine in *L'Abbé C*. Dorothea ("God's gift," whose nickname is Dirty) in *Le Bleu du ciel*. The question one should ask, it seems to me, is: Why is it a woman who embodies most fully the paradoxical combination of pleasure and anguish that characterizes transgression—in whose body, in other words, the contradictory impulses toward excess on the one hand and respect of the limit on the other are played out? Dworkin cannot ask this question, for she has not read Bataille's text carefully enough to notice its specificity.

And yet (this is my last "yes, but"), despite its obvious flaws— perhaps even because of them—Dworkin's willful misreading, or flattening, of *Histoire de l'oeil* provokes at least one important question of anyone interested in modern writing: To what extent are the high-cultural productions of the avant-gardes of our century in a relation of complicity rather than in a relation of rupture vis-à-vis dominant ideologies? From the Surrealists to the *Tel Quel* group and beyond (including some "wings" of postmodernism) twentieth-century avant-gardes have proclaimed their subversive relation to the dominant culture; in a sense, they have lived on (or off) this relation. But insofar as the dominant culture has been not only bourgeois but also patriarchal, the productions of most male avant-garde artists appear anything but subversive.

This was already a conclusion I reached in my reading of Robbe-Grillet...[30] It is also the chief argument of Anne-Marie Dardigna's book, *Les Châteaux d'Eros*. Dardigna reads Bataille, Klossowski, and other French avant-garde writers not, like Dworkin, as "ordinary pornographers" but precisely as pseudo-subversive ones. "The twentieth century," she writes in her conclusion,

> is characterized in literature by the total freedom of the subjec-
> tive instance; the subject can finally tell all about its fantasies,
> its perversions, its hidden desires. That is well and
> good....But what voices are heard then? Always those of men.
> And what do they say? Nothing new: that women are
> dangerous, that they must be dominated, that their "flesh"
> must be conquered by assimilating them [to a male model] or
> by putting them to death...in any case, that they must be
> suppressed.[31]

In this conclusion, Dardigna rejoins, by a different route, the critique of masculine sexual economy—based on the suppression of what is "other" in female sexuality—that one finds in the work of those women writers and philosophers who constituted the French feminist avant-garde of the late 1960s and 1970s: Hélène Cixous, Luce Irigaray, and others associated with what in the United States has come to be known as "new French feminism"....

I want [now] to return to a question I asked only implicitly in my discussion of Robbe-Grillet's *Projet pour une révolution à New York*. What kind of reading is a "good" feminist reading (in quotation marks to acknowledge that the answer can only be subjective, my own) of texts like the ones we have been considering? Texts to which we could add a great many others, from every realm of male avant-garde artistic practice since

Surrealism: Hans Bellmer's dolls (both the objects and the photographs), paintings by Magritte or Dali or David Salle, novels by Sollers or John Hawkes or Robert Coover, photographs by Man Ray or Raoul Ubac, films by Godard or Warhol or Robbe-Grillet, the list is virtually endless.

## FEMINIST POETICS AND THE PORNOGRAPHIC IMAGINATION

Should we, echoing Simone de Beauvoir's question about Sade, ask whether to "burn Bataille"? That question, which Beauvoir asked only rhetorically, but which was also asked (equally rhetorically?) by a French Communist journal around the same time about Kafka, is perhaps—as Bataille suggested in his own essay on Kafka—the permanent temptation of any dogmatism when faced with texts it considers harmful, or even merely irresponsible.[32] But contemporary feminist criticism is, or has been at its best, precisely the opposite of a rigid dogmatism.

If, as I believe, a genuine theory of the avant-garde must include a poetics of gender and if (as I also believe) a genuine poetics of gender is indissociable from a feminist poetics, then a feminist reading of Bataille's and other modern male writers' pornographic fictions must seek to avoid both the blindness of the textual reading, which sees nothing but *écriture,* and the blindness of the ultra-thematic reading, which sees nothing but the "scene and the characters." Such a reading, necessarily thematic but not "ultra," will look at a text, or at a whole *oeuvre* if time and space allow, patiently and carefully, according the work all due respect—but also critically, not letting respect inhibit it.[33]

Patiently and carefully, because like all modern writing with any claim to significance, the fictions of Bataille and other transgressive writers go a long way toward providing the necessary commentary on themselves. Just as *Projet pour une révolution à New York* is also (not only, but also) a book about reading, so *Histoire de l'oeil* is also a book about the very processes that nourish the pornographic imagination. It is no accident that in *Histoire de l'oeil* the narrative of sexual excesses is only part 1 of the work. The second part—which, curiously, none of the commentators I have cited finds worthy of attention—consists of a commentary that traces the fantasmatic elaboration of the obscene narrative from a number of events and people in the narrator's life. The representational content of the fiction is thus retrospectively designated as fantasy—and not only that, but as a fantasy whose source is Oedipal.

The turning point in the narrator's life, we are told, came one day when he heard his mad, blind, syphilitic father cry out, while his mother was in the next room consulting with his doctor: "*Say doc, when you will finish screwing my wife!*" ("*Dis donc, docteur, quand tu aura fini de piner ma femme!*"). "For me," writes the narrator,

> this sentence, which destroyed in one instant the demoralizing effects of a strict upbringing, left behind it a kind of constant obligation, which until now has been involuntarily and unconsciously felt: the necessity to continually find its equivalent in every situation in which I find myself and that is what explains, in large part, *Story of the Eye.*

> Pour moi, cette phrase qui a détruit en un clin d'oeil les effets démoralisants d'une éducation sévère a laissé après elle une sorte d'obligation constante, inconsciemment subie jusqu'ici et non voulue: la nécessité de trouver continuellement son équivalent dans toutes les situations où je me trouve et c'est ce qui explique en grande partie *Histoire de l'oeil*.[34]

"This sentence which destroyed in one instant the demoralizing effects of a strict upbringing...": what the father suddenly reveals (or recalls?) to the son is that the mother's body is sexual. The knowledge that a "strict upbringing" has always tried to repress, in a male child, is that his mother's body is *also* that of a woman. The recognition of the mother's body as female, and desirable—a recognition forced on the son by his blind but still powerful father—is thus designated as the source of the narrator's pornographic imagination. This, I think, might explain why in Bataille's fiction it is always a woman (and in the posthumous *Ma mère*, is the mother herself) in whose body the drama of transgression is played out. For the female body in its duplicity as asexual maternal and sexual feminine, is the very emblem of the contradictory coexistence of transgression and prohibition, purity and defilement, that characterizes both the "inner experience" of eroticism *and* the textual play of the pornographic narrative.

One could also, in a more classically Freudian perspective, suggest that the mother's sexual body traumatizes the son by exhibiting its (and his own potential) "castration." In Bataille's pornography the male protagonist is often split between a passive and an active sexual role; this split is most clearly evident in *L'Abbé C.*, where one of the identical twin brothers is the desired woman's lover, while the other brother, a priest dressed "in skirts," repeatedly witnesses their lovemaking and leaves behind him his own feces as a trace of his *jouissance*. This is strikingly similar to Freud's reconstitution of the primal scene in the case history of the Wolf Man, in which a crucial supposition is that the child reacted to witnessing his parents' lovemaking by passing a stool (it's true that he was only eighteen months old!). Freud interprets this reaction as a sign (or a source?) of his patient's repressed homosexuality, his anal identification with the passive role of the mother.[35]

As far as Bataille's text is concerned, it is clear that whichever interpretation one emphasizes, the focus is on the son's view of the mother's genitals, which invariably leads him to a recognition of sexual difference and to a split in his own experience: either through the combination of fascination and terror provoked by the mother's sexuality (in the first interpretation), or through the combination of fear and desire, manifested in active *versus* passive sexual roles, as concerns his own castration (in the second interpretation). Paradoxical as it may seem, in both instances the real drama exists between the son and the father (who is at once "real" and "symbolic" in Lacan's sense), not between the son and the mother. The mother's body functions as mediation in the Oedipal narrative, whose only true (two) subjects are male.[36]

These observations are the result of a careful reading of Bataille's own text, not against itself but insofar as it comments on itself. Kristeva, in one of her general remarks on Bataille's fiction, wrote: "Contrary to 'objective,' historical or simply novelistic narratives which can be blind to their cause and merely repeat it without knowing it, [Bataille's] 'opération souveraine' consists in 'meditating'...on the Oedipal cause of the fiction and therefore of the narrating-desiring subject."[37] In its self-conscious meditation on its own Oedipal sources, Bataille's pornographic fiction (one finds this meditation, in one form or another, in all of Bataille's novels) is a far cry from the pulp novels or trashy magazine photos that serve up their fantasies straight. The difference between them is, one could argue, the difference between blindness and insight.

But the insight provided by Bataille's text about itself has its own limits. And that is why it must be read critically as well as carefully. Among the questions that Bataille's text cannot ask about itself—because in order to do so it would have to have both a historical and a theoretical distance from itself that it cannot have—are these: is there a model of sexuality possible in our culture that would not necessarily pass through the son's anguished and fascinated perception of the duplicity of the mother's body? Is there a model of *textuality* possible that would not necessarily play out, in discourse, the eternal Oedipal drama of transgression and the Law—a drama that always, ultimately, ends up maintaining the latter?[38]

Harold Bloom, in a moment of mock prophecy (and, one suspects, with some anxiety of his own) once predicted that "the first true break with literary continuity will be brought about in generations to come, if the burgeoning religion of Liberated Woman spreads from its clusters of enthusiasts to dominate the West. Homer will cease to be the inevitable precursor, and the rhetoric and forms of our literature may then break at last from tradition."[39] That time is still a while off, nor am I certain that it is what we should be waiting for. What does appear to me certain is that there will be no genuine renewal, either in a theory of the avant-garde or in its practices, as long as every drama, whether textual or sexual, continues to be envisaged—as in Bataille's pornography and in Harold Bloom's theory of poetry—in terms of a confrontation between an all-powerful father and a traumatized son, a confrontation staged across and over the body of the mother.

## NOTES

1. The works by Georges Bataille referred to in this paragraph are: "La morale de Miller," *Critique*, 1, no. 1 (1946), 3–17; *L'Erotisme* (Paris: Editions de Minuit, 1957); *La Littérature et le Mal* (Paris: Editions Gallimard, 1957); *L'expérience intérieure* (Paris: Editions Gallimard, 1943). Sartre's essay, "Un nouveau mystique," is reprinted in his *Situations*, vol. 1 (Paris: Editions Gallimard, 1947), 143–188.

2. Actually, it was preceded by an even earlier publication, never mentioned by Bataille: a pious pamphlet published in 1918, celebrating the cathedral of Reims, which had been bombed by the Germans. This essay, *Notre-Dame de Reims*, discovered only after Bataille's death, appears as an appendix to Bataille's *Oeuvres Complètes*, vol. 1 (Paris: Editions Gallimard, 1970). It is reprinted and commented on in detail by Denis Hollier in his *La Prise de la Concorde: Essai sur Georges Bataille* (Paris: Editions Gallimard, 1974). *Histoire de l'oeil* is in *Oeuvres complètes*, I, 13–78; *Madame Edwarda* is in *Oeuvres complètes*, vol. 3 (Paris: Editions Gallimard, 1971).

3. *Histoire de l'oeil* was first published in a private edition (134 copies) in 1928, under the pseudonym, "Lord Auch." New, equally limited editions appeared in 1940 and 1941; although all three editions were published in Paris, the second and third gave Burgos and Seville as places of publication, respectively. The work appeared for the first time under Bataille's name in 1967, five years after his death (published by Editions J.-J. Pauvert). *Madame Edwarda* has a similar publishing history, and two other well-known works, *Ma mère* and *Le Mort*, were published only posthumously (in 1966 and 1967, respectively). The only two novels Bataille himself published under his own name are *Le Bleu du Ciel* and *L'Abbé C.*

4. For a transcription of the trial, see *L'Affaire Sade* (Paris: J.-J. Pauvert, 1957). Bataille was one of those testifying, unsuccessfully, on behalf of the publisher and in defense of Sade as a significant writer.

5. Paradoxically, Bataille remained virtually unknown to English-speaking readers until very recently, despite his enormous influence on French theorists who have had a wide and long-standing audience in England and in the United States. Over the past few years, however, Bataille's works have entered the American intellectual scene. See, in particular, the important volume of his selected writings in English, *Visions of Excess: Selected writings, 1927–1939*, ed. Allan Stoekl with Carl L. Lovitt and Donald M. Leslie, Jr. (Minneapolis: University of Minnesota Press, 1985). See also Michele M. Richman, *Reading Georges Bataille: Beyond the Gift* (Baltimore: Johns Hopkins University Press, 1982), the first book on Bataille to be published in English; and Allan Stoekl's *Politics, Writing, Mutilation: The Cases of Bataille, Blanchot, Roussel, Leiris and Ponge* (Minneapolis: University of Minnesota Press, 1985). Denis Hollier's excellent book, *La Prise de la Concorde*, has recently been translated into English (University of Minnesota Press, 1990).

6. Michel Foucault, "Présentation," in Bataille, *Oeuvres Complètes*, I, 5.

7. Philippe Sollers, "Pourquoi Artaud, pourquoi Bataille," in *Artaud*, P. Sollers, ed. (Paris: 10/18, 1973), 9–12.

8. Susan Sontag, "The Pornographic Imagination," in *Styles of Radical Will* (New York: Delta, 1981), 44; hereafter, page numbers are given in parentheses in the text.

9. Philippe Sollers, "Le Toit," in *L'Ecriture et l'expérience des limites* (Paris: Editions du Seuil, 1968), 122.

10. Jacques Derrida, "De l'économie restreinte à l'économie générale," in *L'Ecriture et la différence* (Paris: Editions du Seuil, 1967), 404.

11. Roland Barthes, "La métaphore de l'Oeil," in *Essais critiques* (Paris: Editions du Seuil, 1964), 244. This essay was first published in *Critique*, August-September 1963, in the commemorative issue devoted to Bataille after his death.

12. See Derrida, "De l'économie restreinte à l'économie générale," 404–405: "The greatest force is that of a writing [*écriture*] which, in the most audacious transgression, continues to maintain and to recognize the necessity of the system of prohibitions (knowledge, science, philosophy, work, history, etc.). Writing is always traced between these two sides of the limit." I will return to the implications of this paradoxically conservative view at the end of this essay.

13. Derrida, "De l'économie restreinte à l'économie générale," 373–384.

14. Ibid., 392, 383–384.

15. Kristeva, "L'expérience et la pratique," in *Polylogue*, 123. This essay was first published in the proceedings of the 1972 *décade de Cerisy*.

16. Maurice Blanchot, "L'expérience limite," in *L'Entretien infini* (Paris: Editions Gallimard, 1969), 301.

17. Andrea Dworkin, *Pornography: Men Possessing Women* (New York: Perigee, 1981); Anne-Marie Dardigna, *Les Châteaux d'Eros, ou Les Infortunés du sexe des femmes* (Paris: Masparo, 1981).

18. The essay on *l'Erotisme*, "Le Toit," was first published in *Tel Quel* (1967), then collected in *Logiques* (Paris: Editions du Seuil, 1968), and reprinted in *L'Ecriture et l'expérience des limites*. The essay on *Ma Mère* "Le récit impossible" appeared in *Logiques* but was not reprinted in *L'Ecriture et l'expérience des limites*.

19. The only sustained commentary on one of Bataille's pornographic works by a well-known textual critic is Lucette Finas's book on *Madame Edwarda*, *La Crue* (Paris: Editions Gallimard, 1972). Finas's line-by-line reading, based on a principle of dictionary-inspired free associations to Bataille's text, is extremely interesting and takes greater account of the representational content of the work than does Barthes's reading of *Histoire de l'oeil*.

Finas's main emphasis, however, remains textual; what interests her chiefly is the way "*Madame Edwarda* [as] narrative is constituted by this effort, always disappointed, to envelop Her by him" (219).

In a somewhat different vein, one might also mention Brian Fitch's monograph, *Monde à l'envers, texte reversible: la fiction de Georges Bataille*, (Paris: Lettres Modernes, 1982) devoted exclusively to Bataille's novels. Fitch's elegant readings analyze the various forms of self-reflexive doubling in Bataille's fiction; but Fitch specifically excludes the question of eroticism and erotic representation, on the grounds that "Bataillean eroticism" is an experience to be understood only by reading the theoretical essays, not the novels! (48). Here then is yet another reading of Bataille, a "strictly literary," formalist reading that manages to exclude even the metaphoric notion of transgression central to the textual reading. Bataille is shown to be a highly inventive, self-conscious writer—but one is tempted to say, "So what?"

20. This display was visual as well as verbal in the first (1928) edition of *Histoire de l'oeil*, which contained—printed on heavy paper in large format—eight original lithographs by André Masson, illustrating some of the more "scandalous" scenes. (I saw this edition at the Houghton rare book library at Harvard University.) It is only a small step, after this, to associate the textual critics' "averting of the gaze" with the aversion traditionally inspired by the Medusa's head, which, the myth tells us, had the power to turn men to stone—and which, Freud has told us, is a symbolic representation of the female genitals. I shall argue later that the son's problematic seeing of the mother's genitals is centrally inscribed in *Histoire de l'oeil*, which may then turn out to be a *mise en abyme* of the problematic "seeing" practiced by its critics. In a different perspective, Teresa de Lauretis has related Medusa to the question of female subjectivity and female seeing/spectatorship—see her *Alice Doesn't: Feminism, Semiotics, Cinema* (Bloomington: Indiana University Press, 1984), 109–111, 136 and *passim*. My thanks to Nancy Miller for calling this book to my attention, and for reminding me about the beautiful Gorgon.

21. Derrida, "De l'économie restreinte à l'économie générale," 372.

22. Dworkin, *Pornography*, 167; hereafter page numbers are given in parentheses in the text.

23. Gerard Genette, *Introduction à l'architexte* (Paris: Editions du Seuil, 1979); also *Palimpsestes: La Littérature au second degré* (Paris: Editions du Seuil, 1982).

24. *Histoire de l'oeil*, in *Oeuvres complètes*, I, 13-14. "Je restai quelque temps devant elle, immobile, le sang à la tête et tremblant pendant qu'elle regardait ma verge raide tendre ma culotte. Alors je me couchai à ses pieds sans qu'elle bougeât et, pour la première fois, je vis sa chair 'rose et noire' qui se rafraichissait dans le lait blanc." This is the text of the 1928 edition, which Bataille revised extensively in 1940. The English translation, by Joachim Neugroschel (New York: Berkeley Books, 1982) follows the original version. The translations here are my own.

25. During the discussion that followed the delivery of an earlier version of this essay at the International Poetics Conference at Columbia University (November 1984), Michael Riffaterre suggested that Simone's dipping her genitals in the plate of milk (which the text says was there for the cat, *le chat*) is already inscribed in the word *chat*, which, similar to the English "pussy," has an obscene slang meaning in French. This would therefore, he concluded, be simply an example of Bataille's play with language, for "what she does, after all, is put her *chat* in its natural place, in the milk." The interpretation is ingenious, but whether the shock value or pornographic force of Simone's action is thereby diminished is highly debatable.

26.  Sollers makes a somewhat similar remark apropos of a sentence in *Ma Mère*, noting that the result of such incongruous juxtapositions "will be all the more effective, the greater the spread between the noble aspect (thought) and the inavowable (excrement, sex)" ("Le récit impossible," in *Logiques*, 160).  In fact, this may be a particular variation on the Surrealist theory of metaphor, founded on the idea of incongruous juxtaposition; for a discussion of the link between this aesthetic theory and what I call the "figure of perversion" (Bataille being a case in point), see chapter 7, "Parody, Perversion, Collage: Surrealists at Play."

27.  It is unfortunate that the English translation by Joachim Neugroschel mitigates Bataille's stylistic transgression by rendering "rose et noire" as "pink and dark." There are some other problems with the translation as well (e.g, "cunt" for the less specific term "cul").  Dworkin's reading is based on the English version—but even so, it is reductive.  For another discussion of "the pink and the black" in Bataille, see Hollier's "Bataille's Tomb: A Halloween Story," *October*, 33 (summer 1985), 80ff.

28.  The violence of such a metaphoric equation is made explicit in René Magritte's painting, *Le Viol* (*The Rape*, 1934), which represents a woman's face, the eyes being her breasts, the nose her navel, and the mouth her pubis.  The shock provoked by a first viewing is considerable.  It is reproduced in color in Robert Hughes, *The Shock of the New* (New York: Knopf, 1982), 150.  Here again, Bataille's affinity with Surrealist aesthetics is evident.

29.  The fact that both of the main characters are adolescents is significant, since adolescence is that period when experimentation with sexual roles is indissociable from a more general search for the self.  In both cases, the search is intimately bound up with an awareness of the (parental) Law and the possibilities of its infraction.  This is repeatedly emphasized in *Histoire de l'oeil*.  I consider the Oedipal implications of the fiction later in this chapter.

30.  See both Suleiman's article "Reading Robbe-Grillet" and the chapter of her book *Subversive Intent* from which this article has been taken.  I have slightly abridged Suleiman's original text at this point, as it makes references to other chapters of her book (ed.)

31.  Dardigna, *Les Châteaux d'Eros*, 312–313.  Dardigna's book was published several years after my essay on Robbe-Grillet.  The fact that we arrived at our somewhat similar conclusions independently adds to their weight, I believe.

32.  See Georges Bataille, "Kafka," in *La Littérature et le Mal* (Paris: Editions Gallimard, 1957), 173–196; also Simone de Beauvoir, *Faut-il brûler Sade?* (Paris: Editions Gallimard, 1955).  One sometimes hears (or even reads) people who have not read Beauvoir's book, but know her as a feminist, scoffing at her "inquisitorial" stance.  It is therefore worth emphasizing that Beauvoir did not ask the question about burning seriously (to ask it seriously is already to show who one is) and indeed recognized fully Sade's importance as a thinker, representing a kind of absolute noncompromise that Beauvoir admired.

33.  In *Les Châteaux d'Eros*, Dardigna does devote several interesting chapters to detailed readings of Pierre Klossowski's trilogy, *Les Lois de l'hospitalité*.  But in her latest book, a full-length study of Klossowski's *oeuvre*, Dardigna has virtually abandoned the feminist perspective that gave an edge to her earlier work.  (See Dardigna, *Pierre Klossowski: L'Homme aux simulacres*).  Are respect for and "total immersion" in a writer's work somehow incompatible with critical distance and judgment? A question worth pondering, especially by feminist critics.

34. Bataille, *Oeuvres complètes*, I, 77; Bataille's emphasis. This passage, as well as the whole second part of Histoire de l'oeil, has generally been read as straight autobiography, testifying to Bataille's tormented childhood. (See, for example, Michel Surya, *Bataille: La Mort à l'oeuvre* [Paris: Librairie Séguier, 1987]—a biography which bases most of its account of Bataille's early years on this text.) Whether Bataille is speaking here in his own name or not, the fact is that part 2 (titled "Coincidences") has the same textual status as part 1 (titled "Récit"): it is set in the same type and is in no way marked as being "different" in truth value from the first part. Although the reference, in the sentence I quote, to the title of the work as a whole suggests that its *author* (rather than an invented character) is speaking, this indication is complicated by the fact that the work was signed with a pseudonym—its author was therefore also "invented." At any rate, there is at least as much justification for reading part 2 as part of the fiction as there is for reading it as straight autobiography.

35. See Sigmund Freud, "The Case of the Wolf-Man" in *The Wolf-Man by the Wolf-Man*, Muriel Gardiner, ed. (New York: Basic Books, 1971), 181–191, 214–230.

36. Denis Hollier, in a rich analysis of the father-son relation in Bataille and of its political and psychological implications, has suggested that the son's deepest desire may be a "glorious castration," at once violent and incestuous, at the hands of the father (Hollier, "La tombe de Bataille," unpublished manuscript). In that case, the mother becomes superfluous, and indeed Hollier suggests as much. Is the elimination of the mother, and *a fortiori* of female subjectivity, the "real" logic of Oedipus? For a far-ranging feminist critique of the Oedipal narrative, viewed as the single most powerful narrative model in patriarchal culture, see de Lauretis, *Alice Doesn't*, chap 5. For an analysis of the Oedipal logic which leads to the male child's violent repudiation of the mother see Jessica Benjamin, "The Bonds of Love: Rational Violence and Erotic Domination," *Feminist Studies*, 6, no. 1 (Spring 1980), 144–174.

37. Kristeva, "L'expérience et la pratique," 121.

38. See, for example, the passage I quoted from Derrida in n. 12. The question of whether, and to what extent, the theory of *écriture* is "revolutionary" or even genuinely subversive, is part of the general current debate regarding the politics of the "posts": postmodernism, poststructuralism, deconstruction. I discuss some aspects of the debate in Chapter 8.

39. Harold Bloom, *A Map of Misreading* (New York: Oxford University Press, 1975), 33.

# Index